A PRACTICAL CHINESE GRAMMAR

方明达

Related Titles Published by The Chinese University Press

Business Chinese: An Advanced Reader
《商贸汉语高级读本》
By Songren Cui 崔颂人 著 (2003)

Talk Mandarin Today
By Hong Xiao (2003)

Chinese Language and Culture: An Intermediate Reader
《汉语与文化读本》
By Weijia Huang and Qun Ao 黄伟嘉、敖群 合著 (2002)

Kung Fu (Elementary Putonghua Text)
《功夫》
Edited by John C. Jamieson and Lin Tao
简慕善、林涛 主编 (2002)

A Student Handbook for Chinese Function Words
《汉语虚词学习手册》
By Jiaying Howard 庄稼婴 著 (2002)

A Learners' Handbook of Modern Chinese Written Expression
《现代汉语书面语学习手册》
By Yu Feng 冯禹 著 (2000)

A Guide to Proper Usage of Spoken Chinese
《汉语口语指引》
By Tian Shou-he (1996 second edition)

Chinese-English Dictionary
《汉英小字典》
Edited by Chik Hon Man and Ng Lam Sim Yuk
植汉民、吴林婵玉 合编
(1994 second edition)

Fifty Patterns of Modern Chinese
By Dezhi Han (1993)

English-Cantonese Dictionary
《英粤字典》
Edited by New Asia–Yale-in-China Chinese Language Center,
The Chinese University of Hong Kong (1991)

A PRACTICAL CHINESE GRAMMAR

Hung-nin Samuel Cheung
in collaboration with
Sze-yun Liu and Li-lin Shih

The Chinese University Press

A Practical Chinese Grammar
  Hung-nin Samuel Cheung in collaboration with
  Sze-yun Liu and Li-lin Shih

© **The Chinese University of Hong Kong**, 1994

ISBN 962–201–595–6

First edition   1994
Second printing 1996
Third printing   1997
Fourth printing 1999
Fifth printing   2002
Sixth printing   2003

THE CHINESE UNIVERSITY PRESS
The Chinese University of Hong Kong
SHA TIN, N.T., HONG KONG
Fax: +852 2603 6692
     +852 2603 7355
E-mail: cup@cuhk.edu.hk
Web-site: www.chineseupress.com

Printed in Hong Kong

Contents

Introduction

Ever since the early 1970s when the re-establishment of Sino-US relations generated a surging interest in the study of the Chinese language, there has been an increasing demand for teaching materials compiled in China. The various series published by the Beijing Language Institute, when compared to texts issued overseas and especially those compiled in the United States, are most successful in accurately representing current language use in mainland China. Their 1981 publication entitled *Practical Chinese Reader* has been reprinted twice and remains the primary choice for a beginning text among American colleges that offer Chinese language training. Linguistic currency and cultural relevance notwithstanding, one major drawback of all the Beijing Language Institute series is the inadequacy of grammatical explanations. As noted in the introduction to *Practical Chinese Reader* (*PCR*), the grammar section in each lesson aims at introducing major grammatical points, without attempting a comprehensive analysis. The discussions concentrate primarily on features which are characteristic of the Chinese language and which may pose difficulty for foreign students. However, because grammatical particulars are broken down bit by bit throughout the lessons and presented in a somewhat illogical fashion, the result is a disappointingly insufficient grammar component, at times fragmentary or even confusing. As is always the case, every teacher has his or her own philosophy about grammar and how it should be taught. Many are ready to improvise answers derived from their linguistic experiences when accounting for why the language behaves in a certain manner. Yet, despite such willing and ready effort to supplement what textbooks provide for grammatical explanation, many of us in the field had hoped that the Beijing Language Institute would publish a grammar, which we would readily use as a *PCR* reference. However, no such reference has been produced. In fact, compared with other languages, Chinese has suffered from an unfortunate lack of adequately prepared grammar handbooks which we, teachers and students alike, could consult for detailed and systematic descriptions of sentence patterns and functional words.

In Fall 1986 when I assumed responsibility for the first year Chinese language program at Berkeley, I felt firsthand, and with mounting anxiety, the need for a grammar handbook designed for beginning Chinese students. During the following year, with the help of Mrs. Liu Szeyun and Mrs. Shih Lilin, both veteran instructors in the program, I began compiling grammar notes to supplement the first two volumes of *PCR*, the core text in our curriculum. The divison of labor was like this. Mrs. Liu and Mrs. Shih took turns gathering the preliminary notes and examples, on the basis of which I wrote the discussions and added more examples. After the grammar was circulated among the teaching team members, their remarks and suggestions were incorporated into the notes which I then expanded to book length. This grammar, entitled *Practical Chinese Reader : A Grammar Companion*, was formally adopted in Fall 1988 as a required text. Additional changes and modifications have been made in the course of its use. As we originally scheduled our first year syllabus to cover forty-seven of the fifty lessons in *PCR*, that grammar was three lessons shorter than the textbook. I devoted my sabbatical in Spring 1991 to another round of revisions and wrote the last three lessons.

Because the grammar was initially intended to be a handbook for students using *PCR* as their principal textbook, the grammatical patterns have been arranged in the order in which they appear in *PCR*. Sample sentences, given in both simplified Hanzi 汉字 and 拼音 *pinyin*, are constructed using the new vocabulary of the lessons so as to serve as an additional review of new words and characters for *PCR* readers. However, as most language texts follow approximately the same set of grammar rules in a similar order of presentation, the *Grammar* may in fact serve as a reference for those who are following other textbooks. Insofar as our discussions examine the structural characteristics of the language in detail and include ample illustrations of both general and idiosyncratic usages, the work may also be read on its own as an introduction to Chinese grammar for beginning language students. Hence, to better represent its many functions, the book has now been re-titled *A Practical Chinese Grammar*.

However, because of the association with *PCR* in the format and sequence in which grammar is introduced, we are sometimes limited in our effort to pursue an issue to its fullest extent. For example, although we are not satisfied with the treatment of 了 *le* in *PCR*, we have followed the order in which it is introduced in the book, the perfective 了 in Lesson 27 and the new situation 了 in Lesson 33. Such an arrangement makes explanation of the two 了's in Lessons 28 and 31 or the use of the sentence 一了 in the pattern of imminence 要⋯⋯了 in Lesson 29 a most difficult challenge. In places where we deem it absolutely necessary, we have made modifications, sometimes extensively, by introducing information ahead of the *PCR* schedule so as to elucidate the discussion that follows. Such digressions are of course conducted with caution, minimizing any disruption of the regular *PCR* syllabus. As the intent of this compilation is to provide a firm grasp of grammar upon which students can develop a competent command of the language, we have examined each pattern in depth, describing ramifications that go beyond what is required for a first year textbook. Teachers may choose to abridge the information to suit instructional needs and design. It is a well-known but unfortunate fact that very few advanced Chinese textbooks pay adequate attention to grammar. For example, although the first two *PCR* volumes present fifty lessons each of which contains a section on grammar, the format of the next two volumes changes, giving only explanatory notes of grammatical information in the context of words and phrases. To most textbook writers and language teachers, grammar falls under the charge of the beginning level instruction, a philosophy with which I do not necessarily agree. My personal view on this matter is to adopt a cyclical format of introduction, repeating all the major grammatical patterns over a three-year period, with increasing sophistication in both style and usage. For example, the pattern 是⋯⋯ 的 which embraces the Verb—Object predicate （是 V－O 的 ）has a variant form in which the Object is moved to the end of the sentence （是 V 的 O）. In the *PCR* text, the two forms are simultaneously introduced in Lesson 44. Granted that the postponement would not necessarily pose any great challenge to students who, by this time, have already witnessed all sorts of syntactic movements, is it really necessary or feasible to teach the modified pattern at the time when students may still have problems in distinguishing the use of 了 from that of 是⋯⋯的 ? The fact that the variant form carries its own grammatical restrictions (e.g. the Object cannot be a pronoun) requires memorization of more rules, thereby delaying or even deterring the acquisition process. I would prefer to present only the basic 是⋯⋯的 pattern in a beginning text and reintroduce it at the intermediate level together with its stylistic variation. Such a format of incremental repetition not only provides a systematic review of grammar at each level of learning, but also redistributes the grammatical load into all levels, alloting more time to accomplish a solid foundation. To correct the lopsided emphasis of putting all grammar into the beginning class, the syllabus must be redesigned so that students acquire, at a carefully-measured pace, an ever-growing knowledge and appreciation of the linguistic complexities of Chinese. However, within the present framework, we have hoped to produce a grammar that is designed for beginners and which also contains information pertaining to a higher level of understanding. Therefore, at times when the discussion goes beyond the confines of a first year textbook, it is in anticipation of what students will need in their subsequent linguistic pursuit.

The *Grammar* is prepared for pedagogical use. And, as such, it is both descriptive and prescriptive by design. It attempts to describe linguistic phenomena in an admittedly simple fashion, often representing complex behaviors with a few patterns and paradigms. We are fully aware of the versatile nature of the language and the inadequacy of any set of linguistic rules to capture all syntactic features and encompass the full scope of grammatical and pragmatic applications. In fact, the more we study and teach the language, the more we realize how little we know. In class, when a teacher is short of explanation, he or she often gets out of the embarrassment by resorting to those all too familiar formulaic incantations such as "That's the way we say it," or "That doesn't sound right to a native ear." In spite of the self-justifying voice of authority, we all know deep down that there should be better and more logical reasons to account for all the do's and don'ts in the language. Yet, we also realize that the process of searching for a conclusive and comprehensive answer is long and formidable. Regardless of our interest in theoretical linguistics or in second language acquisition, we are confronted with the same task of describing and explaining the many and often seemingly anomalous phenomena in the language. This grammar introduces some of the observations we have made in our attempt to offer beginners a systematic account of the Chinese language. The book has proven quite successful with our students at Berkeley, and we hope other readers will find it just as rewarding. It is written for an audience in the field of language teaching, but we are sure that many of the controversial issues addressed and the rich collection of sample sentences cited, including examples of ungrammatical usages, will be of great interest to students of linguistics.

For the compilation of the *Grammar*, I would first like to thank Mrs. Liu and Mrs. Shih for their collaboration on this project. Their advice and support have always been a source of inspiration in every phase of the writing and revision of this book. They have also been the vital work force in the operation of our first year language program at Berkeley. Until her retirement in November 1992, Mrs. Shih was the person we always turned to for guidance in matters pertaining to language instruction. She is methodical and meticulous, even in enforcing the transcription rule of removing the dot on the vowel "i" when the tone mark sits upon it. She insists on producing only the most 优美 "exquisite" sentences. As she rightly claims, sample sentences serve not only to illustrate grammatical patterns but also to create and instill a sense of beauty, rhythm and humor. We have diligently abided by this principle of 优美 in our construction and selection of examples. Mrs. Liu began her teaching career at Columbia and has been on the Berkeley faculty since the mid-seventies. She stresses cultural orientation and pragmatic application in language teaching. Many of the discussions in this grammar should indeed be credited to her astute observations. Specifically, topics such as the following were first noted by Mrs. Liu: the distinction between 有 and 在 in terms of ownership and temporary holding as in 我有你的书 "I have your book —— I own a copy of your book" and 你的书在我这儿 "I have your book —— your book is here with me" (Lesson 16); the contrast between the progressive patterns "在 Verb－Object 呢" and "正在 Verb－Object 呢" in highlighting how two actions are viewed in terms of their interaction or lack of it (Lesson 23); the differentiation between 会 and 能 as illustrated in the "typewriting" scenario: 你会打字吗？ vs. 你一分钟能打多少个字？(Lesson 26); the tendency for the 有—comparison to be used more in the interrogative form than in a positive statement: 我有你高吗？ (Lesson 36), etc.

Mrs. Liu always keeps herself abreast of the latest research in second language instruction and its implications for and application to Chinese. Recently she has compiled a set of exercises, entitled *Situational Exercises* (in 39 lessons), to accompany *Practical Chinese Reader*. The workbook contains a variety of challenging exercises designed to practice patterns and vocabulary in contexts that closely simulate real life experiences.

I want to thank all the teaching assistants who have contributed to the project by experimenting with the grammar notes in their instruction. They are, in alphabetical order, Kim Besio, Lucy Borota, Guo Jiansheng, Jean Kim, Sabina Knight, John Kowalis, Linette Lee, Liu Li, Sang Tze-lan, Tsao Chih-lien, Giovanni Vitiello, Jason Chia-chi Wang, Yang Ching-fen, Yang Ying, Yao Da-jun, and Zhang Jie. Many of the fun examples and dialogues included in this *Grammar* are in fact their compositions. I wish to acknowledge Kim Besio, Andrea Goldman, Luo Shaodan and Linda G. Wang for their meticulous efforts in proofreading the manuscript and Christopher Laughrun for his assistance in preparing the Index. In particular, I am indebted to Marjorie Fletcher, who kindly read the entire manuscript with care and made many invaluable editorial changes and suggestions. I want to thank Yao Yao for typing the first draft of the first 47 Lessons using the Tianma computer program, a project which the Department of East Asian Languages generously funded. I am grateful to Ms. Cecilia Chu, our second year instructor, for generously sharing with me her comments on the last three lessons and her many sample sentences which I have used for lessons 48 and 49. I am also thankful to Dr. Ningping Chan for commenting on an earlier version of the *Grammar* and to Ms. Ying Yang for pointing out some of the errors in the manuscript. The entire project was indeed a collaborative effort of many hands. But, above all this *Grammar* was spurred by the needs of the students and it was upon their recommendation that we finally sought publication. Finally, I want to express my gratitude to my teacher, Professor Kun Chang, who once said, "There is less than three-tenths of the language we can claim to have some knowledge about. Be sure not to blow these three-tenths or to bluff on the other seven-tenths." To this date, these words remain my motto in language teaching. It goes without saying that, as primary author, I remain solely responsible for any errors and shortcomings in the *Grammar*. Comments and criticisms are eagerly solicited. As error-making is crucial to language learning, your remarks and suggestions will be important in our effort to revise and improve the text.

CHEUNG, Hung-nin Samuel
University of California, Berkeley
June 15, 1994

Acknowledgements

In this reprint, I wish to thank my readers and friends for their continuous support and encouragement. Many have written to express their appreciation of the *Practical Chinese Grammar* and others have raised questions on various issues including spelling, special word usage and grammatical explanations. I am especially indebted to Ms. Ying Yang, my colleague at UC Berkeley, for her meticulous reading of the grammar, for the many hours she spent with me discussing the use of the book, and for the corrections that she has made in all fifty lessons.

H. Samuel Cheung
Hong Kong, 2002

Lesson 1

1. The Adjective as a Verb

The following dialogue[1] represents one of the most common ways of exchanging greetings in Chinese. Though containing two short sentences, the dialogue introduces a simple but very important grammatical feature of the Chinese language, namely, an adjective behaves like a verb.

(1)　帕兰卡：　古波，你好！
　　　　Palanka:　Gǔbō, nǐ hǎo!
　　　　　　　　How are you, Gubo?
　　　　　　　　(= Hello, Gubo.)

　　　　古波：　你好，帕兰卡！
　　　　Gubo:　Nǐ hǎo, Pàlánkǎ!
　　　　　　　How are you, Palanka?
　　　　　　　(= Hello, Palanka.)

The literal translation of the expression 你好 *nǐ hǎo* is "you fine," where the pronoun 你 "you" is placed directly before the adjective 好 "fine." Tarzan may say "You fine," to Jane, but, in proper English, a verb-to-be is required between a subject and its adjectival predicate. Thus, "You are fine." Such a requirement is, however, absent in the Chinese language. A Chinese adjective may appear all by itself as a predicate without an intervening verb-to-be. In this regard, it behaves very much like a verb, which usually forms the core of a predicate. Some grammarians refer to adjectives in Chinese as quality verbs or stative verbs. Hence, the first rule to learn in Chinese grammar is that *adjectives are verbs*. Usually they are not accompanied by a verb-to-be in predicates.

---

1. Cited from *Practical Chinese Reader*, Vol. 1, Lesson 1.

Lesson 2

1. Question Formation: The 吗—Question

A Chinese sentence generally consists of a subject and a predicate, the latter of which, as noted in the last lesson, may be just an adjective.

> Sentence = Subject + Predicate

To turn a sentence into a question, we may simply attach a particle 吗 *ma* to the end of the sequence without involving a change in word order as required by the English language.

> Affirmative → Interrogative
> 〔Subject + Predicate〕 → 〔Subject + Predicate〕+ 吗？

(1) 你好。　　　　　　　你好吗？
　　Nǐ hǎo.　　　　　　Nǐ hǎo ma?
　　You are fine.　　　　Are you fine?
　　(= Hello.)　　　　　(= How are you?)

The sentence 你好吗？ represents, therefore, not only an idiomatic expression of greeting in Mandarin but also a format for question formation in the Chinese language.

2. Question Formation: The 呢—Question

The second way of asking a question in Chinese is through the use of the interrogative particle 呢 *ne*. The particle indicates not only an interrogation but also that the question itself is related to preceding statements and/or questions. Therefore, one does not start off a dialogue by using a 呢－question. Only when some sort of a verbal context has already been established in the conversation does one begin to use the 呢－form of interrogation. For example, in the following dialogue quoted from Lesson 2 in *Practical Chinese Reader*, Palanka may use 呢 to form her question, which is related to Gubo's inquiry. But Gubo may not use 呢 in his inquiry because that is the very first sentence in the conversation.

(1)　　古波：　　你好吗？
　　　　Gubo:　　Nǐ hǎo ma?
　　　　　　　　How are you?

　　　　帕兰卡：　我很好，你呢？
　　　　Palanka:　Wǒ hěn hǎo, nǐ ne?
　　　　　　　　I'm fine, and how about you?

　　　　古波：　　也很好。
　　　　Gubo:　　Yě hěn hǎo.
　　　　　　　　I'm also fine.

As demonstrated in Palanka's question, 呢 is often attached to the end of a noun or pronoun, with the meaning of "How about X?" The following is another example.

(2)　　古波很好。帕兰卡呢？
　　　　Gūbō hěn hǎo. Pàlánkǎ ne?
　　　　Gubo is fine. How about Palanka?

3. 很 ＋ Adjective

As noted in the previous lesson, an adjective in Chinese can be used as a full predicate all by itself without the help of a verb-to-be. In fact, it is grammatically incorrect to put such a verb in an adjectival sentence. (You may be wondering what exactly is this verb-to-be in Chinese. The verb will be introduced in a later lesson, and, until then, you don't have to worry about making such an error.) However, it is a common practice in Chinese to modify the adjective, *especially in an affirmative sentence*, with the adverb 很 *hěn*, which literally means "very." For example,

(1)　　我很好。
　　　　Wǒ hěn hǎo.
　　　　I'm very well.

In a normal descriptive sentence, 很 is almost always there, standing right in front of the adjective. Because of its high frequency in use, the adverb 很 carries a much weaker force than its English corresponding form "very." It can often be omitted in translation. Therefore,

> （1.a）我很好。
> Wǒ hěn hǎo.
> I'm fine.

4. The Adverb 也

Both 也 *yě* and 很 are adverbs and, as adverbs, they always come *before* the verbs or adjectives they modify. For example,

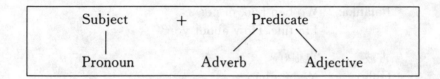

> （1） 我很好。
>   Wǒ hěn hǎo.
>   I'm fine.

> （2） 你也好。
>   Nǐ yě hǎo.
>   You're fine, too.

Because 也 is often translated as "also" or "too," students tend to follow the English word order and place it at the beginning or the end of a sentence, which is grammatically wrong. Remember that *one-syllable adverbs in Chinese always appear between the Subject and the verb.* They never appear in the sentence-final position.

> Subject ＋ 也 ＋ Verb/Adjective

When there are two or more adverbs modifying the same verb/adjective in a sentence, they often follow a set order. In the case when 也 and 很 appear together, the former precedes the latter.

> Subject ＋ 也 ＋ 很 ＋ Verb/Adjective

(3)   我也很好。
        Wǒ yě hěn hǎo.
        I am also fine.

5. Omission of a Subject

When someone asks "How are you?" you can answer by saying either "I'm fine." or, simply, "Fine." In the latter case, the subject is omitted since we can infer from the context just "who" is "fine." Employing such an ellipsis is a very common practice in Chinese, much more so than in English. Whenever the context is clear, the subject of a sentence can be readily omitted. For example, the last two lines in the dialogue cited above provide such a scenario:

(1)   帕兰卡：   我很好，你呢？
        Palanka: Wǒ hěn hǎo, nǐ ne?
                   I'm fine. How about you?

        古波：   也很好。
        Gubo: Yě hěn hǎo.
                   [I'm] also fine.

Lesson 3

1. The Negative Sentence

1.1 A negative sentence is formed by placing the negative marker 不 *bù* before the appropriate verb or adjective.

$$\boxed{\text{Subject} \ + \ 不 \ + \ \text{Verb}}$$

（1）　我不忙。
　　　Wǒ bù máng.
　　　I am not busy.

（2）　他不好。
　　　Tā bù hǎo.
　　　He is not fine.

Again, there is no need to use a verb-to-be to negate an adjective.

1.2 The negative 不, when used in isolation or before a pause, is pronounced in the fourth tone: *bù*. In other positions, however, its tone changes according to the tonal register of the following syllable. Standing in front of a first, second, or third tone, it is pronounced in the fourth tone; when it precedes a fourth tone, it changes to a second tone. The following list demonstrates this tone change phenomenon.

不＋ 1st	：不高　bù gāo　→ bù gāo　"not tall"
不＋ 2nd	：不忙　bù máng → bù máng "not busy"
不＋ 3rd	：不好　bù hǎo　→ bù hǎo　"not fine"
不＋ 4th	：不胖　bù pàng　→ bú pàng　"not fat"

If 不 is followed by a neutral tone syllable, its tonal realization depends on whether the unstressed syllable is originally a fourth tone word. If it is, the preceding 不

takes on a rising tone. In all other cases, the negative is pronounced with a falling tone.

The phenomenon of tonal modification happens to a very small number of words, but those that are affected are extremely common forms in the language. The other high frequency word that shows a similar behavior is the numeral 一 *yī* "one," more about which will come in Lesson 15.

2. The Adverb 都

都 *dōu*, meaning "all" or "every," is a monosyllabic adverb which by definition must appear after the subject and before the verb. The all-inclusiveness represented by 都 refers to the noun phrase standing before it.

> Subject ＋ 都 ＋ Verb

(1)   我们都很忙。
        Wǒmen dōu hěn máng.
        We're all busy.

(2)   哥哥弟弟都很好。
        Gēge dìdi dōu hěn hǎo.
        Both the elder and younger brothers are fine.

It is incorrect to say the following sentence, which follows the English word order. The correct order is given in (4).

(3)   *都他们好。[1]
        *Dōu tāmen hǎo.

(4)   他们都好。
        Tāmen dōu hǎo.
        They are all fine.

---

1. From here on, all incorrect sentences will be marked with an asterisk *.

3. Pronouns and Their Plural Forms

3.1   The following table presents the three primary Chinese pronouns and their plural forms.

	Singular	Plural
1st Person	我 *wǒ*	我们 *wǒmen*
2nd Person	你 *nǐ*	你们 *nǐmen*
3rd Person	他 *tā*	他们 *tāmen*

3.2   In speech, there is only one form for the third person reference, namely *tā*. Orthographically, however, there are two characters, both pronounced the same as *tā*, demonstrating a gender distinction.

Masculine	Feminine
他　　*tā* (he)	她　　*tā* (she)
他们　*tāmen* (they: M)	她们　*tāmen* (they: F)

3.3   The element 们 *men*, always pronounced unstressed with a neutral tone, is the marker of plurality. It is attached to pronouns to form their plural equivalents. It may appear after personal nouns (which is to say, nouns representing people, for example, 哥哥 *gēge* "brother"), but it is a general practice in Chinese not to use it with a noun even when the referents are more than one in number. In fact, it is incorrect to attach 们 to inanimate nouns such as 车 *chē* "cars" or 书 *shū* "books." Often, the context itself suffices to show the distinction between singular and plural. For example, in the following sentence, we can tell that 哥哥 is plural, simply because of the presence of 都 *dōu* in the predicate, an adverb that indicates a plural reference in its preceding noun.

(1)   哥哥都很忙。
　　　Gēge dōu hěn máng.
　　　(My) brothers are all very busy.

3.4   Chinese pronouns do not display case changes as required by the English language. For example, one single form 我 is used for both "I" and "me." The pronoun can also be placed immediately before a human noun to indicate a relationship of possession commonly referred to as that of the "genitive."

```
┌─────────────────────────────────────────────────────┐
│           Pronoun    +    Personal Noun              │
└─────────────────────────────────────────────────────┘
```

(2)   我哥哥
       wǒ gēge
       my brother

(3)   他们弟弟
       tāmen dìdi
       their younger brother

We will learn in a later lesson, however, that if the "possessed" is not in the form of a kinship term or a personal noun, the genitive relationship needs to be grammatically marked. But, until then, enjoy the lack of such a formal requirement.

1. How to Introduce a Person

1.1   The formula used in introducing someone is as follows:

（1）   这是 X 。
Zhè shì X.
This is X.

Like its English equivalent, the Chinese pattern follows a simple subject－predicate construction. The formula, however, uses two new grammatical elements which call for some explanation.

1.2   这 *zhè* is a "demonstrative," corresponding to "this" in English. There is, of course, an equivalent to "that" in Chinese, which we will learn in the following lesson.

1.3   You have guessed right. 是 *shì* is the long-awaited verb-to-be in Chinese. But, *don't use it with an adjective in a descriptive sentence.* An adjective is a full verb and can function as a predicate without the assistance of 是.

1. How to Introduce a Person

Lesson 5

1. The Demonstrative

Lesson 5 introduces the matching demonstrative for 这 *zhe* "this," which appeared in the previous lesson.

这 :	*zhè*	"this"
那 :	*nà*	"that"

（1） 这是车。
Zhè shì chē.
This is a car.

（2） 那是我妈妈。
Nà shì wǒ māma.
That is my mother.

The two demonstratives can sometimes refer to plural things, in which case they will be translated as "these" and "those." Again, the context will clarify the quantity reference.

Notice, however, that unlike their English corresponding forms, 这 and 那 never appear in the Object position all by themselves. This point will be dealt with later.

2. The Possessive Construction

Possession is explicitly marked by a particle 的 *de*, placed immediately after the "possessor." The function of 的 is similar to the use of 's in English to indicate the genitive association.

$$\boxed{\text{Possessor} \;+\; \text{的} \;+\; \text{Possessed}}$$

(1) 我的车
 wǒ de chē
 my car

(2) 他们的大夫
 tāmen de dàifu
 their doctor

(3) 妈妈的书
 māma de shū
 mother's book(s)

The possessive 的 can be omitted when (a) the possessor is represented by a personal pronoun, and (b) the possessed is a "personal" noun such as one's parents, teachers, etc. (Cf. Lesson 3.) Hence, "my mother" is 我妈妈 without an explicit marking of the genitive. However, in the phrase "my mother's car," 的 becomes a compulsory element. The possessor is now a noun rather than a pronoun: 妈妈, and the possessed object, 车, is a thing and not a person. Hence,

(4) 我妈妈的车
 wǒ māma de chē
 my mother's car

3. More on the 吗—Question

3.1 We have learned in Lesson 2 that, when turning a statement into a question, we may simply attach the interrogative particle 吗 to the end of the sentence. The statement can be a descriptive sentence as in (1) or a 是—sentence as in (2), or, for that matter, any sentence type that we shall learn in later lessons.

(1) 你们都好吗?
 Nǐmen dōu hǎo ma?
 Are you all fine?

(2) 这是你的书吗?
 Zhè shì nǐ de shū ma?
 Is this your book?

3.2 To answer these questions, we can give a full positive sentence for a Yes—
answer or a negative sentence for a No—answer. Alternatively, for short answers,
we can simply give the positive verb/adjective or its negative form as the appropriate response. Or, we can use both options in combination, with the short form
first, followed by the full answer. In this regard, the use of the positive/negative
verb as a short answer is essentially the same thing as saying "Yes/No" in English.
In fact, we don't have a word in Chinese for either "Yes" or "No." Hence, the
answers to the above questions are:

	Positive Answers	Negative Answers
(1.a) Short Answers	好。	不好。
	Hǎo.	Bù hǎo.
	Fine.	Not fine.
(1.b) Full Answers:	我们都很好。	我们都不好。
	Wǒmen dōu hěn hǎo.	Wǒmen dōu bù hǎo.
	We're all fine.	We're all not fine.
(1.c) In Combination:	好，我们都很好。	不好，我们都不好。
	Hǎo, wǒmen dōu hěn hǎo.	Bù hǎo, wǒmen dōu bù hǎo.
	Yes, we're all fine.	No, we're all not fine.
(2.a) Short Answers:	是。	不是。
	Shì.	Bú shì.
	Yes.	No.
(2.b) Long Answers:	这是我的书。	这不是我的书。
	Zhè shì wǒ de shū.	Zhè bú shì wǒ de shū.
	This is my book.	This is not my book.
(2.c) In Combination:	是，这是我的书。	不是，这不是我的书。
	Shì, zhè shì wǒ de shū.	Bú shì, zhè bú shì wǒ de shū.
	Yes, this is my book.	No, this isn't my book.

1. Question Formation: The Use of an Interrogative Word

1.1 The third type of question involves the use of an interrogative word that asks for specific information. In English, such questions are formed with words like "who," "what," "where," "when," "why," etc. and are often referred to, for obvious reasons, as the "WH-questions." Two Chinese interrogative words are introduced in this lesson:

（1） 谁 *Shéi* "who": 那是谁？
    Nà shì shéi?
    Who is that?

（2） 哪 *nǎ* "which": 他是哪国人？
    Tā shì nǎ guó rén?
    He is which country's person?
    (= What is his nationality?)

The following are a few points to note about the use of an interrogative−word question.

1.2 The word order in an interrogative word question follows the same sequence as its answer. In other words, phrase the question in the same way it will be answered. Unlike English, Chinese does not require any change in word order.

（3） Q: 那是谁？
    Nà shì shéi?
    Who is that?
    A: 那是我们老师。
    Nà shì wǒmen lǎoshī.
    That is our teacher.

(4)   Q: 这是谁的书？

Zhè shì shéi de shū?

This is "who's" book?

(= Whose book is this?)

A: 这是老师的书。

Zhè shì lǎoshī de shū.

This is the teacher's book.

(5)   Q: 谁不忙？

Shéi bù máng?

Who is not busy?

A: 我不忙。

Wǒ bù máng.

I'm not busy.

1.3 The question particle 吗 never appears in an interrogative−word question. Therefore, it is incorrect to say,

(6)   *那是谁吗？

*Nà shì shéi ma?

Who is that?

1.4 The question word 哪 *nǎ* "which" is always used together with a following noun, forming an interrogative phrase.

(7)   Q: 他是哪国人？

Tā shì nǎ guó rén?

He is which country's person?

(= He is a person from which country?)

(= What is his nationality?)

A: 他是中国人。

Tā shì Zhōngguó rén.

He is Chinese.

Note, however, that in order for 哪 to be connected to the following noun, some intermediary element must stand in between, a grammatical feature that will be introduced in Lesson 15. In other words, it is incorrect to say 哪书 *nǎ shū* for "which book?" 哪国人 is an exception to this rule and may be regarded as an idiomatic expression.

Lesson 7

1. The Interrogative Word 什么

Like its equivalent "what" in English, 什么 *shénme* is probably the most frequently used interrogative word in the Chinese language. It can appear all by itself, as in (1), as the sole interrogative expression, or it can be placed before a noun for more specific identification, as in (2).

(1)　这是什么？
　　　Zhè shì shénme?
　　　What is this?

(2)　这是什么地图？
　　　Zhè shì shénme dìtú?
　　　What map is this?

As described in the previous lesson, the word order in a Chinese question is often quite different from that in English. Chinese uses the same word order for its questions as well as for their answers, a structural parallel that becomes self-evident when the above questions are compared with their respective answers:

(1.a)　这是地图。
　　　　Zhè shì dìtú.
　　　　This is a map.

(2.a)　这是中国地图。
　　　　Zhè shì Zhōngguó dìtú.
　　　　This is a map of China.

2. The Imperative

An imperative sentence in English is usually a "subjectless" sentence, for example, "Look! " To give the same command in Chinese, we have an option as to whether we want to include or omit the relevant subject. Therefore, both of the following sentences are correct.

(1)   看！
        Kàn!
        Look!

(2)   你看！
        Nǐ kàn!
        You look!

Sentence (1), however, sounds harsher and more abrupt than sentence (2).

Lesson 8

1. An Action Sentence

An action sentence involves the use of an action verb, an example of which is 看 *kàn* "to see," introduced in the previous lesson. In this lesson, we are going to learn a few more action verbs, some of which are transitive in use and some intransitive.

进	*jìn*	"to enter"			
喝	*hē*	"to drink"	喝茶	*hē chá*	"to drink tea"
吸	*xī*	"to inhale"	吸烟	*xī yān*	"to inhale smoke" (= "to smoke a cigarette")
看	*kàn*	"to look"	看书	*kàn shū*	"to look at a book" (= "to read a book")

A transitive verb takes an Object, [1] and the Object appears after the verb. The word orders for an action sentence in all three modes are listed as follows:

> Positive: Subject ＋ Verb ＋ Object

(1) 他喝茶。
Tā hē chá.
He drinks tea.

> Negative: Subject ＋ 不 ＋ Verb ＋ Object

(2) 我们不吸烟。
Wǒmen bù xī yān.
We don't smoke.

---

1. As the word "object" can mean either a physical object or a grammatical object, the latter usage is always spelled with a capital "O" 〔 "Object" 〕 in this book.

> Interrogative: Subject + Verb + Object + 吗？

(3)   老师看书吗？
        Lǎoshī kàn shū ma?
        Does the teacher read books?

2. The Polite Request

To make a polite request, we may begin the sentence with the word 请 *qǐng*, literally meaning "please." The subject 你／你们 *nǐ/nǐmen* "you" is often omitted. For example.

(1)   请进！
        Qǐng jìn!
        Please enter!
        (= Come in, please.)

(2)   请喝茶！
        Qǐng hē chá!
        Please drink tea!
        (= Have some tea, please.)

3. The Honorific Pronoun 您

The second person singular pronoun 你 *nǐ* has a variant form 您 *nín*, which marks respect for the addressee. It is normally used to address one's elders or a person whom one meets for the first time. There is, however, no corresponding plural form: *您们.   Within the Chinese culture, it is important to use this honorific form to refer to the person you are speaking with when he/she is senior to you in age or in social status. An even more polite discourse pattern is to begin the conversation with an appropriate term of address and use 您 throughout the dialogue. For example, among the following three ways of offering tea to your teacher, (1) is much more courteous than (2), and (3) displays lack of respect.

(1)   王老师，您喝茶吗？
        Wáng lǎoshī, nín hē chá ma?
        Teacher Wang, would you like to have some tea?

(2)   您喝茶吗？
        Nín hē chá ma?

(3) 你喝茶吗？
     Nǐ hē chá ma?

4. How to Address a Person

To address someone as "Dr. Wang" in Chinese, the word order is to have the last
name first, to be followed by the title: 王大夫 *Wáng dàifu*. By the same token, 丁老
师 *Dīng lǎoshī* is literally "Teacher Ding." There is no English equivalent to 老师 ,
a title that can be used for all teachers, a kindergarten instructor as well a college
professor. The following are some common social titles:

先生	xiānsheng	"Mr.":	王先生	Wáng xiānsheng	"Mr. Wang"
太太	tàitai	"Mrs.":	丁太太	Dīng tàitai	"Mrs. Ding"
小姐	xiǎojie	"Ms.":	古小姐	Gǔ xiǎojie	"Miss Gu"

There is no equivalent to "Ms." in Chinese.

Lesson 9

1. Naming in Chinese

1.1 A personal name in Chinese consists of two parts, the surname 姓 *xìng* and the given name. The surname comes first, followed by the given name. Hence, "the last name first."

1.2 The word 姓 is both a noun and a verb, but it is generally used as a verb in conversation. Thus,

> (1)　我姓丁。
> Wǒ xìng Dīng.
> I am surnamed Ding.
> (= My last name is Ding.)

1.3 To ask for someone's surname, the polite form of inquiry is "您贵姓？", literally "You expensive surname is…?" 贵 marks a honorific reference and is, therefore, never used when referring to oneself. For example,

> (2)　A. 请问，您贵姓？
> 　　　Qǐng wèn, nín guì xìng?
> 　　　May I ask what your last name is?
> 　　B. 我姓丁。
> 　　　Wǒ xìng Dīng.
> 　　　My last name is Ding.
> 　　*我贵姓丁。
> 　　　My expensive last name is Ding.

1.4 To give one's full name, either one of the following forms can be used:

> 我姓 LAST NAME ，我叫 GIVEN NAME 。
> *Wǒ xìng..., Wǒ jiào...*

```
┌─────────────────────────────────────────────────────┐
│        我叫  FULL NAME（ Last  +  Given Names ）       │
└─────────────────────────────────────────────────────┘
```

叫 *jiào* literally means "to call." Its usage in this regard is similar to that of *heissen* in German: "Wie heiβen Sie?" ("What are you called?" for "What's your name?") In general, one would give one's full name even if the question is simply "您贵姓？"

> (3)   A: 请问您贵姓？
>   Qǐng wèn nín guì xìng?
>   B: 我姓丁，我叫丁云。
>   Wǒ xìng Dīng, wǒ jiào Dīng Yún.

2. 请问 "May I ask..."

To express politeness when asking for information, one often begins the question with the phrase 请问 *qǐng wèn.* Its use is similar to that of "May I ask..." or "Excuse me, ..." in English.

> (1)   请问，您是中国人吗？
>   Qǐng wèn, nín shì Zhōngguó rén ma?
>   May I ask, are you Chinese?

> (2)   请问，你吸烟吗？
>   Qǐng wèn, nǐ xī yān ma?
>   Excuse me, do you smoke?

> (3)   请问，他们学习什么？
>   Qǐng wèn, tāmen xúexí shénme?
>   May I ask what are they studying?

Literally, 请 means "please" and 问 "to ask." 问 is a transitive verb, as used in the following sentence:

> (4)   我问你，他是你老师吗？
>   Wǒ wèn nǐ, tā shì nǐ lǎoshī ma?
>   May I ask you: Is he your teacher?

Lesson 10

1. The Verb 在

1.1 The verb 在 *zài* indicates location or presence. To say someone is present or absent, we may simply use 在 to form the sentence.

（1） Positive: 他在。
Tā zài.
He is here.

（2） Negative: 他不在。
Tā bú zài.
He is not here.
(= He's out.)

（3） Interrogative: 他在吗？
Tā zài ma?
Is he here?
(= Is he in?)

1.2 The verb 在 may also be followed by a place word indicating a person's location.

（4） A. 请问，帕兰卡在宿舍吗？
Qǐng wèn, Pàlánkǎ zài sùshè ma?
May I ask if Palanka is at the dorm?
B. 在，她在宿舍。
Zài, tā zài sùshè.
Yes, she is at the dorm.

2. The Locative

The following three locatives are general indicators of localities with reference to the speaker.

这儿 *zhèr*	"here"
那儿 *nàr* (4th tone)	"there"
哪儿 *nǎr* (3rd tone)	"where"

The locatives often appear as Objects of 在, specifying location.

(1)　他在哪儿？
　　　Tā zài nǎr?
　　　Where is he?

(2)　他在这儿，不在那儿。
　　　Tā zài zhèr, bú zài nàr.
　　　He is here, and not there.

The difference between 他在 and 他在这儿 is that the former indicates the presence and the latter the location.

3. Numerals

○	一	二	三	四	五
líng	*yī*	*èr*	*sān*	*sì*	*wǔ*
0	1	2	3	4	5

A room number or a telephone number is to be read as is. For example, 231−5041 is "èr−sān−yī−wǔ−líng−sì−yī."

4. The Interrogative Word 多少

The interrogative word 多少 *duōshao* (literally "many-few") is used to ask for quantity or number: "how many, how much, what." For example, 多少号？ *Duōshao hào* means "What is the number?" Please note that 号 *hào* "number" comes after the interrogative word. The following are a few more examples to illustrate the use of interrogative words in combination with numerals:

(1)　A: 请问，您住哪儿？

　　　　Qǐng wèn, nín zhù nǎr?

　　　　Excuse me, where do you live?

　　B: 我住那儿。

　　　　Wǒ zhù nàr.

　　　　I live there.

　　A: 那儿是多少号？

　　　　Nàr shì duōshao hào?

　　　　What's the number there?

　　B: 那儿是三四一号。

　　　　Nàr shì sān—sì—yī hào.

　　　　It's 341.

(2)　A: 请问，古波在吗？

　　　　Qǐng wèn, Gǔbō zài ma?

　　　　Excuse me, is Gubo here?

　　B: 他不在，他在宿舍。

　　　　Tā bú zài, tā zài sùshè.

　　　　No, he isn't. He is at the dorm.

　　A: 他住多少号？

　　　　Tā zhù duōshao hào?

　　　　What's his room number?

　　B: 他住二〇五号。

　　　　Tā zhù èr—líng—wǔ hào.

　　　　He lives in (room) number 205.

Lesson 11

1. The Double-Object Construction

As in English, certain verbs in Chinese may take two Objects, a Direct Object (DO) representing the thing that is being affected *and* an Indirect Object (IO) representing the person toward whom the action is directed. For example, "I return the book to you." "Book" is the Direct Object and "you" is the Indirect Object. The IO in English is often marked by the preposition "to." In Chinese, the Double-Object construction follows a set word order:

Subject + Verb + IO + DO

(1)　我还你书。
　　　Wǒ huán nǐ shū.
　　　I return the book to you.

Besides 还 *huán* "to return (a borrowed) object," there are quite a few other verbs that can take two Objects. We will have more to say about the pattern in Lesson 15.

2. Time Words

A time word *always* appears before the verb/predicate it modifies. It may stand either before or after the subject. The following examples are all constructed with 现在, the only time word we have learned thus far.

(1)　我现在看书。
　　　Wǒ xiànzài kàn shū.
　　　I am reading a book now.
　　　(= I am reading now.)

(2)   丁老师现在很忙。

Dīng lǎoshī xiànzài hěn máng.

Teacher Ding is busy right now.

(3)   现在我看画报，我不用词典。

Xiànzài wǒ kàn huàbào, wǒ bú yòng cídiǎn.

I'm reading a magazine now. I don't need to use the dictionary.

(4)   请问丁老师现在在吗？

Qǐng wèn Dīng lǎoshī xiànzài zài ma?

Excuse me, is Teacher Ding here now?

Unlike its English equivalent "now" which may appear in a variety of positions in a sentence ("Now, I'm reading." "I'm now reading." "I'm reading now."), 现在 *never* shows up in the sentence final position. It would be wrong to rephrase sentence (1) as (1.a).

(1.a)*我看书现在。

*Wǒ kàn shū xiànzài.

3. The Tentative 一下儿

To express the notion of "doing an action just a little bit," we suffix the verb with the "tentative" marker 一下儿 *yíxiàr*, literally meaning "a bit":

Verb ——一下儿

(1)   看一下儿

kàn yíxiàr

take a look

(2)   用一下儿

yòng yíxiàr

use (it) a little bit/for a short while

The pattern "Verb ——一下儿" is often used when asking for permission to use an object. It softens the tone of the request, almost as if guaranteeing that "I am using it only for a short while."

(3)   我用一下儿您的车，好吗？

Wǒ yòng yíxiàr nín de chē, hǎo ma?

Is it fine if I use your car (for a short while)?

You may have already noticed that the character 一 is pronounced in the first tone as numeral *yī*, but in the second tone in the compound 一下儿 *yíxiàr*. More to come on this tonal change in Lesson 15.

4. Numerals (continued)

六	七	八	九	十
liù	*qī*	*bā*	*jiŭ*	*shí*
6	7	8	9	10

How do you tell your friends that you live in Room 784 or that your phone number is 981−6072? Just read the number as is. Now that you have learned the words for 0−10, you should be able to say any numeral combinations under 100. The challenge in forming the combinations, however, will be postponed until Lesson 15.

Lesson 12

1. The Modification

We know the word for "good" is 好 or 很好 and the word for "friend" is 朋友. Hence, "My friend is good," is 我的朋友很好. But, how do we say "a (very) good friend"? In this case, the adjective "good" or 很好 does not appear in the predicate; rather, it is used attributively, modifying the noun that follows. In Chinese, a "很 + Adjective" combination requires the intervening particle 的 *de* before it can be placed in front of a noun.

> 很 ＋ Adjective ＋ 的 ＋ Noun

（1） 很好的朋友
hěn hǎo de péngyou
a very good friend

（2） 很忙的老师
hěn máng de lǎoshī
a busy teacher

（3） 帕兰卡和古波都是很好的学生。
Pàlánkǎ hé Gǔbō dōu shì hěn hǎo de xuésheng.
Both Palanka and Gubo are good students.

2. The Motion Verb 去

The verb 去 *qù* "to go" may take a place word of destination as its Object. The place word may be a specific place as in sentences (1) and (2), or a general location as in sentences (3) and (4).

> 去 ＋ Destination

(1)   我去中国。
        Wǒ qù Zhōngguó.
        I go to China.

(2)   他现在去宿舍吗？
        Tā xiànzài qù sùshè ma?
        Is he going to the dorm now?

(3)   你们现在去哪儿？
        Nǐmen xiànzài qù nǎr?
        Where are you going now?

(4)   帕兰卡去那儿，古波不去那儿。
        Pàlánkǎ qù nàr, Gǔbō bú qù nàr.
        Palanka is going there and Gubo is not going there.

3. The Adverb 常

常 *cháng* "often" is a monosyllabic adverb and, by defination, it can only appear between a subject and a predicate. It never stands in the sentence initial or final position.

(1)   他常去中国。
        Tā cháng qù Zhōngguó.
        He often goes to China .

(2)   我们常用汉语词典。
        Wǒmen cháng yòng Hànyǔ cídiǎn.
        We often use a Chinese dictionary.

(3)   我常去宿舍看我朋友。
        Wǒ cháng qù sùshè kàn wǒ péngyou.
        I often go to the dorm to see my friends.

4. The Multifunctional 看

By this time, you probably have noticed that the verb 看 *kàn* can mean a variety of things in Chinese:

(1)   看！
        Kàn
        Look!

(2)　我看书。
　　Wǒ kàn shū.
　　I am looking at a book.
　　(= I'm reading a book/I'm reading.)

(3)　我去看朋友。
　　Wǒ qù kàn péngyou.
　　I'm going to see a friend.
　　(= I'm going to look up/to visit a friend.)

*　　*　　*　　*

Although in the initial stages of Chinese language learning the emphasis is usually placed upon familiarization with sounds and tones, quite a bit of grammar has been introduced in the last twelve lessons. Don't worry if you have problems in understanding or absorbing all the details. Most of the patterns will reappear in the ensuing lessons, where we will review their use again. Don't panic or feel discouraged at this point. You have many more weeks ahead of you to develop a better understanding of how Chinese grammar works and to gain a full and competent command of all the rules and regulations. At least, consider the bright side, we have not burdened you with verb conjugations as you would have encountered in learning almost any other language. Chinese is actually a very simple and logical form of speech. Give it time and patience and you will enjoy it immensely.

Lesson 13

1. Question Formation: The Affirmative－Negative Question

1.1 In addition to the three question types that we have learned in the past twelve lessons (such as the 吗－question, the 呢－question and the interrogative word question), there is a fourth way of forming a question, namely by placing the positive verb and its negative counterpart together. Hence, this form is known as the affirmative－negative question. For example, when you want to ask if someone is busy or not, you may put the positive adjective 忙 *máng* immediately before its negative 不忙 *bù máng*, forming the following question:

> （1）　你忙不忙？
> 　　　Nǐ máng bu máng?
> 　　　You busy not busy?
> 　　　(＝ Are you busy?)

Likewise, to ask if someone is coming, you may say,

> （2）　你来不来？
> 　　　Nǐ lái bu lái?
> 　　　Are you coming?

Please note that the negative marker 不 becomes unstressed in this question form.

1.2 If the verb takes an Object, the formula is simply to juxtapose the affirmative and the negative versions of the verb and place the Object at the end.

> Subject ＋ Verb ＋ 不 ＋ Verb ＋ Object?

> （3）　你是不是学生？
> 　　　Nǐ shì bu shì xuésheng?
> 　　　Are you a student?

(4)   你认识不认识他？

Nǐ rènshi bu rènshi tā?

Do you know him?

(5)   你来不来宿舍？

Nǐ lái bu lái sùshè?

Are you coming to the dorm?

If the verb is in two syllables (AB), repeat the entire form in the interrogative: AB 不 AB. A truncated form, as in the following example is generally considered ill-formed in standard Chinese.

(6)   *你认不认识他？

*Nǐ rèn bu rènshi tā?

Do you know him?

To reply to an affirmative–negative question, one picks the positive predicate for a positive answer and the negative predicate for a negative answer. The marker 不 resumes its full tone, with appropriate modification, in the negative answer. (See Lesson 3 for tone change rules.) Thus, the two responses to question (4) are:

(7)   我认识他。

Wǒ rènshi tā.

I know him.

(8)   我不认识他。

Wǒ bú rènshi tā.

I don't know him.

The short answers are:

(7.a) 认识。

Rènshi.

Yes.

(8.a) 不认识。

Bú rènshi.

No.

Do not ever use 是 as a positive short answer, unless the main verb in the question is 是, as is the case in example (3).

1.3 The affirmative—negative question is essentially the same in meaning as a 吗—question, both soliciting either a Yes or a No answer. Thus, they can often be used interchangeably.

> (9.a) 你朋友说汉语吗？
>
> Nǐ péngyou shuō Hànyǔ ma?
>
> Does your friend speak Chinese?
>
> (9.b) 你朋友说不说汉语？
>
> Nǐ péngyou shuō bu shuō Hànyǔ?

In some instances, however, an affirmative—negative form may sound more forceful, emphatic, or even abrupt, than a 吗—question. For example,

> (10.a) 你是中国人吗？
>
> Nǐ shì Zhōngguó rén ma?
>
> Are you Chinese?
>
> (10.b) 你是不是中国人？
>
> Nǐ shì bu shì Zhōngguó rén?

(10.a) is a simple information question asking for someone's identity; (10.b), on the other hand, sounds more like questioning someone's identity.

Another difference between the two question forms is that the affirmative—negative formula is never used for a sentence that contains an adverb such as 很 *hěn*, 都 *dōu* or 也 *yě*. Therefore,

> (11.a) 你们都说中国话吗？
>
> Nǐmen dōu shuō Zhōngguó huà ma?
>
> Do you all speak Chinese?
>
> (11.b) *你们都说不说中国话？
>
> *Nǐmen dōu shuō bu shuō Zhōngguó huà?
>
> (12.a) 你朋友也去吗？
>
> Nǐ péngyou yě qù ma?
>
> Is your friend also going?
>
> (12.b) *你朋友也去不去？
>
> *Nǐ péngyou yě qù bu qù?

As marked by the asterisk, neither (11.b) nor (12.b) is a grammatically correct question.

2. Verbal Expressions in Series

2.1 This construction refers to a series of verbal expressions that are strung together, with one acting as the main predicate and the rest adding more information to the sentence. There are various types of V−V series, each carrying out a different semantic function. The one that we are learning in this lesson pertains to "PURPOSE."

```
Subject + [Verb + Object] + [Verb + Object]
                                      [PURPOSE]
```

(1)   你去商店买书。
      Nǐ qù shāngdiàn mǎi shū.
      You're going to the shop to buy books.

(2)   他来宿舍看朋友。
      Tā lái sùshè kàn péngyou.
      He's coming to the dorm to see a friend.

(3)   老师来帮助我。
      Lǎoshī lái bāngzhù wǒ.
      The teacher is coming to help me.

2.2   The negative pattern of the V−V series is:

```
Subjct + 不 + [Verb + Object] + [Verb + Object]
                                       [PURPOSE]
```

(4)   你不去商店买书。
      Nǐ bú qù shāngdiàn mǎi shū.
      You're not going to the shop to buy books.

(5)   他不来宿舍看朋友。
      Tā bù lái sùshè kàn péngyou.
      He's not coming to the dorm to see his friend(s).

(6)   老师不来帮助我。
      Lǎoshī bù lái bāngzhù wǒ.
      The teacher is not coming to help me.

Is it all right to negate the second verb phrase in a V−V series, yielding a sentence like (5.a)?

(5.a) *他来宿舍不看朋友。

*Tā lái sùshè bú kàn péngyou.

The answer is NO with some qualification. Strictly speaking, the negative of a V−V series with the second verb phrase denoting PURPOSE is formed by placing the marker 不 before the first verb phrase, as shown in the above pattern. Should we negate the second verb phrase, we would be saying something like "Yes, I'm doing this, but for a different purpose." The emphasis of the sentence is quite different from simply saying "I'm not doing this for this purpose." But before further involving ourselves in semantic complications, let's for the time being simply remember that 不 has the entire V−V series as its scope of negation.

2.3 There are two ways to form the interrogative of the V−V series:

(A) The 吗−Question:

(7) 你去商店买书吗？

Nǐ qù shāngdiàn mǎi shū ma?

Are you going to the shop to buy books?

(B) The Yes−No Question:

```
Subject + [ Verb + 不 + Verb + Object ] + [ Verb + Object ]
                                           [ PURPOSE ]
```

(8) 你去不去商店买书？

Nǐ qù bu qù shāngdiàn mǎi shū?

Again, it would be incorrect to place the interrogative on the second verb phrase. Hence, the following sentence is grammatically wrong. As in the case with the negative, (9) may be considered acceptable if and only if the emphasis is on the Purpose expression. It is almost like saying, "I know you are going to the store, but are you going there to buy books?"

(9) *你去商店买不买书？

*Nǐ qù shāngdiàn mǎi bu mǎi shū?

The following are a few more examples to illustrate the use of the Purpose expression:

(10)　你来不来宿舍喝茶看报？

Nǐ lái bu lái sùshè hē chá kàn bào?

Are you coming to the dorm to drink tea and read the newspaper?

(11)　他不常去商店买笔买纸。

Tā bù cháng qù shāngdiàn mǎi bǐ mǎi zhǐ.

He doesn't often go to the store to buy pens and paper.

(12)　丁老师的学生都去中国学习汉语。

Dīng lǎoshī de xuésheng dōu qù Zhōngguó xuéxí Hànyǔ.

Teacher Ding's students all go to China to study Chinese.

3. Positioning of Adverbs in a Sentence

3.1　We have thus far learned three monosyllabic adverbs, namely, 很 "very," 也 "also," and 都 "also." Without exception, they always appear after the subject in a sentence. When more than one adverb appears in the same sentence, they follow a certain order:

也　+　都　+　很

(1)　你很好。
(2)　我也很好。
(3)　我们都很好。
(4)　她们也都很好。

(5)　我买书。
(6)　你也买书。
(7)　我们都买书。
(8)　她们也都买书。

Remember 都 *never* precedes 也.

3.2　When negation applies, the negative marker 不 may appear either before or after the adverb, with a clear distinction in meaning.

(A) 不 and 很

| 不 ＋ 很 ＋ Adjective
not very Adjective | vs. | 很 ＋ 不 ＋ Adjective
very un－Adjective |

(9) 他不很忙。
   Tā bù hěn máng.
   He isn't too busy.

(10) 他很不忙。
   Tā hěn bù máng.
   He's very un－busy.
   (= He's not busy at all.)

(B) 不 and 都

| 不 ＋ 都 ＋ Verb
not all Verb
(not all but some) | vs. | 都 ＋ 不 ＋ Verb
all not Verb
(none at all) |

(11) 他们不都是学生。
   Tāmen bù dōu shì xuésheng.
   Not all of them are students.

(12) 他们都不是学生。
   Tāmen dōu bú shì xuésheng.
   None of them is a student.

(13) 学生不都说汉语。
   Xuésheng bù dōu shuō Hànyǔ.
   Not all the students speak
   Chinese.

(14) 学生都不说汉语。
   Xuésheng dōu bù shuō Hànyǔ.
   None of the students speaks
   Chinese.

(15) 我们不都很忙。
   Wǒmen bù dōu hěn máng.
   Not all of us are busy.

(16) 我们都不很忙。
   Wǒmen dōu bù hěn máng.
   None of us is busy.

(C) 不 and 也: They appear only in one order:

| 也 ＋ 不 ＋ Verb |

(17) 他也不忙。
   Tā yě bù máng.
   He isn't busy either.

（18） 爸爸不来，妈妈也不来。

Bàba bù lái, māma yě bù lái.

Dad isn't coming and mom isn't coming either.

4. The Conjunction 和

4.1   Like "and" in English, the conjunction 和 *hé* is used to join nouns, pronouns, and nominal expressions.

（1） 帕兰卡和古波都说中国话。

Pàlánkǎ hé Gǔbō dōu shuō Zhōngguó huà.

Both Palanka and Gubo speak Chinese.

（2） 爸爸、妈妈、和弟弟都在。

Bàba, māma, hé dìdi dōu zài.

Father, mother, and younger brother are all here.

（3） 我现在学习英语和法语。

Wǒ xiànzài xuéxí Yīngyǔ hé Fǎyǔ.

I'm now studying English and French.

Notice that when the subject phrase contains two or more nouns joined together by 和 , the predicate is usually preceded by the adverb 都 marking the plurality.

4.2   Unlike "and" in English, however, 和 is never used to join clauses; nor is it normally used to join verbs or adjectives. Therefore, it is wrong to say,

（4） *我买书，和他买笔。

*Wǒ mǎi shū, hé tā mǎi bǐ.

I buy books and he buys pens.

（5） *大夫很忙，和老师也很忙。

*Dàifu hěn máng, hé lǎoshī yě hěn máng.

The doctor is busy and the teacher is also busy.

The correct linking of the clauses in (5), for example, is simple juxtaposition, as in (6):

（6） 大夫很忙，老师也很忙。

Dàifu hěn máng, lǎoshī yě hěn máng.

汉吾 = speech
中文 = text

5. A Noun Functioning as an Attribute

5.1   A noun can be used to modify another noun and, as an attribute, it may simply stand before the noun it modifies.

(1)   中国人：   China + person → a Chinese person
(2)   中文书：   Chinese language + book → a Chinese book
(3)   英文报：   English language + newspaper → an English newspaper

There are two words for "the Chinese language," namely 汉语 *Hànyǔ* and 中文 *Zhōngwén*. The difference between the two is a matter of emphasis. While the former pertains more to the speech form, the latter stresses more the written aspect of the language. Thus, the subject we are studying now can be referred to as either 汉语 or 中文. Our textbook may be described as 中文书 *Zhōngwén shū* or 汉语书 *Hànyǔ shū* since it teaches the Chinese language, covering both sounds and characters. However, a Chinese language newspaper is always a 中文报 *Zhōngwén bào* as what we see in it is basically Chinese orthography.

The phrase "a Chinese teacher" is ambigious in English. The teacher may be Chinese but teaching, say, world geography, or he/she may be British but teaching Mandarin. Such ambiguity does not exsit in Chinese. When referring to race or nationality, the term is 中国老师 *Zhōngguó lǎoshī* "a teacher of Chinese descent"; if we are speaking of the subject of instruction, the term is 中文老师 *Zhōngwén lǎoshī* or 汉语老师 *Hànyǔ lǎoshī*. A newspaper printed in China in any language is 中国报 *Zhōngguó bào*, but a Chinese language newspaper printed anywhere in the world is always 中文报 *Zhōngwén bào*. A Chinese name is either 中文名字 *Zhōngwén míngzi* or 中国名字 *Zhōngguó míngzi* since such a name, whomever it is given to, in generally written in characters and not in *pīnyīn,* and it follows a uniquely Chinese naming format such as the last name first, the last name being chosen from a limited set of surnames, and the characters in the given name being carefully selected and combined so as to give a positive reading.

In general, the distinction among 中文, 汉语 and 中国 is quite self-evident. A car made in China is a 中国车 *Zhōngguó chē*, a Chinese pen is a 中国笔 *Zhōngguó bǐ*, a Chinese student (by nationality) is a 中国学生 *Zhōngguó xuésheng*, a Chinese language student is a 中文学生 *Zhōngwén xuésheng*. Please note that while both 中文老师 *Zhōngwén lǎoshī* and 汉语老师 *Hànyǔ lǎoshī* mean "a Chinese language teacher," only 中文学生 *Zhōngwén xuésheng* and not *汉语学生 *Hànyǔ xuésheng* is used to refer to the student.

5.2   In this regard we should also make a brief note of the difference between 中国朋友 *Zhōngguó péngyou* and 中国的朋友 *Zhōngguó de péngyou*. While the former refers to "friends who are Chinese by nationality or descent," the latter are "friends of China." We have already discussed the possessive use of 的 *de* in Lesson 5 and we will have more to say about this grammatical marker in later lessons.

6. The Use of 喂

喂 *wèi* is often glossed as an interjection for informal greeting, an expression equivalent to "hello" or "hey" in English. It is, however, used most often as a telephone greeting, similar to the use of "hello" when answering a phone call. When speaking to a person face-to-face, however, it is very impolite to "greet" the other party by saying 喂. To address someone with 喂 is like calling someone "Hey, you!" in English. Only when speaking to a very close friend or wanting the attention of a total stranger would one use 喂 as a "greeting" interjection; even then it sounds uncouth and rude.

7. How to Ask for Someone's Name

To ask for someone's name, one may say,

(1)   你叫什么名字？
       Nǐ jiào shénme míngzi?
       What's your name?

This question is used, however, only when addressing one's peers or inferiors. It is never used when speaking to elderly persons or one's superiors. To ask for this information, a more appropriate question form, as introduced earlier, is (2), to which the addressee will more often than not give his/her full name.

(2)   您贵姓？
       Nín guì xìng?
       (Literally) What is your expensive last name?

8. The Verb 介绍

The verb 介绍 *jièshào* literally means "to introduce." Its scope of application is, however, much wider than that of the English equivalent. It may be used for introducing a friend, as in (1), or it may be used in the sense of briefing an audience on a certain subject matter, as in (2). It may even be used for making a recommendation, as in (3).

(1) 我们不认识，请你介绍一下儿。
  Wǒmen bú rènshi, qǐng nǐ jièshào yíxiàr.
  We don't know each other. Please introduce us (to each other).

(2) 老师现在介绍北京。
  Lǎoshī xiànzài jièshào Běijīng.
  The teacher is now telling us something about Beijing.

(3) 我不介绍你看他的书。
  Wǒ bú jièshào nǐ kàn tā de shū.
  I don't recommend you read his book.

The last sentence, though a bit complicated in structure, is perfectly clear in terms of the usage of the word 介绍. Also, in sentence (1), the pattern "Verb 一下儿" is adopted so as to soften the tone of the often uneasy or embarrassing task of introducing people to each other. The following is another example of this use of 介绍一下儿.

(4) 她说，"这是我哥哥。来，我介绍一下儿。"
  Tā shuō, "Zhè shì wǒ gēge. Lái, wǒ jièshào yíxiàr."
  She said, "This is my elder brother. Come, let me introduce you."

Lesson 14

1. The 有－Sentence

The verb for "to have, to possess" is 有 *yǒu* in Chinese and its negative is 没有 *méi yǒu* and not *不有. Its interrogative may either be a 吗－question or an affirmative－negative form juxtaposing 有 and 没有.

    (1)   Affirmative: 我们有孩子。
                                    Wǒmen yǒu háizi.
                                    We have children.

    (2)   Negative: 我们没有孩子。
                                    Wǒmen méi yǒu háizi.
                                    We don't have children.

    (3)   Interrogative: (a) 你们有孩子吗？
                                          Nǐmen yǒu háizi ma?
                                      (b) 你们有没有孩子？
                                          Nǐmen yǒu mei yǒu háizi?
                                        Do you have children?

Short answers to a 有－question are 有 for the positive and 没有 for the negative. Like 不 introduced earlier, 没 is pronounced with a full tone in the negative 没有 *méi yǒu* but with a neutral tone in the affirmative－negative form 有没有 *yǒu mei yǒu*. The following are a few more examples:

    (4)   老师有中国地图。
                Lǎoshī yǒu Zhōngguó dìtú.
                The teacher has a map of China.

    (5)   我朋友没有汉语词典。
                Wǒ péngyou méi yǒu Hànyǔ cídiǎn.
                My friend doesn't have a Chinese dictionary.

(6)   丁云的哥哥有没有女朋友？

Dīng Yún de gēge yǒu mei yǒu nǚ péngyou?

Does Ding Yun's elder brother have a girl friend?

(7)   A: 你姐姐有孩子吗？

Nǐ jiějie yǒu háizi ma?

Does your elder sister have kids?

B: 没有。他和他爱人都是大夫。他们很忙……

Méi yǒu. Tā hé tā àiren dōu shì dàifu. Tāmen hěn máng...

No, she doesn't. She and her husband are both doctors. They are busy...

2. The Prepositional Construction

2.1   A prepositional expression in English provides us with additional information pertinent to the main verb in a sentence. For example, "I study *in the library*," "I study *from morning till night*," and "I study *with my friends*." The phrases in italics are all prepositional phrases specifying, in these three cases, the place, time, and company with regard to the main action of "studying." To incorporate information of this kind into a Chinese sentence, we employ a similar mechanism often referred to as the "prepositional construction." One difference between the two languages is that, while an English prepositional phrase appears *after* a verb, a Chinese prepositional construction, in the true meaning of "pre-position," appears *before* it. In other words, instead of saying "He studies at home," the Chinese word order is "He *at home* studies."

2.2   We will learn two kinds of prepositional constructions in this lesson. The first introduces PLACE, as in the following sentences.

(1)   他在书店买书。

Tā zài shūdiàn mǎi shū.

He is buying books in a bookstore.

(2)   我不在银行工作。

Wǒ bú zài yínháng gōngzuò.

I'm not working in a bank.

(3)   你在宿舍写信吗？

Nǐ zài sùshè xiě xìn ma?

Are you writing a letter in the dorm?

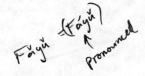

Fǎyǔ [Fáyǔ]
↑
pronounced

We learned in a previous lesson that 在 *zài* is a full verb meaning "to be at (a place), to be present." Therefore, what we have in the above three sentences is basically a V—V series with the first expression specifying PLACE.

> Subject + [Verb + Object] + [Verb + Object]
> [PLACE]

The negative marker 不 is placed at the front of the entire series, i.e. before the first verb. The interrogative generally adopts the 吗—form. The following are a few more examples:

(4) A: 请问，你爱人在哪儿工作？

Qǐng wèn, nǐ àiren zài nǎr gōngzuò?

May I ask where your husband works?

B: 他现在没有工作。他在家学习法语。

Tā xiànzài méi yǒu gōngzuò. Tā zài jiā xuéxí Fǎyǔ.

He doesn't have a job now. He is studying French at home.

(5) 商老师的孩子都不在家住。商老师常去宿舍看他们。

Shāng lǎoshī de háizi dōu bú zài jiā zhù. Shāng lǎoshī cháng qù sùshè kàn tāmen.

Teacher Shang's children don't live at home. Teacher Shang often goes to the dorm to see them.

2.3 The other kind of prepositional construction introduced in this lesson contains a 给 *gěi* phrase for the first component, the meaning of which is "on behalf of someone, for someone's benefit, for someone, to someone." We shall call this a BENEFACTOR expression.

> Subject + [Verb + Object] + [Verb + Object]
> [BENEFACTOR]

(6) 我给弟弟买画报。

Wǒ gěi dìdi mǎi huàbào.

I am buying a pictorial for my younger brother.

(7) 古波不给爸爸写信。

Gǔbō bù gěi bàba xiě xìn.

Gubo doesn't write to his father.

(8)   老师给我们介绍中国吗？

Lǎoshī gěi wǒmen jièshào Zhōngguó ma?

Is the teacher going to tell us something about China?

(9)   我妈妈常给我介绍女朋友。

Wǒ māma cháng gěi wǒ jièshào nǔ péngyou.

My mother often introduces me to girls (girl friends).

The negative and interrogative formations are the same as in section 2.2.

The use of a benefactor expression is not something that a student can introduce at will into a sentence. Certain verbs require this pattern while others may employ a different structure to express a similar notion. For our purposes here, let's remember the following verbs that appear in this paradigm.

给 Someone 买 Something   (buying something for
                                                          someone)

给 Someone 写信   (writing a letter to someone)

给 Someone 介绍 Something/Someone   (introduce something/someone to
                                                          someone)

The following example, however, illustrates the use of a different structure to represent the notion of Benefactor.

(10)   我姐姐问你好。

Wǒ jiějie wèn nǐ hǎo.   [Verb + Object + Object]

My elder sister sends you her regards.

The verb in sentence (10), 问 *wèn* "to ask," requires the use of the Double－Object construction juxtaposing the addressee Object 你 and the content Object 好 "How are you?" In any case, this is an idiomatic form for expressing one's regards. You should remember the form as is.

The following are some examples demonstrating a combined use of prepositional expressions.

(11)   A: 古大夫常在哪儿给他孩子买书？

Gǔ dàifu cháng zài nǎr gěi tā háizi mǎi shū?

Where does Dr. Gu usually purchase books for his children?

B: 古大夫常去学生书店给他孩子买书。

Gǔ dàifu cháng qù Xuéshēng Shūdiàn gěi tā háizi mǎi shū.

Dr. Gu generally goes to Student Books to purchase books for his children.

(12) 丁云在银行工作，她爱人现在在法国工作。丁云常在银行给她爱人写
      信，告诉他她很想他。

      Dīng Yún zài yínháng gōngzuò, tā àiren xiànzài zài Fǎguó gōngzuò.
      Dīng Yún cháng zài yínháng gěi tā àiren xiě xìn, gàosu tā tā hěn
      xiǎng tā.

      Ding Yun works in a bank. Her husband is now working in France.
      Ding Yun often writes to him from the bank, telling him how much
      she misses him.

(13) (A Note)

      帕兰卡，
            我来宿舍看你，你不在。我姐姐给我写信说她很想你。她问你
      好。
                                                                              丁云

      Pàlánkǎ,
      Wǒ lái sùshè kàn nǐ, nǐ bú zài. Wǒ jiějie gěi wǒ xiě xìn shuō tā hěn
      xiǎng nǐ. Tā wèn nǐ hǎo.
                                                                       Dīng Yún

      Palanka,
      I came to the dorm to see you and you aren't here. My sister wrote
      me and said that she was thinking about you a lot. She sends her re-
      gards.
                                                                       Ding Yun

3. The Adverb 常 (continued)

The adverb 常 *cháng*, or its reduplicated form 常常 *chángcháng*, always comes
after the subject in a sentence.

  (1) 我朋友常／常常来看我。
       Wǒ péngyou cháng/chángcháng lái kàn wǒ.
       My friends often come to see me.

  (2) *常常我朋友来看我。

  (3) *我朋友来看我常常。

When the sentence is negated, only the monosyllabic 常 is used. Although 不 may
appear either before or after the adverb with a difference in meaning, 不常 "not
often" is more often used than 常不 "often not." In fact, the latter order appears
only in certain highly idiomatic expressions.

(4)   他不常来看我。

Tā bù cháng lái kàn wǒ.

He doesn't come to see me often.

(= He comes occasionally but not too often.)

(5)   他不常用词典。

Tā bù cháng yòng cídiǎn.

He doesn't use a dictionary too often.

(6)   我爱人不常来看我，我孩子也都不常来看我。

Wǒ àiren bù cháng lái kàn wǒ, wǒ háizi yě dōu bù cháng lái kàn wǒ.

My spouse doesn't often come to see me; and none of my kids often comes to see me either.

The last sentence illustrates the word order of a series of adverbs:

也 + 都 + 常 + verb

4. The Rhetorical Question

A rhetorical question is formed by simply attaching the marker 吗 *ma* to the end of a sentence.

(1)   你不想你爸爸吗？

Nǐ bù xiǎng nǐ bàba ma?

Don't you miss your father?

(2)   他给你写信吗？

Tā gěi nǐ xiě xìn ma?

He writes to you?

The rhetorical 吗 is both phonologically and orthographically identical to the simple interrogative marker 吗. The latter, however, never appears with a negative statement. In other words, if we find 吗 at the end of a negative sentence, as in the sentence "你不想你爸爸吗？", we know this is a rhetorical question. If it appears in a positive sentence, it is then ambiguous as to whether it is a true yes/no inquiry or a rhetorical question. Therefore, out of context, "他给你写信吗？" can have either one of the following two interpretations.

(a) Does he write to you?

(b) He writes to you!? Huh!

But, then, placed in the right context, the ambiguity does not exist.

Lesson 15

1. Numbers

Enumeration in Chinese is based on a simple decimal system involving only ten number words and any combinations thereof for counting under 100.

一	二	三	四	五	六	七	八	九	十
十一	十二	十三	十四	十五	十六	十七	十八	十九	二十
二十一	二十二	二十三	二十四	二十五	二十六	二十七	二十八	二十九	三十
三十一	三十二	三十三	三十四	三十五	三十六	三十七	三十八	三十九	四十
四十一	四十二	四十三	四十四	四十五	四十六	四十七	四十八	四十九	五十
五十一	五十二	五十三	五十四	五十五	五十六	五十七	五十八	五十九	六十
六十一	六十二	六十三	六十四	六十五	六十六	六十七	六十八	六十九	七十
七十一	七十二	七十三	七十四	七十五	七十六	七十七	七十八	七十九	八十
八十一	八十二	八十三	八十四	八十五	八十六	八十七	八十八	八十九	九十
九十一	九十二	九十三	九十四	九十五	九十六	九十七	九十八	九十九	

2. The Measure Word

2.1 When counting things in English, we may simply put the number directly before the noun, as in "three books," "five pens," etc. In some cases, however, we need to insert a "measure" word between the numeral and the noun, as in "a piece of paper," or "two pairs of pants." A measure word is therefore a grammatical element by means of which a numeral is connected to a noun. While the use of a measure word is occasionally required in English, its presence is obligatory at all times in Chinese when a number is placed before a noun. Furthermore, every noun in Chinese has its own specific measure, which should be learned together with the word, much in the same manner as one would memorize the gender of a noun in languages such as French and German.

[Numeral + Measure] + Noun

(1) 一个   孩子
    yíge   háizi
    a child

(2) 十本   书
    shíběn   shū
    ten books

(3) 三十二个   系
    sānshi'èrge   xì
    thirty-two departments

A measure word may demonstrate some kind of a semantic reading that accounts for its use with certain types of objects. For example, the measure word 本 *běn* is generally used as a counter for book-like objects.

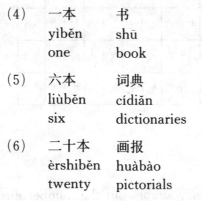

(4) 一本   书
    yìběn   shū
    one   book

(5) 六本   词典
    liùběn   cídiǎn
    six   dictionaries

(6) 二十本   画报
    èrshiběn huàbào
    twenty   pictorials

On the other hand, 个 *ge* is less specific as to its semantic import. It functions primarily as a measure and is extensively employed with all kinds of nouns. In case of doubt about the specific measure for a noun, it is usually safe to use the general 个.

(7)	一个 yíge a	图书馆 túshūguǎn library
(8)	十二个 shí'èrge twelve	朋友 péngyou friends
(9)	五十个 wǔshige fifty	汉字 Hànzì characters
(10)	七十五个 qīshiwǔge seventy-five	本子 běnzi notebooks

In the last example, 本子 chooses 个 over 本 as its measure, primarily to avoid having two 本's in a row.

(11)　我现在去书店买一本新杂志和二十个本子。
Wǒ xiànzài qù shūdiàn mǎi yìběn xīn zázhì hé èrshige běnzi.
I'm now going to the bookstore to buy a new magazine and twenty notebooks.

2.2 Depending on what follows it, the numeral 一 may be pronounced in three different ways:

(A)　yī : When 一 is used all by itself or when it stands at the end of a sequence, it is pronounced in the first tone. For example, 十一 *shíyī*.

(B)　yí + 4th tone: When 一 is followed by a fourth tone syllable, it is pronounced in the second tone. For example, 一件 *yíjiàn* (件 : Measure for clothes).

(C)　yì + 1st/2nd/3rd: When 一 is followed by any of the other tones, it becomes a fourth tone syllable. For example, 一本 *yìběn*.

(D)　yi + a neutral tone: If the neutral tone syllable is originally in the fourth tone, rule (B) applies and 一 is pronounced in the second tone. For example 一个 *yígè* → *yíge*. If the unstressed syllable comes from any of the other three tone categories, then rule (C) applies and 一 is pronounced in the fourth tone.

(E) 一 is always pronounced in the first tone when it is used as or part of an ordinal number. For example, 一二一号 *yīèryī hào* "No. 121".

2.3 The measure is also required in an interrogative sentence asking for a number. The interrogative word appears, again, before the measure. There are two numeral interrogatives in Chinese: 几 *jǐ* and 多少 *duōshao*. 几－M is used for an anticipated number smaller than ten and 多少 is used for any number.

(A) 几－M:

(12) 你们有几个中文老师？
      Nǐmen yǒu jǐge Zhōngwén lǎoshī?
      How many Chinese language teachers do you have?
      (Expecting no more than two or three teachers.)

(13) 你有几个姐姐妹妹？
      Nǐ yǒu jǐge jiějie mèimei?
      How many sisters do you have?
      (Over ten? Not quite likely.)

(B) 多少－M:

(14) 图书馆有多少本中文画报？
      Túshūguǎn yǒu duōshaoběn Zhōngwén huàbào?
      How many Chinese pictorials does the library have?
      (Probably more than ten.)

(15) 你们学院有多少个系？
      Nǐmen xuéyuàn yǒu duōshaoge xì?
      How many departments does your institute have?
      (From a few to a few dozens.)

Please note, however, that 多少 may appear with or without a measure. While the use of the measure may seem optional, there is a slight difference in connotation between the two forms. When the anticipated response is a huge figure, the measure is generally omitted.

(16) 中文系有多少（个）学生？
      Zhōngwén xì yǒu duōshao(ge) xuésheng?
      How many students does the Chinese Department have?

（17）　中国有多少人？

Zhōngguó yǒu duōshao rén?

How many people does China have?

(= What is the population in China?)

Since the Chinese population is in the order of tens of millions, the inclusion of 个 would seem quite inappropriate in the second question.

2.4 The numeral—measure combination stands before the noun it modifies. In a context where the reference is clear, the noun may be omitted but the measure is always retained in the company of the numeral.

（18）　A: 你们有几个孩子？

Nǐmen yǒu jǐge háizi?

How many children do you have?

B: 四个。一个男孩子，三个女孩子。

Sìge. Yíge nánháizi, sānge nǚháizi.

Four. One boy and three girls.

（19）　我和我爱人都学习汉语。我认识七十七个汉字，我爱人认识六十六个。

Wǒ hé wǒ àiren dōu xuéxí Hànyǔ. Wǒ rènshi qīshiqīge Hànzì, wǒ àiren rènshi liùshiliùge.

My spouse and I are both studying Chinese. I know seventy-seven Chinese characters. My spouse knows sixty-six.

3. The Existence 有

The verb 有 *yǒu* indicates possession: "to have". It also marks existence, as in the following sentence:

（1）　阅览室有中文杂志。

Yuèlǎnshì yǒu Zhōngwén zázhì.

(a) The reading room has Chinese magazines.

(b) There are Chinese magazines in the reading room.

The second translation (b) is clearly indicative of this existence use of 有, even though the first translation (a) is just as correct with a possessive verb "to have." In Chinese, the same verb 有 is used for both functions, a linguistic phenomenon observed also in other languages such as French and Japanese. If the subject (or possessor) is an animate noun, it is a possessive 有 ; if the subject is inanimate, then it is an existential 有 .

(2)　　我们有三个老师。
　　　　Wǒmen yǒu sānge lǎoshī.
　　　　We have three teachers.   (Possession)

(3)　　中文系有三个老师。
　　　　Zhōngwén xì yǒu sānge lǎoshī.
　　　　There are three teachers in the Chinese Department.   (Existence)

The negative form of the existence 有 is 没有 *méi yǒu*, and the affirmative−negative form is 有没有 *yǒu mei yǒu*. The negative marker is pronounced in the neutral tone in the 有没有 pattern. The following are more examples of the existence 有 .

(4)　　图书馆没有中文画报。
　　　　Túshūguǎn méi yǒu Zhōngwén huàbào.
　　　　The library doesn't have Chinese pictorials.

(5)　　我们班有二十六个学生。
　　　　Wǒmen bān yǒu èrshiliùge xuésheng.
　　　　Our class has twenty-six students.

(6)　　你们的大学有没有中文系？
　　　　Nǐmen de dàxué yǒu mei yǒu Zhōngwén xì?
　　　　Does your university have a Chinese Department?

(7)　　那儿有三个商店，也有一个书店。那儿没有银行。
　　　　Nàr yǒu sānge shāngdiàn, yě yǒu yíge shūdiàn. Nàr méi yǒu yínháng.
　　　　There are three stores there, and also a bookstore. There are no banks there.

4. The Double−Object Construction (continued)

This pattern has been previously introduced in Lesson 11. To recapitulate, when a verb takes two objects, a Direct Object (DO) representing an object or a thing acted upon and an Indirect Object (IO) representing the person to which the action is directed, IO stands before DO in Mandarin Chinese.

Subject + Verb + IO + DO

(1)　我还他书。
　　　Wǒ húan tā shū.
　　　I return the book to him.

(2)　谁教我们汉字？
　　　Shéi jiāo wǒmen Hànzì?
　　　Who teaches us Chinese characters?

(3)　他告诉我他的名字。
　　　Tā gàosu wǒ tā de míngzi.
　　　He told me his name.

(4)　你问老师什么？
　　　Nǐ wèn lǎoshī shénme?
　　　What are you asking the teacher?

(5)　老师给学生词典。
　　　Lǎoshī gěi xuésheng cídiǎn.
　　　The teacher gives the students a dictionary.

Only a small number of verbs in Chinese may take two grammatical Objects, five of which have been introduced thus far. Other verbs may involve the use of a different grammatical pattern to express the directed goal of an action. For example, the BENEFACTOR pattern we learned in Lesson 14 is one such choice.

(6)　我给他写信。
　　　Wǒ gěi tā xiě xìn.
　　　I write to him.

(7)　我给你介绍我朋友。
　　　Wǒ gěi nǐ jièshào wǒ péngyou.
　　　I'll introduce my friend to you.

The English translation may employ the same structure for both patterns, but we will have to remember which verbs in Chinese take two Objects and which opt for the BENEFACTOR pattern.

(8)　He bought me a dictionary.
(8.a)　他给我买一本词典。
　　　Tā gěi wǒ mǎi yìběn cídiǎn.

(8.b) *他买我一本词典。

　　　 *Tā mǎi wǒ yìběn cídiǎn.

(9)　　 He taught us Chinese.

(9.a)　 他教我们汉语。

　　　 Tā jiāo wǒmen Hànyǔ.

(9.b) *他给我们教汉语。

　　　 *Tā gěi wǒmen jiāo Hànyǔ.

5. The Adverb 还

The adverb 还 *hái* has a variety of meanings and functions, and one of its basic us-ages is to indicate "in addition to," "beside," or "on top of that."

(1)　　 我有三个姐姐，四个妹妹，还有一个哥哥。

　　　 Wǒ yǒu sānge jiějie, sìge mèimei, hái yǒu yíge gēge.

　　　 I have three elder sisters, four younger sisters, and in addition one brother.

Its use is, to a certain extent, very similar to 也, meaning "also." In fact, the above sentence may be rephrased with 也 replacing 还.

(2)　　 我有三个姐姐，四个妹妹，也有一个哥哥。

　　　 Wǒ yǒu sānge jiějie, sìge mèimei, yě yǒu yíge gēge.

There are, however, a few differences between the two adverbs in usage.

(A) 也 marks a parallel situation or relationship between two events or actions. Hence, it is translated as "also" or "too." 还, on the other hand, implies some kind of a surprise. Hence, the translation is "in addition to," "on top of that," etc. Therefore, sentence (2) with 也 is simply a counting of the siblings one has, but sentence (1) with 还 stresses the large number of siblings one has: "Not only do I have seven sisters, I also have one brother."

Here is another pair of examples:

(3)　　 王老师教语法，也教汉字。

　　　 Wáng lǎoshī jiāo yǔfǎ, yě jiāo Hànzì.

　　　 Teacher Wang teaches grammar, and also Chinese characters.

(4)　王老师教语法，还教汉字。

Wáng lǎoshī jiāo yǔfǎ, hái jiāo Hànzì.

Teacher Wang teaches grammar. In addition, he also teaches Chinese characters.

Again, (3) is a simple statement of the subjects Wang teaches. In contrast, (4) is a much more emphatic description of the same teaching assignments: in addition to grammar (which in itself is already a very difficult task), Wang also has to teach characters. 也, therefore, is more of a factual adverb whereas 还 adds to a statement extra emphasis or surprise. The following is an example that uses both 也 and 还 in the same sentence.

(5)　A: 我现在去新图书馆借书。那儿有英语书，也有法语书，还有中文报。你去不去？

Wǒ xiànzài qù xīn túshūguǎn jiè shū. Nàr yǒu Yīngyǔ shū, yě yǒu Fǎyǔ shū, hái yǒu Zhōngwén bào. Nǐ qù bu qù?

I'm going to the new library to borrow books. There are English books and also French books there. In addition, there are even Chinese newspapers. Are you going ?

B: 我也去。我去那儿还地图。

Wǒ yě qù. Wǒ qù nàr huán dìtú.

I'm also going. I'm going there to return a map.

(B) Grammatically, there is a difference in use between the two adverbs.

(a)　　A does X, A 也 does Y.

(b)　　A does X, B 也 does X.

(c)　　A does X, A 还 does Y.

(d)　 *A does X, B 还 does X.

There are two possible forms of parallelism between sentences. The first is a parallel between predicates as in (a) and (c), namely the same person is performing different tasks. The other parallel is between subjects, that is to say different people performing the same task as in (b) and (d). 也 can be used to mark both types of parallelism, whereas 还 only highlights the parallel between predicates. In other words, the use of 还 in (d) is incorrect. The following are examples of this contrast between the two adverbs.

(6)   我教语法，（我）也教汉字。   (Parallel between the predicates)
        Wǒ jiāo yǔfǎ, (wǒ) yě jiāo Hànzì.
        I teach grammar and I teach Chinese characters too.

(7)   我教语法，你也教语法。   (Parallel between the subjects)
        Wǒ jiāo yǔfǎ, nǐ yě jiāo yǔfǎ.
        I teach grammar and you teach grammar too.

(8)   我教语法，（我）还教汉字。   (Parallel between the predicates)
        Wǒ jiāo yǔfǎ, (wǒ) hái jiāo Hànzì.
        I teach grammar and, in addition, I teach Chinese characters too.

(9)   *我教语法，你还教语法。   (Parallel between the subjects)
        *Wǒ jiāo yǔfǎ, nǐ hái jiāo yǔfǎ.
        I teach grammar and, in addition, you teach grammar too.

The difference between (6) and (8) is a matter of emphasis, as explained above.

Also note that the character for 还 is identical with that of 还 *huán* "return," as shown in sentence (5).

Lesson 16

1. The Measure Word (continued)

1.1 A measure word is required between a numeral and a noun. It is also required whenever a demonstrative is used before a noun.

> Demonstrative + Measure + Noun

(1) 这本书
zhè běn shū
this book

(2) 那张票
nà zhāng piào
that ticket

(3) 哪条裙子
nǎ tiáo qúnzi
which skirt

If a noun is modified by both a demonstrative and a numeral, the former comes before the latter, to be followed by the measure:

> Demonstrative + Numeral + Measure + Noun

(4) 这五个朋友
zhè wǔge péngyou
these five friends

(5) 那十二件衬衫
nà shí'èrjiàn chènshān
those twelve shirts

(6)   哪四张地图
        nǎ sìzhāng dìtú
        which four maps

1.2   As illustrated in the second pattern above, a noun phrase in Chinese may contain a demonstrative, a numeral, a measure and the noun itself. The first three elements form one structural unit, modifying the following head noun.

$$\boxed{[\text{ Demonstrative } + \text{ Numeral } + \text{ Measure }] \; + \text{ Noun }}$$

In speech, a slight pause may occur between the modifying unit and the head noun. In fact, as noted in the last lesson, the head noun may be left unsaid if the reference is clear from the context.

(7)   A. 你有几本书？
            Nǐ yǒu jǐběn shū?
            How many books do you have?
        B. 我有四本。
            Wǒ yǒu sìběn.
            I have four.
        A. 这四本都是中文书吗？
            Zhè sìběn dōu shì Zhōngwén shū ma?
            Are all these four Chinese books?
        B. 不，一本是中文书，三本是英文书。
            Bù, yìběn shì Zhōngwén shū, sānběn shì Yīngwén shū.
            No, one of them is Chinese, three are English.

As the reference 书 is established in the initial question, the head noun is omitted from all the other noun phrases in the above dialogue.

1.3   The new measure words introduced in this lesson are 张 *zhāng*, 条 *tiáo*, and 件 *jiàn*. 张 is used primary for objects with a smooth flat surface.

(8)   一张报
        yìzhāng bào
        a newspaper

(9)   三张纸
        sānzhāng zhǐ
        three pieces of paper

(10)   三十张京剧票
     sānshizhāng jīngjù piào
     thirty Beijing Opera tickets

件 and 条 are both used as measures for clothing. 件 is used generally for upper garments such as 一件衬衫 *yíjiàn chènshān* "a shirt," 三件大衣 *sānjiàn dàyī* "three overcoats," etc. 条, on the other hand, is assigned specifically to items such as 裤子 *kùzi* "pants" and 裙子 *qúnzi* "a skirt." Also, please note that while "pants, trousers" are always counted as plural ("a pair of") in English, their Chinese equivalents are measured in singular terms. Hence, 一条裤子 *yìtiáo kùzi*.

2. The Numeral 两

You may already be wondering why we have not been using the number "2" in our practice of counting things with measures. We have deliberately avoided that number because there are two words for "two" in Chinese: 二 *èr* and 两 *liǎng*. In counting numbers, 2 is 二. In counting things, 2 becomes 两 when it stands before a measure word. However, 2 remains as 二 in all number combinations (such as 12, 20, 22, 32, etc.) whether or not it is followed by a measure. Thus,

(11)   两张票
     liǎngzhāng piào
     two tickets

(12)   十二本词典
     shí'èrběn cídiǎn
     twelve dictionaries

(13)   二十个本子
     èrshige běnzi
     twenty notebooks

(14)   这两本书
     zhè liǎngběn shū
     these two books

(15)   那二十二个孩子
     nà èrshi'èrge háizi
     those twenty-two kids

(16)   哪两条裙子
     nǎ liǎngtiáo qúnzi
     which two skirts

（17） 这五十二张纸
zhè wǔshi'èrzhāng zhǐ
these fifty-two sheets of paper

3. The Use of 的 in a 是—Sentence

3.1   The particle 的 *de* is basically a marker of the modification construction. Whenever a noun is modified by an adjective, a pronoun or another noun (or even a sentence, as we shall learn later), 的 appears in between, marking the first segment as an attributive.

[Modifier　+　的] ＋ Noun

（1）　我的书
wǒ de shū
my books

（2）　图书馆的书
túshūguǎn de shū
books of the library

（3）　新的书
xīn de shū
new books

The first example has been introduced earlier (Lesson 5) as a possessive sentence. Actually, a possessive sentence is a sub-type of the modification construction and the possessive particle 的 is in fact the general marker of modification. Grammatically speaking, 我的 (Pronoun ＋ 的) and 图书馆的 (Noun ＋ 的) in examples (1) and (2) function just like 新的 (Adjective ＋ 的) in example (3) in that they all are telling us something extra about the noun 书 . That additional information may pertain to its ownership, its location, or simply its quality of newness.

Here are some more examples of a modified noun phrase in a full sentence.

（4）　这本书是图书馆的书。
Zhè běn shū shì túshūguǎn de shū.
This book is the library's book.

（5）　那张地图是我的地图。
Nà zhāng dìtú shì wǒ de dìtú.
That map is my map.

(6)　　这条裙子是新的<u>裙子</u>。

　　　　Zhè tiáo qúnzi shì xīn de <u>qúnzi</u>.

　　　　This skirt is a new skirt.

3.2　The head noun in a modification construction may sometimes be omitted if its reference can be clearly inferred from the context. Hence, the head nouns underlined in the previous three examples, (4) to (6), can all be deleted; they are redundant of the subject nominals in their respective sentences. The shortened versions sound more natural and are preferred.

(4.a)　这本书是图书馆的。

(5.a)　那张地图是我的。

(6.a)　这条裙子是新的。

In other words, when there is no ambiguity in the context, a modification segment, namely, "Modifier ＋ 的," can appear as an independent unit without its accompanying noun.

(7)　　我有两本中文书，一本是新的，一本是旧的。

　　　　Wǒ yǒu liǎngběn Zhōngwén shū, yìběn shì xīn de, yìběn shì jiù de.

　　　　I have two Chinese books, one is a new one, one is an old one.

(8)　　那个老师不是我们系的；他是法语系的。

　　　　Nà ge lǎoshī bú shì wǒmen xì de; tā shì Fǎyǔ xì de.

　　　　That teacher is not (a member) of our Department; he is (a member) of the French Department.

(9)　　这件大衣是黑的，不是我的。我的是蓝的。

　　　　Zhè jiàn dàyī shì hēi de, bú shì wǒ de. Wǒ de shì lán de.

　　　　This coat is black, it is not mine. Mine is a blue one.

3.3　Now, compare the following two sentences:

(10)　　这是我的书。

　　　　Zhè shì wǒ de shū.

　　　　This is my book.

(11)　　这本书是我的。

　　　　Zhè běn shū shì wǒ de.

　　　　This book is mine.

Both sentences describe ownership. However, while sentence (11) stresses exclusively the ownership, sentence (10) is more of an identification. They answer two different questions:

(12) 这是什么？
      Zhè shì shénme?
      What is this?
      → This is my book.

(13) 这本书是谁的？
      Zhè běn shū shì shéi de?
      Whose book is this?
      → This book is mine.

3.4. Now, compare another pair of sentences:

(14) 那本书很新。
      Nà běn shū hěn xīn.
      That book is new.

(15) 那本书是新的。
      Nà běn shū shì xīn de.
      That book is a new one.

The two sentences are very much alike in meaning, both describing the newness of a book. But, there are actually two very different kinds of newness involved here: the categorical newness and the descriptive newness. By "categorical" we mean the object referred to is either in the category of being new or not being new. For example, all of us have purchased new books. So, categorically, all our books are new. But if my book, though a new one, is somewhat soiled or slightly creased, then mine may not be as "new" as yours, in which case this "new" is a descriptive condition that allows different degrees of variation. This dichotomy between the categorical and the descriptive, or between absolute and relative, is linguistically represented by two different patterns in Chinese:

Categorical: 是 ＋ Adjective ＋ 的

Descriptive: 很 ＋ Adjective

The presence of 很 (literally "very") underscores the relativity of the condition as represented by the Adjective. Another pair of examples is:

    (16)   这件衬衫是蓝的。
                Zhè jiàn chènshān shì lán de.
                This shirt is a blue one.

    (17)   这件衬衫不太蓝。
                Zhè jiàn chènshān bú tài lán.
                This shirt is not too blue.

Sentence (16) is saying that the shirt is a blue one, not yellow or white or of any other color. It doesn't matter whether it is of a darker shade of blue or a lighter shade; it is categorically "blue." Sentence (17), however, stresses the particular hue of blue, as in comparison with other blue objects. Therefore, it is possible to say:

    (18)   这件衬衫是蓝的，可是不太蓝。
                Zhè jiàn chènshān shì lán de, kěshì bú tài lán.
                This shirt is blue in color, but not too blue.

The following are a few more examples:

    (19)   她的大衣不是新的，是旧的。
                Tā de dàyī bú shì xīn de, shì jiù de.
                Her overcoat is not a new one; it is an old one.

    (20)   他的衬衫是白的，裤子是黑的。
                Tā de chènshān shì bái de, kùzi shì hēi de.
                His shirt is white and his pants are black in color.

    (21)   他给我五张纸。那五张不都是白的。一张是白的，四张是绿的。
                Tā gěi wǒ wǔzhāng zhǐ. Nà wǔzhāng bù dōu shì bái de. Yìzhāng shì bái de, sìzhāng shì lǜ de.
                He gave me five sheets of paper. Not all five sheets are white. One sheet is white, four are green.

    (22)   张老师给我两张票，一张是白的，一张是蓝的。白的是京剧票，蓝的是电影票。
                Zhāng lǎoshī gěi wǒ liǎngzhāng piào, yìzhāng shì bái de, yìzhāng shì lán de. Bái de shì jīngjù piào, lán de shì diànyīng piào.
                Teacher Zhang gave me two tickets. One is white and one is blue. The white one is an opera ticket and the blue one is a movie ticket.

（23） 那本杂志是旧的，你有新的吗？

Nà běn zázhì shì jiù de, nǐ yǒu xīn de ma?

That magazine is an old one. Do you have the new one?

（24） 这条裙子太大。我穿那条黑的。

Zhè tiáo qúnzi tài dà. Wǒ chuān nà tiáo hēi de.

This skirt is too big. I'll wear that black one.

3.5　The modification marker 的 between the modifier and its head noun is some-times omitted under the following conditions:

(A) In a possessive construction, as described in Lesson 5, 的 may be deleted if the possessor is a pronoun and the possessed refers to a person.

（25）	我爸爸	vs.	古波<u>的</u>爸爸	vs.	我的书
	wǒ bàba		Gǔbō de bàba		wǒ de shū
	my father		Gubo's father		my book

(B) When a noun is modified by another noun which describes its attributive characteristics, the 的 marker in between is often omitted.

（26） 中国地图

Zhōngguó dìtú

a map of China

（27） 学生宿舍

xuésheng sùshè

student dormitory

（28） 京剧票

jīngjù piào

Beijing Opera ticket

In some cases, the presence or absence of 的 results in a different reading, as shown in the following examples.

（29）	中国朋友	vs.	中国的朋友
	Zhōngguó péngyou		Zhōngguó de péngyou
	a Chinese friend		a friend of China

As explained in Lesson 13, "Noun 的 Noun" often stands for a possessive reading whereas "Noun + Noun" represents an attributive use.

(C) When a noun is modified by a single-syllable adjective, 的 is often omitted:

    (30) 新地图
           xīn dìtú
           a new map

    (31) 白大衣
           bái dàyī
           a white overcoat

    (32) 大书店
           dà shūdiàn
           a big bookstore

However, when a noun is modified by more than one single-syllable adjective, all except the last adjective keeps the marker 的.

    (33) 新的白大衣
           xīn de bái dàyī
           a new white overcoat

As a result of the close binding between an adjective and its noun without the intervention of 的, the "Adjective + Noun" form may become a lexical unit, carrying a specific or idiomatic meaning.

    (34) 大图书馆
           dà túshūguǎn
           (a) "a big library," a literal reading for which we can also say 大的图书馆
           (b) "the main library," a specialized reading that does not allow the inclusion of 的.

3.6. The following demonstrates a gradual build-up in a nominal phrase, utilizing the various grammatical features we have learned so far.

(35)
蓝裙子	lán qúnzi	blue skirt
旧的蓝裙子	jiù de lán qúnzi	old blue skirt
两条旧的蓝裙子	liǎngtiáo jiù de lán qúnzi	two old blue skirts
这两条旧的蓝裙子	zhè liǎngtiáo jiù de lán qúnzi	these two old blue skirts
我的这两条旧的蓝裙子	wǒ de zhè liǎngtiáo jiù de lán qúnzi	these two old blue skirts of mine

4. The Locative Construction

4.1   Certain verbs in Chinese require the use of place words as their Objects. Among others, these include the three verbs we have already seen: 在 *zài* "to be at," *lái* "to come" and 去 *qù* "to go." For example, it is grammatically correct to say "come to me" in English, where the Object of "come" is a simple personal pronoun "me." But, translating this literally into Chinese, as in (1), yields an incorrect sentence.

> (1)   *来我。
>   *Lái wǒ.
>   Come to me.

Since the Object of 来 has to be a place word and 我 is not one, we need to attach a locative word to 我 so as to turn it into an acceptable Object. Common locatives used for this purpose are 这儿 "here" and 那儿 "there." Hence, the correct form for (1) is,

> (2)   来我这儿。
>   Lái wǒ zhèr.
>   Come to me.

The choice between 这儿 and 那儿 depends mainly on the spatial reference.

> (3)   他去张大夫那儿。
>   Tā qù Zhāng dàifu nàr.
>   He went to Dr. Zhang.

> (4)   朋友常常来我这儿。
>   Péngyou chángcháng lái wǒ zhèr.
>   Friends often come to me/my place.

> (5)   老师的笔在谁那儿？
>   Lǎoshī de bǐ zài shéi nàr?
>   The teacher's pen is with whom?
>   (= Who has the teacher's pen?)

> (6)   你的裙子在妈妈那儿。
>   Nǐ de qúnzi zài māma nàr.
>   Your skirt is with Mom.
>   (= Mom has your skirt)

In the last two examples where the English version may use the verb "to have," it is not possible to rephrase the Chinese sentences with 有. Unlike its English counterpart, 有 marks possession that has a more permanent nature. In both (5) and (6), the emphasis is not so much on ownership as it is on the present location of the objects. In (6), for example, Mom may be holding *your* skirt now, but it is still *your* skirt. To indicate this temporary "possession" or current location, we use the 在一 pattern in Chinese.

4.2   As explained in Lesson 14, a 在一place unit can be used as the first verbal expression in a V一V series, in which the 在一place expression denotes the location where the action takes place.

(7)   你弟弟在图书馆看杂志。
      Nǐ dìdi zài túshūguǎn kàn zázhì.
      Your brother is reading magazines in the library.

(8)   你弟弟在我这儿看杂志。
      Nǐ dìdi zài wǒ zhèr kàn zázhì.
      Your brother is reading magazines at my place.

Sentence (7) has a real place word as the Object of 在; in sentence (8) we have a derived place word, which is formed by attaching 这儿 to 我. The derivation is necessary since 我 cannot serve as the Object of 在.

4.3   Another very important pattern is the use of a locative Object after the preposition 从 *cóng* "from" to indicate place of origin.

```
┌─────────────────────────────────────────┐
│        [从  +  Place Word]    +   Verb   │
│               [ORIGIN]                   │
└─────────────────────────────────────────┘
```

(9)   他从中国来。
      Tā cóng Zhōngguó lái.
      He's coming from China.

(10) 我从家去。
      Wǒ cóng jiā qù.
      I am going from my house.

(11) 你从宿舍去。
      Nǐ cóng sùshè qù.
      You're going from the dorm.

(12)　你从我这儿去。

Nǐ cóng wǒ zhèr qù.

You're going from my place.

(13)　他从老师那儿来。

Tā cóng lǎoshī nàr lái.

He's coming from the teacher's place.

In sentences (12) and (13), the place word Objects are formed, in each case, by attaching an appropriate locative to the noun/pronoun. 从 is a member of the locative construction family; but, unlike 来 and 去 (which are verbs *per se*), 从 is a preposition that can never stand on its own without a following verb. For this reason, sentence (14) below is incorrect. In other words, the 从－expression can only function as the first V in a V－V series. Such a word or preposition is often referred to in Chinese grammar as a Coverb because its main function is to assist another verb in a V－V paradigm. In this regard, 从 is also very different from 在, which can function as either a full verb or a coverb as represented by sentences (16) and (17).

(14)　*他从中国。

Tā cóng Zhōngguó.

He is from China.

(15)　你们也去宿舍找朋友喝茶吗？你们从哪儿去？从图书馆去吗？

Nǐmen yě qù sùshè zhǎo péngyou hē chá ma? Nǐmen cóng nǎr qù? Cóng túshūguǎn qù ma?

Are you also going to the dorm to drink tea with your friends? Where are you going from? From the library?

(16)　他在这儿。

Tā zài zhèr.

He is here.

(17)　他在这儿写信。

Tā zài zhèr xiě xìn.

He is writing a letter here.

When a sentence involves both an expression of origin and one of destination, there is a fixed order to follow in forming a grammatical sentence.

```
[从 + Place  Word]    + Verb + Place  Word
[ORIGIN]                        [DESTINATION]
```

(18) 他从中国去美国。
     Tā cóng Zhōngguó qù Měiguó.
     He goes from China to America.

(19) 他从我这儿去书店。
     Tā cóng wǒ zhèr qù shūdiàn.
     He goes from my place to the bookstore.

(20) 他从宿舍去你那儿。
     Tā cóng sùshè qù nǐ nàr.
     He goes from the dorm to your place.

(21) 他从我这儿去你那儿。
     Tā cóng wǒ zhèr qù nǐ nàr.
     He goes from my place to your place.
     (= He goes from me to you.)

(22) 他从哪儿去王老师那儿？
     Tā cóng nǎr qù Wáng lǎoshī nàr?
     From where does he go to Teacher Wang's place?

Note that in each case when there is a need for a place word, a locative is employed to turn the noun/pronoun into an appropriate place Object.

1. How to Tell Time

1.1 Basic time units:

点 *diǎn* "o'clock"
分 *fēn* "minute"
刻 *kè* "quarter"

These time units are measure words *per se*; numbers can be placed directly before them.

X o'clock: X 点（钟）(钟 *zhōng* "clock" is the proper noun used in time measurement.)

X o'clock Y minutes: X 点 Y 分 (if Y is less than ten, the numeral is preceded by 零 *líng*.)

X o'clock 15 minutes: (a) X 点十五分
                             (b) X 点一刻 "X o'clock and one quarter"

X o'clock 30 minutes: (a) X 点三十分
                             (b) X 点半 "X o'clock and a half"

X o'clock 45 minutes: (a) X 点四十五分
                             (b) X 点三刻, "X o'clock and three quarters"
                             (c) 差一刻 X + 1 点, "lacking one quarter, it'll be the next hour."

The following are examples of various time expressions:

	点 diǎn	分 fēn
1:00	一点（钟）	
1:01	一点	零一分
2:02	两点	零二分
3:05	三点	零五分
4:10	四点	十分
5:12	五点	十二分
6:15	六点	十五分／六点一刻
7:20	七点	二十分
8:22	八点	二十二分
9:30	九点	三十分／九点半
10:45	十点	四十五分／十点三刻／差一刻十一点
11:55	十一点	五十五分／差五分十二点
12:00	十二点（钟）	

Please note that for "two o'clock," the numeral is always 两 and never 二：两点. However, for "X o'clock and two minutes," it is always X 点零二分, and never 两分.

1.2 How to Ask the Time: The interrogative word used in asking for time is generally 几 *jǐ*, followed by the pertinent time unit.

(1)　现在几点？

Xiànzài jǐdiǎn?

What o'clock is it now?

(= What time is it now?)

(2)   A: 请问现在几点几分？

Qǐngwèn xiànzài jǐdiǎn jǐfēn?

Excuse me, what time is it now?

B: 我的表现在十点十分，教室的钟现在十点十三分。

Wǒ de biǎo xiànzài shídiǎn shífēn, jiàoshì de zhōng xiànzài shídiǎn shísānfēn.

My watch is now ten minutes past ten, but the clock in the
classroom is thirteen minutes past ten.

Please note that the verb 是 is not required in forming a positive sentence or a
question. In the negative, however, 是 is always persent.

(3)   现在不是两点零二分，现在是差两分两点。

Xiànzài bú shì liǎngdiǎn líng èrfēn, xiànzài shì chà liǎngfēn liǎngdiǎn.

It's not two minutes past two, but two minutes before two.

1.3 Time Units in Combination: If there is more than one time unit in an expression, the sequence follows a general order with the larger preceding the smaller.
Hence,

(4)   2:10   两点十分

(5)   7:15 p.m.   晚上七点一刻

In example （5）, 晚上 *wǎnshang* "evening" represents a part of a day, a period of
which the "o'clock" unit is but a sub-division. Therefore, unlike English, Chinese
takes "p.m." before "hour."

This placement principle is a very important one in the Chinese language, applicable to both time specification and spatial description. The largest unit should always be placed first, followed by all the other units in a descending order of magni-
tude. For example, information on date and time should be given in this set order:

年 + 月 + 日 +	上午 / 下午 / 晚上	+ 点 + 分 + 秒
nián yuè rì	shàngwǔ/xiàwǔ/wǎnshang	diǎn fēn miǎo
year month day	period of day	hour minute second

2. The Time Word Construction

2.1   To describe when an action takes place, English uses a prepositional phrase that comes after the verbal expression. For example, "I go to the library *at seven o'clock,*" or "*... in the evening.*" Or, the two phrases may be combined, "*... at seven o'clock in the evening .*" In Chinese, however, a time expression always comes before the verb. In fact, it may even appear before the subject, at the very beginning of the sentence.

$$\boxed{\text{(Time) + Subject + (Time) + Verb}}$$

(1)   七点我去图书馆
(2)   我七点去图书馆
(3)   晚上我去图书馆
(4)   我晚上去图书馆
(5)   晚上七点我去图书馆
(6)   我晚上七点去图书馆

(7)   我们晚上去看电影。
       Wǒmen wǎnshang qù kàn diànyǐng.
       We'll go see a movie in the evening.

(8)   两点一刻老师来教室。
       Liǎngdiǎn yíkè lǎoshī lái jiàoshì.
       The teacher is coming to the classroom at a quarter past two.

(9)   你几点上课？
       Nǐ jǐdiǎn shàng kè?
       What time do you go to class?
       (= When is your class?)

(10)   晚上八点你作什么？
       Wǎnshang bādiǎn nǐ zuò shénme?
       What do you do at eight o'clock in the evening?

(11)   我六点钟从他那儿走路去食堂。
       Wǒ liùdiǎn zhōng cóng tā nàr zǒu lù qù shítáng.
       I'll walk to the dining hall from his place at six o'clock.

(12)   你现在去哪儿？
       Nǐ xiànzài qù nǎr?
       Where are you going now?

In the last example, 现在 is a time word and is, therefore, placed before the verb.

Another difference between Chinese and English in terms of formation of a time expression is that while English employs a prepositional construction ("*at* eight o'clock," "*in* the evening," etc.), a time word in Chinese stands on its own without the assistance of another element. Therefore, it is grammatically incorrect to say the following sentence using 在 to introduce the time word.

(13) *我在三点上课。

     *Wǒ zài sāndiǎn shàng kè.

     I go to class at three o'clock.

2.2 A time word may also be used as a modifier as in the following phrases:

(14)   九点的课   "a nine o'clock class"
(15)   两点半的电影   "a 2:30 movie"
(16)   十点三刻的票   "a 10:45 ticket"
(17)   八点零五分的车   "an 8:05 train"

As expected, 的 appears between the time modifier and the head noun. The following are more examples:

(18)   我七点半来找你，我们一起去看八点的电影，好吗？

        Wǒ qīdiǎnbàn lái zhǎo nǐ, wǒmen yìqǐ qù kàn bādiǎn de diànyǐng, hǎo ma?

        I'll come to look for you at half-past seven; we'll go see an eight o'clock movie together. How about it?

(19)   我现在去上十点钟的课。

        Wǒ xiànzài qù shàng shídiǎn zhōng de kè.

        I'm going to attend my ten o'clock class now.

(20)   这张票是几点的？

        Zhè zhāng piào shì jǐdiǎn de?

        This ticket is for what (hour's) performance?

2.3 以前 and 以后 : A time expression may be a simple time word such as 七点 "seven o'clock." Or, it may be a compound expression representing a more general time frame. For example, 七点以前 *qīdiǎn yǐqián* "before seven o'clock," or 七点以后 *qīdiǎn yǐhòu* "after seven o'clock." Both compound expressions share the same structural pattern:

X   以前／以后

The X can stand for a specific time as in sentences (21) and (22), or it can be an event which is used as a special reference point, as in sentences (22), (23) and (25). In all cases, the expressions come before the main verbs.

（21）　我三点以前在家，四点半以后我有事儿。
　　　　Wǒ sāndiǎn yǐqián zài jiā, sìdiǎnbàn yǐhòu wǒ yǒu shìr.
　　　　I am home before three o'clock, and I'll be busy after half-past four.

（22）　五点一刻以前，我没事儿。我在中文系的图书馆看杂志。
　　　　Wǔdiǎn yíkè yǐqián, wǒ méi shìr. Wǒ zài Zhōngwénxì de túshūguǎn
　　　　kàn zázhì.
　　　　I'm free before a quarter past five and I'll be reading magazines in the library of the Chinese Department.

（23）　你上课以前来找我。
　　　　Nǐ shàng kè yǐqián lái zhǎo wǒ.
　　　　Come look for me before class.

（24）　回家以后，我学习汉语。
　　　　Huí jiā yǐhòu, wǒ xuéxí Hànyǔ.
　　　　I study Chinese after I return home.

（25）　来美国以后，我常常去咖啡馆喝咖啡。
　　　　Lái Měiguó yǐhòu, wǒ chángcháng qù kāfēiguǎn hē kāfēi.
　　　　Since I came to America, I have been going a lot to coffee shops to have coffee.

In other words, the X in the formula can be simply a time word, or a more complicated verbal expression, or, as we will learn later, a complex sentence.

3. Verbal Expressions in Series (continued)

In addition to the place expression, the benefactor expression and the origin expression, the following are some of the other major types of V－V series in Chinese.

3.1   The Expression of Accompaniment:

```
         [跟   Person   一起]   +   Verb
         [COMPANY]
```

(1)   我们跟老师一起去图书馆。
      Wǒmen gēn lǎoshī yìqǐ qù túshūguǎn.
      We go to the library together with the teacher.

(2)   我跟我弟弟一起去看电影。
      Wǒ gēn wǒ dìdi yìqǐ qù kàn diànyǐng.
      I'll go see a movie together with my younger brother.

(3)   你在他那儿等一下儿，我去阅览室找张先生。我们跟他一起去买词
      典。
      Nǐ zài tā nàr děng yíxiàr, wǒ qù yuèlǎnshì zhǎo Zhāng xiānsheng.
      Wǒmen gēn tā yìqǐ qù mǎi cídiǎn.
      Please wait at his place. I'll go to the reading room to look for Mr.
      Zhang. We'll go together with him to buy a dictionary.

The company expression consists of the verb 跟 *gēn* "to follow, with," the Object referring to the company, and the adverb 一起 *yìqǐ* "together." You should note,
however, that when the company is included in the subject expression as in the
answer in the following dialogue, then 一起 may be used all by itself, standing before the verb.

(4)   A: 下班以后，你跟你爱人一起去食堂吗？
         Xià bān yǐhòu, nǐ gēn nǐ àiren yìqǐ qù shítáng ma?
         After work, will you be going to the cafeteria together with your
         wife?
      B: 对了，我们一起去食堂。
         Duìle, wǒmen yìqǐ qù shítáng.
         Correct, we'll be going to the cafeteria together.

3.2   The Expression of Means of Conveyance:

```
              [CONVEYANCE]   +   Verb
```

(5)　　我们坐车去邮局。

Wǒmen zuò chē qù yóujú.

We go to the post office by car.

(6)　　他们走（路）来这儿。

Tāmen zǒu(lù) lái zhèr.

They come here on foot.

(7)　　下班以后，我和爸爸在书店等妈妈。我们一起坐车回家。

Xià bān yǐhòu, wǒ hé bàba zài shūdiàn děng māma. Wǒmen yìqǐ zuò chē huí jiā.

After work, Dad and I will wait for Mom at the bookstore. We'll go home together by car.

The conveyance expression is in itself a Verb－Object construction, the Object being, in most cases, the means of transportation. Some common conveyance phrases are 坐车 *zuò chē* "sit-car: to ride a car: by car," 走路 *zǒu lù* "walk-road: to walk: on foot." In example (6), the Object 路 "road" may be left out. There are different vehicles (bus, boat, plane, etc.) one can 坐 "ride," but one always walks on 路 "road."

3.3　The Expression of Instrument :

```
[用  INSTRUMENT]  +  Verb
```

(8)　　我们用笔写字。

Wǒmen yòng bǐ xiě zì.

We write with a pen.

(9)　　老师用汉语介绍语法。

Lǎoshī yòng Hànyǔ jièshào yǔfǎ.

The teacher introduces grammar in Chinese.

(10)　　晚上七点以后，他在教室用英语介绍汉语语法。

Wǎnshang qīdiǎn yǐhòu, tā zài jiàoshì yòng Yīngyǔ jièshào Hànyǔ yǔfǎ.

After seven o'clock in the evening, he'll be in the classroom explaining Chinese grammar in English.

The instrumental expression is also a Verb－Object construction. The verb is 用 *yòng* "to use" and the Object refers to the instrument or means.

3.4 When a sentence contains a series of verbal constructions that denote the place, the company, the means, etc., there is usually a preferred order for stringing them together. The following are a few examples.

(11)　我下课以后　跟我朋友一起　从教室　　走路　　去　图书馆。
　　　　Time　　Accompaniment　Origin　　Conveyance　Main Verb
　　　　When　　with/Whom　　from Where　How　　　　Action

Wǒ xià kè yǐhòu gēn wǒ péngyou yìqǐ cóng jiàoshì zǒu lù qù túshū-guǎn.

After class, I'll walk from the classroom to the library together with my friends.

(12)　晚上八点以后，王老师 在教室 给学生　　用英语　介绍这个法国电影。
　　　　When　　　　　　　Where　for Whom　with What　Action

Wǎnshang bādiǎn yǐhòu, Wáng lǎoshī zài jiàoshì gěi xuésheng yòng Yīngyǔ jièshào zhè ge Fǎguó diànyǐng.

Teacher Wang will be talking about this French movie in English in the classroom after eight o'clock in the evening.

(13)　我　现在　　跟你一起　　走路　　去那儿　坐车，　　好吗？
　　　　When　with/Whom　How　　Action　for What

Wǒ xiànzài gēn nǐ yìqǐ zǒu lù qù nàr zuò chē, hǎo ma?

Shall I now walk with you there to catch the bus?

Please compare the following two sentences:

(14)　我们坐车去那儿。
　　　　Wǒmen zuò chē qù nàr.

(15)　我们去那儿坐车。
　　　　Wǒmen qù nàr zuò chē.

If 坐车 appears before 去那儿, it is a conveyance expression, describing how to get there. If it appears after the main verb, it is a purpose expression, explaining why to go there.

Lesson 18

1. The Use of 每 as a Demonstrative

1.1 每 *měi* is a demonstrative, meaning "each and every." Like all demonstratives, it requires the assistance of a measure word before it can be placed before a noun.

$$\boxed{\text{每} \; + \; \text{Measure} \; + \; \text{Noun}}$$

(1) 每个老师都很忙。
Měi ge lǎoshī dōu hěn máng.
Every teacher is busy.

(2) 每本书都是新的。
Měi běn shū dōu shì xīn de.
Every book is a new one.
(= All the books are new.)

There are, however, some nouns in Chinese which behave like measure words, thereby not requiring another measure in the above pattern. 天 *tiān* "day" is one such example. (In this sense, 天 may be regarded as a measure word in its own right.)

(3) 我们每天九点上课。
Wǒmen měi tiān jiǔdiǎn shàng kè.
We go to class at nine every day.

(4) 我每天六点一刻起床。
Wǒ měi tiān liùdiǎn yíkè qǐ chuáng.
I get up at a quarter past six every day.

Another example is 课 *kè* "lesson."

  (5) 每课有几个汉字？
     Měi kè yǒu jǐge Hànzì?
     How many Chinese characters are there in each lesson?

There is still a third category of nouns for which the use of a measure in the above pattern is optional. The membership in this category is rather small; thus far we have seen only two.

  (6) 每（个）人有十二个本子。
     Měi (ge) rén yǒu shí'èrge běnzi.
     Each person has twelve notebooks.

  (7) 每（个）班都教汉字。
     Měi (ge) bān dōu jiāo Hànzì.
     Chinese characters are taught in every class.

1.2 It is general practice to add 都 to the predicate of a 每－sentence. The demonstrative 每 denotes "each and every," but its connotation is all-inclusion. Therefore, 都 is used to highlight plurality.

  (8) 每个学生都来找他。
     Měi ge xuésheng dōu lái zhǎo tā.
     Every student comes to look for him.

  (9) 每个阅览室都有中文词典。
     Měi ge yuèlǎnshì dōu yǒu Zhōngwén cídiǎn.
     There is a Chinese dictionary in every reading room.

However, in forming a question with an interrogative numeral in the predicate, 都 is never used.

  (10) 每（个）班有几个老师？
     Měi (ge) bān yǒu jǐge lǎoshī?
     How many teachers does each class have?

  (11) 每个学生买多少张票？
     Měi ge xuésheng mǎi duōshaozhāng piào?
     How many tickets does each student buy?

（12）*每个宿舍都有几个学生？

　　　 *Měi ge sùshè dōu yǒu jǐge xuésheng?

　　　 How many students does each dorm have?

Nor is 都 used when answering these questions, as demonstrated in the following dialogue.

（13）　A. 每班有几个男学生？

　　　　　 Měi bān yǒu jǐge nán xuésheng?

　　　　　 How many male students does each class have?

　　　　B. 每班有十二个男学生。

　　　　　 Měi bān yǒu shí'èrge nán xuésheng.

　　　　　 There are twelve male students in each class.

Please note that in the English translation only "each" and not "every" is used in this same environment. Substituting "each" for "every" in the above sentences, (10) — (13), is unacceptable.

　　　 Now, when the predicate contains a numeral expression that is not in the form of an interrogative word, the use of 都 may be optional. However, the semantic distinction between the inclusion of 都 and its omission is very subtle, even for a native speaker.

（14）　每个学生（都）有四本中文书。

　　　　 Měi ge xuésheng (dōu) yǒu sìběn Zhōngwén shū.

　　　　 Every student has four Chinese books.

（15）　每个人（都）有两个工作。

　　　　 Měi ge rén (dōu) yǒu liǎngge gōngzuò.

　　　　 Everyone has two jobs.

In the above two examples, the choice of 都 seems to place more emphasis on the all inclusive implication of the description and indicate that there are no exceptions to the statements. To facilitate our learning at this stage, however, let us simply say that the use of 都 is strongly preferred in a 每－sentence, except when it serves as an answer to a 几／多少－question.

1.3 When 每 appears with the Object of a sentence, 都 is not used before the verb. The adverb is absent for a very simple reason. As noted earlier, 都 stands in front of a verb, marking the plurality of the nominal standing *before* it. It never refers to a nominal that follows. When 每 appears with an Object, it is by definition positioned after the verb and thereby disqualified from the concomitant use of 都 .

(16) 老师给每个学生两本杂志。

Lǎoshī gěi měi ge xuésheng liǎngběn zázhì.

The teacher gives each student two magazines.

(17) *老师都给每个学生两本杂志。

*Lǎoshī dōu gěi měi ge xúesheng liǎngběn zázhì.

(18) 他问每个人一个问题。

Tā wèn měi ge rén yíge wèntí.

He asked each person a question.

In this connection, we should also point out that the use of the "每－都" pattern serves to highlight the uniformity or sameness of a situation as expressed in the predicate. In this usage, 都 must come before the predicate it modifies. Hence, the sentence below is incorrect because 都 is placed before the verb rather than the entire predicate. 九点 is part of that routine pattern and should therefore be included in the scope of 都 . The sentence may be rephrased as either (20.a) or (20.b).

(19) *帕兰卡每天七点一刻都起床。

*Pàlánkǎ měi tiān qīdiǎn yíkè dōu qǐ chuáng.

Palanka gets up at a quarter past seven everyday.

(20).a 帕兰卡每天都七点一刻起床。

(20).b 帕兰卡每天七点一刻起床。

2. The Time Word 有时候

The time word 有时候 *yǒu shíhou* "sometimes" is often used in pairs, each unit standing before the predicate that represents an occasional happening.

(1) 我晚上有时候十点睡觉，有时候十点半睡觉。

Wǒ wǎnshang yǒu shíhou shídiǎn shuì jiào, yǒu shíhou shídiǎnbàn shuì jiào.

I sometimes go to bed at ten in the evening and sometimes at half past ten.

(2)   下课以后，我有时候回家听美国现代音乐，有时候去蓝老师那儿听中
国古典音乐。

Xià kè yǐhòu, wǒ yǒu shíhou huí jiā tīng Měiguó xiàndài yīnyuè,
yǒu shíhou qù Lán lǎoshī nàr tīng Zhōngguó gǔdiǎn yīnyuè.

After class, I sometimes go home to listen to modern American
music, and sometimes I go to Teacher Lan's place to listen to classical Chinese music.

(3)   A. 你每天吃饭以前都喝一杯红酒吗？

Nǐ měi tiān chī fàn yǐqián dōu hē yìbēi hóng jiǔ ma?

Do you always have a glass of red wine before your meal every
day?

B. 我有时候喝一杯红酒，有时候喝一杯白酒，有时候喝一杯橘子水，
不喝酒。

Wǒ yǒu shíhou hē yìbēi hóng jiǔ, yǒu shíhou hē yìbēi bái jiǔ,
yǒu shíhou hē yìbēi júzishuǐ, bù hē jiǔ.

Sometimes I have a glass of red wine, sometimes I have a white
wine. Sometimes I drink orange juice and don't drink wine.

In the last example, 有时候 appears three times.

3. The Adjective 多

Like all adjectives, 多 *duō* "many, much" may be used either attributively or predicatively, i.e. it can stand before a noun as its modifier or it may constitute a predicate all by itself. The following is an example of its predicative use:

(1)   他的书很多，也很新。

Tā de shū hěn duō, yě hěn xīn.

His books are many, and new too.

But, when it functions as an attribute, 多 behaves somewhat differently from other
adjectives. For one thing, it can never appear alone to modify a noun; it always requires the presence of some adverb such as 很 before it.

(2)   * 多朋友   vs.   新朋友
       *duō péngyou   xīn péngyou
       many friends   new friends

(3)　很多朋友

　　　hěn duō péngyou

　　　many friends

(4)　我们班有很多女学生。

　　　Wǒmen bān yǒu hěn duō nǚ xuésheng.

　　　There are a lot of female students in our class.

(5)　他每天喝很多咖啡。

　　　Tā měi tiān hē hěn duō kāfēi.

　　　He drinks a lot of coffee everyday.

It has been noted (Cf. Lesson 16) that when a monosyllable adjective modifies a noun, the modification marker 的 is generally omitted. Thus, 新的书→新书 "new book." However, when the adjective is modified by 很, the marker resurfaces, as in the following example.

(6)　他没有很新的杂志。

　　　Tā méi yǒu hěn xīn de zázhì.

　　　He doesn't have any new magazines.

(7)　*他没有很新杂志。

　　　*Tā méi yǒu hěn xīn zázhì.

In other words, 的 is required in the attributive use of 很 + Adjective:

```
┌─────────────────────────────────────────────┐
│        [很  +  Adjective]  +  的  +  Noun      │
└─────────────────────────────────────────────┘
```

But, as illustrated in examples (2) to (5), the use of 的 becomes optional in the case of 多; in fact, its absence is more common than its presence.

```
┌─────────────────────────────────────────────┐
│        [很  +  多]  +  （的）  +  Noun          │
└─────────────────────────────────────────────┘
```

The following is a summary of the idiosyncratic behavior of 多 as compared with that of a regular adjective such as 新:

(8)　　新书　　　　　　　　　　　*多书
　　　　xīn shū　　　　　　　　　*duō shū

　　*　很新书　　　　　　　　　很多书
　　*　hěn xīn shū　　　　　　　hěn duō shū

　　　很新的书　　　　　　　　很多（的）书
　　　hěn xīn de shū　　　　　hěn duō (de) shū

少 *shǎo*, the antonym of 多,　shares this anomalous behavior. But, for some strange euphemistic reasons, " 很少 Noun" is often rephrased as a negative of 很 多 , as illustrated in the following sentence.

(9)　　他有很少书。　　　　　　他没有很多书。
　　　Tā yǒu hěn shǎo shū.　　Tā méi yǒu hěn duō shū.
　　　He has few books.　　　　He doesn't have many books.

1. The Alternative Question

There are four major types of question formation in Chinese: (a) the Interrogative Particle Question, including the 吗—Question and the 呢—Question; (b) the Affirmative—Negative Question; (c) the Interrogative—Word Question; and (d) the Alternative Question. The last is the subject of this lesson.

An alternative question provides two (or more) choices and asks the addressee to make his/her selection. For example, in offering your friend a drink, you may ask "What would you like?" or "Would you like to have coffee or tea?" The former is an interrogative—word question, the latter an alternative question. To answer the first question, your friend needs to supply you with the name of a drink; to answer the second question, he/she has to pick one of the two alternatives suggested. In English, the alternative question is marked by the conjunction "or." In Chinese, the marker is 还是 *háishì*.

(1)　你来还是去？
　　　Nǐ lái háishì qù?
　　　Are you coming or going?

(2)　你喝茶还是喝咖啡？
　　　Nǐ hē chá háishì hē kāfēi?
　　　Do you drink tea or coffee?

Please note that, whereas the English "or" may be put directly before the noun in the second alternative, as in (2) "...or *coffee*?", the Chinese 还是 has to appear before the entire predicate, treating the "Verb + Object" as a whole unit. Therefore, in sentence (2), even when the choice is between 茶 and 咖啡, we still need to repeat the verb 喝 in the second clause. Or, to put it in another way, the selection in Chinese is not between "coffee" and "tea," but rather between "drinking tea" and "drinking coffee." The following is a list of all the possible forms of alternative combinations, each illustrated by a sentence.

(A) Choice between the verb and its negative counterpart:

$$\boxed{\text{Subject} \ + \ \text{Verb} \ + \ \text{还是} \ + \ \text{不—Verb?}}$$

(3)   你来还是不来？

Nǐ lái háishì bù lái?

Are you coming or not coming?

(B) Choice between two verbs:

$$\boxed{\text{Subject} \ + \ \text{Verb}_1 \ + \ \text{还是} \ + \ \text{Verb}_2 ?}$$

(4)   你来还是去？

Nǐ lái háishì qù?

Are you coming or going?

(C) Choice between two predicates with different verbs and Objects:

$$\boxed{\text{Subject} + \text{Verb}_1 \ - \ \text{Object}_1 \ + \ \text{还是} \ + \ \text{Verb}_2 \ - \ \text{Object}_2 ?}$$

(5)   你来学校还是回宿舍？

Nǐ lái xuéxiào háishì huí sùshè?

Are you coming to school or going back to the dorm?

(D) Choice between two predicates with different Objects:

$$\boxed{\text{Subject} + \text{Verb} - \text{Object}_1 \ + \ \text{还是} \ + \ \text{Verb} - \text{Object}_2 ?}$$

(6)   你去图书馆还是去食堂？

Nǐ qù túshūguǎn háishì qù shítáng?

Are you going to the library or the dining hall?

(E) Choice between two predicates with same Objects but different verbs:

$$\boxed{\text{Subject} + \text{Verb}_1 \ - \ \text{Object} \ + \ \text{还是} \ + \ \text{Verb}_2 \ - \ \text{Object?}}$$

（7）　你借书还是还书？

Nǐ jiè shū háishì huán shū?

Are you borrowing books or returning books?

(F) Choice between elements other than the two predicates:

> Subject + X_1 + Verb − Object + 还是　X_2 + Verb − Object?

（8）　你上午上课还是下午上课？

Nǐ shàngwǔ shàng kè háishì xiàwǔ shàng kè?

Do you have class in the morning or in the afternoon?

(G) Choice between two sentences or two subjects with identical or different predicates:

> Sentence₁　+　还是　+　Sentence₂?

（9）　你来还是我去？

Nǐ lái háishì wǒ qù?

Are you coming or am I going?

（10）　你去还是我去？

Nǐ qù háishì wǒ qù?

Are you going or am I going?

In any case, the rule to remember is that the verb has to be repeated in each of the alternatives. The connector 还是 is to be placed before the second alternative. In a sentence where the choice pertains to time, place, manner, etc., of an action, the verb still has to be repeated to complete the formula. Sentence (8), for example, poses a choice between time elements. The following are more examples of this nature:

（11）　你从家来还是从宿舍来？   (origin)

Nǐ cóng jiā lái háishì cóng sùshè lái?

Are you coming from home or from the dorm?

（12）　你坐车来还是走路来？   (conveyance)

Nǐ zuò chē lái háishì zǒu lù lái?

Are you coming by car or on foot?

(13)   你跟你姐姐一起来还是跟你哥哥一起来？   (company)
        Nǐ gēn nǐ jiějie yìqǐ lái háishì gēn nǐ gēge yìqǐ lái?
        Are you coming with your sister or your brother?

(14)   你用汉语介绍还是用英语介绍？   (means)
        Nǐ yòng Hànyǔ jièshào háishì yòng Yīngyǔ jièshào?
        Are you going to introduce (this) in Chinese or in English?

(15)   你给你爱人买大衣还是给你朋友买大衣？   (benefactor)
        Nǐ gěi nǐ àiren mǎi dàyī háishì gěi nǐ péngyou mǎi dàyī?
        Are you buying an overcoat for your wife or for your friend?

Now, if the main verb in the formula is 是, then theoretically the alternative question would look like (16), where there would be two 是 succeeding each other. However, one is deleted in speech, yielding (17) as the correct form. In fact, (16) would be considered linguistically unacceptable.

(16)   *你 [是学生] 还是 [是老师] ？
        Nǐ [shì xuésheng] háishì [shì lǎoshī] ?
        Are you a student or a teacher?

(17)   你是学生还是老师？
        Nǐ shì xuésheng háishì lǎoshī?

(18)   这件衬衫是你的还是我的？
        Zhè jiàn chènshān shì nǐ de háishì wǒ de?
        Is this shirt yours or mine?

When two identical elements are immediate to each other, then fusion into one element is quite a common process in the Chinese language. We will witness more of this process in the future lessons. The following are a few more examples of the alternative question type, where the two alternative segments are a little more varied in structure.

(19)   你回宿舍休息还是跟你女朋友一起去看电影？
        Nǐ huí sùshè xiūxi háishì gēn nǐ nǚ péngyou yìqǐ qù kàn diànyǐng?
        Are you going back to the dorm to rest or are you going to see a movie together with your girl friend?

(20)   她上午来看你还是你下午去找她？
        Tā shàngwǔ lái kàn nǐ háishì nǐ xiàwǔ qù zhǎo tā?
        Is she coming to see you in the morning or are you going to look for her in the afternoon?

(21)   你晚上跟我一起去图书馆看书，还是一个人在家听音乐？

Nǐ wǎnshang gēn wǒ yìqǐ qù túshūguǎn kàn shū, háishì yí ge rén zài jiā tīng yīnyuè?

Do you want to go with me to the library this evening and study, or do you want to stay home and listen to music by yourself?

2. The Pivotal Construction

2.1   In spite of its rather technical nomenclature, the pivotal construction is actually a very simple sentence type that exists in all languages. For example, we can see that the following English sentence has a total of three nouns and two verbs.

(1)   John   invited   Mary to drink   beer.
        $[N_1]$ $[V_1]$ $[N_2] [V_2]$ $[N_3]$

N_1 "John" is the subject of V_1 "invite" and N_3 "beer" is the Object of V_2 "drink." How is N_2 "Mary" grammatically related to the two verbs? It is clearly the Object of V_1, "... invited Mary"; at the same time, it is also the subject of V_2 "Mary... to drink." In other words, N_2 holds a dual identity, Object of the first verb and subject of the second verb. Hence, it is the pivot of two verbal units. A pivotal sentence in Chinese is constructed in the same manner as in English.

$$\text{Subject} + \text{Verb}_1 + \left\{ \begin{array}{c} \text{Object} \\ \text{Subject} \end{array} \right\} + \text{Verb}_2 + \text{Object}$$

(2)   古波请帕兰卡喝啤酒。

Gūbō qǐng Pàlánkǎ hē píjiǔ.

Gubo invites Palanka to drink beer.

(3)   我们请老师唱中国歌儿。

Wǒmen qǐng lǎoshī chàng Zhōngguó gēr.

We ask the teacher to sing a Chinese song.

(4)   他不请他朋友去他家。

Tā bù qǐng tā péngyou qù tā jiā.

He wouldn't invite his friends to his house.

(5)   老师让学生写汉字。

Lǎoshī ràng xuésheng xiě Hànzì.

The teacher asks students to write Chinese characters.

(6)   大夫不让他喝咖啡。
       Dàifu bú ràng tā hē kāfēi.
       The doctor won't let him have coffee.

2.2   There are only a limited number of verbs in Chinese that may appear in a pivotal construction. Two of them are introduced here: 请 *qǐng* and 让 *ràng*. Literally, 请 means "to invite" and 让 "to allow." Thus, even though both are used for "asking someone to do something," 请 represents a more courteous request. Children 请 their parents to do something, but parents 让 their children to perform a task.

(7)   孩子请爸爸唱一个歌儿。
       Háizi qǐng bàba chàng yíge gēr.
       The children asked their father to sing a song.

(8)   爸爸让孩子唱一个歌儿。
       Bàba ràng háizi chàng yíge gēr.
       Father asked the child to sing a song.

Other points to note with regard to the use of 请 and 让 are:

(A) The pattern for making a polite request, namely 请 + Verb (as in 请进 *qǐng jìn* "Please come in," and 请喝茶 *qǐng hē chá* "Please have some tea."), is actually a truncated version of 请 + 你 + Verb. The pivotal object is omitted in the pattern, and 请 is often translated as "please." 请问 *qǐng wèn* "May I ask" is an idiomatic compound marking the beginning of a polite inquiry.

(B) 请 also means "to invite," in which case its Object can also be pivotal in function. For example, in the following sentence, 你 is the Object of 请 but also the subject of 看京剧.

(9)   我请你看京剧。
       Wǒ qǐng nǐ kàn jīngjù.
       I invite you to see a Beijing Opera.

In some cases, a 请—sentence may be ambiguous as to whether it is an invitation or a request.

(10)   我请他喝咖啡。
       Wǒ qǐng tā hē kāfēi.

This sentence could mean either (a) a request: "I ask him to drink coffee (and not do anything else)," or (b) a treat: "I buy him a coffee." The context in general will decide which is the intended reading.

There are two kinds of "ask" in English: "to ask someone a question" and "to ask someone to do something." They correspond to different verbs in Chinese as demonstrated in the following pair of sentences.

(11) 我问他晚上来不来。

Wǒ wèn tā wǎnshang lái bu lái.

I asked him if he'd be coming in the evening.

(12) 我请他晚上来。

Wǒ qǐng tā wǎnshang lái.

I asked him to come in the evening.

Sentence (13) juxtaposes both *qǐng* and *wèn* in the same sentence.

(13) 我们请他去问王老师一个语法问题。

Wǒmen qǐng tā qù wèn Wáng lǎoshī yíge yǔfǎ wèntí.

We asked him to go ask Teacher Wang a grammar question.

(C) Depending on the context, a 让—sentence connotes either request or permission. Its negative, 不让 Verb, however, is always a prohibition.

(14) 老师让我用英文说。

Lǎoshī ràng wǒ yòng Yīngwén shuō.

(a) The teacher asked me to speak in English.

(b) The teacher let me speak in English.

(15) 老师不让学生上课说英文。

Lǎoshī bú ràng xuésheng shàng kè shuō Yīngwén.

The teacher does not allow students to speak English in class.

(16) 妈妈不让孩子吃饭以前吃太多糖。

Māma bú ràng háizi chī fàn yǐqián chī tài duō táng.

The mother doesn't let her child eat too much candy before meals.

We should also note that the Chinese counterpart of the word "tell" in English can be either 告诉 *gàosu* or 让 *ràng* depending on the context, a distinction that is quite evident in the following examples.

（17）　她告诉我们她穿红的。

　　　　Tā gàosu wǒmen tā chuān hóng de.

　　　　She told us that she would wear red.

（18）　她让我们穿红的。

　　　　Tā ràng wǒmen chuān hóng de.

　　　　She told us to wear red.

The contrast between 告诉 and 让 is similar to that between 问 and 请. The first member of each pair takes a whole statement or question as its Object. On the other hand, both 让 and 请 are pivotal verbs, requesting someone to perform a certain task. Like example (13), the following has both 让 and 告诉 in the same sentence.

（19）　乐老师让我告诉你们，他欢迎你们晚上八点以后去他家听中国音乐。

　　　　Yuè lǎoshī ràng wǒ gàosu nǐmen, tā huānyíng nǐmen wǎnshang bā-diǎn yǐhòu qù tā jiā tīng Zhōngguó yīnyuè.

　　　　Teacher Yue asked me to tell you that he'd welcome you to go to his place after eight o'clock in the evening to listen to Chinese music.

3. A Verbal Unit Functioning as an Object

3.1   Thus far, we have seen only a nominal (a noun or a pronoun) appearing in the Object slot in a sentence.

（1）　我喜欢你。

　　　　Wǒ xǐhuan nǐ.

　　　　I like you.

（2）　我很喜欢我的小妹妹。

　　　　Wǒ hěn xǐhuan wǒ de xiǎo mèimei.

　　　　I like my little sister very much.

（3）　你喜欢哪一个歌儿？

　　　　Nǐ xǐhuan nǎ yíge gēr?

　　　　Which song do you like?

However, as one's likings may include not only people and things but actions or events as well, the verb 喜欢 may take another verb, a Verb−Object unit, or even a whole sentence as its Object.

(4) 我喜欢学习。
Wǒ xǐhuan xuéxí.
I like to study.

(5) 我喜欢听音乐。
Wǒ xǐhuan tīng yīnyuè.
I like to listen to music.

(6) 我喜欢看中国电影。
Wǒ xǐhuan kàn Zhōngguó diànyǐng.
I like to see Chinese movies.

(7) 你喜欢喝什么茶？
Nǐ xǐhuan hē shénme chá?
What kind of tea do you like to drink?

(8) 我喜欢去图书馆看书。
Wǒ xǐhuan qù túshūguǎn kàn shū.
I like going to the library to read.

(9) 我不喜欢你吸烟。
Wǒ bù xǐhuan nǐ xī yān.
I don't like you to smoke.

(10) 帕兰卡喜欢不喜欢穿裙子？
Pàlánkǎ xǐhuan bu xǐhuan chuān qúnzi?
Does Palanka like to wear skirts?

Please compare the following sets of Chinese and English sentences:

（a） 我喜欢咖啡。   （喜欢 ＋ Object）
（b） 我喜欢喝咖啡。   （喜欢 ＋ ［Verb＋Object］）
（c） I like coffee.   （like ＋ Object）
（d） I like to drink coffee.   （like ＋ ［Verb＋Object］）

Even though these are all grammatical sentences in the two languages respectively, the preferred form is (b) in Chinese but (c) in English. In other words, to the Chinese mind, what you like is "coffee-drinking" rather than "coffee," as is the case in English.

3.2 Other verbs, among the ones that we have learned, that can take a verbal Object include 学 *xué* "to learn," 想 *xiǎng* "to think, want," and 要 *yào* "to want."

(11)　学：(a) 学 + Noun:　　　　　　　　我学汉语。

Wǒ xúe Hànyǔ.

I am studying Chinese.

(b) 学 + Verb:　　　　　　　　我学说，不学写。

Wǒ xué shuō, bù xué xiě.

I'm learning how to speak (it) and not how to write (it).

(c) 学 + [Verb + Object] :　我学写汉字。

Wǒ xué xiě Hànzì.

I am learning how to write Chinese characters.

(12)　想：(a) 想 + Noun:　　　　　　　　我很想我爸爸。

Wǒ hěn xiǎng wǒ bàba.

I miss my father.

(b) 想 + [Verb + Object] :　我很想看中国电影。

Wǒ hěn xiǎng kàn Zhōngguó diànyǐng.

I want to see a Chinese movie very much.

(c) 想 + [Verb + Object + X] :　　　你想去哪儿喝咖啡？

Nǐ xiǎng qù nǎr hē kāfēi?

Where do you want to go for coffee?

Sentence (12.a) represents an idiomatic reading of the verb 想 : to think of a person a lot connotes "missing the person very much."

(13)　要：(a) 要 + Interrogative:　　你要什么？

Nǐ yào shénme?

What do you want?

(b) 要 + Noun:　　　　　　我要一杯咖啡。

Wǒ yào yìbēi kāfēi.

I want a cup of coffee.

(c) 要 + [Verb + Interrogative] :　　　你要吃什么？

Nǐ yào chī shénme?

What do you want to eat?

When followed by a verbal unit in the pattern 要／想 + [Verb + (Object)] , 要 generally indicates a stronger desire than 想 . But 要 is the idiomatic verb to use for ordering food in a restaurant; it is used by both the waiter and the customer. The following dialogue illustrates this function of 要.

(14)　A: 先生，您要什么？
　　　　　Xiānsheng, nín yào shénme?
　　　　　What would you like to have, sir?

　　　　B: 我要一瓶英国啤酒。
　　　　　Wǒ yào yìpíng Yīngguó píjiǔ.
　　　　　I'd like to have an English beer.

　　　　A: 您呢，小姐？
　　　　　Nín ne, xiǎojie?
　　　　　What about you, Miss?

　　　　B: 我要一杯橘子水。你们有中国茶吗？我还要一杯花茶。
　　　　　Wǒ yào yìbēi júzishuǐ. Nǐmen yǒu Zhōngguó chá ma? Wǒ hái yào yìbēi huāchá.
　　　　　I want a glass of orange juice. Do you have Chinese tea? I also want a cup of jasmine tea.

4. The Prohibitive 别

Like its counterpart in English, an imperative sentence in Chinese is often "subject-less."

(1)　看！
　　　Kàn!
　　　Look!

(2)　别看！
　　　Bié kàn!
　　　Don't look!

别 *bié* is the negative imperative marker. It is to be distinguished from 不, which does not imply command or request.

(3)　别喝那杯桔子水。
　　　Bié hē nà bēi júzishuǐ.
　　　Don't drink that glass of orange juice!

(4)　晚上请别听音乐。
　　　Wǎnshang qǐng bié tīng yīnyuè.
　　　Please don't listen to music in the evening.

(5)   大夫说，"晚上睡觉以前别喝太多咖啡。"
       Dàifu shuō, "Wǎnshang shuì jiào yǐqián bié hē tài duō kāfēi."
       The doctor said, "Don't drink too much coffee before you go to
       sleep in the evening."

In some cases, the omitted subject may be reintroduced into the sentence for emphasis, as shown in the following examples.

(6)   你来看。
       Nǐ lái kàn.
       Come and look!

(7)   你别听他的。
       Nǐ bié tīng tā de.
       Don't listen to him!
       (他的 *tā de* is a short form of 他的话 *tā de huà* "his words.")

5. The Tag Question

A tag question is a short question attached to the end of a statement, asking for
confirmation. "N'est-ce pas?" in French is a typical example of this form of interrogative. A Chinese tag question is usually formed with 是 as the verb: ……是
吗？ or ……是不是？ 对 "correct" may also perform in this role: ……对吗？ or
……对不对？

(1)   美国人喜欢喝咖啡，是吗？
       Měiguó rén xǐhuan hē kāfēi, shì ma?
       American people like to drink coffee, don't they?

(2)   你很想家，是吗？
       Nǐ hěn xiǎng jiā, shì ma?
       You are homesick, aren't you?

(3)   他不喝啤酒，是吗？
       Tā bù hē píjiǔ, shì ma?
       He doesn't drink beer, does he?

(4)   这条裙子太大，是不是？
       Zhè tiáo qúnzi tài dà, shì bu shì?
       This skirt is too big, isn't it?

(5)　你喜欢喝红茶，不喜欢喝绿茶，对吗？

Nǐ xǐhuan hē hóngchá, bù xǐhuan hē lǜchá, duì ma?

You like black tea and not green tea. Right?

(6)　这不是古典音乐，对不对？

Zhè bú shì gǔdiǎn yīnyuè, duì bu duì?

This isn't classical music, (is that) right?

(7)　白老师很喜欢唱歌儿，对不对？

Bái lǎoshī hěn xǐhuan chàng gēr, duì bu duì?

Teacher Bai likes to sing, (isn't that) right?

Please note that English generally uses a negative tag question for a positive sentence and a positive tag question for a negative sentence, as shown in the translations for the above sentences. By comparison, the tag question in Chinese is much simpler in formation. It matters little whether the preceding statement is positive or not; the question form remains the same.

Lesson 20

1. How to Tell the Date

1.1 Year: ⋯⋯年 : Read off the number as is and put 年 *nián* at the end.

  (1) 1900: 一九零零年
         yī-jiǔ-líng-líng-nián
  (2) 1902: 一九零二年
         yī-jiǔ-líng-èr-nián
  (3) 1942: 一九四二年
         yī-jiǔ-sì-èr-nián
  (4) 1987: 一九八七年
         yī-jiǔ-bā-qī-nián
  (5) 2001: 二零零一年
         èr-líng-líng-yī-nián

Please note that in all the above examples, 一 is always pronounced with the first tone regardless of the following tone. The reason is that in this usage the numeral is an ordinal number and ordinal numbers do not participate in tone change.

Another thing to note is that the word 年 is a measure word and can be placed directly after a numeral. Therefore, 一年 *yìnián* "one year," 两年 *liǎngnián* "two years," etc. Notice that in this case 一 is pronounced with a changed tone (the fourth tone in front of a second tone syllable) since it is now a cardinal number.

1.2 Month: ⋯⋯月 : Naming months is an extremely easy task in Chinese; the twelve months are referred to by their ordinal numbers. Hence,

January:	一月	*yīyuè*	(first month)	(notice the use of first tone on 一)
February:	二月	*èryuè*	(second month)	(notice the use of 二 and not 两)
March:	三月	*sānyuè*	(third month)	
April:	四月	*sìyuè*	(fourth month)	

May:	五月	*wǔyuè*	(fifth month)
June:	六月	*liùyuè*	(sixth month)
July:	七月	*qīyuè*	(seventh month)
August:	八月	*bāyuè*	(eighth month)
September:	九月	*jiǔyuè*	(ninth month)
October:	十月	*shíyuè*	(tenth month)
November:	十一月	*shíyīyuè*	(eleventh month) (first tone on 一)
December:	十二月	*shí'èryuè*	(twelfth month)

月 is a noun, whose measure word is 个. Therefore,

（6）　一个月
　　　　yíge yuè
　　　　one month

（7）　两个月
　　　　liǎngge yuè
　　　　two months

（8）　十二个月
　　　　shí'èrge yuè
　　　　twelve months

Please note the following differences:

Numeral ＋ 月	Numeral ＋ 个 ＋ 月
Name of Month:	**Number of Months:**
一月　*yīyuè*　"January" (1st tone)	一个月 *yíge yuè* (2nd tone) "1 month"
二月　*èryuè*　"February"	两个月 *liǎngge yuè*　　　"2 months"
三月　*sānyuè* "March"	三个月 *sānge yuè*　　　"3 months"
...	...

1.3 Days of the Month: When referring to a day in a month, either 日 *rì* or 号 *hào* is used as an indicator and placed after the appropriate number. 号 is more often used in the spoken language than 日.

一号	*yīhào*	"1st of the Month"	(first tone on 一)
二号	*èrhào*	"2nd of Month"	
......			
二十一号	*èrshiyīhào*	"21st of Month"	(neutral tone on 十)

......

三十号 *sānshihào* "30th of Month"   (neutral tone on 十)

1.4 Days of the Week: In Chinese, a week begins with Monday and ends with Sunday. Except for Sunday, the days of the week are named with ordinal numbers. There are two words for Sunday: 星期日 *xīngqīrì* and 星期天 *xīngqītiān*, the former being more common in writing.

星期一	*xīngqīyī*	Monday (first tone on 一)
星期二	*xīngqī'èr*	Tuesday
星期三	*xīngqīsān*	Wednesday
星期四	*xīngqīsì*	Thursday
星期五	*xīngqīwǔ*	Friday
星期六	*xīngqīliù*	Saturday
星期日 / 星期天	*xīngqīrì/ xīngqītiān*	Sunday

The word 星期 *xīngqī* "week" is also a noun, its measure word being 个. Thus, 一个星期 *yíge xīngqī* is "one week" and 两个星期 *liǎngge xīngqī* is "two weeks."

1.5 Ordering of Date Indicators:

Year + Month + Day + Day of Week

一九八零年五月二号	May 2, 1980
一九八七年十月十九号星期一	October 19, 1987, Monday
一九九二年二月二十九号星期六	February 29, 1992, Saturday
一九九九年十二月三十一号	December 31, 1999
二零零零年一月一号	January 1, 2000

The specification of a date follows the general principle described in Lesson 17: the larger unit comes before the smaller unit. The following example includes all temporal elements arranged in the proper order.

(9)   一九八七年一月一号星期四上午十一点三十分
       yījiǔbāqīnián yīyuè yīhào xīngqīsì shàngwǔ shíyīdiǎn sānshifēn
       Thursday, January 1, 1987, at 11:30 a.m.

1.6 How to Ask for Dates:

(10) 今天星期几？

Jīntiān xīngqījǐ?

What day of the week is it today?

(11) 今天几号？

Jīntiān jǐhào?

What day of the month is it today?

(12) 今天几月几号？

Jīntiān jǐyuè jǐhào?

What is today's date?

(13) 今天几月几号星期几？

Jīntiān jǐyuè jǐhào xīngqījǐ?

What is the date today?

(= What day is it?)

(14) 这个月是几月？

Zhè ge yuè shì jǐyuè?

What month is this?

(15) 今年是一九九几年？

Jīnnián shì yījiǔjiǔjǐnián?

What year is it now?

(= Nineteen ninety-what?)

The following two question forms are rather specific in reference. The first asks for horoscopic information and the second refers to a past or historical event.

(16) 今年是什么年？

Jīnnián shì shénme nián?

What year is this?

(= The year of the dragon?)

(17) 那年是哪年？

Nà nián shì nǎ nián?

What year was that year?

1.7 How to say "This DATE," "Last DATE," and "Next DATE" in Chinese: There are two ways of providing such information as summarized in the following chart:

Last DATE		This DATE		Next DATE	
昨天	*zuótiān*	今天	*jīntiān*	明天	*míngtiān*
去年	*qùnián*	今年	*jīnnián*	明年	*míngnián*
上个月	*shàng ge yuè*	这个月	*zhè ge yuè*	下个月	*xià ge yuè*
上个星期	*shàng ge xīngqī*	这个星期	*zhè ge xīngqī*	下个星期	*xià ge xīngqī*
上个星期日	*shàng ge xīngqīrì*	这个星期日	*zhè ge xīngqīrì*	下个星期日	*xià ge xīngqīrì*

(A) 天 and 年 are of the same category, utilizing 今 *jīn* for the present and 明 *míng* for the future. As for the past, 昨 *zuó* is used for 天 and 去 *qù* for 年 . (Cf. a similar use of "go" in the English expression "the bygone year." Also, "day" and "year" share the same prefix "yester-" in English: "yesterday" and "yesteryear"). Another characteristic feature of these words is that they are both measures by themselves. Hence, numerals can be placed directly before them. For example, 三年 *sānnián* "three years"; 两天 *liǎngtiān* "two days."

(B) 月 and 星期 form another category, where the marker for the present is 这个 "this," the marker for the past is 上个 (literally "the above..."), and the marker for the future is 下个 (literally "the below..."). Also, 月 and 星期 generally require the presence of a measure word when a cardinal number is used. For example, 一个 月 *yíge yuè* "one month" (Cf. 一月 *yīyuè* "January"), 两个星期 *liǎngge xīngqī* "two weeks."

(C) Another thing to note is that in English we often use "last X" or "next X" to refer to a past or future date. That "past" or "future" reading is, however, based on a direct reference to the present moment or the moment of the speech act. For example, when we say "last May" in English, we could be referring to May of this year if it is now, say, September, or we could mean May of the previous year if it is now January. In Chinese, however, we use the entire temporal cycle (for example, in this case, the calendar year) as one unit. A past marker refers to a time unit in the previous cycle and a future marker refers to what is in the coming cycle. If the date falls in the same cycle as the present, it is always referred to as "this..." regardless of whether that particular date has passed or not . For example, if we are now in October, then,

(18)   今年七月
         jīnnián qīyuè
         July of this year
         (= last July)

(19) 今年十二月
      jīnnián shí'èryuè
      December of this year
      (= the coming December)

(20) 去年七月
      qùnián qīyuè
      July of last year
      (= a year before this last July)

(21) 去年十二月
      qùnián shí'èryuè
      December of last year
      (= last December)

(22) 明年七月
      míngnián qīyuè
      July of next year
      (= next July)

(23) 明年十二月
      míngnián shí'èryuè
      December of next year
      (= a year from this coming December)

Or, if today is Wednesday, then:

(24) 这个星期一
      zhè ge xīngqīyī
      Monday of this week
      (= last Monday)

(25) 这个星期六
      zhè ge xīngqīliù
      Saturday of this week
      (= coming Saturday)

(26) 上个星期一
      shàng ge xīngqīyī
      Monday of last week
      (= a week before last Monday)

(27) 上个星期六
      shàng ge xīngqīliù
      Saturday of last week (= last Saturday)

(28)   下个星期一
       xià ge xīngqīyī
       Monday of next week
       (= next Monday)

(29)   下个星期六
       xià ge xīngqīliù
       Saturday of next week
       (= a week from this coming Saturday)

Complications arise when the day in question is a Sunday, which is considered the first day of a week in the Western calendar but the end of the week to a Chinese speaker. If we compare the following two representations of the same month but in different arrangements of the days of the week, we will understand why there is such a drastic divergence in naming Sundays between the two languages.

S	M	T	W	T	F	S
	1	2	3	4	5	6
7	8	9	10	11	12	13
14	15	16	17	18	19	20
21	22	23	24	25	26	27
28	29	30	31			

一	二	三	四	五	六	日
1	2	3	4	5	6	7
8	9	10	11	12	13	14
15	16	17	18	19	20	21
22	23	24	25	26	27	28
29	30	31				

Today: 17th
14th: last Sunday
21st: next Sunday
28th: a week from the coming Sunday

今天：   十七号
十四号：   上个星期天
二十一号：这个星期天
二十八号：下个星期天

According to the Western calendar, the fourteenth should be included in the same weekly cycle as the seventeenth and should have been referred to as 这个星期天 in Chinese. However, as the Chinese week ends on a Sunday, the fourteenth actually belongs to the previous cycle and is therefore referred to as 上个星期天.

1.8   The following is a set of examples to illustrate the use of date expressions in various sentence structures.

(30)   我哥哥去年和今年都在北京大学工作，他每个月都给我写信。
       Wǒ gēge qùnián hé jīnnián dōu zài Běijīng Dàxué gōngzuò. Tā měi ge yuè dōu gěi wǒ xiě xìn.
       My elder brother worked at Beijing University both last year and this year. He wrote to me every month.

(31) 请问明年二月有二十八天还是有二十九天？

Qǐng wèn míngnián èryuè yǒu èrshíbātiān háishì yǒu èrshíjiǔtiān?

Excuse me, does February of next year have twenty-eight days or twenty-nine days?

(32) 那个人很有意思。他的生日是四月一号。

Nà ge rén hěn yǒu yìsi. Tā de shēngri shì sìyuè yīhào.

That man is interesting. His birthday is April 1st.

(33) 五月十六号晚上八点半学校有一个舞会，欢迎同学们都来参加。

Wǔyuè shíliùhào wǎnshang bādiǎnbàn xuéxiào yǒu yíge wǔhuì, huānyíng tóngxuémen dōu lái cānjiā.

On May 16th, there will be a dance party at school in the evening at half-past eight. All fellow-students are welcome to attend.

(34) A: 你什么时候有空儿？

Nǐ shénme shíhou yǒu kòngr?

When are you available?

B: 我上午十点以后，下午两点半以前没事儿。

Wǒ shàngwǔ shídiǎn yǐhòu, xiàwǔ liǎngdiǎnbàn yǐqián méi shìr.

I am free between ten o'clock in the morning and 2:30 in the afternoon.

(35) A: 请问有十一月二号晚上音乐会的票吗？

Qǐng wèn yǒu shíyīyuè èrhào wǎnshang yīnyuèhuì de piào ma?

Excuse me, do you have tickets for the concert on the evening of November 2nd?

B: 对不起，十一月二号没有音乐会。

Duìbuqǐ, shíyīyuè èrhào méi yǒu yīnyuèhuì.

I'm sorry, but there is no concert on November 2nd.

(36) 以前每个星期二上午十一点我上谢老师的辅导课。今天我告诉谢老师以后我还上星期四白老师的辅导课。

Yǐqián měi ge xīngqī'èr shàngwǔ shíyīdiǎn wǒ shàng Xiè lǎoshī de fǔdǎo kè. Jīntiān wǒ gàosu Xiè lǎoshī yǐhòu wǒ hái shàng xīngqīsì Bái lǎoshī de fǔdǎo kè.

In the past I attended Teacher Xie's tutorial class every Tuesday at eleven o'clock in the morning. Today I told Teacher Xie that in the future I would also like to go to Teacher Bai's tutorials on Thursdays.

2. How to Inquire about Someone's Age

The word for "age" is 岁 *suì*, often translated as "...years old." It is therefore to be distinguished from 年 *nián*, which simply means "year." The pattern for stating age is:

```
                    Numeral 一岁
```

(1)   这个小孩儿今年三岁。
       Zhè ge xiǎoháir jīnnián sānsuì.
       This child is three years old this year.

(2)   他去年十五岁。
       Tā qùnián shíwǔsuì.
       He was fifteen years old last year.

(3)   王老师今年不是五十二岁。
       Wáng lǎoshī jīnnián bú shì wǔshí'èrsuì.
       Teacher Wang is not fifty-two years old this year.

If the age is a two-digit figure, the marker 岁 may be omitted.

(4)   A: 我孩子今年六岁。
          Wǒ háizi jīnnián liùsuì.
          My child is six this year.
       B: 你爱人呢？
          Nǐ àirén ne?
          What about your wife?
       A: 她今年二十八。
          Tā jīnnián èrshibā.
          She is twenty-eight.

To ask for someone's age, there are different patterns covering different age ranges.

(A) For a child younger than ten:

(5)   你今年几岁？
       Nǐ jīnnián jǐsuì?

(B) For someone older than ten or an adult:

　　(6)　你今年多大？

　　　　　Nǐ jīnnián duō dà?

　　　　　(Literally "How big are you?")

　　(7)　你今年多少岁？

　　　　　Nǐ jīnnián duōshaosuì?

(C) For an older person, say, above fifty:

　　(8)　您今年多大岁数？

　　　　　Nín jīnnián duō dà suìshù?

　　(9)　您今年多大年纪？

　　　　　Nín jīnnián duō dà niánjì?

　　　　　(*niánjì* is another word meaning "age.")

3. The Nominal Predicate

We have learned from the previous lesson that when telling or asking for time, the verb-to-be 是 is not required. In other words, the predicate is made up primarily of a noun or a nominal expression without an intervening verb. Hence, it is referred to as a nominal predicate. Sentences giving dates, ages, etc., are often formed with nominal predicates.

　　(1)　A: 现在几点？

　　　　　　Xiànzài jǐdiǎn?

　　　　　　What time is it?

　　　　　B: 现在三点半。

　　　　　　Xiànzài sāndiǎnbàn.

　　　　　　It's half-past three.

　　(2)　A: 今天几号？

　　　　　　Jīntiān jǐhào?

　　　　　　What day of the month is it?

　　　　　B: 今天七号。

　　　　　　Jīntiān qīhào.

　　　　　　It's the seventh.

(3)   A: 他今年多大？

Tā jīnnián duō dà?

How old is he?

B: 他今年二十岁。

Tā jīnnián èrshisuì.

He is twenty years old.

In actuality, however, a nominal predicate is derived from a verbal predicate that contains 是, a verb that is often deleted in speech. Therefore, it is grammatically correct, though stylistically perhaps less preferable, to say,

(4)   现在（是）两点钟。

Xiànzài (shì) liǎngdiǎn zhōng.

It is now two o'clock.

(5)   我今年（是）三十岁。

Wǒ jīnnián (shì) sānshisuì.

I'm thirty this year.

The verb 是 nevertheless resurfaces in the negative as well as in the affirmative—negative question form:

(6)   今天不是三十号。

Jīntiān bú shì sānshihào.

Today is not the thirtieth.

(7)   你哥哥今年是不是二十二岁？

Nǐ gēge jīnnián shì bu shì èrshi'èrsuì?

Is your brother twenty-two years old?

4. Topic and Comment

The following conversation, taken from *PCR* Lesson 20, contains a very interesting phenomenon that requires some explanation.

(1)   王老师：今天的语法你们有问题吗？

Jīntiān de yǔfǎ nǐmen yǒu wèntí ma?

Do you have questions about today's grammar?

古波： 我有两个问题。帕兰卡也有问题。

Wǒ yǒu liǎngge wèntí. Pàlánkǎ yě yǒu wèntí.

I have two questions. Palanka also has some questions.

王老师：好，下午我来给你们辅导。
Hǎo, xiàwǔ wǒ lái gěi nǐmen fǔdǎo.
OK, I'll come and help you this afternoon.

The question that Teacher Wang poses contains two units: 今天的语法 and 你们有问题吗. Grammatically, the latter constitutes one sentence unit, the structure of which is diagrammed below:

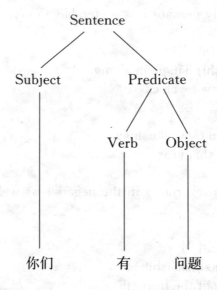

Then, how is 今天的语法 connected to this self-contained sentential unit? Semantically, it represents what the 问题 "questions" concern: questions about the grammar. It also represents the topic of the conversation. When Teacher Wang directs his conversation to the theme of teaching, he asks if Palanka and Gubo have any questions with regard to grammar. Gubo answers by saying that he has two questions and that Palanka has problems too. Teacher Wang then assures them that he will be available for tutorial assistance that afternoon. Thus, 今天的语法 forms the subject matter or topic of a discourse that spans across three or four sentences. A topic is a discoursal notion, acting more like the subject matter of a conversation rather than the subject of a sentence. Once a topic is raised and established, the rest of a sentence or a dialogue functions as a comment or comments on this topic. A topic is generally placed at the beginning of a dialogue, and its comments may range from one predicate or one sentence to a series of sentences or even the entire text. One speaker may identify a topic and comment on it, and other speakers may join in, making further comments without repeating the topic itself. As long as the topic remains unchanged in a conversation, it is not necessary to repeat it in each sentence. In other words, a topic operates on a discoursal level and is, therefore, beyond the grammatical confines of a sentence. It may be the subject of a sentence but it may also very well be syntactically unrelated to the sentence, as demonstrated by the particular sequence cited in the beginning of our discussion. 今天的语法 is the topic and the sentential unit " 你们有问题吗？" is an immediate comment on it. It remains the topic for " 我有两个问题 " and " 我来给你们辅导 ." If the subject of a sentence happens to be the topic of a conversation, it may be omitted after its initial identification. For example, in the following question and answer, 那枝笔 is the topic as well as the subject of each of the two sentences. It appears only in the first and is understood in the second.

> (2)   A: 那枝笔是红的还是黑的？
>   Nà zhī bǐ shì hóng de háishì hēi de?
>   Is that pen a red one or a black one?
>   B: 是红的。
>   Shì hóng de.
>   It is a red one.

Like many other East Asian languages, Chinese is essentially a topic-prominent language, a linguistic characteristic that accounts for its abundant use of "subject-less" sentences in speech. English, on the other hand, is a subject-prominent language, which means that grammatically it is necessary to include a subject in each sentence even if such a grammatical subject may just be a "dummy" element, as in "*It* is a pleasure to meet you," or "*It* is cold today." Evidently, the word "it" appears in the above sentences simply to fill the subject slots. There are occasional instances in English where topicalization is put to work. For example, "That I don't know." The pronoun "that" is actually the Object of "know" but has been moved to the front of the sentence for emphasis. It now serves as the topic of the sentence, a sentence that can be paraphrased as "As for that, I don't know anything about it." While the use of topicalization is quite infrequent in English, it is an extremely common phenomenon in Chinese. We will encounter more of such a utilization of the "Topic－Comment" mechanism in the lessons to come. In fact, the sooner we learn to recognize it and use it correctly in our own speech, the more we will be able to comprehend and speak like a native person.

5. 知道 vs. 认识

The verb 知道 *zhīdao*, generally glossed as "to know," is to be distinguished from another verb 认识 *rènshi,* which means "to know, to be familiar with, to recognize." The difference between the two verbs may be best captured by the following sentence:

(1)   我知道丁云是谁，（但是）我不认识她。
       Wǒ zhīdao Dīng Yún shì shéi, (dànshì) wǒ bú rènshi tā.
       I know who Ding Yun is but I don't know her (personally).

知道 represents a factual knowledge: "to know about, to be informed about," whereas 认识 connotes a cognitive awareness or familiarity: "to know, to recognize, to identify." The same distinction is found in French between "savoir" and "reconnaître." If you are presented with a totally strange Chinese character for identification, you should use 不认识 and not 不知道 to express your inability to recognize it.

(2)   我不认识这个字。
       Wǒ bú rènshi zhè ge zì.
       I don't know this character.

(3)   *我不知道这个字。
       *Wǒ bù zhīdao zhè ge zì.

However, if you do recognize the form but are unable to recall its use or meaning, then you should use 不知道 and not 不认识 to state your lack of linguistic knowledge.

(4)   我不知道这个字的意思。
       Wǒ bù zhīdao zhè ge zì de yìsi.
       I don't know the meaning of this character.

(5)   *我不认识这个字的意思。
       *Wǒ bú rènshi zhè ge zì de yìsi.

The following are a few more examples to illustrate the difference:

(6)   我知道你家的地址。
       Wǒ zhīdao nǐ jiā de dìzhǐ.
       I know the address of your house.
       (—— But I may not recognize the house when I see it.)

(7)   我认识你家。
       Wǒ rènshi nǐ jiā.
       I know/recognize your house.
       (—— But I may not know the address.)

(8)　A: 小白是我同学，你也认识她吗？你知道她现在的地址吗？

Xiǎo Bái shì wǒ tóngxué, nǐ yě rènshi tā ma? Nǐ zhīdao tā xiànzài de dìzhǐ ma?

Little Bai is my classmate. Do you know her too? Do you know her current address?

B: 我知道这个人，但是我不认识她。她的地址，我也不知道。

Wǒ zhīdao zhè ge rén, dànshì wǒ bú rènshi tā. Tā de dìzhǐ, wǒ yě bù zhīdao.

I know of this person but I don't know her personally. I don't know her address either.

(9)　你认识张老师吗？你知道他今天在哪个教室上课吗？

Nǐ rènshi Zhāng lǎoshī ma? Nǐ zhīdao tā jīntiān zài nǎ ge jiàoshì shàng kè ma?

Do you know Teacher Zhang? Do you know which classroom he teaches in today?

The second half of sentence （9） actually contains two questions: (a) 你知道……吗？ and (b) 他今天在哪个教室上课？As the (b) question is embedded in (a), the interrogative particle 吗 is separated from its basic sentence, dangling at the end of the sequence.

6. More on 以前 and 以后

As we learned in Lesson 17, 以前 and 以后 may be appended or "suffixed" to a time word or an action expression to indicate "before" or "after" that referential point: X 以前/以后.

(1)　我每天早上八点以后，十二点以前，都在图书馆看书。

Wǒ měi tiān zǎoshang bādiǎn yǐhòu, shí'èrdiǎn yǐqián, dōu zài túshūguǎn kàn shū.

I study in the library every morning between eight and twelve.

However, if the reference point X either coincides with the present or can be understood from the context, then X may be simply omitted from the pattern. In other words, 以前 or 以后 may stand all by itself as a time word modifying the rest of the sentence.

(2)　以前他常常不来上课。

Yǐqián tā chángcháng bù lái shàng kè.

In the past (= before now), he often missed classes.

(3)   以后，我请你们来我家听音乐。

Yǐhòu, wǒ qǐng nǐmen lái wǒ jiā tīng yīnyuè.

In the future (= from now on), I'll invite you to my house to listen to music.

(4)   上课以前，我告诉丁老师说，你的语法课很有意思，以后我一定每天都来上。

Shàng kè yǐqián, wǒ gàosu Dīng lǎoshī shuō, nǐ de yǔfǎ kè hěn yǒu yìsi, yǐhòu wǒ yídìng měi tiān dōu lái shàng.

Before class, I told Teacher Ding that your grammar class was interesting and I would be attending it every day in the future.

(5)   我有他以前的地址，没有现在的。

Wǒ yǒu tā yǐqián de dìzhǐ, méi yǒu xiànzài de.

I have his old address but not the current one.

7. How to Make an Apology and How to Respond to One

Like "I'm sorry" in English, 对不起 *duì bu qǐ* is an extremely common expression in daily speech in Chinese. If you come to class late, or if you forget to prepare for your class, or if you didn't do well in the quiz, or if..., you offer your apology by saying " 对不起 ." It is an expression to acknowledge your failure or your mistake. In this sense, it is a little different from its English "equivalent." For, in English, the phrase "I'm sorry" may connote sadness or sympathy. If your friend has lost a relative, you may express your condolences by saying "I'm sorry (to hear that)." But, the use of " 对不起 " in this context would be extremely inappropriate, unless of course you were responsible for the tragedy.

In response to 对不起, one says 没关系 *méi guānxi* "(literally) of no relation, of no importance → it doesn't matter," thereby releasing the other party from obligation or duty or guilty feelings. So, if you are truly mad at someone for a gross misbehavior, then however earnestly that someone repeats 对不起 to you, you will not utter 没关系 until you are really ready to forgive him.

The following are examples illustrating the use of these two idiomatic phrases:

(1)   A. 我星期日上午来看你，好吗？

Wǒ xīngqīrì shàngwǔ lái kàn nǐ, hǎo ma?

I'll come visit you on Sunday morning, OK?

B. 对不起，星期日上午我朋友结婚。我没空儿。

Duì bu qǐ, xīngqīrì shàngwǔ wǒ péngyou jiē hūn, wǒ méi kòngr.

I'm sorry, but my friend is getting married on Sunday morning. I won't have any free time.

A. 没关系。

Méi guānxi.

It doesn't matter.

(2) A. 今天不是十六号。这不是今天的报。请问你们有十九号的报吗？

Jīntiān bú shì shíliùhào. Zhè bú shì jīntiān de bào. Qǐng wèn nǐmen yǒu shíjiǔhào de bào ma?

Today isn't the sixteenth. This isn't today's newspaper. Excuse me, do you have the nineteenth's newspaper?

B. 我们没有。对不起。

Wǒmen méi yǒu. Duì bu qǐ.

Sorry, we don't.

A. 没关系。

Méi guānxi.

That's quite all right.

Lesson 21

1. The Relative Clause Construction

As is the case in English, a nominal in Chinese may be modified by a variety of elements that tell us something more about the nominal itself. We have seen the use of an adjective or another noun as a nominal attribute.

（1）　新（的）书
　　　 xīn (de) shū
　　　 a new book　　　　　　　　　　[Adjective＋的＋Noun]

（2）　老师的书
　　　 lǎoshī de shū
　　　 the teacher's book　　　　　　 [Noun＋的＋Noun]

（3）　中文书
　　　 Zhōngwén shū
　　　 a Chinese book　　　　　　　　[Noun＋Noun]

The marker for the construction, 的 *de*, invariably comes between the modifying element and the noun that is being modified. The marker, however, may be omitted under certain circumstances (as specified in previous lessons) and the modified noun (or, head noun) may be omitted if it is clear from the context.

A noun may also be modified by a verb. Examples of the use of a modifying verb in English are "a *crying* baby" (= a baby that cries), "an *interesting* book" (= a book that interests the reader), "a *walking* encyclopedia" (metaphorical usage), etc. However, as these examples illustrate, a modifying verb in English may come either before a noun ("crying + N") or after it ("N that cries"). And, when the modifying verbal unit is put after the noun, it requires a special syntactic pattern generally referred to as the relative clause construction.

a crying baby	=	a baby that cries
[Modifier ＋ Noun]		[Noun ＋ Modifier]

A relative clause in English is basically a modifying clause that comes immediately after the noun it qualifies and is generally marked by a relative pronoun, "who, whom, which, that," etc. In other words, how to modify a nominal is a rather complicated linguistic process in English. The positioning of a modifying unit depends on whether it carries a full finite verb or a participle form. In contrast, the nominal modification in Chinese is a simple or even mechanical matter. A modifying unit, regardless of its makeup (be it a noun, an adjective, a verb, a Verb−Object unit, or a whole sentence), always comes before the noun it modifies. The following are examples to illustrate the range of such a modifying verbal unit in Chinese. 的 is the ubiquitous marker and is never deleted in such a construction.

(4)　　参加的同学
　　　　cānjiā de tóngxué
　　　　the classmate who attends

(5)　　参加舞会的同学
　　　　cānjiā wǔhuì de tóngxué
　　　　the classmate who attends the party

(6)　　来参加舞会的同学
　　　　lái cānjiā wǔhuì de tóngxué
　　　　the classmate who comes to attend the party

(7)　　今天来参加舞会的同学
　　　　jīntiān lái cānjiā wǔhuì de tóngxué
　　　　the classmate who comes to attend the party today

(8)　　今天跟他一起来参加舞会的同学
　　　　jīntiān gēn tā yìqǐ lái cānjiā wǔhuì de tóngxué
　　　　the classmate who comes to attend the party together with him

(9)　　参加的舞会
　　　　cānjiā de wǔhuì
　　　　the party which (X) attended

(10)　　你参加的舞会
　　　　nǐ cānjiā de wǔhuì
　　　　the party which you attended

(11)　　你去参加的舞会
　　　　nǐ qù cānjiā de wǔhuì
　　　　the party which you went to attend

(12) 你昨天去参加的舞会
　　　nǐ zuótiān qù cānjiā de wǔhuì
　　　the party which you went to attend yesterday

(13) 你昨天跟你同学一起去参加的舞会
　　　nǐ zuótiān gēn nǐ tóngxué yìqǐ qù cānjiā de wǔhuì
　　　the party which you went to attend yesterday together with your classmates

Now, supposing we have a scenario of 丁云跟朋友一起去参加舞会 and we want to identify this friend as 古波, we need to take the following grammatical steps to produce such an identification sentence. First, as 朋友 will be the focus of the new sentence, we need to set it as the subject: ⋯⋯朋友是古波. Then, we need to turn the rest of the information into a modifying clause: "Information ＋ 的 ＋ 朋友⋯⋯" Hence, the identification will now be in the form of (14).

(14) 跟丁云一起去参加舞会的那个朋友是古波。
　　　Gēn Dīng Yún yìqǐ qù cānjiā wǔhuì de nà ge péngyou shì Gǔbō.
　　　The friend who went to the dance party with Ding Yun was Gubo.

Or, if we want to comment on the party by saying it was a lot of fun, we will select 舞会 as the subject and turn the other information into a relative clause modifying the head noun. Hence.

(15) 丁云跟朋友一起去参加的那个舞会很有意思。
　　　Dīng Yún gēn péngyou yìqǐ qù cānjiā de nà ge wǔhuì hěn yǒu yìsi.
　　　The party that Ding Yun went to with her friend was a lot of fun.

The following are a few examples to illustrate how to combine sentences together to form a complex relative clause construction. In all cases, the (a) sentences are to become the modifying clauses. The items underlined are to be used as the head nouns.

(16) (a) 那个同学从中国来。
　　　(b) 那个同学很想家。
　　　(c) 那个从中国来的同学很想家。
　　　　　Nà ge cóng Zhōngguó lái de tóngxué hěn xiǎng jiā.
　　　　　That student who came from China is really homesick.

(17) (a) 你送他礼物。

(b) 礼物是什么？

(c) 你送他的礼物是什么？

Nǐ sòng tā de lǐwù shì shénme?

What is the present you gave him?

(18) (a) 这个人常常来找你。

(b) 你喜欢不喜欢他？

(c) 你喜欢不喜欢这个常常来找你的人？

Nǐ xǐhuan bù xǐhuan zhè ge chángcháng lái zhǎo nǐ de rén?

Do you like this man who often comes to see you?

(19) (a) 老师去年在法国写这本书。

(b) 老师让我看这本书。

(c) 老师让我看他去年在法国写的这本书。

Lǎoshī ràng wǒ kàn tā qùnián zài Fǎguó xiě de zhè běn shū.

The teacher told me to read this book which he wrote in France last year.

(20) (a) 我那天从中国来美国。

(b) 那天是十月三十号。

(c) 我从中国来美国的那天是十月三十号。

Wǒ cóng Zhōngguó lái Měiguó de nà tiān shì shíyuè sān-shíhào.

The day I came to America from China was October 30th.

Next are a few more examples of full sentences containing relative clauses. The head nouns are in parentheses and their modifying clauses are underlined.

(21) 今天晚上跟他一起来参加舞会的（同学）很多。

Jīntiān wǎnshang gēn tā yìqǐ lái cānjiā wǔhùi de (tóngxué) hěn duō.

Students who came with him to attend the dancing party were many.

(= There were many students who came to the party with him.)

(22) 你昨天跟你同学一起去参加的（舞会）是谁的？

Nǐ zuótiān gēn nǐ tóngxué yìqǐ qù cānjiā de (wǔhùi) shì shéi de?

The party that you went to with your classmates was whose?

(= Whose party was it that you went to with your classmates yesterday?)

(23)   这是我给你买的（花儿）。
Zhè shì wǒ gěi nǐ mǎi de (huār).
These are the flowers that I bought for you.

(24)   他是教我们汉语的（王老师）。
Tā shì jiāo wǒmen Hànyǔ de (Wáng lǎoshī).
He is Teacher Wang, who teaches us Chinese.

(25)   他给我一张他昨天买的（京剧票）。
Tā gěi wǒ yìzhāng tā zuótiān mǎi de (jīngjù piào).
He gave me a Beijing Opera ticket which he bought yesterday.

(26)   我们每天上汉语课的（教室）在二二二号。
Wǒmen měi tiān shàng Hànyǔ kè de (jiàoshì) zài 222 hào.
The classroom where we have our Chinese class every day is Room 222.

(27)   我们去看他的（那天）是星期天。
Wǒmen qù kàn tā de (nà tiān) shì xīngqītiān.
The day when we went to see him was Sunday.

The next group of sentences demonstrate the use of the pattern in a larger discursive context.

(28)   你看，这是我在中国给你买的新年礼物。漂亮吗？
Nǐ kàn, zhè shì wǒ zài Zhōngguó gěi nǐ mǎi de xīnnián lǐwù.
Piàoliang ma?
Look, this is the New Year present that I bought for you in China.
Is it pretty?

(29)   那个给我们开门的孩子真好看。她是王老师的女儿吗？
Nà ge gěi wǒmen kāi mén de háizi zhēn hǎokàn. Tā shì Wáng lǎo
shī de nǚ'ér ma?
That child who opened the door for us is really pretty. Is she
Teacher Wang's daughter?

(30)   我真喜欢上个星期五晚上跟我跳舞的那个年轻人。你知道他是谁吗？
Wǒ zhēn xǐhuān shàngge xīngqīwǔ wǎnshang gēn wǒ tiào wǔ de nà
ge niánqīng rén. Nǐ zhīdao tā shì shéi ma?
I really like that young man who danced with me last Friday night.
Do you know who he is?

(31)　上个星期，两个从英国来的学生来找你。一个我不认识，一个是去年跟我们一起在中国学习汉语的同学。

Shàngge xīngqī, liǎngge cóng Yīngguó lái de xuésheng lái zhǎo nǐ. Yíge wǒ bú rènshi, yíge shì qùnián gēn wǒmen yìqǐ zài Zhōngguó xuéxí Hànyǔ de tóngxué.

Last week, two students from England came to look for you. One I didn't know, and the other was the classmate who studied Chinese together with us in China last year.

Because of the difference in word order between Chinese and English, the relative clause construction may pose certain difficulty for beginning students. It will take quite a bit of practice, switching a modifying clause from a post-nominal position to a pre-nominal position, to acquire the Chinese speech habit. But, as long as you re-member that the general principle in Chinese is that a modifying element always comes before whatever it modifies, you will at least be able to conceptually under-stand the construction. When you translate either from English to Chinese or vice versa, you first have to decide what is modifying what and then choose the order appropriate to that target language.

2. The Adjectival Predicate

2.1   This section is actually a review of our previous discussion of the use of an adjective. When an adjective is used predicatively, it does not need a verb-to-be to help it constitute a predicate.

(1)　*他今天是高兴。

Tā jīntiān shì gāoxìng.

He is happy today.

On the other hand, a predicative adjective generally appears with some kind of a degree adverb.

Degree Adverb   +   Adjective

(2)　很大　　　　　"(very) big"
(3)　太小（了）　　"too small"
(4)　真高兴　　　　"really happy"
(5)　更年轻　　　　"even younger"
(6)　非常好看　　　"extremely pretty"

(A) Of the five adverbs listed above, 很 *hěn* is the most common one. In fact, its presence, unless specifically stressed, does not necessarily indicate emphasis. 他很忙 may simply mean "He is busy," and not necessarily "He is very busy." 太 *tài* with an optional 了 at the end of the sentence marks "excessiveness."

(B) 真 *zhēn*, literally meaning "real, true, genuine," may function as a degree adverb as in 真 Adjective "really Adjective."

(7)   她送我们的花儿真好看。
    Tā sòng wǒmen de huār zhēn hǎokàn.
    The flowers she gave us are really pretty.

(8)   他们都说你作的饭真好吃。你什么时候请我们去你家吃饭？
    Tāmen dōu shuō nǐ zuò de fàn zhēn hǎochī. Nǐ shénme shíhòu qǐng wǒmen qù nǐ jiā chī fàn?
    They all said that the food you cooked was really tasty. So, when will you invite us to your house for dinner?

(C) 非常 *fēicháng*, literally meaning "extraordinary," is generally used as a very strong degree adverb as in 非常 Adjective "extremely Adjective."

(9)   你们来看我，我非常高兴。
    Nǐmen lái kàn wǒ, wǒ fēicháng gāoxìng.
    I'm extremely happy that you came to see me.

(10)   这两本书都是我朋友送我的新年礼物，非常有意思。你看看。
    Zhè liǎngběn shū dōu shì wǒ péngyou sòng wǒ de xīnnián lǐwù, fēicháng yǒu yìsi. Nǐ kànkan.
    Both of these two books are presents which my friend gave me for the New Year. They're extremely interesting. Take a look.

(D) 更 *gèng*, placed before an adjective, implies some kind of an implicit comparison: "even more Adjective."

(11)   日本车更好。
    Rìběn chē gèng hǎo.
    Japanese cars are even better.
    (Implying that some other cars are good but Japanese cars are even better.)

(12)   白先生在银行工作，不太忙。他儿子在图书馆工作，每天十点上班，
两点下班，更不忙。

Bái xiānsheng zài yínháng gōngzuò, bú tài máng. Tā érzi zài túshūguǎn gōngzuò, měi tiān shídiǎn shàng bān, liǎngdiǎn xià bān, gèng
bù máng.

Mr. Bai works at the bank; (he's) not too busy. His son works at the
library; he goes in at ten o'clock and gets off at two o'clock. He's
even less busy.

2.2   In question formation, only the 吗—form is used and not the affirmative—
negative pattern.

(13)   这本中文书真好看吗？
Zhè běn Zhōngwén shū zhēn hǎokàn ma?
Is this Chinese book truly interesting?
(= good to look at)?

(14)   *这本中文书真好看不真好看？
*Zhè běn Zhōngwén shū zhēn hǎokàn bù zhēn hǎokàn?

2.3   In negative formation, the ordering of the negative marker and the degree
adverb is rather idiosyncratic. Some adverbs may prefer a certain sequence and, for
other adverbs, a different ordering may result in a completely different reading.

(15)   不 [很 Adjective] : not very Adjective   不很高兴   "not very happy"
(16)   很 [不 Adjective] : very unAdjective   很不高兴   "very unhappy"
(17)   不 [太 Adjective] : not too Adjective   不太年轻   "not too young"
(18)   太 [不 Adjective] : too unAdjective   太不好看了 "too unsightly"
(19)   *不 [真 Adjective]
(20)   真 [不 Adjective] : truly unAdjective   真不乾净   "truly dirty"
(21)   *不 [非常 Adjective]
(22)   非常 [不 Adjective] : extremely unAdjective 非常不好   "extremely bad"
(23)   *不 [更 Adjective]
(24)   更 [不 Adjective] : even more unAdjective 更不漂亮   "even less pretty"

2.4   If a predicative adjective appears without the accompaniment of a degree
adverb, it is always a case of implicit comparison. That is to say a sentence like 这

本书好 . "This book is good." carries the following connotation: "This book is good and that book is not." In other words, the pattern "Subject + Adjective" is not a simple description, as is the case in English. 很 is seldomly used in a contrastive description.

(25)　你的衬衫乾净，裤子不乾净。
　　　Nǐ de chènshān gānjing, kùzi bù gānjing.
　　　Your shirt is clean, but not your pants.

(26)　这个图书馆的书多，那个图书馆的书少。
　　　Zhè ge túshūguǎn de shū duō, nà ge túshūguǎn de shū shǎo.
　　　The books of this library are many, and the books of that library are few.
　　　(= This library has a large collection of books and that library a small collection.)

(27)　他女儿年轻，他儿子更年轻。
　　　Tā nǚ'ér niánqīng, tā érzi gèng niánqīng.
　　　His daughter is young and his son is even younger.

(28)　英国车好，日本车更好。我有三辆日本车。
　　　Yīngguó chē hǎo, Rìběn chē gèng hǎo. Wǒ yǒu sānliàng Rìběn chē.
　　　British cars are good but Japanese cars are even better. I have three Japanese cars.

3. The Transitive Quality Verb

There are certain verbs in Chinese that can be modified by a degree adverb and, in this manner, they are very much like adjectives (or status verbs). Unlike adjectives, however, they take Objects. Hence, they are sometimes referred to as "Transitive Quality Verbs"; "transitive" because they take Objects, and "quality" because they behave like adjectives. The same set of degree adverbs that modify adjectives is also compatible with this category of verbs. Examples of transitive quality verbs are:

(A) 喜欢　*xǐhuan* "to like":

(1)　我非常喜欢你。
　　　Wǒ feīcháng xǐhuan nǐ.
　　　I am extremely fond of you.

(2)　　我非常喜欢喝桔子水。

Wǒ fēicháng xǐhuan hē júzishuǐ.

I like (to drink) orange juice a lot.

(B) 想 *xiǎng* "to want/to miss":

(3)　　帕兰卡在中国学习，她很想她爸爸妈妈。

Pàlánkǎ zài Zhōngguó xúexí, tā hěn xiǎng tā bàba māma.

Palanka is studying in China. She misses her parents very much.

(4)　　我真想去看今天晚上的京剧。

Wǒ zhēn xiǎng qù kàn jīntiān wǎnshang de jīngjù.

I really want to go see tonight's Beijing Opera.

(C) 象 *xiàng* "to resemble":

(5)　　你儿子太象你哥哥了。

Nǐ érzi tài xiàng nǐ gēge le.

Your son looks incredibly like your brother.

(6)　　在图书馆工作的王太太有一个非常漂亮的女儿。我们都说她真象妈妈。王太太很高兴。

Zài túshūguǎn gōngzuò de Wáng tàitai yǒu yíge fēicháng piàoliang de nǚ'ér. Wǒmen dōu shuō tā zhēn xiàng māma. Wáng tàitai hěn gāoxìng.

Mrs. Wang, who works at the library, has an extremely beautiful daughter. We all said that she really looks like her mother. Mrs. Wang was very happy.

(D) 感谢 *gǎnxiè* "to thank/to be grateful":

(7)　　我们感谢你，我们更感谢你太太。

Wǒmen gǎnxiè nǐ, wǒmen gèng gǎnxiè nǐ tàitai.

We are very grateful to you, but we are even more grateful to your wife.

As in the case of adjectives, a quality verb, when modified by 很, does not appear in an affirmative－negative question form.

(8) *你女儿很象不很象你？

    *Nǐ nǚ'ér hěn xiàng bu hěn xiàng nǐ?

    Does your daughter look like you?

(9) 你女儿象不象你？

    Nǐ nǚ'ér xiàng bu xiàng nǐ?

(10) 你女儿很象你吗？

    Nǐ nǚ'ér hěn xiàng nǐ ma?

4. Reduplication of Verbs

4.1 A verb denoting an action may be repeated in the form of [Verb + Verb] to express the meaning of "to do it a little bit." The repeated syllable is always in the neutral tone.

(1)   请你想想这个问题。

      Qǐng nǐ xiǎngxiang zhè ge wèntí.

      Please think about this problem a little bit.

(2)   请你给我们介绍介绍中国的民歌。

      Qǐng nǐ gěi wǒmen jièshaojièshao Zhōngguó de míngē.

      Please tell us a little bit about Chinese folksongs.

With a two-syllable verb, say AB, as in sentence (2), the pattern for repetition is ABAB with the main stress falling on the first and the third syllables.

4.2 When a verb is reduplicated, it indicates a tentative notion, a trivialization of an action either in terms of the time it takes to carry out the action or the consequences of the action. The pattern is, therefore, often used for the following purposes:

(A) To describe a "short" action which a person hopes or intends to undertake.

(3)   走走 zǒuzou:

      take a walk (for twenty minutes but not for two hours)

(4)   下课以后，我们常常去咖啡馆坐坐，喝喝咖啡。

      Xià kè yǐhòu, wǒmen chángcháng qù kāfēiguǎn zuòzuo, hēhe kāfēi.

      After class, we often go to the coffee shop (and sit there) for a while and have some coffee.

The reduplication often appears after another verb that represents the effort one expends to achieve that undertaking. For example, in sentence (4), 去咖啡馆 precedes both verbal reduplications, 坐坐 and 喝喝咖啡 .

(B) To express the idea of trying to do something.

（5）　我说说，你听对不对。
　　　　Wǒ shuōshuo, nǐ tīng duì bu duì.
　　　　I'll try to say this; listen and see whether it's correct.

（6）　我今天下午去找找他，看他在不在。
　　　　Wǒ jīntiān xiàwǔ qù zhǎozhao tā, kàn tā zài bu zài.
　　　　I'll go to look for him this afternoon and see whether he is in.

(C) To soften the tone of a command, a request, or a suggestion.

（7）　老师让我们想想这个问题。
　　　　Lǎoshī ràng wǒmen xiǎngxiang zhè ge wèntí.
　　　　The teacher asks us to think about this problem a little bit.

（8）　请你开开门。
　　　　Qǐng nǐ kāikai mén.
　　　　Please open the door.

（9）　我用用你的词典，好吗？
　　　　Wǒ yòngyong nǐ de cídiǎn, hǎo ma?
　　　　May I use your dictionary for a little while?

（10）　他写的汉字非常漂亮。你看看。
　　　　Tā xiě de Hànzì fēicháng piàoliang. Nǐ kànkan.
　　　　(Take a) Look! The Chinese characters he wrote are extremely beautiful.

（11）　你们现在没事儿，来我家坐坐，休息休息。
　　　　Nǐmen xiànzài méi shìr, lái wǒ jiā zuòzuo, xiūxixiuxi.
　　　　Now that you don't have anything to do, come to my house and relax a little bit.

The reduplication occurs only with volitional action verbs, i.e. verbs representing actions that one carries out by intention. Adjectives, transitive quality verbs, and the verbs 是, 在, and 有 do not undergo this reduplication.

5. The Particle 吧

The particle 吧 *ba* attached to the end of a sentence signals a request or a suggestion. Its presence also tends to soften the tone of such a request or suggestion.

(1)   坐！   Zuò!   (Sit!)

(2)   请坐！   Qǐng zuò!   (Sit, please!)

(3)   坐吧！   Zuò ba!   (Why don't you sit down?)

(4)   请坐吧！ Qǐng zuò ba!   (Why don't you sit down please?)

(5)   休息休息吧，好吗？
      Xiūxixiūxi ba, hǎo ma?
      Let's rest for a while, OK?

(6)   你来这儿吧！
      Nǐ lái zhèr ba!
      Why don't you come over here?

(7)   我们跳舞吧！
      Wǒmen tiào wǔ ba!
      Let's dance!

(8)   请你给我们说说吧。
      Qǐng nǐ gěi wǒmen shuōshuo ba.
      Please tell us a little bit about it.

(9)   妈妈告诉儿子说，"你现在穿的衬衫不乾净，也不好看。别穿这件，穿那件吧。"
      Māma gàosu érzi shuō, "Nǐ xiànzài chuān de chènshān bù gānjing, yě bù hǎokàn. Bié chuān zhè jiàn, chuān nà jiàn ba."
      The mother told her son (by saying), "The shirt you're wearing now isn't clean, and it doesn't look good either. Don't wear this one. Wear that one."

(10) A: 我想请你跳舞。
         Wǒ xiǎng qǐng nǐ tiào wǔ.
         I'd like to ask you to dance with me.
      B: 你请丁云跳吧。我现在没空儿。
         Nǐ qǐng Dīng Yún tiào ba. Wǒ xiànzài méi kòngr.
         Why don't you ask Ding Yun to dance? I'm busy right now.

1. Position Words

1.1 As the term suggests, a position word specifies a location and the specification is made in reference to something else. In English, for example, "outside" is a position word, but, without the proper context, the reference point is not clear: "outside of what?" "Outside of a room" or "outside of a building"? The "outside" of a room could still be the "inside" of a building. In other words, the notion of a position is a relative one and it is important to know the actual reference point. In our example above, is it "the room" or "the building" that is being used as the base in relation to which the position "outside" is established? Once the question is answered and the reference is named or understood from the context, it may be omitted from the sentence. Thus, if the following statement is made inside a classroom, the reference point is evidently clear to both the speaker and the addressee.

There is a man waiting outside. (...waiting outside of the classroom.)

Some of the common position words in Chinese for expressing spatial relational terms are:

里边	*lǐbiān*	"inside"	vs.	外边	*wàibiān*	"outside"
前边	*qiánbiān*	"front"	vs.	后边	*hòubiān*	"back"
上边	*shàngbiān*	"top"	vs.	下边	*xiàbiān*	"bottom"
左边	*zuǒbiān*	"left"	vs.	右边	*yòubiān*	"right"
旁边	*pángbiān*	"side, flank"				
中间	*zhōngjiān*	"middle"				
对面	*duìmiàn*	"opposite"				

Please notice that the first four pairs are all formed with the suffix 边 *biān*, which literally means "side." Though it is marked as a first tone syllable, it is always pronounced with a slightly weakened pitch. In 旁边, however, 边 retains its full tone: *pángbiān*.

1.2 To specify the reference point in a positional word unit in Chinese, the ordering is quite different from that in English, as illustrated in the following:

Chinese [Noun + Position]		English [Position + Noun]	
书	上边	on top of	the book
照片	下边	under	the picture
教室	里边	inside	the classroom
邮局	外边	outside of	the post office
厨房	前边	in front of	the kitchen
卧室	后边	behind	the bedroom
桌子	左边	to the left of	the desk
椅子	右边	to the right of	the chair
客厅	旁边	by the side of	the living room
洗澡间	中间	in the middle of	the bathroom
学校	对面	opposite of	the school

If we remember the basic principle in Chinese syntax that a modifier always comes before the noun it modifies, then the sequential ordering in a positional unit is quite easy to understand. The position word serves as the head noun and the reference phrase functions as a modifier, telling us more about the position, namely the positioning in reference to "what." The marker 的, however, is never used in this pattern.

Although we will have much more to say about the use of the position expressions in the next few sections, we should point out at the outset that the application of "Place ＋里边" is not quite the same as that of "in a Place." 里边 is never used in a 在－expression when the Place Word is a geographical name or when it stands for a building or an organization.

(1) 他在北京学习。
      Tā zài Běijīng xuéxí.
      He studies in Beijing.

(2) *他在北京里边学习。
      *Tā zài Běijīng lǐbiān xuéxí.

(3) 他在银行工作。
      Tā zài yínháng gōngzuò.
      He works in a bank.

（4） *他在银行里边工作。

　　　　*Tā zài yínháng lǐbiān gōngzuò.

It is obvious that the focus of sentence (1) is that "he studies *in/at* Beijing" and not "*inside* Beijing." For the same reason, sentence (4) would be correct only if it were to mean "He works inside the bank and not on the outside or at the front."

1.3 A position word may also be used to modify a noun, in which case the former will stand before the latter in the pattern. 的 is obligatory in this case. The order is the exact opposite of what we find in English, as illustrated in the following:

Chinese [Position 的 Noun]	English [Noun + Position]
上边　的　衬衫	the shirt on the top
下边　的　信	the letter beneath
外边　的　窗户	the windows outside
里边　的　人	the people inside
左边　的　房间	the room on the left
右边　的　花儿	the flowers on the right
旁边　的　银行	the bank by the side
对面　的　车	the car on the opposite side
中间　的　花园	the garden in the middle

1.4 If we combine the pattern in 1.2 with that in 1.3, we have a complete modification unit with a positional reference. This is diagrammed as below:

[Noun　+　Position]　的　Noun

床	上边的	衬衫	the shirt on the bed
书	下边的	笔	the pen under the book
学校	外边的	邮局	the post office outside of the campus
食堂	里边的	桌子	the tables inside the dining hall
图书馆	前边的	咖啡馆	the cafe in front of the library
宿舍	后边的	操场	the field behind the dorm

卧室	左边的	厕所	the lavatory to the left of the bedroom
书房	右边的	客厅	the living room to the right of the study
门	旁边的	窗户	the window next to the door
洗澡间	对面的	房间	the room opposite to the bathroom
邮局和宿舍	中间的	咖啡馆	the cafe between the post office and the dorm

As expected, the word order in English is a complete reversal of the sequence in Chinese. And, precisely because of this drastic discrepancy, beginning students in either language may experience difficulty in translation or composition that involves the use of a positional unit. We need to be extra careful when expressing positional information. If not, we may be imparting an inaccurate message or simply uttering a nonsense sentence.

(5) 学校左边   vs.   左边的学校
     the left side of the school   the school on the left

(6) 报下边的书   vs.   书下边的报
     the book under the paper   the paper under the book

(7) 床上边的人   vs.   *人上边的床
     the person in bed   *the bed on the person

2. The Location Sentence

Positional units often appear in three types of sentences: those indicating location, existence and identification. The latter two types are discussed in Sections 3 and 4.

   As we have learned in an earlier lesson, we use the following pattern with the verb 在 to indicate the location of an object or a person, whose reference is known to both the speaker and the addressee. (In English, such specific reference is indicated by the use of the definite article "the.")

Noun ＋ 在 ＋ PLACE.

[The Noun is at PLACE.]

What kind of words may serve as PLACE expressions? The following is a list of identifiable types of elements that may appear in such a role.

(A) The locatives: 这儿，那儿，哪儿：

    (1)   老师在这儿。
            Lǎoshī zài zhèr.
            The teacher is here.

    (2)   厕所在哪儿？
            Cèsuǒ zài nǎr?
            Where is the bathroom?

(B) Noun ＋ 这儿／那儿：

    (3)   你的裙子在你妹妹那儿。
            Nǐ de qúnzi zài nǐ mèimei nàr.
            Your skirt is there with your sister.

    (4)   我的唱片在谁那儿？
            Wǒ de chàngpiàn zài shéi nàr?
            Who has my album?

For a review of this pattern, please refer back to Lesson 16: Section 4.

(C) A real place word such as a place name, a building, or an organization, etc. :

    (5)   我们现在在美国。
            Wǒmen xiànzài zài Měiguó.
            We are now in America.

    (6)   他昨天晚上不在宿舍，他在我家听音乐。
            Tā zuótiān wǎnshang bú zài sùshè, tā zài wǒ jiā tīng yīnyuè.
            He wasn't at the dorm last night. He was at my house, listening to
            music.

(D) A positional unit:

    (7)   图书馆在左边。
            Túshūguǎn zài zuǒbiān.
            The library is to the left.

    (8)   图书馆在书店左边。
            Túshūguán zài shūdiàn zuǒbiān.
            The library is to the left of the bookstore.

(9) 我们去的那个电影院在一个咖啡馆旁边。

Wǒmen qù de nà ge diànyǐngyuàn zài yíge kāfēiguǎn pángbiān.

The movie theater we are going to is right next to a cafe.

3. The Existence Sentence

3.1 An existence sentence tells what can be found at a certain place. The most common syntactic indicator of an existence sentence in English is "There is/are..." For example,

> There is a book on the desk.
> On the desk, there is a book.

The above two sentences are basically the same in meaning, even though the PLACE expression appears at the end of sentence (a) but at the beginning of sentence (b). In Chinese, there is only one order:

> PLACE WORD   有   Object
> [There is NOUN at PLACE]

---

(1) 桌子上边有书。

Zhuōzi shàngbiān yǒu shū.

There is a book on the desk.

The particular verb used in this pattern for existence is 有, a verb that also functions as a possessive verb meaning "to have". This double usage of 有 closely resembles that of "avoir" in French, which marks possession as well as existence. The negative form is, of course, marked by 没：没有 *méi yǒu*. The following are more sentences illustrating the use of various types of PLACE expressions in the pattern.

(A) The locatives: 这儿，那儿，哪儿：

(2) 这儿有很多很漂亮的花儿。

Zhèr yǒu hěn duō hěn piàoliang de huār.

There are a lot of beautiful flowers here.

(3) 这儿哪儿有银行？

Zhèr nǎr yǒu yínháng?

Where is there a bank here?

(B) Noun ＋ 这儿／那儿：

 (4) 我这儿有很多新照片。
   Wǒ zhèr yǒu hěn duō xīn zhàopiàn.
   There are a lot of new pictures here with me.

 (5) 王老师那儿没有汉语词典。
   Wáng lǎoshī nàr méi yǒu Hànyǔ cídiǎn.
   There isn't a Chinese dictionary where Teacher Wang is.

(C) An actual place name or a noun that stands for a place, a building, or an organization:

 (6) 北京有一个非常好的图书馆。
   Běijīng yǒu yíge fēicháng hǎo de túshūguǎn.
   There is a very good library in Beijing.

 (7) 我们的图书馆没有法语词典。
   Wǒmen de túshūguǎn méi yǒu Fǎyǔ cídiǎn.
   There isn't a French dictionary in our library.

 (8) 左边的房子有很多窗户，右边的房子没有窗户。
   Zuǒbiān de fángzi yǒu hěn duō chuānghu, yòubiān de fángzi méi yǒu chuānghu.
   The house on the left has a lot of windows, the house on the right has none.

(D) A positional unit:

 (9) 上边有一个洗澡间。
   Shàngbiān yǒu yíge xǐzǎojiān.
   There is a bathroom above.

 (10) 上边的卧室有一个洗澡间。
   Shàngbiān de wòshì yǒu yíge xǐzǎojiān.
   There is a bathroom in the bedroom above.

 (11) 客厅上边的卧室有一个洗澡间。
   Kètīng shàngbiān de wòshì yǒu yíge xǐzǎojiān.
   There is a bathroom in the bedroom above the living room.

3.2 What exactly is the difference between a location sentence and an existence sentence? They both involve the same two linguistic units: a noun and a place word.

If this noun (be it a person, a thing, or even another place) represents something we already know about, and our task now is to locate it or find out where it is, then we use the location pattern. Hence, in English, we use the definite article "the" before the noun in the pattern "*The* Noun is at PLACE." On the other hand, if we know about the PLACE (PLACE being the old information), and we are now trying to find out what is to be found, or not to be found, at this known PLACE, then we use the existence pattern. Hence, the use of an indefinite article "a/an" in the pattern "There is *a* Noun at PLACE." This semantic distinction is handled in a different manner in Chinese. We utilize two different patterns involving two different verbs, namely 有 and 在. A good example to illustrate the difference in usage between the two patterns is the way we would phrase our question when we want to find a bathroom. If we are driving in the countryside all surrounded by trees and wild flowers, we are not even sure whether there is a bathroom around. Hence, the question to ask when we see a passerby is about existence:

（12） 请问这儿有厕所吗？

Qǐng wèn, zhèr yǒu cèsuǒ ma?

Excuse me. Is there a bathroom here?

However, the question will be phrased quite differently when we are, say, at a friend's house. As all modern houses should be adequately equipped with such facilities, it is safe to skip the existence question and proceed with the location form:

（13） 请问厕所在哪儿？

Qǐng wèn, cèsuǒ zài nǎr?

Excuse me. Where is the bathroom?

4. The Identification Sentence

> PLACE ＋ 是 ＋ NOUN
>
> [What is at PLACE is NOUN.]

An identification sentence is very much like an existence sentence, both in meaning as well as in word order. We will first look at the following two examples:

（1） 桌子上边有一本中文书。   (Existence)

Zhuōzi shàngbiān yǒu yìběn Zhōngwén shū.

There is a Chinese book on the table.

(2)　桌子上边是一本中文书。　　　　　　　　　　　(Identification)
　　　Zhuōzi shàngbiān shì yìběn Zhōngwén shū.
　　　What is on the table is a Chinese book.

Syntactically, the PLACE expression occupies the sentence initial position in both patterns. Semantically, the PLACE expression represents known information. The difference between the two patterns is that in the identification sentence, we know there is something on the table, and our task is to identify what it is. This is not so with the existence sentence, which tells us whether something "exists" at the PLACE, and, if so, what it is. In other words, the existence of something is confirmed in an existence sentence but assumed in an identification sentence. The following pair of questions again demonstrate the same kind of situational difference.

(3)　你前边有人吗？
　　　Nǐ qiánbiān yǒu rén ma?
　　　Is there any one in front of you?

(4)　你前边是谁？
　　　Nǐ qiánbiān shì shéi?
　　　Who is in front of you?

On a pitch-dark night when it is impossible to see very far ahead, one would ask (3) just to find out if there is anyone else around. If one sees, in spite of the darkness, that there is a shadow of a person in the front, the immediate concern is of course to find out who this mystery person is. Thus, the use of the identification form in (4).

　　The noun in an identification sentence may be definite or indefinite in reference. For example, sentence (2) carries an indefinite Object, but the Object in the following sentence is definite.

(5)　桌子上边是我们的中文书。　　　　　　　　　　(Identification)
　　　Zhuōzi shàngbiān shì wǒmen de Zhōngwén shū.
　　　That which is on the table is our Chinese book.

Now, compare sentence (5) with sentence (6):

(6)　我们的中文书在桌子上边。　　　　　　　　　　　(Location)
　　　Wǒmen de Zhōngwén shū zài zhuōzi shàngbiān.
　　　Our Chinese book is on the table.

Sentence (6) starts out with a known object as the topic and proceeds with the comment on its whereabouts. Sentence (5), on the other hand, starts out with a known place as the topic and proceeds with the new information as to what is to be found there. The identified object, in this case, happens to be a definite object, namely "our Chinese book." Generally speaking, if the new information pertains to PLACE, we use the LOCATION pattern; if it pertains to a NOUN, we use the EXISTENCE pattern. In the latter case, we may opt for the IDENTIFICATION pattern if we already know something exists but we don't know what that something is. Interrogatives best reflect this distinction between what is known and what is not known.

（7）　Location:　　　图书馆在哪儿？
　　　　　　　　　　Túshūguǎn zài nǎr?
　　　　　　　　　　Where is the library?

（8）　Existence:　　　图书馆后边有什么？
　　　　　　　　　　Túshūguǎn hòubiān yǒu shénme?
　　　　　　　　　　What is there behind the library?

（9）　Identification:　图书馆后边是什么？
　　　　　　　　　　Túshūguǎn hòubiān shì shénme?
　　　　　　　　　　What is it that is behind the library?

The following are more sentences illustrating the use of the identification pattern with various types of PLACE expressions:

(A)　The locatives: 这儿，那儿，哪儿：

　　（10）　这儿是图书馆。
　　　　　　Zhèr shì túshūguǎn.
　　　　　　Here is the library.

(B)　Noun ＋ 这儿／那儿：

　　（11）　我这儿是一本法文杂志。
　　　　　　Wǒ zhèr shì yìběn Fǎwén zázhì.
　　　　　　What I have here is a French magazine.

(C)　A real place word such as a place name, a building or an organization, etc., is incompatible with this pattern.

(D)   A positional unit:

(12)   左边是食堂
Zuǒbiān shì shítáng.
That which is on the left side is our dining hall.

(13)   图书馆左边是食堂。
Túshūguǎn zuǒbiān shì shítáng.
That which is on the left side of the library is our dining hall.

4.2   The following are a few more examples to contextualize the various types of sentences involving the use of place words and positional expressions. If you are able to identify the types and understand why each is employed in its particular context, you are already developing a feeling for the way in which the Chinese see and choose to represent the complex relations between space and objects in different linguistic schemes.

(14)   书房对面不是饭厅，是客厅。洗澡间在客厅和厨房中间。
Shūfáng duìmiàn bú shì fàntīng, shì kètīng. Xǐzǎojiān zài kètīng hé chúfáng zhōngjiān.
Opposite the study room is not the dining room; it is the living room. The bathroom is between the living room and the kitchen.

(15)   卧室里边有一张桌子和四把椅子。桌子上边有两杯咖啡。
Wòshì lǐbiān yǒu yìzhāng zhuōzi hé sìbǎ yǐzi. Zhuōzi shàngbiān yǒu liǎngbēi kāfēi.
There are four chairs and one table inside the bedroom. On the table, there are two cups of coffee.

(16)   上边的报是今天的，下边的是四号的。星期一的报在中间。
Shàngbiān de bào shì jīntiān de, xiàbiān de shì sìhào de. Xīngqīyī de bào zài zhōngjiān.
The newspaper on top is today's; the one on the bottom is the fourth's. Monday's paper is in the middle.

(17)   右边的窗户外边有一个小花园。花园后边是车房。
Yòubiān de chuānghu wàibiān yǒu yíge xiǎo huāyuán. Huāyuán hòubiān shì chēfáng.
There is a little garden outside of the window on the right. Behind the garden is the garage.

（18） 请问，你们这儿有厕所吗？在哪儿？现在有人用吗？

Qǐng wèn, nǐmen zhèr yǒu cèsuǒ ma? Zài nǎr? Xiànzài yǒu rén yòng ma?

Excuse me. Do you have a restroom here? Where is it? Is anyone using it right now?

（19） 我们现在在学校前边。我左边是一个银行，右边是一个咖啡馆。每个星期五下午，咖啡馆里边总有很多人。

Wǒmen xiànzài zài xuéxiào qiánbiān. Wǒ zuǒbiān shì yíge yínháng, yòubiān shì yíge kāfēiguǎn. Měi ge xīngqīwǔ xiàwǔ, kāfēiguǎn lǐbiān zǒng yǒu hěn duō rén.

Right now we are in front of the school. To my left is a bank; to my right, a cafe. There are always a lot of people in the cafe every Friday afternoon.

（20） 我的卧室后边有一个小房间，房间里边有一个窗户，窗户下边是两张旧床，床旁边有两把新椅子。我和姐姐以前用的旧桌子也在这个房间里边。桌子上边的书真不少，都是妈妈的。

Wǒ de wòshì hòubiān yǒu yíge xiǎo fángjiān, fángjiān lǐbiān yǒu yíge chuānghu, chuānghu xiàbiān shì liǎngzhāng jiù chuáng, chuáng pángbiān yǒu liǎngbǎ xīn yǐzi. Wǒ hé jiějie yǐqián yòng de jiù zhuōzi yě zài zhè ge fángjiān lǐbiān. Zhuōzi shàngbiān de shū zhēn bù shǎo, dōu shì māma de.

There is a small room behind my bedroom, and the room has a window. Under the window there are two used beds. By the beds there are two new chairs. The old desks that my elder sister and I used to use are also inside this room. There are quite a few books on the desks, and they are all mom's.

1. The Progressive Aspect

1.1 Beginning with this lesson, we will be looking at the demarcation of aspect in the Chinese language. Aspect is a universal grammatical notion relating to the particular status of an action or event. When we speak of an action, we may view it as a process consisting of a series of phases, including the beginning, continuation, repetition, completion, etc. Each of these phases is an aspect that may be selected for emphasis in conversation. For example, the aspectual emphases of the following two English sentences are different: the first one stresses the progression of the eating process whereas in the second sentence, its completion.

> (a) *I was eating lunch* when he called.
> (b) *I had already eaten lunch* when he called.

Regardless of the time of occurrence, an action may always be characterized with an emphasis on one of its aspects. Hence, as exemplified by the following three sentences, the progressive may appear in all three time schemes in English: the past, the present and the future.

> (c) *What were you doing* yesterday when he called?　　(past)
> (d) *What are you doing* now?　　(present)
> (e) *What will you be doing* this time tomorrow morning?　　(future)

Sentences (c), (d), and (e) differ in *tense*, as indicated by the explicit marking on the verb-to-be: *were doing*, *are doing* and *will be doing*. The progressive aspect in each case, however, is invariably formed by the auxiliary verb-to-be and the present participle (Verb-ing). The English language uses various means to indicate tense and aspect and allows combinations thereof as required by individual situations. The Chinese language, on the other hand, has no tense markers for its verbs. When necessary, time words, such as 昨天, 现在, 明天, etc., are used to specify the temporal context, but the verb itself always remains uninflected.

(1)   我去年在北京大学学习汉语。
       Wǒ qùnián zài Běijīng Dàxué xuéxí Hànyǔ.
       I studied Chinese at Beijing University last year.

(2)   我现在在北京大学学习汉语。
       Wǒ xiànzài zài Běijīng Dàxué xuéxí Hànyǔ.
       I am now studying Chinese at Beijing University.

In this regard, the Chinese language may be described as void of tenses. As for aspect, there are quite a few cases in Mandarin, each involving a different marking format. The distinction between tense and aspect is an important dichotomy to which we will return for more elaboration in later lessons. In this lesson, we will make our first acquaintance with the marking and the use of the progressive in Chinese.

1.2   The Marking of the Progressive: To mark the ongoing aspect of an action in Chinese, we may place the verb 在 *zài* before the predicate and /or the particle 呢 *ne* after it. In forming this pattern, there are three options from which to choose, with practically no difference in meaning.

(A) 在 + Predicate + 呢	
(B) 在 + Predicate	
(C) Predicate + 呢	

Examples of the variations are:

(3.a) 我在看报呢。
       Wǒ zài kàn bào ne.
       I'm in the midst of reading a newspaper.
(3.b) 我在看报。
       Wǒ zài kàn bào.
(3.c) 我看报呢。
       Wǒ kàn bào ne.

In forming a question, however, the third pattern "Predicate + 呢," is stylistically the least preferable of the three choices. For example,

(4.a) 你在看电视呢吗？

Nǐ zài kàn diànshì ne ma?

Are you watching T.V. ?

(4.b) 你在看电视吗？

Nǐ zài kàn diànshì ma?

(4.c) （你看电视呢吗？）

(Nǐ kàn diànshì ne ma?)

(5.a) 他在作甚么呢？

Tā zài zuò shénme ne?

What is he doing?

(5.b) 他在作甚么？

Tā zài zuò shénme?

(5.c) （他作甚么呢？）

（Tā zuò shénme ne?）

To negate a progressive sentence, we need to use 没有 *méiyou* instead of 不 before the verbal unit, with or without 在 . The final 呢 , however, has to be dropped. 没有 may be shortened to 没 when standing before a verb, but it has to appear in its full form when used as a short answer. As a compound negative marker, *méiyou* is spelled as one word. The following are some examples.

(6)   Question: 你在看电视呢吗？

Nǐ zài kàn diànshì ne ma?

Are you watching T.V.?

Negative Answer: 没有，我没（有）在看电视。

Méiyou, wǒ méi(you) zài kàn diànshì.

No, I'm not watching T.V.

(7)   Question: 早上八点钟的时候，你在打电话呢吗？

Zǎoshang bādiǎn zhōng de shíhòu, nǐ zài dǎ diànhuà ne ma?

Were you using the phone this morning at eight o'clock?

Negative Answer: 没有，我没（有）（在）打电话，我在听新闻呢。

Méiyou, wǒ méi(you) (zài) dǎ diànhuà, wǒ zài tīng xīnwén ne.

No, I wasn't using the phone. I was listening to the news.

(8)   Question: 他在睡觉呢吗？

Tā zài shuì jiào ne ma?

Is he taking a nap?

Negative Answer: 他没（有）（在）睡觉，他在整理房间呢。

Tā méi(you) (zài) shuì jiào, tā zài zhěnglǐ fáng-jiān ne.

He isn't taking a nap; he is in the midst of clean-ing his room.

The optionality of 在 depends on whether the negative answer is followed by a positive description of what actually took place instead at the time in question. If there is such a follow-up statement as in (7) and (8), 在 is optional: 没（有）（在） Verb .... Otherwise, 在 remains intact in the pattern as in (6), a sentence that consists solely of a negative response.

As you may have noticed, the progressive indicator 在 is in itself a full loca-tive verb meaning "to be at..." This use of a locative form to mark the progressive aspect readily reminds us of a similar practice in English: "in the middle of doing something" or "in the midst of Verb-ing," Because of this double status of 在, it may serve both functions in the same sentence as illustrated in (9).

(9)   我们在花园里玩儿呢。

Wǒmen zài huāyuánli wánr ne.

We're playing in the garden.

Sentence (9) is made up of two major components: (a) Location: 在花园里; and (b) Progressive: 在玩儿呢. In fact, we may envision that there are two 在's in the sequence, each playing a different grammatical role, but the two necessarily fuse into one. For this reason, (10) is an incorrect sentence in Mandarin.

(10) *我们<u>在</u><u>在</u>花园里玩儿呢。

Wǒmen <u>zài</u> <u>zài</u> huāyuánli wánr ne.

1.3 The Use of 正: In the following English sentences, the meanings are essen-tially the same even though there is a slight difference in emphasis.

(a) I was in the middle of cooking when he dropped in.
(b) I was *right* in the middle of cooking when he dropped in.

Both sentences report the intersection of two actions: his appearance disturbing the progress of my cooking. The use of the adverb "right" in (b) underscores that timely or untimely interception or interruption, thereby making the sentence more vivid in its narrative effect. A similar device is available in Chinese, namely the adding of the adverb 正 *zhèng* before the verbal sequence:

正在	Verb (Object) 呢
zhèng zài	Verb (Object) ne

Incidentally, like its counterpart in English, the word 正 also means "proper, right." The inclusion of 正 pinpoints an ongoing action to a specific point in time, which may be explicitly expressed by a time word as in (11), or a time clause in the form of ……的时候 "when..." as in (12), or it may be implicitly inferred from the context as in (13).

(11) 他们现在正在上课呢。
Tāmen xiànzài zhèng zài shàng kè ne.
They are in class right now.

(12) 你昨天来找他的时候，他正在洗澡呢。
Nǐ zuótiān lái zhǎo tā de shíhòu, tā zhèng zài xǐ zǎo ne.
When you came to visit him yesterday, he was right in the middle of taking a shower.

(13) 他们正在跳舞呢。
Tāmen zhèng zài tiào wǔ ne.
(At this very moment.) They are in the midst of dancing.

Sentence (12) describes two actions: the visit and the host being in the shower. The two events are temporally interrelated; in fact, the juxtaposition of the two clauses and the use of the progressive plus 正 in the second clause underscore the bad timing of the first action. It was a wrong time for the visitor to appear at the doorstep, or that was the reason why the host did not answer the door in time. However, when there are two activities that go on at the same time but are unrelated to each other, hence not a case of interception, then 正 is not used with the progressive. For example,

(14) 每天下午你学习的时候，你弟弟在作甚么呢？
Měi tiān xiàwǔ nǐ xuéxí de shíhòu, nǐ dìdi zài zuò shénme ne?
What does your brother do every afternoon when you are studying?

(15)   昨天晚上王太太作饭的时候，李先生在洗衣服。

Zuótiān wǎnshang Wáng tàitai zuò fàn de shíhòu, Lǐ xiānsheng zài xǐ yīfu.

Last evening when Mrs. Wang was cooking, Mr. Li was doing his laundry.

Now, compare sentence (15) with sentence (16) where 正 is used , and the difference in terms of interception becomes apparent.

(16)   昨天晚上你作饭的时候，我正在洗衣服呢。

Zuótiān wǎnshang nǐ zuò fàn de shíhòu, wǒ zhèng zài xǐ yīfu ne.

Last evening when you were cooking, I was right in the middle of doing laundry.

Sentence (15) provides a scenario with two parallel but unrelated activities, each actor probably oblivious of what the other was doing. The scenario in sentence (16) is, on the other hand, quite different: I knew you were cooking, but I was also busily engaged in another household chore at that time; and, so, don't blame me for not helping out.

The following are a few more sentences to illustrate the use of the progressive in Chinese.

(17)   我叫张红去接电话的时候，她正在跟孩子们玩儿呢。

Wǒ jiào Zhāng Hóng qù jiē diànhuà de shíhòu, tā zhèng zài gēn háizimen wánr ne.

When I asked Zhang Hong to go answer the phone, she was in the midst of playing with the kids.

(18)   A: 你开车去接他们的时候，他们正在作甚么呢？他们在看电视新闻吗？

Nǐ kāi chē qù jiē tāmen de shíhòu, tāmen zhèng zài zuò shénme ne? Tāmen zhèng zài kàn diànshì xīnwén ma?

When you drove over to pick them up, what were they doing? Were they watching the T.V. news?

B: 没有，张先生在睡觉，张太太在整理花园呢。

Méiyou, Zhāng xiānsheng zài shuì jiào, Zhāng tàitai zài zhěnglǐ huāyuán ne.

No, Mr. Zhang was taking a nap and Mrs. Zhang was cleaning the garden.

（19）　今天我从学校开车去接我太太的时候，我儿子在大学对面的电影院前
　　　　边等他女朋友呢。

Jīntiān wǒ cóng xuéxiào kāi chē qù jiē wǒ tàitai de shíhòu, wǒ érzi zài dàxué duìmiàn de diànyīngyuàn qiánbiān děng tā nǔ péngyou ne.

Today while I was driving from school to pick up my wife, my son was waiting for his girl friend in front of the movie theater opposite the university.

（20）　A: 喂，是丁云家吗？

Wèi, shì Dīng Yún jiā ma?

Hello, is this Ding Yun's house?

　　　　B: 是啊，您找她吗？请等一等。

Shì a, nín zhǎo tā ma? Qǐng děngyiděng.

Yes. Are you looking for her? Just a moment.

　　　　A: 丁云，你在作什么呢？

Dīng Yún, nǐ zài zuò shénme ne?

Ding Yun, what were you doing?

　　　　C: 我正在看电视新闻呢。新闻说，美国工人代表团今天正在中国访
　　　　　问。他们明天去参观工厂。

Wǒ zhèng zài kàn diànshì xīnwén. Xīnwén shuō, Měiguó gōngrén dàibiǎotuán jīntiān zhèng zài Zhōngguó fǎngwèn. Tāmen míngtiān qù cānguān gōngchǎng.

I was just watching news on T.V. The news said that an American workers' delegation is visiting China right now. Tomorrow they are going to go visit the factories.

1.4 Aside from marking an ongoing action, the English progressive form, otherwise known as the continuous tense, may also be used to indicate a future event:

　　　　She *is coming* tomorrow.

The Chinese progressive, however, is only used for a progressive action. There are certain verbs in Chinese that are idiosyncratically non-progressive by nature and are therefore incompatible with the 在……呢 pattern. They include 来 *lái* "to come," 去 *qù* "to go," 走 *zǒu* "to leave," 死 *sǐ* "to die," and a few others. It is for this reason that the following sentence is incorrect in Chinese even though its counterpart is perfectly fine in English.

（21） *他在死呢。

　　　　*Tā zài sǐ ne.

　　　　He is dying.

To the Chinese mind, death is seen as an absolute state which a person has either entered or not. In other words, a person is either dead or alive. To describe an imminent death, the Chinese would say something like "He is about to die," but never "He is dying."

　　　Another idiosyncracy in the use of the progressive is that the same ongoing aspect may be stressed in one language but ignored in another. For example, if a person comes to the door, we would say in English "Who are you looking for?" While the situation does represent an ongoing action, a Chinese speaker would stress "who" rather than the progressive aspect of the action. Therefore, he would simply ask,

（22）　你找谁？

　　　　Nǐ zhǎo shéi?

As is always the case, when to use a pattern and when not to do so is a matter of linguistic idiomacy that can be acquired only through constant practice and repeated corrections of errors. Aspect is a relatively easy concept to understand, but its use in Chinese often poses a great challenge to beginners. However, since Chinese is a tense-less language, the task of tackling Time is only half as formidable as that of studying any of the European languages where there is always a complex interplay of tense and aspect.

2. The Particle 吧 (continued)

The basic function of the particle 吧 *ba* is to indicate uncertainty or supposition. When added to a statement, it softens the tone by implying that the speaker is merely making a suggestion or estimation. For example,

（1）　　这个汉字不对。

　　　　Zhè ge Hànzì bú duì.

　　　　This Chinese character is wrong.

（2）　　这个汉字不对吧。

　　　　Zhè ge Hànzì bú duì ba.

　　　　This Chinese character is wrong, I guess.

Sentence (1) is an authoritative statement that a teacher would say when correcting his/her student's mistake. Sentence (2), on the other hand, suggests doubt, hesitation, or noncommitment either because the speaker truly lacks the expertise to make a fair judgment or because the speaker wishes to tone down his/her judgment by phrasing it in the form of a conjecture. In other words, the use of 吧 is a convenient means to readily change what would otherwise sound abrupt or even offensive into a polite request or suggestion. The following are a few more examples of this suggestive use of 吧.

(3) 这是我的。
  Zhè shì wǒ de.
  This is mine.

(4) 这是我的吧。
  Zhè shì wǒ de ba.
  This is mine, right?

(5) 我们去看电影。
  Wǒmen qù kàn diànyǐng.
  We will go see a movie.

(6) 我们去看电影吧。
  Wǒmen qù kàn diànyǐng ba.
  Let's go see a movie.

(7) 你走！
  Nǐ zǒu!
  Get out!

(8) 你走吧！
  Nǐ zǒu ba!
  Why don't you leave?

3. Position Words (continued)

We have learned in Lesson 22 that most of the position words are formed by attaching the suffix 边 *biān* to directional forms such as 上 *shàng*, 下 *xià*, 里 *lǐ*, 外 *wài*…. Furthermore, the reference point in a positional unit may be specified by placing the pertinent noun immediately before it, as in 书上边 *shū shàngbiān* "on top of the book." There are, however, certain combinations that allow the deletion of the suffix 边 and these units often carry idiomatic readings.

(1.a) 书上边   vs.   (1.b) 书上
     shū shàngbiān   shūshang
     on top of the book   in the book
     above the book

(2.a) 书里边   vs.   (2.b) 书里
     shū lǐbiān   shūli
     inside the book   in the book

(3.a) 城里边   vs.   (3.b) 城里
     chéng lǐbiān   chéngli
     inside the city   in the city, down-
                                                      town

(4.a) 床上边   vs.   (4.b) 床上
     chuáng shàngbiān   chuángshang
     on top of the bed   on the bed, in bed

(5.a) 桌子上边有一个窗户。
     Zhuōzi shàngbiān yǒu yíge chuānghu.
     There is a window above the desk.

(5.b) 桌子上有一个电视。
     Zhuōzishang yǒu yíge diànshì.
     There is a T.V. set on the desk.

(6.a) 墙上边有门。
     *Qiáng shangbiān yǒu mén.
     There is a door in the wall.

(6.b) 墙上有门。
     Qiángshang yǒu mén.

In each of the above pairs, the (a) form represents a literal reading of the positional unit whereas the (b) version a specialized usage. (6.a) is incorrect because we don't normally find a door on top of a wall. In (6.b) 墙上 is translated as "in the wall" rather than "on the wall." The time word 晚上 *wǎnshang* is actually another example of idiomatization, a process by means of which a spatial term is borrowed for temporal reference. When the locational unit gets truncated, the directional form is often pronounced in the neutral tone. For example, 城里边 *chéng lǐbiān* → 城里 *chéngli*. There are, however, certain exceptions which require memorization. For example, in contrast with 城里 *chéngli*, 城外 *chéngwài* "outside of the city" is pronounced with a full tone on 外.

In this connection, we should also note that some of the positional forms may carry two possible readings that are different but related in meaning. For example, 卧室后边 can mean either "at the back of the bedroom" or "behind the bedroom." Similarly, 教室前边 can be either "at the front of the classroom" or "in front of the classroom." As shown in the following examples, the ambiguity readily disappears once the proper context is given.

(7)   厨房后边有一个小花园。

Chúfáng hòubian yǒu yíge xiǎo huāyuán.

There is a small garden behind the kitchen.

(8)   厨房后边有一张桌子，几把椅子。

Chúfáng hòubian yǒu yìzhāng zhuōzi, jǐbǎ yǐzi.

There are a table and a few chairs at the back of the kitchen.

4. Reduplication of Verbs (continued)

As discussed in Lesson 21, a verb may be repeated (XX or XYXY) to indicate a tentative notion or to express a trivializing effect: "to do something a little bit." The reduplication for monosyllabic verbs has a variant pattern which places a neutral tone numeral 一 *yi* in between: X 一 X. The repeated syllable regains its tone in the process.

(1)   等等：等一等

děngdeng: děngyiděng

wait a bit

(2)   走走：走一走

zǒuzou: zǒuyizǒu

take a walk

(3)   这是我写的字，请你看一看。

Zhè shì wǒ xiě de zì, qǐng nǐ kànyikàn.

These are the characters I wrote. Please take a look.

(4)   这课的语法，我们有很多问题。我们去问（一）问丁老师吧。

Zhè kè de yǔfǎ, wǒmen yǒu hěn duō wèntí. Wǒmen qù wèn(yi) wèn Dīng lǎoshī ba.

We have many questions on this lesson's grammar. Let's go ask Teacher Ding.

Generally speaking, there is no difference in meaning between XX and X 一 X. Disyllabic verbs never participate in this variation. Therefore, while 睡睡 *shuìshui* may be modified as 睡一睡 *shuìyishuì* "take a nap," the only tentative form for 休息 *xiūxi* is 休息休息 *xiūxixiūxi* "rest a little" and never *休息一休息 *xiūxiyixiūxi*.

5. Lexical Differentiation: 参观，访问，and 看

As you may have noticed, there are some Chinese words that seem to be similar in meaning but actually are very different in usage. For example, 参观 and 访问 are often glossed alike in a dictionary with a definition such as "to visit," which is of course inadequate and misleading. 参观 means to visit and tour a place, usually a building, an institute, or an establishment, but never a city, a country, or a person. Therefore,

> (1)   参观学校
>   cānguān xuéxiào
>   visit a school

> (2)   参观工厂
>   cānguān gōngchǎng
>   visit a factory

> (3)   参观图书馆
>   cānguān túshūguǎn
>   visit a library

> (4)   *参观中国
>   cānguān Zhōngguó
>   visit China

> (5)   *参观北京
>   cānguān Běijīng
>   visit Beijing

> (6)   *参观朋友
>   cānguān péngyou
>   visit a friend

访问, on the other hand, means to visit and interview a person. It connotes some kind of an official visit and may not be used to refer to the casual drop-by of a friend. Therefore.

> (7)   Ted Koppel 想去中国访问邓小平。
>   Ted Koppel xiǎng qù Zhōngguó fǎngwèn Dèng Xiǎopíng.
>   Ted Koppel wants to go to China and interview Deng Xiaoping.

(8)   *我想明年去中国访问我的好朋友。

　　　 *Wǒ xiǎng míngnián qù Zhōngguó fǎngwèn wǒ de hǎo péngyou.

　　　 I want to go and visit my good friend in China next year.

In a situation like (8) where one is visiting a friend, the proper verb to use in Chinese is simply 看 *kàn* "to see, to visit."

(9)   我想明年去中国看我的好朋友。

　　　 Wǒ xiǎng míngnián qù Zhōngguó kàn wǒ de hǎo péngyou.

In some situations, 访问 may be used with a place, as in sentence (10), but it is used only when the general purpose of such a visit is to meet with, hence "to interview," the official people there.

(10)   总统今年想去访问日本。

　　　 Zǒngtǒng jīnnián xiǎng qù fǎngwèn Rìběn.

　　　 President hopes to visit Japan this year.

Now, if the purpose of a China trip is simply for sightseeing and some shopping, then what is the proper word to use to describe such a visit? 参观 is incorrect since the destination is not an institution but the country and its many cities; 访问 is inappropriate since the visit is not official; 看 is also a wrong choice because this verb takes a person and not a place as its Object. There is a verb in the Chinese lexicon meaning "to take a trip to, to tour," which we will learn later. And, until then, we will be content to use 玩儿 *wánr*, literally "to play," to refer to this fun activity.

(11)   我很想去中国玩儿。

　　　 Wǒ hěn xiǎng qù Zhōngguó wánr.

　　　 I really want to go and visit China.

Lesson 24

---

1. The Indefinite Measure Word

1.1 A measure word is required when the noun is qualified by a numeral, such as 三本书 *sānběn shū* "three books." It is also required when the noun is preceded by a demonstrative, for example, 这本书 *zhè běn shū* "this book." In the latter case, even though there is no numeral explicitly stated, the implied number is singular. Hence, "this book" and not "these books." Then, how do we say "these books" where the number is plural but the reference is unspecified or indefinite? In Chinese, an indefinite measure word is used for this purpose.

The indefinite measure word for countable nouns is 些 *xiē*.

这些人	*zhè xiē rén*	"these people"
那些车	*nà xiē chē*	"those cars"
哪些书	*nǎ xiē shū*	"which books?"

The indefinite measure does appear with the numeral for one（一）much in the same manner as the use of "a" in "a few of" or "a bit of" in English.

一些朋友	*yìxiē péngyou*	"a few/some friends"
一些票	*yìxiē piào*	"a few/some tickets"

One main syntactic feature to note here is that, unlike the use of "some Noun" in English which may occupy the subject position in a sentence (For example, "Some friends are waiting for you outside."), the " 一些 Noun" unit nevers appears as a subject in Chinese.

(1)　　我在中国有一些朋友。
　　　　Wǒ zài Zhōngguó yǒu yìxiē péngyou.
　　　　I have a few friends in China.

(2)　　*一些朋友来看你。
　　　　Yìxiē péngyou lái kàn nǐ.
　　　　A few friends came to see you.

A few more sentences to illustrate the use of 些：

(3) 老师今天给我们介绍北京，还给我们看一些中国农村的照片。

Lǎoshī jīntiān gěi wǒmen jièshào Běijīng, hái gěi wǒmen kàn yìxiē
Zhōngguó nóngcūn de zhàopiàn.

Today the teacher talked to us about Beijing and showed us some
pictures of Chinese villages.

(4) 这些生词很难，我们都不太懂。下课以后，我们一起去问王老师吧。

Zhè xiē shēngcí hěn nán, wǒmen dōu bú tài dǒng. Xià kè yǐhòu,
wǒmen yìqǐ qù wèn Wáng lǎoshī ba.

These new words are very difficult and we don't quite understand
them. Let's go and ask Teacher Wang together after class.

(5) 你昨天买的那些裙子都很漂亮。你穿哪一条去参加今天晚上的舞会？

Nǐ zuótiān mǎi de nà xiē qúnzi dōu hěn piàoliang. Nǐ chuān nǎ
yìtiáo qù cānjiā jīntiān wǎnshang de wǔhuì?

The skirts you bought yesterday are all very pretty. Which one will
you wear for tonight's dance party?

1.2 Another indefinite measure word in Chinese is 点儿 *diǎnr*, often used for un-
countable things to indicate a small amount. Hence, 一点儿咖啡 *yìdiǎnr kāfēi* for
"some coffee/a little coffee." Sometimes, 一点儿 *yìdiǎnr* may be used interchangeably with 一些 *yìxiē* to modify the same noun, in which case the former refers to
an even smaller quantity than the latter. For example,

(6) 我有一点儿事儿请你帮助。

Wǒ yǒu yìdiǎnr shìr qǐng nǐ bāngzhù.

I have something on which I need your help.

(7) 我有一些事儿请你帮助。

Wǒ yǒu yìxiē shìr qǐng nǐ bāngzhù.

I have a few things on which I need your help.

Other examples are:

(8) 下星期二是古波的生日。我们一起给他买一点儿礼物，你说好吗？

Xià xīngqī'èr shì Gǔbō de shēngrì. Wǒmen yìqǐ gěi tā mǎi yìdiǎnr
lǐwù. Nǐ shuō hǎo ma?

Next Tuesday is Gubo's birthday. Let's get him some gift together.
What do you say?

（9）　这个酒有一点儿问题。我们别喝吧。

Zhè ge jiŭ yŏu yìdiănr wèntí. Wŏmen bié hē ba.

There is some problem with this wine. Let's not drink it.

（10）　这束花儿是给你的，这点儿糖是给你妹妹的。

Zhè shù huār shì gěi nĭ de, zhè diănr táng shì gěi nĭ mèimei de.

The flowers are for you and the candy is for your sister.

（11）　吃点儿面包吧。

Chī diănr miànbāo ba.

Have some bread.

（12）　你去买点儿鸡蛋。

Nĭ qù măi diănr jīdàn.

Go buy some eggs.

In the last two examples, 点儿 is a short form of 一点儿.

Lesson 25

1. The Complement of Degree

1.1 A complement refers to a grammatical unit, generally made up of a verbal or an adjectival expression, that appears after the main verb in a sentence and enhances its meaning. The Chinese language contains various types of complements and the particular type we are learning in this lesson is called "the Complement of Degree." First, a few examples of this complement construction.

(1)　他吃得很多。
　　　Tā chī de hěn duō.
　　　He ate a lot.

(2)　他写得真好。
　　　Tā xiě de zhēn hǎo.
　　　He writes really well.

(3)　他来得很晚。
　　　Tā lái de hěn wǎn.
　　　He came very late.

Structurally, the complement construction can be diagrammed as below:

Verb ＋ 得 ＋ Complement

得 is the marker for the complement; it is phonetically identical with but graphically different from the modification marker 的. The complement of degree itself is usually an adjective, which in turn requires the modification of a degree adverb. As in the case of a predicative adjective, if no degree adverb is used in the complement, it implies comparison.

（4） 帕兰卡唱得好听，古波唱得不好听。

Pàlánkǎ chàng de hǎotīng, Gǔbō chàng de bù hǎotīng.

Palanka sings well and Gubo doesn't.

Semantically, the complement of degree indicates the manner in which the action is carried out or the extent to which the action generates a result. In other words, it focuses our attention not so much on the action itself as on the state that arises from that action. For example, sentence (1) tells not only of the action of eating but also, specifically, of the consumption quantity. Sentence (2) describes an action of writing, with special emphasis on its quality. Sentence (3) is essentially concerned with the lateness of the action of coming. In all three cases, the resultative states are each represented by a stative verb (an adjective). Hence, we can revise the above diagram as below:

```
Verb  +  得  +        Complement
                     /            \
              Degree Adverb    Adjective
```

1.2 You may want to ask, at this point, why it is that the complement unit does not appear before the verb. We have mentioned more than once that all modifying units in Chinese come before the modified units. It is obvious that the complement is functionally modifying the verb, and, as such, it should occupy a pre-verbal rather than a post-verbal position. The placement of the complement after the verb, therefore, seems to be a violation of this general rule. It should be noted, however, that Chinese often utilizes word order to reflect the time sequence that pertains to an action. In other words, what occurs first in real life also appears first in a linguistic description, and what happens later appears later in a sentence. The best example to illustrate this temporal linear ordering is the following:

（5） 他从食堂去图书馆。

Tā cóng shítáng qù túshūguǎn.

He went from the cafeteria to the library.

This sentence begins with the point of origin, continues with the motion, and concludes with the point of destination, a linguistic sequence that parallels the order in which the events occur. The complement structure observes the same principle. A complement is primarily concerned with the ensuing or resultative state of action. Since result follows action, it is only logical to have a complement appear after a verb. Hence, Verb－Complement.

1.3 The negative falls on the complement unit and the affirmative-negative question is also formed within the complement.

```
Negative:       Verb  ＋  得  ＋  ［不＋ Complement］
Interrogative:  Verb  ＋  得  ＋  ［Complement ＋ 不 ＋ Complement］
```

(6)   他回答得不对。
       Tā huídá de bú duì.
       He didn't answer correctly.

(7)   古波学得认真不认真？
       Gŭbō xué de rènzhēn bu rènzhēn?
       Does Gubo study conscientiously?

(8)   爸爸走得很快吗？
       Bàba zŏu de hěn kuài ma?
       Does father walk fast?

Sentence (8) shows a question formation of the 吗－type, and does not require any explanation. There is another interrogative pattern which places 怎么样 *zěnmeyàng* in the complement slot, forming essentially a "How?" question.

```
           Verb  ＋  得  ＋  怎么样？
```

(9)   他准备得怎么样？
       Tā zhŭnbèi de zěnmeyàng?
       How did he do in his preparation?

(10)   A: 你工作得怎么样？
          Nĭ gōngzuò de zěnmeyàng?
          How are you doing in your job?
       B: 我工作得很好。
          Wŏ gōngzùo de hěn hăo.
          I'm doing well with my job.

1.4   A verb may take an Object and it also may be followed by a complement. In the case when it takes both units, there is an ordering problem: what comes first? The answer is that the Object comes first and the complement comes second. However, the verb itself is to be repeated, so that each unit has its own governing verb. Hence,

Verb−Object   Verb−Complement

(11)   他说英语说得很慢。

Tā shuō Yīngyǔ shuō de hěn màn.

He speaks English slowly.

(12)   他回答问题回答得非常好。

Tā huídá wèntí huídá de fēicháng hǎo.

He answered questions very well.

(13)   他写汉字写得很不整齐。

Tā xiě Hànzì xiě de hěn bù zhěngqí.

He doesn't write Chinese characters neatly at all.

(14)   他吃饭吃得多不多？

Tā chī fàn chī de duō bu duō?

Does he eat much?

(15)   他整理房间整理得怎么样？

Tā zhěnglǐ fángjiān zhěnglǐ de zěnmeyàng?

How did he do in cleaning the room?

1.5   When a complement expression is introduced into a sentence, it becomes the focus of the utterance and needs to be highlighted. One of the ways to highlight the message is to reserve the verb exclusively for the complement unit and remove the Object from the verbal domain. To have both the Object and the complement clustered in the same verbal unit can result in a confusion as to what truly serves as the main message of the sentence. There are different ways of displacing the Object, one being the afore-described means of establishing another verbal unit, namely repeating the verb for the Object. Another option is to move the Object to the front of the sentence, either before the predicate or before the entire sentence. This movement is commonly known as topicalization, a process which we have briefly discussed in Lesson 20. We may prepose an Object if we decide to choose it as the topic of our sentence or conversation. The Object has to represent some known information. The definiteness may be either inferred from the context or, as often is the case, explicitly marked by a definite demonstrative（such as 这个 and 那个）or a specific modifying clause. The following is a summary of the three possible arrangements in a sentence that contains both an Object and a complement.

(A)　Subject + Verb + Object + Verb + Complement

(B)　Subject + Object + Verb + Complement

(C)　Object + Subject + Verb + Complement

Please note that the last two options do not require the repetition of the verb.

（16.a）他学汉语学得很不错。

　　　　Tā xué Hànyǔ xué de hěn bú cuò.

　　　　He is doing quite well in his studying of Chinese.

（16.b）他汉语学得很不错。

　　　　Tā Hànyǔ xué de hěn bú cuò.

（16.c）汉语他学得很不错。

　　　　Hànyǔ tā xué de hěn bú cuò.

（17.a）他回答那些问题回答得很快。

　　　　Tā huídá nà xiē wèntí huídá de hěn kuài.

　　　　He answered those questions expeditiously.

（17.b）他那些问题回答得很快。

　　　　Tā nà xiē wèntí huídá de hěn kuài.

（17.c）那些问题他回答得很快。

　　　　Nà xiē wèntí tā huídá de hěn kuài.

（18.a）他回答老师问的问题回答得很对。

　　　　Tā huídá lǎoshī wèn de wèntí huídá de hěn duì.

　　　　He correctly answered the questions the teacher asked.

（18.b）他，老师问的问题回答得很对。

　　　　Tā, lǎoshī wèn de wèntí huídá de hěn duì.

（18.c）老师问的问题，他回答得很对。

　　　　Lǎoshī wèn de wèntí, tā huídá de hěn duì.

Generally speaking, if the Object expression is a lengthy and/or complicated unit, the usual practice is to place it at the very front of the sentence so that the rest of the sentence may be unambiguously reserved for the complement. In other words, of the three possible alternatives in the last set, (18.c) is the best choice.

(19)　我们班的这些学生作练习作得不认真，生词也准备得不太好。

Wǒmen bān de zhè xiē xuésheng zuò liànxí zuò de bú rènzhēn, shēngcí yě zhǔnbèi de bú tài hǎo.

These students in our class don't do their exercises diligently. They don't prepare their new words well either.

(20)　A: 那位老师念课文念得怎么样？

Nà wèi lǎoshī niàn kèwén niàn de zěnmeyàng?

How did that teacher read the text?

　　　B: 她念得不快也不慢，她念得很清楚。

Tā niàn de bú kuài yě bú màn, tā niàn de hěn qīngchu.

She read it neither quickly nor slowly. She read it very clearly.

(21)　A: 你写汉字写得真不错。

Nǐ xiě Hànzì xiě de zhēn bú cuò.

You write Chinese characters really quite well.

　　　B: 哪里。我写得不太整齐。

Nǎli. Wǒ xiě de bú tài zhěngqí.

Not at all. I don't write very neatly.

(22)　A: 我今天作的菜怎么样？

Wǒ jīntiān zuò de cài zěnmeyàng?

How are the dishes I made today?

　　　B: 作得真好。

Zuò de zhēn hǎo.

They are cooked really well.

(23)　A: 那个说中文说得很流利的小姑娘是谁，你认识吗？

Nà ge shuō Zhōngwén shuō de hěn liúlì de xiǎo gūniang shì shéi, nǐ rènshi ma?

Who is that young girl who speaks fluent Chinese? Do you know her?

　　　B: 她是王大夫的女儿。她唱中国歌儿也唱得非常好听。

Tā shì Wáng dàifu de nǚ'ér. Tā chàng Zhōngguó gēr yě chàng de fēicháng hǎotīng.

She is Dr. Wang's daughter. She also sings Chinese songs very beautifully.

In the last sentence where the predicate includes the adverb 也, the modifying element is sandwiched between the Verb — Object and the Verb — Complement units. The adverb is in fact structurally part of the Verb — Complement segment as there can be a slight pause after the Verb — Object. As described earlier, the complement is the focus of the sentence, constituting therefore the immediate domain of the adverbial modification. The adverb may indeed appear right before the adjective in the complement expression, as shown in the following:

(24.a) *……他也整理房间整理得很乾净。

　　　　 *…Tā yě zhěnglǐ fángjiān zhěnglǐ de hěn gānjing.

　　　　 …He also cleans his room tidily.

(24.b) ……他整理房间也整理得很乾净。

　　　　 …Tā zhěnglǐ fángjiān yě zhěnglǐ de hěn gānjing.

(24.c) ……他整理房间整理得也很乾净。

　　　　 …Tā zhěnglǐ fángjiān zhěnglǐ de yě hěn gānjing.

The complement construction may be considered to be another form of the topic—comment mechanism characteristic of the Chinese language. The Verb—Object segment can be viewed as the topic on which the Verb—Complement functions as the comment. In sentence (23), we are describing two different skills that the young girl possesses: her linguistic facility and her singing talent. Speaker A marvels at her fluency in Chinese and speaker B compliments her on her achievements by saying something like "Even in singing Chinese songs, she can do very well too." The following is another example to illustrate this positioning of an adverb in a complement construction.

(25)　　A: 我现在身体不太好，每天吃饭都吃得不太多。

　　　　　　 Wǒ xiànzài shēntǐ bú tài hǎo, měi tiān chī fàn dōu chī de bú tài duō.

　　　　　　 My health is not too good now. I don't eat very much every day.

　　　　 B: 睡觉呢？

　　　　　　 Shuì jiào ne?

　　　　　　 How about sleeping?

　　　　 A: 睡得也不太好。

　　　　　　 Shuì de yě bú tài hǎo.

　　　　　　 I don't sleep too well either.

The conversation in (25) also clearly shows the topic—comment relationship between the Verb—Object 睡觉 and the Verb—Complement 睡得不好. The latter is a response to the question posed in the form of a Verb—Object unit.

2. The Adverb 再

再 *zài* is an adverb used to mark the repetition of an action that has yet to take place. The monosyllabic adverb always stands before the verb it modifies.

（1）   你再吃一点儿吧。
          Nǐ zài chī yìdiǎnr ba.
          Eat some more!

（2）   你作的鱼汤真不错。我想再喝一点儿。
          Nǐ zuò de yú tāng zhēn bú cuò. Wǒ xiǎng zài hē yìdiǎnr.
          The fish soup you made is marvelous. I want to have some more.

（3）   我们明年再去中国参观北京大学。
          Wǒmen míngnián zài qù Zhōngguó cānguān Běijīng Dàxué.
          We will go to China again next year to visit Beijing University.

（4）   现在太晚了，我们明天再谈吧。
          Xiànzài tài wǎn le, wǒmen míngtiān zài tán ba.
          It's too late now. We'll talk (about it) tomorrow.

The expression for bidding farewell 再见 *zàijiàn* is constructed on this notion of "yet to take place" : "see you again → goodbye." For completed events, there is another adverb to indicate recurrence, which we will learn in a later lesson.

3. More on the Particle 呢

呢 *ne* is an interrogative particle which indicates that the question it marks is related to a previous question, statement, or even a nonlinguistic context. Theoretically speaking, we do not begin a conversation with a 呢－question. The only time this construction is used to start a dialogue is when we ask for the whereabouts of someone/something. Say, when you enter a room and see Gubo there, you may wish to find out where Palanka is by asking, " 帕兰卡呢 ?" Since you saw Gubo in the room, his location has been established. Therefore, when you ask for Palanka's location, the question is related to this prior observation even though it is not expressed linguistically. In other words, 呢 serves the function of marking a "related" question.

呢 may be used in the following types of interrogatives:

(A) Interrogative—Word Questions:

(1) 他们现在回宿舍。我们去哪儿呢？

Tāmen xiànzài huí sùshè. Wǒmen qù nǎr ne?

They are going back to the dorm now. Where are we going?

(2) 老师不懂。我去问谁呢？

Lǎoshī bù dǒng. Wǒ qù wèn shéi ne?

(Even) The teacher doesn't understand it. Whom shall I go ask?

(B) Affirmative—Negative Questions:

(3) 这课语法非常难。你是好学生。你懂不懂这课语法呢？

Zhè kè yǔfǎ fēicháng nán. Nǐ shì hǎo xuésheng. Nǐ dǒng bu dǒng zhè kè yǔfǎ ne?

The grammar of this lesson is hard. You're a good student. Do you understand the grammar in this lesson?

(4) A: 他中文说得很流利。

Tā Zhōngwén shuō de hěn liúlì.

He speaks fluent Chinese.

B: 汉字呢？写得整齐不整齐呢？

Hànzì ne? Xiě de zhěngqí bu zhěngqí ne?

What about Chinese characters? Does he write neatly?

(C) Alternative Questions:

(5) 你现在去还是明天去呢？

Nǐ xiànzài qù háishì míngtiān qù ne?

Are you going now or tomorrow?

(6) 你不喝咖啡。你喝什么呢？喝橘子水呢还是喝茶呢？

Nǐ bù hē kāfēi. Nǐ hē shénme ne? Hē júzishuǐ ne háishì hē chá ne?

You don't drink coffee. Then what will you have? Orange juice or tea?

4. The Honorific Measure 位

The measure word for a person is 个 *ge*. However, to show respect for the person addressed or referred to, we may use 位 *wèi* as a preferable alternative. Hence,

(1)   他是一位作事非常认真的老师。

Tā shì yíwèi zuò shì fēicháng rènzhēn de lǎoshī.

He is a teacher who is very conscientious about his work.

(2)   来，让我介绍一下儿。这位是王大夫。这位是张老师。

Lái, ràng wǒ jièshào yíxiàr. Zhè wèi shì Wáng dàifu, zhè wèi shì Zhāng lǎoshī.

Come, let me introduce you. This is Dr. Wang, and this is Teacher Zhang.

(3)   喂，请问您是哪位？

Wèi, qǐng wèn nín shì nǎ wèi?

Hello, may I ask who you are?

Sometimes 位 may be used among close friends in a playful tone as a term of teasing, as illustrated in the following examples.

Gubo to Palanka and Ding Yun:

(4)   两位小姐，来吧。

Liǎngwèi xiǎojie, lái ba.

You two young ladies, come along.

(5)   你这位先生作的鱼汤真难喝。

Nǐ zhè wèi xiānsheng zuò de yútāng zhēn nán hē.

What terrible fish soup you have made, Mister.

The most common situation where one would use the honorific 位 is in a restaurant when the waiter asks, 几位？ *jǐ wèi?* "How many in your party?" According to the general rule of linguistic propriety, one would expect the customer to answer the question by using the common measure 个 *ge*: 四个 *sìge* for, say, "Four." However, for some strange reasons or just as a matter of substitution, the most common form of response employs 位 instead of 个, with no implied sense of self-aggrandisement. This is one of the few cases where pragmatics takes priority over linguistic logic.

5. How to Respond to Compliments

The proper way to acknowledge a compliment in Chinese is to humbly deny what you have been praised for. If someone makes a flattering remark about what you are wearing: "你今天穿得真漂亮！", you should respond by saying, with a heartfelt smile on your face, that the clothes are just plain old rags or they were purchased at a bargain price. If you return the compliment by saying, as you would in English,

"谢谢" or some other comments such as "I like them too," or "I think so too," your Chinese admirer may be taken aback at such unabashed pomposity. In fact, he/she may think that as you eagerly agree with the compliment, you have in effect displayed distasteful signs of self-contentment, ill-manners, or even arrogance. So, while it is perfectly acceptable in the West to receive a compliment graciously, it is important in Chinese etiquette to make, at least, a verbal negation of the complimentary words. One useful expression of denial to know is 哪里 *nǎli*, literally meaning "where." The connotation is "Where on earth did you get such an idea?" For emphasis, the expression may be repeated more than once and/or used in conjunction with another statement of denial. The following are some examples.

(1)　　A: 你的女朋友真漂亮。
　　　　　Nǐ de nǚ péngyou zhēn piàoliang.
　　　　　Your girlfriend is really attractive.
　　　　B: 哪里，哪里。
　　　　　Nǎli, nǎli.
　　　　　You think so? Thank you.

(2)　　A: 你这条红裙子非常好看。
　　　　　Nǐ zhè tiáo hóng qúnzi fēicháng hǎokàn.
　　　　　Your red skirt is really very pretty.
　　　　B: 哪里，哪里。是一条旧裙子。
　　　　　Nǎli, nǎli. Shì yìtiáo jiù qúnzi.
　　　　　Really? It's just an old skirt.

(3)　　A: 你说汉语说得很流利。
　　　　　Nǐ shuō Hànyǔ shuō de hěn liúlì.
　　　　　You speak very fluent Chinese.
　　　　B: 哪里，我说得不太好。
　　　　　Nǎli, wǒ shuō de bú tài hǎo.
　　　　　No, I don't speak well at all.

Lesson 26

1. The Optative Verbs

1.1 The word "optative" means "expressing a wish or desire." In the Indo-European languages, a verb may appear in an optative mood to express a wish or desire. In Chinese, such modal marking is done by an auxiliary verb, often referred to as a modal auxiliary or an optative verb. An optative is different from a regular verb in that it does not carry a substantive denotation of an action; on the other hand, it indicates the ability, possibility, intention, or wishes of carrying out such an action. As an auxiliary, it generally appears in the company of a verb.

> Positive: Auxiliary   +   Verb
>
> Negative: 不   +   Auxiliary   +   Verb
>
> Question: (a) Auxiliary   +   Verb   +   吗？
>
>   (b) [Auxiliary 不 Auxiliary]   +   Verb?

（1）　我想去中国参观访问。

        Wǒ xiǎng qù Zhōngguó cānguān fǎngwèn.

        I want to go and visit China.

（2）　你不应该在教室里吸烟。

        Nǐ bù yīnggāi zài jiàoshìli xī yān.

        You should not smoke in the classroom.

（3）　他会不会游泳？

        Tā huì bu huì yóu yǒng?

        Does he know how to swim?

Unlike a regular verb, an optative verb may not be reduplicated (*会会); nor can it be followed by a suffix such as 了 *le* (*会了), a grammatical element on which we will have more to say in the following lessons.

As an auxiliary is essentially a marker of the optative mode of the following verb, its actual semantic connotations may vary in different contexts. It may cover a rather broad range of modal usages, so much so that its functions may overlap with those of another auxiliary. Auxiliaries are generally rather difficult to master in a foreign language; just think of the multifarious meanings and uses of auxiliaries such as "can," "may," "should," etc. in English. The following is a general description of the behaviors of the six most common auxiliaries in Chinese.

1.2 想 + Verb: Some of the auxiliaries are derivatives of actual substantive verbs. 想 *xiǎng* is one such example. Its basic meaning is "to think of/about." As an auxiliary, it marks the intention or desire of doing something, which is to say, "thinking of doing it."

(4)   Verb: 她想妈妈
       Tā xiǎng māma.
       She's thinking about her mother.
       (= She misses her mother.)

(5)   Auxiliary: 她想去看妈妈。
       Tā xiǎng qù kàn māma.
       She's thinking about going to see her mother.
       (= She wants to go see her mother.)

(6)   这个星期六你想去看电影吗？
       Zhè ge xīngqīliù nǐ xiǎng qù kàn diànyǐng ma?
       Do you want to go see a movie this coming Saturday?

(7)   我不想去看电影，我想在家休息。
       Wǒ bù xiǎng qù kàn diànyǐng, wǒ xiǎng zài jiā xiūxi.
       I don't want to go see a movie; I want to rest at home.

(8)   每个人都想找一个理想的工作，可是找一个理想的工作不容易。
       Měi ge rén dōu xiǎng zhǎo yíge lǐxiǎng de gōngzuò, kěshì zhǎo yíge lǐxiǎng de gōngzuò bù róngyi.
       Every one wants to look for an ideal job, but finding an ideal job is not easy.

1.3 要 + Verb: The basic meaning of 要 *yào* is "to desire." As an optative verb, it marks a strong desire to carry out the action as represented by the verb.

(9) Verb: 孩子要牛奶。

Háizi yào niúnǎi.

The child wants milk.

(10) Auxiliary: 孩子要喝牛奶。

Háizi yào hē niúnǎi.

The child wants to drink milk.

(11) 你明天要不要去城里看朋友？

Nǐ míngtiān yào bu yào qù chéngli kàn péngyou?

Do you want to go into town to see friends tomorrow?

(12) 你要去厕所吗？

Nǐ yào qù cèsuǒ ma?

Do you want to go to the bathroom?

The negative of "要 + Verb" is, however, "不想 + Verb" and not "不要 + Verb." The latter may be acceptable in some dialects but not in Standard Mandarin. In fact, "不要 + Verb" is the pattern to use for phrasing a strong negative imperative, as in sentence (15).

(13) 他不想听京剧，他要听民歌。

Tā bù xiǎng tīng Jīngjù, tā yào tīng míngē.

He doesn't want to listen to Beijing Opera; he wants to listen to folk songs.

(14) 我现在不想喝啤酒，你呢？

Wǒ xiànzài bù xiǎng hē píjiǔ, nǐ ne?

I don't want to drink beer now. What about you?

(15) 你晚上不要开车！

Nǐ wǎnshang bú yào kāi chē!

Don't drive at night.

1.3.1 The Differences between 想 and 要: As both 想 and 要 are markers of intention, the two are sometimes used interchangeably. The latter, however, represents a stronger intention than the former: 想 connotes more of a "wish" and 要 more of a "will." 想 stresses the wishing or planning of taking an action and 要 the urge or demand for carrying it out. For example, of the following two sentences, (16) implies a much stronger determination than (17).

(16) 我要学游泳。

Wǒ yào xué yóu yǒng.

I want to take swimming lessons.

(17) 我想学游泳。

Wǒ xiǎng xué yóu yǒng.

I'd like to take swimming lessons.

Another difference between the two optatives is that 想 may be modified by a degree adverb and 要 may not.

(18) 我很想研究这个作家。

Wǒ hěn xiǎng yánjiū zhè ge zuòjiā.

I really want to do research on this writer.

(19) *我很要研究中国文学。

*Wǒ hěn yào yánjiū Zhōngguó wénxué.

I really want to do research on Chinese literature.

1.3.2   The Extended Use of 要: 要 may be also used to indicate a demand, a necessity imposed from the external world. In this usage "要 + Verb" means "have to Verb; should Verb." Sometimes the adverb 一定 *yídìng* may be added to the pattern to further underscore the importance or urgency of the demand: "一定要 + Verb."

(20) 老师要认真教，学生要认真学。

Lǎoshī yào rènzhēn jiāo, xuésheng yào rènzhēn xué.

Teachers should be conscientious in teaching and students should (also) be conscientious in studying.

(21) 对不起，现在我要去上课。我们晚上再谈吧。

Duì bu qǐ, xiànzài wǒ yào qù shàng kè. Wǒmen wǎnshang zài tán ba.

Sorry, I have to go to a class now. We'll talk (about it) in the evening.

(22) 写字一定要写得慢。

Xiě zì yídìng yào xiě de màn.

You definitely have to write characters slowly.

It is in fact this function of 要 that we see in the pattern of the negative imperative "不要 + Verb" described above: the demand or command is to refrain from doing something. Just as in English where the negative of "should Verb" is not "should not Verb" but "don't have to Verb," "要 ＋ Verb" and "不要 ＋ Verb" do not form a natural pair of affirmation and negation. The proper negative counterpart to 要 in this usage is 不用 *bú yòng*.

(23) 老师说这九个字不用写。

Lǎoshī shuō zhè jiǔge zì bú yòng xiě.

The teacher said that (we) didn't have to write these nine characters.

(24) A: 明天要上课吗？

Míngtiān yào shàng kè ma?

Do we have to go to school tomorrow?

B: 明天是星期天，不用上课。

Míngtiān shì xīngqītiān, bú yòng shàng kè.

Tomorrow is Sunday. No need to go to school.

1.3.3 想 with a Sentential Object: In this connection, we will also mention another use of the verb 想 that may pose certain problems for beginning students. 想 may take a whole sentence as its Object, much in the same manner as "think" in English.

(25) 我想他明天会来上课。

Wǒ xiǎng tā míngtiān huì lái shàng kè.

I think he will come to class tomorrow.

But, unlike English, the negation of the above sentence is not to negate the verb 想, as you would with "think," but to negate the verb in the embedded sentence. In other words, we don't say in Chinese "I don't think this is the case." The idiomatic form should be "I think this is not the case."

(26.a) 我想他明天不会来上课。

Wǒ xiǎng tā míngtiān bú huì lái shàng kè.

I think he will not come to class tomorrow.

(= I don't think he'll be coming to class tomorrow.)

(26.b) *我不想他明天会来上课。

*Wǒ bù xiǎng tā míngtiān huì lái shàng kè.

(27.a) 我想你今天晚上不用来吧。

Wǒ xiǎng nǐ jīntiān wǎnshang bú yòng lái ba.

I don't think you have to come tonight.

(27.b)*我不想你今天晚上要来吧。

　　　　*Wǒ bù xiǎng nǐ jīntiān wǎnshang yào lái ba.

1.4 能 ＋ Verb: The optative 能 marks the ability of carrying out an action.

(28)　　他现在能看中文杂志。

　　　　Tā xiànzài néng kàn Zhōngwén zázhì.

　　　　He is able to read Chinese magazines now.

(29)　　A: 你能不能翻译这本鲁迅的小说？

　　　　　　Nǐ néng bu néng fānyì zhè běn Lǔ Xùn de xiǎoshuō?

　　　　　　Are you able to translate this story by Lu Xun?

　　　　B: 我不能，我弟弟能。他在研究鲁迅呢。

　　　　　　Wǒ bù néng, wǒ dìdi néng, tā zài yánjiū Lǔ Xùn ne.

　　　　　　I can't, but my younger brother can. He is working on Lu Xun now.

(30)　　每天练习游泳，以后一定能游得很快。

　　　　Měi tiān liànxí yóu yǒng, yǐhòu yídìng néng yóu de hěn kuài.

　　　　If you practise swimming every day, you will for sure be able to swim very fast in the future.

Like the English auxiliary "can," 能 represents two kinds of "ability," namely, "ability" on the part of the person and "ability" conditioned by external factors. The above three sentences are examples of the first reading of 能: the actors either possess or lack the necessary skills to perform the respective tasks. The following sentences illustrate the use of the "circumstantial" 能.

(31)　　我今天下午没有课，我能跟你一起去看电影。

　　　　Wǒ jīntiān xiàwǔ méi yǒu kè, wǒ néng gēn nǐ yìqǐ qù kàn diànyǐng.

　　　　I don't have classes this afternoon; I can go see a movie with you.

(32)　　这儿能不能吸烟？

　　　　Zhèr néng bu néng xī yān?

　　　　Can one smoke here?

　　　　(＝ Is smoking allowed here?)

(33)　　爸爸说弟弟练习作得不好，今天晚上不能看电视。

　　　　Bàba shuō dìdi liànxí zuò de bù hǎo, jīntiān wǎnshang bù néng kàn diànshì.

　　　　My father said that (since) he didn't do his homework well, my younger brother couldn't watch T.V. tonight.

The next pair of sentences provides a contrast between these two meanings of 能. Sentence (34) shows that the inability to teach is due to one's own deficiency in swimming; hence, the "inner" ability. What the speaker lacks in sentence (35), however, is not skill but time; thus the "circumstantial" inability.

(34)　我不会游泳，（所以）不能教你游泳。
　　　Wǒ bú huì yóu yǒng, (suǒyǐ) bù néng jiāo nǐ yóu yǒng.
　　　I don't swim; therefore, I can't teach you to swim.

(35)　我现在有事儿，（所以）不能教你游泳。
　　　Wǒ xiànzài yǒu shìr, (suǒyǐ) bù néng jiāo nǐ yóu yǒng.
　　　I'm busy right now; therefore, I can't teach you to swim.

For the use of 会 in sentence (34), see the next section.

1.5 会 ＋ Verb: 会 may be used as a regular verb or an optative auxiliary, carrying the same meaning of "to know how to."

(36)　Verb: 你会英语吗？
　　　　　Nǐ huì Yīngyǔ ma?
　　　　　Do you know English?

(37)　Auxiliary: 你会说英语吗？
　　　　　　　　Nǐ huì shuō Yīngyǔ ma?
　　　　　　　　Do you know how to speak English?

(38)　A: 你们会不会作中国饭？
　　　　Nǐmen huì bu huì zuò Zhōngguó fàn?
　　　　Do you know how to cook Chinese food?
　　　B: 他不会作饭，我会。
　　　　Tā bú huì zuò fàn, wǒ huì.
　　　　He doesn't know how to cook, but I do.

1.5.1 The Differences between 能 and 会: Both 能 and 会 may be translated as "can." However, 会 connotes more specifically an acquired skill, an "ability" that is obtained through learning. Once you have mastered that skill, you will always have it with you. But external conditions and other factors may prevent you from implementing that skill at times. In other words, you may always 会 but not necessarily 能 under all circumstances.

(39)　我会游泳，可是今天我不舒服，所以不能去游泳。

Wǒ huì yóu yǒng, kěshì jīntiān wǒ bù shūfu, suǒyǐ bù néng qù yóu yǒng.

I know how to swim; but I don't feel well today and so I can't go to swim.

(40)　他不会说日语，可是他能用汉字表达他的意思。

Tā bú huì shuō Rìyǔ, kěshì tā néng yòng Hànzì biǎodá tā de yìsi.

He doesn't (know how to) speak Japanese, but he is able to express his ideas with Chinese characters.

(41)　他们都会打字。丁云一分钟能打八十个字，王大年一分钟能打五十五个字。你说你用谁呢？

Tāmen dōu huì dǎ zì. Dīng Yún yìfēn zhōng néng dǎ bāshige zì, Wáng Dànián yìfēn zhōng néng dǎ wǔshiwǔge zì. Nǐ shuō nǐ yòng shéi ne?

They both can type. Ding Yun can type eighty words per minute and Wang Danian fifty-five words a minute. Which one would you say you would hire?

Sentence (40) contrasts the inability（不会）as a result of not having had any proper training in the language with the ability（能）to manage a special situation by using Chinese characters, or the *kanji* to interact with the Japanese. In (41), 会 tells the basic ability of "to know how to type," and 能 marks the different levels of proficiency. Generally speaking, 会 is more concerned with the acquisition of the basic skill while 能 refers more to the different phases of achievement or the various conditions under which the skill is implemented.

1.5.2 The auxiliary 会 may also be used to indicate "possibility": "It's likely or possible that something will happen."

(42)　明天他会来上课。

Míngtiān tā huì lái shàng kè.

He will come to class tomorrow.

(43)　王大年不会请我们吃晚饭吧。

Wáng Dànián bú huì qǐng wǒmen chī wǎnfàn ba.

It's not likely that Wang Danian is going to invite us to dinner.

This 会 is often translated as "will" or "is going to." It is, however, not to be construed as a future tense marker. The difference between sentence (42) and the sentence below is that, while sentence (44) is a simple statement of "his coming" tomorrow, sentence (42) stresses the possibility or likelihood of such an event. In other words, 会 is an optative marker and not a tense indicator.

(44) 他明天来上课。
Tā míngtiān lái shàng kè.
He will come to class tomorrow.

(45) 不会下雨，我们走吧。
Bú huì xià yǔ, wǒmen zǒu ba.
It's not going to rain. Let's go.

(46) 你下午会不会在家？我能不能来看你？
Nǐ xiàwǔ huì bu huì zài jiā? Wǒ néng bu néng lái kàn nǐ?
Will you be home this afternoon? Can I come to see you?

The possibility 会 is, of course, to be distinguished from the ability 会, as demonstrated by the following pair of sentences.

(47) 他会开车，可是开得不快。
Tā huì kāi chē, kěshì kāi de bú kuài.
He knows how to drive, but he doesn't drive fast.

(48) 下午他会开车去。
Xiàwǔ tā huì kāi chē qù.
He will go by car this afternoon.

1.6 可以 + Verb: 可以 *kěyǐ* in its positive form is identical with 能 both in meaning and in use. It marks "internal ability" as well as "circumstantial permissibility."

(49) 他每天可以写五百个汉字。
Tā měi tiān kěyǐ xiě wǔbǎige Hànzì.
He can write five hundred Chinese characters a day.

(50) 我现在没有事儿，可以来教你作鱼汤。
Wǒ xiànzài méi yǒu shìr, kěyǐ lái jiāo nǐ zuò yú tāng.
I'm not busy right now. I can come over to teach you how to make fish soup.

In both cases, the optative 可以 may be replaced by 能 without affecting the meaning of the sentences. However, in asking for permission, 可以 is used more often than 能.

(51)   我可以用一下儿您的电话吗？
        Wǒ kěyǐ yòng yíxiàr nín de diànhuà ma?
        May I use your phone?

(52)   我可以进来吗？
        Wǒ kěyǐ jìnlái ma?
        May I come in?

The negative of "可以 + Verb" is "不能 + Verb." In other words, 能 and 可以 share the same negative form. "不可以 + Verb," on the other hand, indicates "prohibition."

(53)   我不能去。
        Wǒ bù néng qù.
        I can't go.
        (— Because I am sick or I don't know the way.)

(54)   你不可以去。
        Nǐ bù kěyǐ qù.
        You can't go.
        (— You are not allowed to go.)

1.7 应该 + Verb: The optative 应该 *yīnggāi* marks a moral obligation or a practical necessity: "ought to, should."

(55)   他想以后去中国访问，他现在就应该学习汉语。
        Tā xiǎng yǐhòu qù Zhōngguó fǎngwèn, tā xiànzài jiù yīnggāi xuéxí Hànyǔ.
        He wants to go visit China in the future; he should be studying Chinese now.

(56)   睡觉以前，应该不应该洗澡？
        Shuì jiào yǐqián, yīnggāi bu yīnggāi xǐ zǎo?
        Should one take a shower before going to bed?

(57)   你以后应该常常给我写信。
        Nǐ yǐhòu yīnggāi chángcháng gěi wǒ xiě xìn.
        You should write me often in the future.

There are two optative verbs in Chinese to describe necessity or obligation: 要 and 应该 . Generally speaking, the two are interchangeable in this usage, and they both form their negatives by adopting a different auxiliary: 不用 .

（58） A: 明天要不要上课？

Míngtiān yào bu yào shàng kè?

Do we have to go to school tomorrow?

B: 明天是星期六，不用上课；可是今天应该上课。

Míngtiān shì xīngqīliù, bú yòng shàng kè; Kěshì jīntiān yīnggāi shàng kè.

Tomorrow is Saturday. You don't have to go to school. But you should be going to school today.

Like 不要 , the negative form " 不应该 ＋ Verb" indicates that it is an obligation not to do such a thing.

（59） 小朋友不应该看这本杂志。

Xiǎo péngyou bù yīnggāi kàn zhè běn zázhì.

Our young friends should not read this magazine.

（60） 你身体不好，应该常常锻炼，不应该吸烟。

Nǐ shēntǐ bù hǎo, yīnggāi chángcháng duànliàn, bù yīnggāi xī yān.

Your health is not good. You ought to exercise more often and you shouldn't smoke.

1.7.1 In addition to the reading of "obligation," 应该 may also be used like "should" in the sense of expressing "expectation" or "a logical conclusion."

（61） 这个句子不太难，他应该会翻译吧。

Zhè ge jùzi bú tài nán, tā yīnggāi huì fānyì ba.

This sentence is not too hard. He should be able to translate it.

（62） 你请丁云吃饺子吧。她是中国人，应该喜欢吃饺子。

Nǐ qǐng Dīng Yún chī jiǎozi ba. Tā shì Zhōngguó rén, yīnggāi xǐhuan chī jiǎozi.

Why don't you treat Ding Yun to some dumplings? She is Chinese and should like dumplings.

1.8 Summary: The following is a table summarizing the various uses of the auxiliaries we have learned in this lesson. As each auxiliary may have more than one function and its meaning may change in the negative form, the many and complex behaviors of this special class of verbs cannot be fully captured below. We will conclude our discussion with two lists of Chinese sentences to further prepare you for, and alert you to, the kind of difficulty you may encounter while learning the optative verbs. The first list, (63) to (70), consists of sentences using different optatives which may all be rendered as "can" in English. The second group, (71) to (77), demonstrates a mixed use of the optatives, some of which may even be used in combinations.

	Positive	Negative
will likely Verb	会	不会
know how to Verb	会	不会
able to Verb	能 / 可以	不能
ought to Verb	要 / 应该	不用
want to Verb	想 / 要	不想
allowed to Verb	可以	
prohibited to Verb		不可以
should not Verb		不要 / 不应该

(63)　我会游泳，可是我不能游得很快。

　　　Wǒ huì yóu yǒng, kěshì wǒ bù néng yóu de hěn kuài.

　　　I can swim, but I can't swim too fast.

(64)　我不会游泳。你能教我吗？

　　　Wǒ bú huì yóu yǒng. Nǐ néng jiāo wǒ ma?

　　　I can't swim. Can you teach me?

(65)　你能晚上游泳吗？

　　　Nǐ néng wǎnshang yóu yǒng ma?

　　　Can you swim at night?

(66)　这条河不乾净。不可以在这儿游泳。

　　　Zhè tiáo hé bù gānjing. Bù kěyǐ zài zhèr yóu yǒng.

　　　This river is polluted. You can't swim here.

(67)　晚上没事儿，我们可以去游泳。

　　　Wǎnshang méi shìr, wǒmen kěyǐ qù yóu yǒng.

　　　We will be free in the evening. We can go swimming.

(68)　你工作很忙，不会去游泳吧。

　　　Nǐ gōngzuò hěn máng, bú huì qù yóu yǒng ba.

　　　You have a lot of work to do. You can't be going swimming?

(69)　我明天要上班，不能跟你去游泳。

　　　Wǒ míngtiān yào shàng bān, bù néng gēn nǐ qù yóu yǒng.

　　　I have to go to work tomorrow. I can't go swimming with you.

(70)　妈妈说，明天不用上课，你们可以去游泳。

　　　Māma shuō, míngtiān bú yòng shàng kè, nǐmen kěyǐ qù yóu yǒng.

　　　Mother said, "There is no school tomorrow. You can go swimming."

(71)　A: 这些生词很难，我不会念，也不会用。你能现在来帮助我吗？

　　　　Zhè xiē shēngcí hěn nán, wǒ bú huì niàn, yě bú huì yòng. Nǐ néng xiànzài lái bāngzhù wǒ ma?

　　　　These new words are difficult. I don't know how to say them or how to use them. Can you come and help me now?

　　　B: 对不起，我现在不能来，我要去学画画儿。

　　　　Duì bu qǐ, wǒ xiànzài bù néng lái, wǒ yào qù xué huà huàr.

　　　　Sorry, I can't come now. I have to go to a painting class.

　　　A: 晚上呢？

　　　　Wǎnshang ne?

　　　　What about this evening?

　　　B: 今天晚上或者明天上午都可以。

　　　　Jīn tiān wǎnshang huòzhě míngtiān shàngwǔ dōu kěyǐ.

　　　　Either this evening or tomorrow morning is fine.

(72)　我的女朋友一定要会作中国饭。

　　　Wǒ de nǚ péngyou yídìng yào huì zuò Zhōngguó fàn.

　　　My girl friend has to know how to cook Chinese food.

(73)　你画画儿画得真不错，可是没有人买。你应该请那位有名的作家在你的画儿上写几个字，我想总会有一点儿帮助吧。

Nǐ huà huàr huà de zhēn bú cuò, kěshì méi yǒu rén mǎi. Nǐ yīnggāi qǐng nà wèi yǒumíng de zuòjiā zài huàrshang xiě jǐge zì. Wǒ xiǎng zǒng huì yǒu yìdiǎnr bāngzhù ba.

Your paintings are really not bad but there are no buyers. You should ask that famous writer to write a few words on your pictures. I think it would certainly help a little bit.

(74)　这儿能停车吗？我想去买一点儿火腿、鸡蛋。明天上午要用。

Zhèr néng tíng chē ma? Wǒ xiǎng qù mǎi yìdiǎnr huǒtuǐ, jīdàn. Míngtiān shàngwǔ yào yòng.

Can we park here? I want to go buy some ham and eggs. I need to use them tomorrow morning.

(75)　大夫说，你不应该吸烟，不可以喝咖啡，鸡蛋也不要吃得太多。你应该常常锻炼。常常锻炼，身体一定会好。

Dàifu shuō, nǐ bù yīnggāi xī yān, bù kěyǐ hē kāfēi, jīdàn yě bú yào chī de tài duō. Nǐ yīnggāi chángcháng duànliàn. Chángcháng duànliàn, shēntǐ yídìng huì hǎo.

The doctor says that you shouldn't smoke and you can't drink coffee. You shouldn't eat too many eggs either. You should do exercises regularly. If you do exercises regularly, your health will for sure be good.

(76)　我明天上午不用上班，应该能来。

Wǒ míngtiān shàngwǔ bú yòng shàng bān, yīnggāi néng lái.

I don't have to go to work tomorrow. I should be able to come.

(77)　想当翻译，应该要会说流利的汉语和英语。

Xiǎng dāng fānyì, yīnggāi yào huì shuō liúlì de Hànyǔ hé Yīngyǔ.

If you want to be an interpreter, you have to be proficient in both Chinese and English.

2. The Adverb 还　(continued)

As illustrated in the following two sentences, the adverb 还 *hái* has basically two meanings: "in addition" and "still."

(1)　我有四个姐姐，还有三个妹妹。

Wǒ yǒu sìge jiějie, hái yǒu sānge mèimei.

I have four elder sisters, and, in addition, three younger ones.

(2)   他还在睡觉呢。

Tā hái zài shuì jiào ne.

He is still asleep.

In Lesson 15, we discussed the use of 还 in its first meaning and contrasted its be-havior with that of 也 . Besides being a marker of the notion "also, additionally," 还 also functions as a temporal adverb, indicating that "the situation is *still* the case." The action or state represented by the verb began in the past and continues into the present. If I used to have three younger sisters and I still have three, without hav-ing lost any over the years, I can describe my good fortune in the following sen-tence, which is of course to be distinguished from sentence (1).

(3)   我以前有三个妹妹，现在还有三个妹妹。

Wǒ yǐqián yǒu sānge mèimei, xiànzài háiyǒu sānge mèimei.

A few more examples of this second meaning of 还 :

(4)   我的孩子今年三岁，可是还不会走路。

Wǒ de háizi jīnnián sānsuì, kěshì hái bú huì zǒu lù.

My child is three this year but he still can't walk.

(5)   你作的面包真好吃，我还想再吃一点儿。可以吗？

Nǐ zuò de miànbāo zhēn hǎochī, wǒ hái xiǎng zài chī yìdiǎnr. Kěyǐ ma?

The bread you made is really good. I (still) want to have some more. May I?

(6)   A: 我们走吧。

Wǒmen zǒu ba.

Let's go.

B: 还早呢，我还要再跟丁云谈谈。

Hái zǎo ne. Wǒ hái yào zài gēn Dīng Yún tántan.

It's still early. I still need to talk to Ding Yun more.

(7)   他说汉语，有时候说得没有问题，有时候说得不太对。我想他语法了解得还不太清楚。

Tā shuō Hànyǔ, yǒu shíhòu shuō de méi yǒu wèntí, yǒu shíhòu shuō de bú tài duì. Wǒ xiǎng tā yǔfǎ liǎojiě de hái bú tài qīngchu.

When he speaks Chinese, sometimes he speaks with no problem while other times he speaks inaccurately. I think he still doesn't understand Chinese grammar too clearly.

3. The Connector 或者

Both 或者 *huòzhě* and 还是 *háishì* are used to join alternatives together. In English, they are both translated as "or." In actual usage, 或者 and 还是 are quite different. 还是 is used primarily in a choice-type interrogative while 或者 is used to join non-disjunctive alternatives together. The following is cited from Y. R. Chao's *Mandarin Primer* (pp. 145 − 146) to illustrate such a distinction:

The written sentence "Are you going today or tomorrow?" is ambiguous. (a) Spoken with a rising intonation on "today" (with or without a pause) and with a falling intonation on "tomorrow," it is a disjunctive question and the person answering is expected to make a choice between "today" and "tomorrow." (b) If the same words are spoken with a gradually rising intonation with no pause, then it is a yes-or-no question and the person answering is expected to say "Yes (I am going today or tomorrow)" or "No (I am not going either today or tomorrow)." In Chinese, different words are used for the two kinds of "or's." 还是 is used in the first case, while 或者 is used in the second. Thus,

你要铅笔还是要钢笔？
Nǐ yào qiānbǐ háishì yào gāngbǐ?
Do you want a pencil or a pen?
(= Which do you want?)

你要铅笔或者钢笔吗？
Nǐ yào qiānbǐ huòzhě gāngbǐ ma?
Do you (or do you not) want a pencil or a pen?

Note that in a statement — unless it contains an indirect disjunctive question — "or" will always be translated by 或者.

The following are more examples of the use of 或者. Please note that since the 或者 expression links two or more alternatives together, it is plural in reference. If the expression stands before the verb in a sentence as in (2) and (3), the predicate is usually modified by 都.

(1)   我不想当大夫，我要研究中国文学或者当翻译。
        Wǒ bù xiǎng dāng dàifu, wǒ yào yánjiū Zhōngguó wénxué huòzhě dāng fānyì.
        I don't want to be a doctor. I want to do research in Chinese literature or become an interpreter.

(2)　A: 阅览室里能吸烟吗？

　　　Yuèlǎnshìli néng xī yān ma?

　　　Can I smoke in the reading room?

　　B: 不可以。阅览室或者教室里都不可以吸烟。

　　　Bù kěyǐ. Yuèlǎnshì huòzhě jiàoshìli dōu bù kěyǐ xī yān.

　　　No. There is no smoking in reading rooms or in classrooms.

(3)　你想锻炼身体，走路或者游泳都很好。

　　　Nǐ xiǎng duànliàn shēntǐ, zǒu lù huòzhě yóu yǒng dōu hěn hǎo.

　　　If you want to exercise, either walking or swimming is good.

4. The Adverb 就

The adverb 就 *jiù* is a temporal marker for a verb/adjective, stressing the imminence or urgency of the action/state. It may also indicate that an event takes place sooner or earlier than expected. Please compare the following two sentences:

(1)　我今年想去中国。

　　　Wǒ jīnnián xiǎng qù Zhōngguó.

(2)　我今年就想去中国。

　　　Wǒ jīnnián jiù xiǎng qù Zhōngguó.

Sentence (1) is a simple statement of one's wish of going to China. Sentence (2), on the other hand, contains the adverb 就, underscoring the urgency of the plan. Hence, the sentence means "I want to go to China as early as this year." Other examples are:

(3)　我八点就可以回家。

　　　Wǒ bādiǎn jiù kěyǐ huí jiā.

　　　I can return home as early as eight o'clock.

(4)　我现在就去。

　　　Wǒ xiànzài jiù qù.

　　　I'll go right away.

(5)　在美国十八岁就可以开车。可是在中国呢，十八岁还不可以开车。对吗？

　　　Zài Měiguó shíbāsuì jiù kěyǐ kāi chē. Kěshì zài Zhōngguó ne, shíbāsuì hái bù kěyǐ kāi chē. Duì ma?

　　　The minimum age for driving in America is (as young as) eighteen. But in China an eighteen-year-old person is still not allowed to drive. Right?

(6)   我小时候就很喜欢看小说。现在还常常去图书馆借鲁迅或者郭沫若的
        小说来看。
        Wǒ xiǎo shíhòu jiù hěn xǐhuan kàn xiǎoshuō. Xiànzài hái cháng-
        cháng qù túshūguǎn jiè Lǔ Xùn huòzhě Guō Mòruò de xiǎoshuō lái
        kàn.
        Even when I was young I liked to read fiction. I still often go to the
        library to check out stories by Lu Xun or Guo Moruo.

5. A Special Numeral 俩

In colloquial Mandarin, 两个 *liǎngge* may be shortened to 俩 *liǎ*. The short form is
often used when referring to people.

(1)   请你们俩都来。
        Qǐng nǐmen liǎ dōu lái.
        Both of you are invited to come.

(2)   他们俩都是很有名的作家。
        Tāmen liǎ dōu shì hěn yǒumíng de zuòjiā.
        They are both famous writers.

Lesson 27

1. The Perfective 了

1.1 了 *le* is one of the most difficult grammatical features in the Chinese language. It serves a variety of functions and may appear either after a verb or at the end of a sentence. In this lesson, we will examine the use of the post-verbal 了 , or, simply, the verb—了 .

The verbal 了 is primarily used to mark the completion aspect of a verb. The concept of completion of an action is to be distinguished from the concept of a past action. As discussed in Lesson 23, in English "tense" refers to the time context in which an action takes place; hence, there is a three-way differentiation: the past, the present and the future. English verbs are inflected for the present and the past; the future tense is expressed by another device using an auxiliary. For example, eat—ate—will eat, sing—sang—will sing, walk—walked—will walk. However, in each of the three time frames, an action can be viewed with an emphasis on a particular phase along the course of its progress. We may choose to focus our attention on its beginning, its continuation, or its completion. In any case, each of these stages is referred to as an "aspect." A past action has all these aspects, so does a present action and a future action. Therefore, in English, the "perfective," or the "completive," may appear in the present tense, the past tense or the future tense.

> Past perfect: I *had* already arriv*ed* (when he called).
> Present perfect: I *have* already arriv*ed*.
> Future perfect: I *shall have* arriv*ed* (by eight tomorrow evening).

"Perfect" refers essentially to the completion or perfection aspect of an action, signifying that the action as represented by the verb has attained its completion by a certain reference point in time. The Chinese verb—了 serves to mark this perfective aspect. It is an aspect marker and *not* a past tense indicator. The verb—了 can appear with a future action, a present action, or a past action, as long as the context calls for its use.

However, as a past action is generally also an accomplished action, the verb—了 is often used in such a temporal context. But, if the perfective aspect is not stressed in the context, the verb－了 is not used even when the verb refers to a past action. The following are some situations in which the inclusion of the verb－了 is incorrect.

(A) When the sentence describes a habitual action in the past, we do not use this 了.

> (1)　　他以前常常来看我。
>   Tā yǐqián chángcháng lái kàn wǒ.
>   He often came to see me in the past.

> cf.(2)　　他昨天来了。
>   Tā zuótiān lái le.
>   He came yesterday.

Sentence (2) reports a specific event that took place *yesterday* and, hence, is completed by now. The first sentence, on the other hand, states a general or habitual situation in the past. Because the action was repeated on a regular basis, the emphasis is not on its perfective aspect. The same distinction may be found in English, where only sentence (1) may be rephrased with "used to come." However, unlike English which requires a past tense form, either "came" or "used," the verb 来 in (1) is not marked for either tense or aspect. The time element is explicitly indicated by the time word 以前.

(B) When the sentence reports a state or status which is generally viewed in its entirety and not measured in terms of its various aspectual phases, we do not use the perfective 了.

> (3)　　他去年在中国学习汉语。
>   Tā qùnián zài Zhōngguó xuéxí Hànyǔ.
>   He was studying Chinese in China last year.

This sentence describes his previous status as a Chinese language student for the entire year. The focus is evidently on the continuous state and not on its conclusion. The main verb 学习 is, therefore, not suffixed with the perfective 了. Again, the time word 去年 delineates the temporal context of the situation.

Verbs such as 是, 姓, 有, etc. which pertain to status descriptions do not normally appear with the perfective 了.

(4) 他以前是我老师。

Tā yǐqián shì wǒ lǎoshī.

He used to be my teacher.

(5) 王老师以前姓文。

Wáng lǎoshī yǐqián xìng Wén.

Teacher Wang's name used to be Wen.

(6) 几年以前，这儿都是电影院。

Jǐnián yǐqián, zhèr dōu shì diànyǐngyuàn.

A few years ago, this place was full of movie theaters.

(7) 我小时候有很多中国朋友。

Wǒ xiǎo shíhòu yǒu hěn duō Zhōngguó péngyou.

I used to have a lot of Chinese friends when I was young.

(C) When the sentence makes a descriptive statement with an adjective, we do not use the perfective 了. Adjectives are stative verbs in Chinese. And, as *stative* verbs, they do not normally appear in the perfective mode.

(8) 这个作家以前很有名。

Zhè ge zuòjiā yǐqián hěn yǒumíng.

This author used to be very famous.

(9) 昨天的酒会不太有意思。

Zuótiān de jiǔhuì bú tài yǒu yìsi.

The reception yesterday wasn't particularly interesting.

(D) When the sentence contains the degree complement construction, which is essentially a description of the state of achievement, we do not use the perfective 了.

(10) 你昨天跳舞跳得很好。

Nǐ zuótiān tiàowǔ tiào de hěn hǎo.

You danced very well yesterday.

(E) When the sentence gives reported speech, either directly or indirectly, we do not use the perfective 了. As the emphasis is more on what is being said rather than the completion of the speech act itself, the quotation always begins with a simple verb such as, 说, 问, etc.

（11） 老师问我们："你们想去参加招待会吗？"我们说："我们都很想去。"
Lǎoshī wèn wǒmen, "Nǐmen xiǎng qù cānjiā zhāodàihuì ma?"
Wǒmen shuō, "Wǒmen dōu hěn xiǎng qù."
The teacher asked us, "Would you want to go to the reception?" We said, "We all want to go."

（12） 他说他不会翻译今天的课文。
Tā shuō tā bú huì fānyì jīntiān de kèwén.
He said he didn't know how to translate today's text.

The above discussion on the non-use of the verb－了 may have provided some idea about the nature and behavior of this aspect marker. Unfortunately, this knowledge does not necessarily guarantee that you will know how to use it, or not to use it, correctly. One cue that you might find useful from English is that when you have to use the perfect form "to have *Verb*-ed" to describe an action, you probably will have to use the verb－了 for the same description in Chinese.

1.2 Now, some grammatical rules to remember with regard to the use of the verb －了. As different patterns are involved depending on whether the verb phrase contains an Object, our discussion will be divided into several sections.

1.2.1 When the verb does not take an Object, the aspectual 了 appears immediately after the verb. The negative of "Verb ＋了" is "没（有）＋ Verb." The perfective 了 is cancelled by the presence of 没有 in the negative pattern.

Positive:	Subject ＋ Verb －了	(has taken place)
Negative:	(a) Subject ＋没（有）＋ Verb (b) Subject ＋还没（有）＋ Verb ＋呢	(not taken place) (not taken place yet, but would later)
Interrogative:	(a) Subject ＋ Verb －了＋吗？ (b) Subject ＋ Verb －了＋没有？ (c) Subject ＋ Verb ＋没＋ Verb?	

(13)　电影开始了吗？

Diànyǐng kāishǐ le ma?

Has the movie started?

(14)　电影开始了。

Diànyǐng kāishǐ le.

The movie has started.

(15)　电影还没开始呢。

Diànyǐng hái méi kāishǐ ne.

The movie hasn't started yet.

(16)　今天他们很忙，都没休息。

Jīntiān tāmen hěn máng, dōu méi xiūxi.

They have all been very busy today. They didn't take a break.

(17)　老师讲得很清楚，学生都懂了。

Lǎoshī jiǎng de hěn qīngchu, xuésheng dōu dǒng le.

The teacher explained it clearly, and all the students understood it.

(18)　你现在可以来，我们还没有睡呢。

Nǐ xiànzài kěyǐ lái, wǒmen hái méiyou shuì ne.

You can come now. We haven't gone to bed yet.

(19)　没有，我今天没有喝酒。

Méiyou, wǒ jīntiān méiyou hē jiǔ.

No, I didn't drink alcohol today.

There are actually two negative patterns, "Subject ＋没(有)＋Verb" and "Subject ＋ 还没(有)＋Verb ＋呢," both employing 没有 *méi you* as the negative marker. The first pattern, "没有＋ Verb" as exemplified in (16), is a simple negation: the event did not take place. The second pattern, "还没有＋ Verb ＋呢" as in (18), connotes more than negation. It implies that such an event is expected to take place but has not yet taken place. (Compare the distinction in English between "did not happen" and "has not happened yet.") In either case, the negative marker is considered one unit and is spelled as one word: *méiyou*. (Cf. 没有 *méiyǒu,* which is the negative of the possessive verb 有.) 没有 may be used as a short answer all by itself, as in (19); when it appears together with the verb, it may be shortened to "没 Verb." The following are two more examples to illustrate the difference between the two negative patterns.

(20)　昨天他身体不好，所以没锻炼。

Zuótiān tā shēntǐ bù hǎo, suǒyǐ méi duànliàn.

He wasn't well yesterday. So he didn't do his physical training.

（21）　我们还没锻炼呢。我们在等王老师呢。

Wǒmen hái méi duànliàn ne. Wǒmen zài děng Wáng lǎoshī ne.

We haven't started our physical training yet. We're still waiting for Teacher Wang.

For the interrogative, there are again the 吗－form and the affirmative－negative version. For the latter, the V－not－V may appear in two orders: "Subject + Verb－了＋没有?" and "Subject + Verb + 没 Verb?" In the former, Verb－了＋没有?, the negative ending没有may not be further reduced to a single syllable没. In the latter, however, the reduction is obligatory: Verb+没 Verb? The following is a set of examples to illustrate the three options:

（22）　他们走了吗？

Tāmen zǒule ma?

Have they left?

（23）　他们走了没有？

Tāmen zǒule méiyou?

（24）　他们走没走？

Tāmen zǒu mei zǒu?

1.2.2 When the verb in the perfective mode appears with an Object, the picture becomes complicated. Depending on the nature of the nominal expression, the Object may be placed in different positions in a sentence. Such complications, however, pertain essentially to the formation of the positive sentence. Therefore, to facilitate our discussion, we will begin with the formation of the negative and the interrogative patterns.

Negative:	Subject + 没(有) Verb + Object. Subject +还没(有) Verb + Object +呢
Interrogative:	Subject + Verb－了 + Object +吗? Subject + Verb－了 + Object +没有? Subject + Verb－没 Verb + Object?

（25）　A: 你吃了饭没有？

Nǐ chīle fàn méiyou?

Have you eaten?

B: 我还没吃饭呢。你给我准备一点儿吃的，好吗？

Wǒ hái méi chī fàn ne. Nǐ gěi wǒ zhǔnbèi yìdiǎnr chī de, hǎo ma?

I haven't eaten yet. Can you prepare something for me to eat?

(26) A: 你要了桔子水吗？

Nǐ yàole júzishuǐ ma?

Did you order orange juice?

B: 不对，我没要桔子水。你喝吧。

Bú duì, wǒ méi yào júzishuǐ. Nǐ hē ba.

Wrong, I didn't order orange juice. Why don't you have it?

(27) A: 去年你去没去中国？

Qùnián nǐ qù mei qù Zhōngguó?

Did you go to China last year?

B: 我去年太忙了，没有去中国。

Wǒ qùnián tài máng le, méiyou qù Zhōngguó.

I was too busy last year. I didn't go to China.

The verb phrases in (25) and (27), 吃饭 and 去中国 respectively, are not quite the same in terms of the semantic specificity of the Objects. 饭 in 吃饭 is a generic Object representing any food and not necessarily "cooked rice" that one eats for lunch or dinner. On the other hand, by virtue of its being a proper name, 中国 is very specific in its reference. The Object in 要桔子水 in (26) is also a specific nominal since it refers to the glass of orange juice that has been brought over by mistake. Specific or not, the Object nominals in the above sentences all occur in a post-verbal position. Such unanimity is, however, limited only to the negative and the interrogative patterns. For the positive sentences, the positioning varies according to the specificity of the Object nominals.

A nominal may be considered specific in reference when it is a proper noun （中国） or when it is preceded by some kind of a special modifier. The modifier may be a numeral－measure expression （三本书）, a demonstrative－measure unit （这本书）, an attribute （中文书，好看的书，你的书）, or a relative clause （你喜欢看的书）. As specification is generally achieved by means of either quantification or qualification, the modified nominal will henceforth be referred to as a *Q/Q nominal*. In our following discussion, a Q/Q nominal will also include by extension proper names and personal pronouns since they are by nature specific in reference. In a perfective sentence in the positive mode, a Q/Q Object may occupy its usual post-verbal slot, as exemplified by the following sentences.

$$\boxed{\text{Subject} \quad + \quad \text{Verb} - \mathcal{T} \quad + \quad \text{Q/Q Object}}$$

(28) 他买了三本书。
Tā mǎile sānběn shū.
He bought three books.

(29) 他买了那本书。
Tā mǎile nà běn shū.
He bought that book.

(30) 他买了一本中文书。
Tā mǎile yìběn Zhōngwén shū.
He bought a Chinese book.

(31) 他买了你喜欢看的书。
Tā mǎile nǐ xǐhuan kàn de shū.
He bought the books which you like to read.

(32) 他买了 *War and Peace*。
Tā mǎile *War and Peace.*
He bought *War and Peace.*

In the negative and interrogative patterns, the Q/Q Object may again occur after the verb. The following are more examples to illustrate the behavior of a Q/Q Object in dialogues which combine questions with answers in both positive and negative forms.

(33) A: 你准备了翻译没有？
Nǐ zhǔnbèile fānyì méiyou?
Did you prepare the translation?
B: 对不起，我还没有作今天的翻译呢。我明天交，可以吗？
Duì bu qǐ, wǒ hái méiyou zuò jīntiān de fānyì ne. Wǒ míngtiān jiāo, kěyǐ ma?
Sorry, I haven't done today's translation yet. Can I turn it in tomorrow?

(34) A: 昨天他作了几个汤。我尝了鱼汤，作得真不错。你尝了那个鸡蛋汤没有？怎么样？
Zuótiān tā zuòle jǐge tāng. Wǒ chángle yú tāng, zuò de zhēn bú cuò. Nǐ chángle nà ge jīdàn tāng méiyou? Zěnmeyàng?
He made several soups yesterday. I tried the fish soup, and it was very good. Did you try that egg soup? How was it?

B: 我没喝鱼汤，也没喝鸡蛋汤。我到的时候，汤都没有了。

Wǒ méi hē yú tāng, yě méi hē jīdàn tāng. Wǒ dào de shíhòu, tāng dōu méi yǒu le.

I didn't drink the fish soup or the egg soup. By the time I arrived, all the soups were gone.

(35) A: 你们参观农村的时候，访问没访问那儿的人？

Nǐmen cānguān nóngcūn de shíhòu, fǎngwèn mei fǎngwèn nàr de rén?

When you visited the villages, did you talk to the people there?

B: 我们访问了一些农民，他们都说很想来美国看看。

Wǒmen fǎngwènle yìxiē nóngmín, tāmen dōu shuō hěn xiǎng lái Měiguó kànkan.

We interviewed some farmers. They all said that they would very much like to come to America and take a look.

1.2.3 If the Q/Q Object is definite in reference, it may also be moved to the very front of the sentence as the topic. The definiteness of a nominal may be explicitly marked by a demonstrative as in (36) or it may be inferred from the context as in (37) and (38).

> Object, Subject + Verb 一了

(36) 那个问题，我们谈了。

Nà ge wèntí, wǒmen tán le.

We have discussed that problem.

(37) 今天的报我们都看了。

Jīntiān de bào wǒmen dōu kàn le.

We have all read today's paper.

(38) 小说，我看了，可是还没有还。

Xiǎoshuō, wǒ kàn le, kěshì hái méiyou huán.

I read *the* novel but I haven't returned it yet.

A Q/Q Object is not necessarily definite in reference. A nominal is definite only when its referent is known to both the speaker and the addressee. A nominal like 一本书 is of course non-definite in reference: the referent can be any book. On the other hand, a Q/Q nominal like 那本好看的书 has a clear and definite reference. The choice is one particular book known to both the speaker and the addressee: *that* interesting book. In contrast, 一本好看的书 is a Q/Q nominal with a non-definite reference. The choice is rather specific: not any book but an interesting one. Yet, the reference is not particular enough to be associated with any special title known to both the speaker and the addressee. Generally speaking, if the quantifier in the nominal is " 一 ＋ Measure" (一个, 一本, etc.), it is always considered indefinite in reference and is therefore not qualified for topicalization. In most cases, a definite nominal is marked by the definite article "the" in English. If the Object is rendered with an indefinite article "a/an" in the English version, it is most likely an indefinite nominal and cannot be topicalized. Compare the following two sentences:

（39）　我看了一本很有意思的小说。

　　　　Wǒ kànle yìběn hěn yǒu yìsi de xiǎoshuō.

　　　　I read an interesting novel.

（39.a）*一本很有意思的小说，我看了。

　　　　*yìběn hěn yǒu yìsi de xiǎoshuō, wǒ kàn le.

（40）　我看了那本很有意思的小说。

　　　　Wǒ kànle nà běn hěn yǒu yìsi de xiǎoshuō.

　　　　I read that interesting novel.

（40.a）那本很有意思的小说，我看了。

　　　　Nà běn hěn yǒu yìsi de xiǎoshuō, wǒ kàn le.

Both (39) and (40) contain Q/Q Objects and are, therefore, readily qualified for the use of the perfective 了. Yet, the two Objects are not the same in definiteness, a distinction that explains why only (40) and not (39) may undergo topicalization.

Topicalization may also occur in the negative and interrogative patterns, and the following are a few examples of such a process.

（41）　A: 你尝了妈妈作的菜没有？

　　　　　Nǐ chángle māma zuò de cài méiyou?

　　　　　Have you tried the dish that Mom made?

　　　　B: 妈妈作的菜，我还没尝；你作的，我尝了。非常好吃。

　　　　　Māma zuò de cài, wǒ hái méi cháng; nǐ zuò de, wǒ cháng le. Fēicháng hǎochī.

　　　　　I haven't tried Mom's dish yet, but I have tried yours. It is delicious.

（42）　A: 课文，我还没有准备呢。

　　　　　Kèwén, wǒ hái méiyou zhǔnbèi ne.

　　　　　I haven't read the text yet.

B: 语法呢，你看没看？

Yǔfǎ ne, nǐ kàn mei kàn?

What about grammar? Have you looked at it?

1.2.4 If the Object in a perfective sentence does not carry a Q/Q modifier, then the sequence of "Verb－了＋Object" would represent an incomplete sentence. Why? A few words of explanation are in order to account for the difference in behavior between a Q/Q nominal and a non-Q/Q nominal.

When the predicate of a sentence consists of a verb without an Object, the focus of the sentence naturally falls on the action itself. On the other hand, when a verb does require an accompanying Object, the predicate then contains two pieces of information, either of which can become the focus of attention: what is being done (the Verb) or what is being acted upon (the Object). In a perfective mode when the verb is suffixed with 了, the attention is drawn to the action and, specifically, its conclusion. As the conclusion of an action is reached only at a certain point in time, such a temporal stance needs to be specified in the sentence to justify the use of the perfective 了. In other words, a sentence like (43) is incomplete precisely because it contains a perfective verb but it does not specify the reference point in time.

(43) *他吃了饭。

*Tā chīle fàn.

He ate.

The requirement may, however, be suspended if the focus of the sentence is switched to the Object. Compare (43) with the following sentence where the Object is 两碗饭.

(44) 他吃了两碗饭。

Tā chīle liǎngwǎn fàn.

He ate two bowls of rice.

Although both nominals contain the same noun 饭, they belong to different types of Objects: the generic and the specific. As described earlier in our discussion, 饭 in (43) is a generic Object, whose reference may be "rice" or "spaghetti" or anything that one eats at a meal. In fact, 吃饭 may be considered to be a compound word describing the action of having a meal: "meal-eating." There are a large number of Verb－Object compounds in the Chinese language whose Objects are more like dummy elements than substantial nominals. For example, 走路 *zǒu lù* "walk road: to walk," 游泳 *yóu yǒng* "swim swim: to swim," 洗澡 *xǐ zǎo* "wash bath: to take a bath," 睡觉 *shuì jiào* "sleep a sleep: to sleep," 写字 *xiě zì* "write character: to write,"

结婚 *jié hūn* "to tie marriage: to wed," 喝酒 *hē jiǔ* "drink wine: to drink," etc. When a predicate is made up of a Verb and a generic Object, the focus is always on the action as represented by the Verb－Object compound. When the Verb－Object action is cast in the perfective mode, some additional element has to be added to the sentence to provide the necessary reference point for the aspect. However, when the Object is being modified by an attribute or a quantifier, the Q/Q nominal becomes a specific semantic unit. Thus, in contrast to the generic 饭, 两碗饭 in (44) means precisely "two bowls of rice" and never "two bowls of noodles" or any other type of food. As the Object turns specific in reference, it also becomes the focal point of the sentence, thereby relaxing the temporal constraint in using the perfective 了. Hence, with a Q/Q Object, sentence (44) is grammatical. The following are a few sentences to contrast the grammaticality between a Q/Q nominal and a generic Object in a perfective sentence.

(45.a) *他写了字。
　　　 *Tā xiěle zì.
　　　　He wrote characters.
(45.b) 他写了一些中国字。
　　　 Tā xiěle yìxiē Zhōngguó zì.
　　　　He wrote some Chinese characters.

(46.a) *他画了画儿。
　　　 *Tā huàle huàr.
　　　　He drew.
(46.b) 他画了一张很好看的画儿。
　　　 Tā huàle yìzhāng hěn hǎokàn de huàr.
　　　　He drew a beautiful picture.

(47.a) *他喝了酒。
　　　 *Tā hēle jiǔ.
　　　　He drank.
(47.b) 他喝了那杯葡萄酒。
　　　 Tā hēle nà bēi pútao jiǔ.
　　　　He drank that glass of wine.

(48.a) *他唱了歌儿。
　　　 *Tā chàngle gēr.
　　　　He sang.
(48.b) 他唱了美国国歌。
　　　 Tā chàngle Měiguó guógē.
　　　　He sang the American National Anthem.

All the above (a) sentences may become grammatical if they are set in a larger discursive context where there is a clear indication of the temporal reference point. In our next lesson, we will learn how to provide such a temporal context where the perfective 了 may be used with a generic Object. At this point, you may recall some of the Object-less sentences we described in 1.2.1 and wonder why we did not find them to be violating the conditions we have established for using the perfective 了. A sentence like (14) or (49) does not have an Object or an aspectual reference point. How do we account for the grammaticality?

(14)　电影开始了。
　　　Diànyǐng kāishǐ le.
　　　The movie has started.

(49)　他们走了。
　　　Tāmen zǒu le.
　　　They left.

The answer will also be given in Lesson 28 when we further examine the behavior of the perfective 了.

For the negative and interrogative sentences, it matters little what kind of an Object occurs after the verb. These sentences follow the general patterns described in 1.2.2. A few examples will suffice to demonstrate the formation:

(50)　A: 你喝没喝酒？
　　　　Nǐ hē mei hē jiǔ?
　　　　Did you have any alcohol?
　　　B: 我没喝。
　　　　Wǒ méi hē.
　　　　I didn't drink at all.

(51)　你没看书，也没写字。你作了些什么？
　　　Nǐ méi kàn shū, yě méi xiě zì. Nǐ zuòle xiē shénme?
　　　You didn't do your reading or your writing. What did you do?

(52)　我昨天晚上没睡觉，我复习了十几课的生词。
　　　Wǒ zuótiān wǎnshang méi shuì jiào. Wǒ fùxíle shíjǐkè de shēngcí.
　　　I didn't sleep last night. I reviewed the vocabulary for more than ten lessons.

(53) A: 你洗了澡没有？

　　　　Nǐ xǐle zǎo méiyou?

　　　　Have you taken a shower?

　　　B: 没有，我还没有洗澡呢。

　　　　Méiyou, wǒ hái méiyou xǐ zǎo ne.

　　　　No, I haven't taken a shower yet.

(54) A: 你今天上午写没写信？

　　　　Nǐ jīntiān shàngwǔ xiě mei xiě xìn?

　　　　Did you write a letter this morning?

　　　B: 我没写信，可是我给他打了一个电话。

　　　　Wǒ méi xiě xìn, kěshì wǒ gěi tā dǎle yíge diànhuà.

　　　　I didn't write, but I gave him a call.

(55) A: 老师回答了那两个问题吗？

　　　　Lǎoshī huídále nà liǎngge wèntí ma?

　　　　Has the teacher answered those two questions?

　　　B: 那两个问题，老师都还没回答呢。

　　　　Nà liǎngge wèntí, lǎoshī dōu hái méi huídá ne.

　　　　The teacher hasn't answered those two questions yet.

1.2.5 Before we conclude our discussion of 了 in this lesson, we should point out that whenever we describe a past action with a quantified Object, we always use the perfective 了. It is true that the perfective aspect is not to be confused with the past tense, and, as illustrated in 1.1, there are many conditions where a past action does not require the use of 了. However when a verb for a past action takes an Object containing a quantifier, the verb has to be cast in the perfective form.

(56) 你吃了几个饺子？

　　　Nǐ chīle jǐge jiǎozi?

　　　How many dumplings did you eat?

(57) 我昨天买了一件红衬衫。

　　　Wǒ zuótiān mǎile yíjiàn hóng chènshān.

　　　I bought a red shirt yesterday.

(58) 老师让我回答了三个语法问题。

　　　Lǎoshī ràng wǒ huídále sānge yǔfǎ wèntí.

　　　The teacher made me answer three grammar questions.

1.3 Summary: The following is a table that sums up our discussion of 了 in this lesson. The patterns are divided into two main categories, those with intransitive verbs and those with transitive verbs. In the second category, further divisions are

...osed Object, the Q/Q
...strated with one sim-
...ntences and 喝酒 for

...rogative
...?
...有?
...有?
...Verb?
...息?
...Verb 了吗?
...了吗?
...Verb 了没有?
...了没有?
...Verb 没 Verb?
...没喝?
...Q/Q 吗?
...杯红酒吗?
...Q/Q 没有?
...杯红酒没有?
...没 Verb Q/Q?
...那杯红酒?
...了 Object 吗?
...酒吗?
...了 Object 没有?
...酒没有?
...没 Verb Object?
...喝酒?

Order ID: 108-1112451-2608203

Thank you for buying from ASOA on Amazon Marketplace.

Shipping Address:
Jing Lu
954 Nattinger Way
San Jose, CA 95125

Order Date:	Jul 23, 2015
Shipping Service:	Standard
Buyer Name:	Jing Lu
Seller Name:	ASOA

Quantity	Product Details
1	**A Practical Chinese Grammar (Mandarin) [Paperback] [2002] Cheung, Samuel Hung-nin; Liu, Sze-yun; Shih, Li-lin** SKU: I8-Z1FQ-9UN8 ASIN: 9622015956 Listing ID: 0101P1OPFMM Order Item ID: 15338052459042 Condition: Used - Acceptable Comments: Pretty good shape, but has minor wear and tear, and a few markings inside the book.

Returning your item:
Go to "Your Account" on Amazon.com, click "Your Orders" and then click the "seller profile" link for this order to get information about the return and refund policies that apply.

2. The Adverb 又

In a previous lesson, we learned how to use the adverb 再 *zài* to indicate the repetition of an action that has yet to take place. If the repetition has already taken place, we need to use a different adverb, namely 又 *yòu*, as the modifier.

再 ＋ Verb: to do it again (projected)

又 ＋ Verb: to have done it again (completed)

For example, if someone who came yesterday is here again, we may describe the repeated presence as 又来了. If he is expected to show up again tomorrow, the projection is 再来. If a person who did not come yesterday (Negative Verb: 没有来) is again absent today, the repeated absence is 又 ＋ Negative Verb: 又没有来. If he is not going to show up again tomorrow, the projection is 再 ＋ Negative Verb: 再不来.

Now if the person who did not come yesterday（没有来）came today, his arrival is of course 来了. On the other hand, if the person who came yesterday（来了）and who was expected to come again today（再来）did not show up after all, the absence may be characterized as 没有再来. As the expected event, namely 再来, did not happen, the negative is formed with 没有, which sits before the verb phrase.

The following is a summary of this difference between 再 and 又. They may be used with both positive and negative verbs and they may refer to past actions as well as future events. Regardless of the time frame (past, present or future), projection of recurrence is marked by 再 and completion by 又. Please note the difference in word order between the following two negative patterns:

又没 Verb "(it didn't happen first and) it didn't happen again"

没再 Verb "(it happened first but) it didn't happen again"

昨天 今天 明天	came: 来了 came: 又来了 will come: 再来	didn't come: 没来 didn't come: 又没来 won't come: 再不来
昨天 今天	came: 来了 didn't come: 没再来	didn't come: 没来 came: 来了

Some examples to illustrate the difference between the two adverbs:

(1) 你今天去找他，他不在。你明天再去找他吧。

Nǐ jīntiān qù zhǎo tā, tā bú zài. Nǐ míngtiān zài qù zhǎo tā ba.

You went to look for him today and he wasn't there. Why don't you go look for him again tomorrow?

(2) 我昨天去找他，他不在。今天给他打电话，他又不在。

Wǒ zuótiān qù zhǎo tā, tā bú zài. Jīntiān gěi tā dǎ diànhuà, tā yòu bú zài.

I went to look for him yesterday and he wasn't there. I tried to call him today and, again, he wasn't in.

(3) 他昨天上午来了，下午又来了，可是晚上没有再来。

Tā zuótiān shàngwǔ láile, xiàwǔ yòu láile, kěshì wǎnshang méiyou zài lái.

He came yesterday morning, and he came again in the afternoon. But he didn't come again in the evening.

(4) 他昨天没来上课，今天又没来上课。明天再不来上课，我们一起去他家找他。

Tā zuótiān méi lái shàng kè, jīntiān yòu méi lái shàng kè. Míngtiān zài bù lái shàng kè, wǒmen yìqǐ qù tā jiā zhǎo tā.

He didn't come to class yesterday; he didn't come today either. If he is absent again tomorrow, we'll go to his house to look for him.

(5) 我又尝了一下儿你作的菜。真不错。我还想再尝尝，可以吗？

Wǒ yòu chángle yíxiàr nǐ zuò de cài. Zhēn bú cuò. Wǒ hái xiǎng zài chángchang, kěyǐ ma?

I tried your dish again and it's really good. I'd like to taste it once more. May I?

(6) 那位有名的大夫去年常常来我们学校参观。今年他没再来。不知道他以后会不会再来。

Nà wèi yǒumíng de dàifu qùnián chángcháng lái wǒmen xuéxiào cānguān. Jīnnián tā méi zài lái. Bù zhīdao tā yǐhòu huì bu huì zài lái.

Last year, that famous doctor often came to visit our school. He didn't come this year. I wonder if he will come again in the future.

(7) 昨天爸爸又没回家。他一定又跟那个女人在一起。

Zuótiān bàba yòu méi huí jiā. Tā yídìng yòu gēn nà ge nǚrén zài yìqǐ.

Dad didn't come home again yesterday. He must have been with that woman again.

(8) 他说："对不起，我又要走了。"
她说："我们以后什么时候能再在一起？"

Tā shuō, "Duì bu qǐ, wǒ yòu yào zǒu le."
Tā shuō, "Wǒmen yǐhòu shénme shíhòu néng zài zài yìqǐ?"

He said, "I'm sorry. I have to go again."
She asked, "When shall we be together again in the future?"

(9) 他上个月给我打了两个电话，以后没有再打。

Tā shàng ge yuè gěi wǒ dǎle liǎngge diànhuà, yǐhòu méiyou zài dǎ.

He called me twice last month but hasn't called since.

3. The Collective Pronoun 大家

The pronoun for "all" or "everybody" is 大家 *dàjiā*, a compound that literally means "the big family." It refers particularly to "all who are present" or "all concerned parties." The pronoun may be used by itself, as in (1) and (2), or in conjunction with a personal pronoun, as in (3) and (4). The inclusive adverb 都 is often added to the predicate when the 大家 expression occurs before the verb. It is absent in sentence (4) simply because 大家 appears postverbally.

(1) 大家请到楼下喝咖啡吧。
Dàjiā qǐng dào lóuxià hē kāfēi ba.
Everybody please go downstairs for coffee.

(2) 我们大家都不喝酒，我们叫茶或者桔子水吧。
Wǒmen dàjiā dōu bù hē jiǔ, wǒmen jiào chá huòzhě júzishuǐ ba.
None of us drinks wine. Let's order tea or orange juice.

(3) 他们大家都说帕兰卡学习得真不错。

Tāmen dàjiā dōu shuō Pàlánkǎ xuéxí de zhēn bú cuò.

They all said that Palanka did very well in her studies.

(4) 我今天请大家来是想谢谢大家的帮助。

Wǒ jīntiān qǐng dàjiā lái shì xiǎng xièxie dàjiā de bāngzhù.

I have invited all of you here today just to thank you for your help.

4. The Preposition 为

The expression for proposing a toast is " 为 Reason/Person 干杯," literally "to dry the glass for Reason/Person." Structurally, the phrase consists of two units, joined together as verbal expressions in series. 干杯 *gān bēi* is the main verbal unit and the modifying segment is formed with the preposition, or coverb, 为 *wèi* which means "for, for the reason of, for the sake of, on behalf of." In modern Mandarin, the coverbial 为 appears only is certain idiomatic expressions or set patterns. The following are a few examples of this "toast" expression.

(1) 为我们的朋友干杯。

Wèi wǒmen de péngyou gān bēi.

A toast to our friends.

(2) 为我们的友谊干杯。

Wèi wǒmen de yǒuyì gān bēi.

To our friendship!

(3) 他说为大家的友谊干杯。我干了一杯。他又说为我们的学习干杯。我
又干了一杯。我说，"对不起，为我们的健康，我们不要再干吧。"

Tā shuō wèi dàjiā de yǒuyì gān bēi. Wǒ gānle yìbēi. Tā yòu shuō wèi wǒmen de xuéxí gān bēi. Wǒ yòu gānle yìbēi. Wǒ shuō, "Duì bu qǐ, wèi wǒmen de jiànkāng, wǒmen bú yào zài gān ba."

He proposed a toast to our friendship. I drank to it. He proposed another toast to our studies. I drank again. I said, "Excuse me, but for our health's sake, let's not propose any more toasts!"

Lesson 28

1. The Modal Particle 了

1.1　It has been noted that when a verb-了 construction takes a non-Q/Q Object, the sequence stands as an incomplete sentence. It may, however, appear in a longer sentence where there is a second verbal expression, which takes place only after the completion of the first action. For example, there are two actions, "eating" and "going to see a movie": "eating" takes place first and only after the meal is finished will "movie-going" follow. Then, in Chinese, the first action "eating: 吃饭 *chī fàn*" will appear in the perfective mode with the verbal 了, to be followed by the second action "movie-going: 去看电影 *qù kàn diànyǐng.*"

（1）　我吃了饭去看电影。
　　　Wǒ chīle fàn qù kàn diànyǐng.
　　　I'll go see a movie after I eat.

Action₁	Action₂
Verb-了 + Object	Verb + Object

In other words, the perfective aspect of the first action is to be viewed from the stand point of the second action. When the second action takes place, the first action will have been completed. If the actions follow each other closely, the immediacy may be marked by the adverb 就 *jiù*, which literally means "immediately after that" or "as a consequence." The monosyllabic adverb appears in the second clause and sits before the predicate. The following are more examples to illustrate this pattern.

（2）　你到了法国就给我写信。
　　　Nǐ dàole Fǎguó jiù gěi wǒ xiě xìn.
　　　Write to me when you get to France.

(3)   我们都不会打乒乓球。你明天下了课以后，能来教我们吗？

Wǒmen dōu bú huì dǎ pīngpāngqiú. Nǐ míngtiān xiàle kè yǐhòu, néng lái jiāo wǒmen ma?

None of us knows how to play table tennis. Can you come and teach us after class tomorrow?

(4)   你要买一顶帽子吗？好，我们明天吃了早饭就去商店看看。

Nǐ yào mǎi yìdīng màozi ma? Hǎo, wǒmen míngtiān chīle zǎofàn jiù qù shāngdiàn kànkan.

You want to buy a hat? OK, we'll go the stores tomorrow right after breakfast.

(5)   你们放了假以后想去哪儿玩儿？

Nǐmen fàngle jià yǐhòu xiǎng qù nǎr wánr?

Where do you want to go for your vacation?

(6)   你买了冰鞋，我们就去滑冰。

Nǐ mǎile bīngxié, wǒmen jiù qù huá bīng.

Once you have bought ice skates, we'll go ice skating.

All the above sentences are set in a future time framework. The pattern of marking the sequential ordering of two actions with 了 and/or 就 is, however, applicable to past events as well. Compare the following two sentences:

(7)   我明天吃了饭就去看电影。

Wǒ míngtiān chīle fàn jiù qù kàn diànyǐng.

I will go see a movie tomorrow after I eat.

(8)   我昨天吃了饭就去看电影了。

Wǒ zuótiān chīle fàn jiù qù kàn diànyǐng le.

I went to see a movie yesterday after I had eaten.

The major structural difference between the two sentences is that (8) contains an additional 了 at the end. The sentence-final 了 is a modal particle, the nature and use of which we will briefly describe in the following section. More discussion will be devoted to this topic in the next few lessons. For the time being, we will provide more examples to demonstrate the distinction in use between the two patterns. Sentences (9) and (10) are set in the future and sentences (11) to (14) in the past. Sentences (15) and (16) do not require the final particle 了 as they both represent habitual actions, even though one relates a previous situation and the other a current one.

> Future: Verb－了 ＋ Object,（就）＋Verb ＋ Object

> Past: Verb－了 ＋ Object,（就）＋Verb ＋ Object 了

(9)   我现在在准备行李呢。我整理了箱子以后，还要去买一些吃的。
Wǒ xiànzài zài zhǔnbèi xíngli ne. Wǒ zhěnglǐle xiāngzi yǐhòu, hái yào qù mǎi yìxiē chī de.
I'm in the middle of packing. When I have packed my bags, I still have to go buy some food.

(10) 我们明天吃了午饭就去办签证，办了签证，我们就去买火车票。
Wǒmen míngtiān chīle wǔfàn jiù qù bàn qiānzhèng. Bànle qiānzhèng, wǒmen jiù qù mǎi huǒchē piào.
We will go get our visas after lunch tomorrow. Afterwards, we'll go buy the train tickets.

(11) 我吃了早饭就跟朋友去看电影了。看了电影以后，我们又去公园了。我们玩儿得很高兴。
Wǒ chīle zǎofàn jiù gēn péngyou qù kàn diànyǐng le. Kànle diànyǐng yǐhòu, wǒmen yòu qù gōngyuán le. Wǒmen wánr de hěn gāoxìng.
After breakfast, I went to see a movie with a friend. After the movie, we went to the park. We had a great time.

(12) 我昨天下午没去图书馆复习。我下了课就去看足球赛了。
Wǒ zuótiān xiàwǔ méi qù túshūguǎn fùxí. Wǒ xiàle kè jiù qù kàn zúqiú sài le.
I didn't go to the library to do my review yesterday afternoon. After class, I went to see a football game.

(13) 他到了那儿就给爸爸妈妈打电话了。他说他很想家。
Tā dàole nàr jiù gěi bàba māma dǎ diànhuà le. Tā shuō tā hěn xiǎng jiā.
As soon as he arrived there, he called his parents, telling them he was really homesick.

(14) 他下了班就去城里看朋友了。他晚上没回家。
Tā xiàle bān jiù qù chéngli kàn péngyou le. Tā wǎnshang méi huí jiā.
Right after he got off from work, he went into town to see a friend. He didn't go home that night.

(15)   现在我每天吃了午饭以后总要休息三十分钟。

Xiànzài wǒ měi tiān chīle wǔfàn yǐhòu zǒng yào xiūxi sānshifēn zhōng.

Every day, I need to rest for thirty minutes after lunch.

(16)   我以前每天吃了午饭以后都要休息三十分钟。

Wǒ yǐqián měi tiān chīle wǔfàn yǐhòu dōu yào xiūxi sānshifēn zhōng.

In the past, I had to rest for thirty minutes after lunch every day.

(17)   我昨天回家以后，给你打了三个电话。

Wǒ zuótiān huí jiā yǐhòu, gěi nǐ dǎle sānge diànhuà.

I called you three times after I had returned home yesterday.

The last sentence seems to have violated our description of the use of 了. The first action 回家 is not cast in the perfective mode and the sentence lacks a final 了 to indicate that this is a past event. The first verb phrase can actually be rephrased as 回了家, as it is the first action in the series. However, as 回家 is a compound verb containing a generic Object, it may appear without the intervening aspect marker. On the other hand, 三个电话 in the second clause is a Q/Q Object, and a past action with a Q/Q Object does not normally take a final 了.

1.2   The primary function of the sentence-final 了 is to indicate a new situation or a change in situation.

(18)   我们现在吃饭了。

Wǒmen xiànzài chī fàn le.

Now we shall eat.

We were not eating before but we shall now begin eating. To express such a change in status, the particle 了 is used and positioned at the very end of the sentence. Therefore, the basic difference between a verb-了 and a sentence-了 is that the former appears right after the verb (before the Object) but the latter at the very end of the whole sentence.

Verb-了: Subject + Verb-了 + Object

Sentence-了: Subject + Verb + Object + 了

Semantically, the verb－了 indicates completion and the sentence－了 indicates a change in situation. The two notions are very different but related. When we say the function of the verb－了 is to stress the completive aspect of an action, we have to know from what standpoint this action is viewed. In other words, completion in reference to what? The reference point could be another action, as in the sentences we examined in the last section. Or it can be the moment when the action is described or referred to. If so, the sentence－了 has to be used, indicating that it is as of now that the pertinent action has taken place.

Subject ＋ Verb－了 ＋ Object ＋ 了

Therefore, we have two 了's in the same sequence, the first to indicate completion, the second to provide a reference point. Since it is in reference to the present moment of the speech act that the completion of the action is stressed, the action is of course a past action. Consequently, it is a common practice to use a final 了 in a sentence to describe a past action when the verb takes on a perfective 了 and a non-Q/Q Object. Even when a time word such as 昨天 *zuótiān* "yesterday" or 去年 *qùnián* "last year" is explicitly stated in the sentence, the final 了 has to be present to make the sentence complete. That is, the action might have taken place last year, but it is only when the action is viewed from the present standpoint that its perfective aspect is stressed.

> (19) 我昨天买了书了。
> Wǒ zuótiān mǎile shū le.
> I bought books yesterday.

In speech, it is a common practice to delete the first 了 in the pattern, rendering (19) into (20):

Subject ＋ Verb ＋ Object ＋ 了

> (20) 我昨天买书了。
> Wǒ zuótiān mǎi shū le.
> I bought books yesterday.

The truncated pattern is identical in form with that of a simple sentence－了: "Subject ＋ Verb ＋ Object ＋ 了." In fact, out of context, sentence (20) could have two meanings:

(a) with 了 as marker of a new situation: I had never bought any books in my life, and yesterday was my first time to go book-buying.

(b) with 了 representing the truncated pattern: I bought books yesterday. A simple description of what I accomplished yesterday.

The ambiguity can of course be readily resolved once the proper context is supplied. The following are more examples of the double 一了 pattern and its variation.

(21)　昨天晚上我给你打电话了。你不在。你去哪儿了？

Zuótiān wǎnshang wǒ gěi nǐ dǎ diànhuà le. Nǐ bú zài. Nǐ qù nǎr le?

I called you last night and you weren't there. Where did you go?

(22)　他喝了酒了，不应该开车。

Tā hēle jiǔ le, bù yīnggāi kāi chē.

He had some drinks. He shouldn't be driving.

(23)　去年暑假我去中国了。我没学习中文。

Qùnián shǔjià wǒ qù Zhōngguó le. Wǒ méi xuéxí Zhōngwén.

I went to China last summer. I didn't study Chinese.

(24)　"你星期日去商店了，对不对？你买什么了？""我给孩子买了一双冰鞋。"

"Nǐ xīngqīrì qù shāngdiàn le, duì bu duì? Nǐ mǎi shénme le?" "Wǒ gěi háizi mǎile yìshuāng bīngxié."

"You went to the stores on Sunday, right? What did you buy?" "I bought a pair of ice skates for my child."

(25)　妈妈今天作鱼汤了。你们都在这儿吃饭吧。

Māma jīntiān zuò yútāng le. Nǐmen dōu zài zhèr chī fàn ba.

Mom has made some fish soup today. Why don't you all stay for dinner?

(26)　爸爸问我考了试了没有。我说考了，考得很好。弟弟还没考呢。

Bàba wèn wǒ kǎole shì le méiyou. Wǒ shuō kǎo le, kǎo de hěn hǎo. Dìdi hái méi kǎo ne.

Dad asked me if I had had my test. I said I had and I did well. Younger brother hadn't had his test yet.

The last sentence also provides us with an example of the negative and interrogative. The negative pattern follows what we have learned in the last lesson. The negative marker is 没有 or 还没有……呢, depending on whether there is an implied meaning of "not yet but would eventually." The formation of the interrogative is a bit complex. As the perfective 了 is omissible, there is a variety of interrogative forms that can be summed up in the following paradigms.

```
Verb （了） Object （了） 吗？
Verb （了） Object （了） 没有？
Verb 没 Verb Object？
```

The third pattern deletes both 了's in the juxtaposition of the positive (Verb) and the negative (没 Verb). In the first two patterns, however, either one of the 了's, or both, may appear in the interrogative, thereby producing the following set of question forms.

```
Verb 一了 Object 了 吗？
Verb 一了 Object 了 没有？
Verb 一了 Object 吗？
Verb 一了 Object 没有？
Verb Object 了 吗？
Verb Object 了 没有？
```

Including the pattern "Verb 没 Verb Object," there is a total of seven possible ways to form a question in the perfective mode. They are not equally common in occurrence. Some speakers may prefer certain forms over the others. The following are more examples for illustration.

(27) 你听新闻了没有？代表团昨天来没来我们工厂访问？你知道吗？

Nǐ tīng xīnwén le méiyou? Dàibiǎotuán zuótiān lái mei lái wǒmen gōngchǎng fǎngwèn? Nǐ zhīdao ma?

Did you listen to the news? Did the delegation come to our factory for a visit? Do you know?

(28) 古波办了签证没有？他想什么时候去法国？

Gūbō bànle qiānzhèng méiyou? Tā xiǎng shénme shíhòu qù Fǎguó?

Has Gubo gotten his visa? When does he want to leave for France?

(29)   A: 去年寒假，你去北京了没有？

Qùnián hánjià, nǐ qù Běijīng le méiyou?

Did you go to Beijing last year during winter vacation?

B: 我没去北京，我去 New York 看朋友了。

Wǒ méi qù Běijīng, wǒ qù New York kàn péngyou le.

I didn't go to Beijing. I went to New York to see some friends.

(30)   你们吃没吃午饭？没吃，我这儿有饺子。

Nǐmen chī mei chī wǔfàn? Méi chī, wǒ zhèr yǒu jiǎozi.

Have you had lunch? If not, I have some dumplings here.

(31)   A: 你看了课文了吗？你作了翻译没有？

Nǐ kànle kèwén le ma? Nǐ zuòle fānyì méiyou?

Did you read the text? Did you do the translation?

B: 我也没看课文，也没作翻译。

Wǒ yě méi kàn kèwén, yě méi zuò fānyì.

I didn't read the text and I didn't do the translation either.

A: 那，你这几天作什么了？

Nà, nǐ zhè jǐtiān zuò shénme le?

Then, what did you do these last few days?

(32)   你买票了吗？你买了几张票？

Nǐ mǎi piào le ma? Nǐ mǎile jǐzhāng piào?

Have you bought the tickets? How many did you buy?

One point to note is that if the predicate contains an adverb like 都, the interrogative never appears in the "Verb 没 Verb" pattern. Thus,

(33.a)*你们都洗没洗澡？

*Nǐmen dōu xǐ mei xǐ zǎo?

Have you all taken your showers?

(33.b) 你们都洗澡了吗？

Nǐmen dōu xǐ zǎo le ma?

(33.c) 你们都洗了澡没有？

Nǐmen dōu xǐ le zǎo méiyou?

1.3 In our description of the aspectual 了 in Lesson 27, we raised two questions concerning its use:

(A) How do we resolve the problem of ungrammaticality in a sentence like *他喝了酒, where the perfective verb is followed by a non‑Q/Q Object?

(B) How do we account for the grammaticality of a sentence like 他休息了, where the perfective verb carries no Object at all?

It is evident from the discussion thus far that the key to solving the first problem is to provide the sentence一了, which serves as the reference point for the aspectual marking: 他喝了酒了. Our answer to the second question also pertains to this sentence一了. When a transitive verb takes on both types of 了, the two elements are separated by the Object: Verb一了 + Object + 了. But, when an intransitive verb appears in the same pattern, it is followed by two 了's in a row: Verb一了 + 了, a redundancy that is not acceptable in Chinese. Hence, one must be deleted, resulting in a deceptively simple one 了 sequence.

> Subject ＋ Verb一了 ＋ 了 → Subject ＋ Verb ＋ 了

（34） （他走了了。 ＝ ）他走了。
　　　 Tā zǒu le le.
　　　 He has left.

Again, out of context, the sequence 他走了 could have two possible readings:

(a) with 了 as a marker of new situation: He is now to leave.
(b) with 了 as fusion of two 了's: He is gone.

However, when the sentence is said or heard in a proper context, confusion is not likely to arise. The following sentences illustrate how meanings are differentiated through contextualization.

（35） 招待会现在开始了。请进来吧。
　　　 Zhāodàihuì xiànzài kāishǐ le. Qǐng jìnlái ba.
　　　 The reception is to begin now. Please come in.

（36） 音乐会已经开始了。请别进来。
　　　 Yīnyuè huì yǐjīng kāishǐ le. Qǐng bié jìnlái.
　　　 The concert has already started. Please don't come in.

The following are more examples of an intransitive verb in a perfective sentence.

(37)   A: 今天下午我去看足球赛了。

      Jīntiān xiàwǔ wǒ qù kàn zúqiú sài le.

      I went to see the football match this afternoon.

      B: 谁赢了？

      Shéi yíng le?

      Who won?

      A: 我们队又输了。五比七，真气人。

      Wǒmen duì yòu shū le. Wǔ bǐ qī, zhēn qì rén.

      Our team lost again, 5 to 7. It's really annoying.

(38)   昨天晚上你给我们打电话的时候，我们都睡了。所以没有人接。

      Zuótiān wǎnshang nǐ gěi wǒmen dǎ diànhuà de shíhòu, wǒmen dōu shuì le. Suǒyǐ méi yǒu rén jiē.

      When you called last night, we were already asleep. So, no one answered the phone.

(39)   你来得太晚了，他们都出发了。

      Nǐ lái de tài wǎn le. Tāmen dōu chūfā le.

      You came too late. They had all departed.

1.4   As the negative form of the perfective is constructed with 没有, students may wrongly infer that the interrogative can be formed with 有没有 : *有没有 Verb. In some of the southern dialects, this is indeed an acceptable pattern, and may be used as an alternative to "Verb一了没有." Therefore, students who have been exposed to southern Mandarin will have to be extra careful when phrasing perfective questions. There may be a variety of ways of asking the following question in Standard Mandarin, but (a) is definitely not one of them.

(40)   Did you see a movie yesterday?

(40.a) *你昨天有没有看电影？

      *Nǐ zuótiān yǒu mei yǒu kàn diànyǐng?

For the same reason, we never respond to a "Verb一了没有？" question with 有 as the short answer. The positive form is always "Verb一了."

(41)   A: 你昨天看电影了没有？

      Nǐ zuótiān kàn diànyǐng le méiyou?

      Did you go see a movie yesterday?

      B: 看了，我昨天看了一个法国电影。

      Kànle, wǒ zuótiān kànle yíge Fǎguó diànyǐng.

      I did. I saw a French movie yesterday.

2. The Measure Word 双

The measure word 双 *shuāng* is used for things that usually exist or are used in pairs. For example, 一双筷子 *yìshuāng kuàizi* "a pair of chopsticks," 一双鞋 *yìshuāng xié* "a pair of shoes," etc. There are objects that are measured in sets of two in English but which are considered to be single items in Chinese. The best example is, of course, 一条裤子 *yìtiáo kùzi* "a pair of pants." As is always the case, we need to remember which noun is accompanied by which measure word.

(1)   这双鞋太旧了，不能再穿。我们去买一双新的吧。
       Zhè shuāng xié tài jiù le, bù néng zài chuān. Wǒmen qù mǎi yìshuāng xīn de ba.
       This pair of shoes is too worn out. I can't wear them any more. Let's go buy a new pair.

Lesson 29

1. The Imminent Aspect

1.1   We learned in Lesson 28 that the modal particle 了 may be used to express a new situation or a change of state. If such a change is impending or an action is going to take place, we may add the auxiliary 要 *yào* to the predicate to indicate imminence.

要　＋　〔Verb　＋　Object〕　＋　了

(1)　飞机要起飞了。
　　　Fēijī yào qǐfēi le.
　　　The plane is about to take off.

(2)　我们要吃午饭了。
　　　Wǒmen yào chī wǔfàn le.
　　　We're going to have our lunch.

(3)　爸爸要给我们照相了。
　　　Bàba yào gěi wǒmen zhào xiàng le.
　　　Father is about to take a picture for us.

1.2   The degree of imminence may be enhanced by placing the adverb 就 *jiù* "immediately" before the auxiliary.

就　＋　要　＋　〔Verb　＋　Object〕　＋　了

(4)　飞机就要起飞了。
　　　Fēijī jiù yào qǐfēi le.
　　　The plane is going to take off momentarily.

(5) 我们就要回家了。
　　 Wǒmen jiù yào huí jiā le.
　　 We are just about to go home.

(6) 他们就要来接我们了。
　　 Tāmen jiù yào lái jiē wǒmen le.
　　 They'll be coming to pick us up very soon.

Please note, however, that when 就 is used, 要 becomes optional in the pattern. In other words, sentences (4) to (6) may all be said without the auxiliary and there is no difference in meaning or emphasis.

(4.a) 飞机就起飞了。
(5.a) 我们就回家了。
(6.a) 他们就来接我们了。

1.3 There is another adverb, 快 *kuài* (literally "fast, soon"), that may also appear in this pattern and, when it does, the auxiliary 要 again becomes optional.

$$\boxed{\text{快}\ +\ （\text{要}）\ +\ [\text{Verb}\ +\ \text{Object}]\ +\ \text{了}}$$

(7) 船快（要）开了。你们快跑吧。
　　 Chuán kuài (yào) kāi le. Nǐmen kuài pǎo ba.
　　 The ship is leaving soon. Please run fast.

(8) 快下课了。
　　 Kuài xià kè le.
　　 The class is about to be over.

(9) 学校快（要）放假了。
　　 Xuéxiào kuài (yào) fàng jià le.
　　 School will be over soon.

However, unlike 就, which increases the degree of immediacy, and contrary to its basic meaning "fast," 快 tends to slightly mitigate the urgency. Hence, the three patterns are now arranged in the following order of decreasing imminence.

	Degree of imminence
就（要）Verbal 了	1st
要　Verbal 了	2nd
快（要）Verbal 了	3rd

The effects that adverbs can have on an expression of imminent action may be compared to those of "immediately" and "soon" in English. To modify a statement like "I'm coming" with "immediately" adds to the immediacy of the action: "I'm coming immediately." The same sentence said with "soon" sounds less urgent: "I'm coming soon."

1.4 Another difference among the three patterns of marking imminence is that a time expression may co-occur with either pattern of 要 or 就（要）, but not with 快（要）.

(10)　他们明天就（要）走了。
　　　Tāmen míngtiān jiù (yào) zǒu le.
　　　They are leaving (as soon as) tomorrow.

(11)　我们今年要去中国学习了。
　　　Wǒmen jīnnián yào qù Zhōngguó xuéxí le.
　　　We are (soon) going to China to study this year.

(12)　*电影八点快（要）开始了。
　　　*Diànyǐng bādiǎn kuài (yào) kāishǐ le.
　　　The movie will (soon) start at eight o'clock.

1.5 To sum up, the three patterns marking the imminent aspect of an action or situation are dissimilar in the following ways:

	Degree of Imminence	Co-occurrence with Time
要　　 Verbal 了	2nd	yes
就（要）Verbal 了	1st	yes
快（要）Verbal 了	3rd	no

1.6 To negate a sentence with a new situation particle 了, we use 没有 or 还没有. Hence, the negative counterpart of a sentence with the imminent marker is always formed with （还）没有. The interrogative form generally takes the 吗-type over the other possibilities.

（13）　A: 学校快要考试了吗？

　　　　　　Xuéxiào kuài yào kǎo shì le ma?

　　　　　　Are exams coming up soon?

　　　　B: 没有。我们放了春假以后考试。

　　　　　　Méiyou. Wǒmen fàngle chūnjià yǐhòu kǎo shì.

　　　　　　No, we'll have our exams after the spring break.

（14）　A: 就要下课了吗？

　　　　　　Jiù yào xià kè le ma?

　　　　　　Will the class be over real soon?

　　　　B: 还没有呢。我们十点下课。现在是九点三刻。请你再等十五分钟。

　　　　　　Hái méiyou ne. Wǒmen shídiǎn xià kè. Xiànzài shì jiǔdiǎn sānkè. Qǐng nǐ zài děng shíwǔfēn zhōng.

　　　　　　No. We get out at ten o'clock. It's now nine forty-five. Could you wait for another fifteen minutes?

（15）　A: 球赛快开始了吗？

　　　　　　Qiú sài kuài kāishǐ le ma?

　　　　　　Is the ball game going to start soon?

　　　　B: 没有。裁判还没来呢。

　　　　　　Méiyou. Cáipàn hái méi lái ne.

　　　　　　No. The referee isn't here yet.

1.7 To review, the optative auxiliary 要 may serve to mark three kinds of modality:

(A) Volition/Desire (Cf. Lesson 26): The negative is 不想.

(16) 我不想坐船，我要坐飞机。
Wǒ bù xiǎng zuò chuán, wǒ yào zuò fēijī.
I don't want to take the ship; I want to fly.

(B) Necessity/Obligation (Cf. Lesson 26): The negative is 不用.

(17) 我不认识路，你一定要来接我。
Wǒ bú rènshi lù, nǐ yídìng yào lái jiē wǒ.
I don't know the way. You definitely have to come and meet me.

(18) 你不用来接我，我可以坐车去。
Nǐ bú yòng lái jiē wǒ, wǒ kěyǐ zuò chē qù.
You don't have to come and pick me up. I can take the bus to get there.

(C) Imminence: The following are more examples of the various patterns of imminence.

(19) 快一点儿吧。我叫的汽车就要来了。
Kuài yìdiǎnr ba. Wǒ jiào de qìchē jiù yào lái le.
Hurry up! The cab I called will be here any moment.

(20) 你们准备准备，老师要给我们照相了。
Nǐmen zhǔnbèi zhǔnbèi, lǎoshī yào gěi wǒmen zhào xiàng le.
Get ready. The teacher is going to take our picture.

(21) 明天就要开学了。我真不愿意上学。
Míngtiān jiù yào kāi xué le. Wǒ zhēn bú yuànyì shàng xué.
School will start tomorrow. I really don't want to go back to school.

(22) 上船吧，船快要开了。
Shàng chuán ba, chuán kuài yào kāi le.
The ship is about to leave. Get on board.

Depending on the context, the following sentence may mean either necessity or imminence.

(23) 我要走了。
Wǒ yào zǒu le.
(a) I've got to go.
(b) I'm leaving.

If the adverb 一定 is added to the sentence, there can be only one reading:

（24） 我一定要走了。
      Wǒ yídìng yào zǒu le.
      I definitely have to go.

If the sentence is phrased with 就 or 快, again there can be only one reading, namely, "about to happen."

（25） 我就 / 快要走了。
      Wǒ jiù/kuài yào zǒu le.
      I'm leaving soon.

2. The Optative 会

As an auxiliary placed before a verb, 会 *huì* may indicate either "to know how to" or "it's likely that," both of which have been described in Lesson 26. Here are a few more examples to illustrate these two uses:

（A） Ability:

（1） 他会开飞机，可是不会开车。
      Tā huì kāi fēijī, kěshì bú huì kāi chē.
      He knows how to fly a plane but he doesn't know how to drive a car.

（B） Possibility:

（2） 我明年会去中国留学，所以我们很快会在北京见面。
      Wǒ míngnián huì qù Zhōngguó liú xué, suǒyǐ wǒmen hěn kuài huì zài Běijīng jiànmiàn.
      I'm (probably) going to China to study next year, so (it's likely that) we'll be seeing each other in Beijing soon.

（3） 你难过的时候会笑吗？
      Nǐ nánguò de shíhòu huì xiào ma?
      Do you laugh when you are sad?

（4） 他们明天就要去日本旅行了。你们会去机场送行吗？

Tāmen míngtiān jiù yào qù Rìběn lǚxíng le. Nǐmen huì qù jīchǎng sòngxíng ma?

They will be traveling to Japan as soon as tomorrow. Will you go to the airport to see them off?

（C）Combined:

（5） 他不会开车，所以明天不会开车来机场接你。

Tā bú huì kāi chē, suǒyǐ míngtiān bú huì kāi chē lái jīchǎng jiē nǐ.

He doesn't know how to drive, so he won't be coming by car to meet you at the airport tomorrow.

（6） 他不会跳舞，也不愿意学。明天的舞会，他不会去吧。

Tā bú huì tiào wǔ, yě bú yuànyì xué. Míngtiān de wǔhuì, tā bú huì qù ba.

He doesn't know how to dance and he doesn't want to learn how to dance either. He probably won't be going to the dance party tomorrow.

（7） A: 你结婚的时候，会请谁照相？

Nǐ jié hūn de shíhòu, huì qǐng shéi zhào xiàng?

Who will you ask to take pictures at your wedding?

B: 我会请一个很会照相的人给我们照相。

Wǒ huì qǐng yíge hěn huì zhào xiàng de rén gěi wǒmen zhào xiàng.

I'll ask someone who really knows how to take pictures to be our photographer.

3. The Prohibitive 别 (continued)

3.1 A negative imperative is formed by putting 别 *bié* before the verb, a pattern we first learned in Lesson 19.

别 ＋ ［Verb ＋ Object］

（1） 你喝了很多酒，所以今天晚上别开车。

Nǐ hēle hěn duō jiǔ, suǒyǐ jīntiān wǎnshang bié kāi chē.

You have had a lot to drink. So, don't drive tonight.

（2） 孩子睡了，请别唱歌儿。

Háizi shuìle, qǐng bié chàng gēr.

The child is asleep. Please don't sing.

A variant form of 别 is 不要 *bú yào*, a negative auxiliary that was introduced in Lesson 26. As explained in that lesson, 不要 is not the negative counterpart of 要 in marking "necessity" or "demand." On the contrary, it indicates the "demand for refraining from an action. " In this sense, 不要 and 别 may be used interchangeably.

（3） 请不要离开我。

Qǐng bú yào líkāi wǒ.

Please don't leave me!

（4） 请不要忘了作这个练习。

Qǐng bú yào wàngle zuò zhè ge liànxí.

Please don't forget to do this exercise.

3.2 A modified version of the prohibitive pattern involves the use of 了 at the end. Semantically, it implies that an action has been going on for a while and the request or demand is to stop doing it now. For example, if you and your friend are going to a party and you don't want to bring up certain topics which you know will bore the other guests, you may advise him in advance by saying,

（5） 我们别谈这些问题。

Wǒmen bié tán zhè xiē wèntí.

Let's not talk about these problems.

On the other hand, if your guests have already been engaged in a conversation which is getting more controversial by the minute, you want to stop the arguments by saying,

（6） 我们别谈这些问题了。

Wǒmen bié tán zhè xiē wèntí le.

Let's not talk about these problems any more.

The sentence-final 了 marks precisely this interruption, requesting a change of the subject. Here are a few more examples,

```
        别  +  ［Verb  +  Object］  +  了
```

(7) 别难过了，我一定会常给你写信。

　　　Bié nánguò le, wǒ yídìng huì cháng gěi nǐ xiě xìn.

　　　Don't be sad!(Stop being sad!)I definitely will write to you often.

(8) 我们现在上汉语课，请不要再说英语了。

　　　Wǒmen xiànzài shàng Hànyǔ kè, qǐng bú yào zài shuō Yīngyǔ le.

　　　We'll now begin our Chinese class; please don't speak English any more.

(9) 上船吧，别再照相了。船快要开了。

　　　Shàng chuán ba, bié zài zhào xiàng le. Chuán kuài yào kāi le.

　　　You'd better stop taking pictures and get on board now. The ship is going to depart soon.

Unlike the above examples, sentence (10) is not an illustration of the "别……了" pattern. Rather, it consists of a perfective verb 忘了, literally "to have forgotten," placed directly after the negative imperative 别.

(10) 别忘了，一定要来信。

　　　Bié wàngle, yídìng yào lái xìn.

　　　Don't forget, you've got to write.

The verb 忘 often appears in the perfective mode, as the emphasis of the word is on the result of "having forgotten" rather than the process of "forgetting." One could in fact consider 忘了 a compound verb, with the perfective suffix as a built-in element. Hence, "forget me not" is 别忘了我 and not *别忘我了. A few more examples of 忘了：

(11) A: 对不起，我又忘了你是哪天生日。

　　　　　Duì bu qǐ, wǒ yòu wàngle nǐ shì nǎ tiān shēngri.

　　　　　Sorry, I forgot again when your birthday was.

　　　B: 三月八号。以后别再忘了。

　　　　　Sānyuè bāhào. Yǐhòu bié zài wàngle.

　　　　　March 8. Don't ever forget it again.

(12)　今天晚上别睡得太晚。别忘了你明天早上要坐七点的飞机。

Jīntiān wǎnshang biè shuì de tài wǎn. Biè wàngle nǐ míngtiān zǎoshang yào zuò qīdiǎn de fēijī.

Don't go to bed too late tonight. Don't forget you have to catch a seven o'clock plane tomorrow morning.

4. The Sentential Predicate Construction

Though both of the following sentences are grammatical and essentially the same in meaning, (2) sounds more idiomatic in Chinese and (1) more like a translation from English.

(1)　他有很大的眼睛。

　　　Tā yǒu hěn dà de yǎnjing.

(2)　他眼睛很大。

　　　Tā yǎnjing hěn dà.

　　　He has big eyes.

Structurally, sentence (2) can be diagrammed like this:

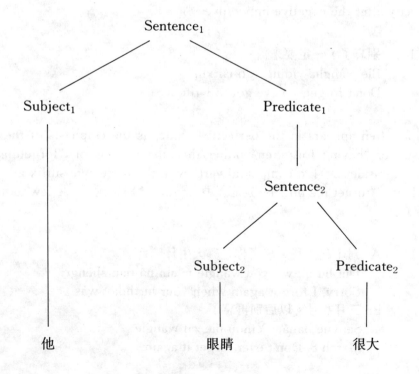

In other words, the main predicate （眼睛很大） is in itself a complete sentence unit: 眼睛 is the subject and 很大 is the predicate. It is therefore referred to as a sentential predicate. The main subject of the sentence, 他, is actually the topic of the statement or conversation. We are now talking about him, so, what about him? Comments follow: his eyes are big, or his nose is tall, etc., each of which is a sentence by itself, with its own subject and predicate. Therefore, the correct but cumbersome (and, hence, not preferred) way of translating the sentence is "As for him, his eyes are big." In this manner, Subject$_2$ （眼睛） may be viewed as bearing a part-whole relationship with Subject$_1$（他）. (Eyes being part of the body.) But, even in sentences where we do not necessarily see such a "componential" relationship, the construction is still frequently used when a series of sentential comments, mostly descriptive and/or contrastive, are made on an identified topic.

(3)   这个孩子眼睛很大，鼻子很高，可是头发太少了。
      Zhè ge háizi yǎnjing hěn dà, bízi hěn gāo, kěshì tóufa tài shǎo le.
      This kid has big eyes and a tall nose, but he has too little hair.

(4)   我身体很好，工作很忙。
      Wǒ shēntǐ hěn hǎo, gōngzuò hěn máng.
      I am busy but in good health.
      (= As for me, my body is good, and my work is busy.)

(5)   这个大学校园很大，学生很多，老师都很有名。
      Zhè ge dàxué xiàoyuán hěn dà, xuésheng hěn duō, lǎoshī dōu hěn yǒumíng.
      This university has a big campus, a large student population and a renowned faculty.

(6)   妈妈说，"你身体不好，你坐火车或者汽车旅行，我都不放心。"
      Māma shuō, "Nǐ shēntǐ bù hǎo, nǐ zuò huǒchē huòzhě qìchē lǚxíng, wǒ dōu bú fàngxīn."
      Mom said, "You are not in good health. Whether you'll be traveling by plane or by car, I'll be worried. "

(7)   你房间里东西太多了。你有空儿整理一下儿吗？
      Nǐ fángjiānli dōngxi tài duō le. Nǐ yǒu kòngr zhěnglǐ yíxiàr ma?
      You have too many things in your room. Do you have time to clean it up?

(8)   她工作认真，学习也很努力，所以进步很快。
      Tā gōngzuò rènzhēn, xuéxí yě hěn nǔlì, suǒyǐ jìnbù hěn kuài.
      She is both conscientious about her work and diligent in her studies. So, she is making speedy progress.

5. Adjective 一点儿

When 一点儿 *yìdiǎnr* is attached to the end of an adjective, it indicates a slight increase in degree of the quality as represented by the adjective: "a little bit more Adjective." The pattern is used most frequently in making requests.

(1)　请快一点儿。
　　　Qǐng kuài yìdiǎnr.
　　　A little faster, please!

(2)　请你明天来得早一点儿。
　　　Qǐng nǐ míngtiān lái de zǎo yìdiǎnr.
　　　Please come a little earlier tomorrow.

(3)　这件衬衫不好看，我要一件红一点儿的。
　　　Zhè jiàn chènshān bù hǎokàn, wǒ yào yíjiàn hóng yìdiǎnr de.
　　　This blouse is not pretty. I want one that is a little redder.

(4)　爸爸要给我们照相了。大家站得紧一点儿。
　　　Bàba yào gěi wǒmen zhào xiàng le. Dàjiā zhàn de jǐn yìdiǎnr.
　　　Dad is going to take a picture for us. Let's stand a little closer together.

(5)　请你说得慢一点儿。我的中文不太好。
　　　Qǐng nǐ shuō de màn yìdiǎnr. Wǒ de Zhōngwén bú tài hǎo.
　　　Can you speak a little more slowly? My Chinese is not too good.

In Sentences (2), (4) and (5), the 一点儿 expressions are used as complements of degree.

Please note that "a little more Adjective" is different from "a little too Adjective." Only the former is an equivalent to "Adjective 一点儿" in Chinese. We will learn how to say the latter in a later lesson.

6. The Conjunction 所以

The conjunction 所以 *suǒyǐ* "therefore" is often placed in the consequence clause in a string of sentences representing a cause-and-effect relationship. It generally appears before the subject of that clause.

(1)　今天放假，所以他一定不会来。
　　　Jīntiān fàng jià, suǒyǐ tā yídìng bú huì lái.
　　　Today is a holiday, and so he certainly won't come.

(2) 她常常游泳，所以身体很健康。

Tā chángcháng yóu yǒng, suǒyǐ shēntǐ hěn jiànkāng.

She swims regularly and so she is in good shape.

(3) 我不放心，所以来看你。

Wǒ bú fàng xīn, suǒyǐ lái kàn nǐ.

I was worried, and so I came to see you.

(4) 我下个星期就要结婚了。他知道了以后，一定会很难过。所以你别告诉他。

Wǒ xià ge xīngqī jiù yào jié hūn le. Tā zhīdao le yǐhòu, yídìng huì hěn nánguò. Suǒyǐ nǐ bié gàosu tā.

I'm getting married next week. He'll certainly be very upset when he learns about it. So, don't tell him.

(5) 夏天去中国旅行的人太多了，所以我想秋天去。

Xiàtiān qù Zhōngguó lǚxíng de rén tài duō le, suǒyǐ wǒ xiǎng qiū-tiān qù.

Too many people travel to China in the summer. So, I want to go in the fall.

Lesson 30

1. The Preposition 离

The literal meaning of 离 *lí* is "to depart, to leave," as in the compound 离开 *líkāi* with the same meaning. As a coverb, it forms a prepositional pattern indicating distance in space or time.

> X 离 Y 很远 (X is far from Y)

> X 离 Y 很近 (X is close to Y)

It is obvious that the X's and Y's in the above sentence paradigms have to be nouns of place or time, and the main predicates often involve the use of an adjective of distance, namely, 远 *yuǎn* "far" or 近 *jìn* "near."

(1) 我们家离学校很近。
Wǒmen jiā lí xuéxiào hěn jìn.
Our house is very close to school.

(2) 上海离北京不太远。
Shànghǎi lí Běijīng bú tài yuǎn.
Shanghai is not too far from Beijing.

(3) 我想他不会来送你，他家离机场太远了。
Wǒ xiǎng tā bú huì lái sòng nǐ, tā jiā lí jīchǎng tài yuǎn le.
I don't think he'll come to see you off. He lives too far from the airport.

(4) 现在离圣诞节很近了，所以商店都很忙。
Xiànzài lí Shèngdànjié hěn jìn le, suǒyǐ shāngdiàn dōu hěn máng.
It's close to Christmas now; the shops are all very busy.

(5)   离考试还很远呢。不用星期六星期天都在图书馆准备吧。

Lí kǎoshì hái hěn yuǎn ne. Bú yòng xīngqīliù xīngqītiān dōu zài túshūguǎn zhǔnbèi ba.

The exams are still quite far away. We don't have to study in the library on both Saturdays and Sundays, do we?

(6)   A: 这儿离北京还有多远啊？

Zhèr lí Běijīng hái yǒu duō yuǎn a?

How much farther is Beijing from here?

B: 没多远了。我们快要到了。

Méi duō yuǎn le. Wǒmen kuài yào dào le.

Not too far now. We'll be there soon.

It is interesting to note that in the last sentence where the Chinese version has 这儿离北京 , the English translation is "Beijing *from here*." In measuring the distance between two points, we may identify one of them as the base or the reference point from which the span extends. In English, such a gauging point generally appears with *from*. In the above example, "here" is where the speaker is and, therefore, becomes the base: "from here." the 离 pattern in Chinese, however, is not bound by such a referential restriction. Either point may occur as the Object of the coverb 离 . In fact, as exemplifed by (7) and (8), while there are two ways of forming the same question in Chinese, there is, however, only one acceptable order in English.

(7)   那个图书馆离这儿有多远？我们可以走路去吗？

Nà ge túshūguǎn lí zhèr yǒu duō yuǎn? Wǒmen kěyǐ zǒu lù qù ma?

How far is that library from here? Can we go there on foot?

(8)   这儿离那个图书馆有多远？我们可以走路去吗？

Zhèr lí nà ge túshūguǎn yǒu duō yuǎn? Wǒmen kěyǐ zǒu lù qù ma?

*How far is here from that library? Can we go there on foot?

The same distinction between "from" and "to" is found between 从 *cóng* and 到 *dào* in Chinese as the former always marks the point of origin and the latter the destination point. Hence, sentence (6) may be rephrased only in one order:

(6.a)   从这儿到北京还有多远啊？

Cóng zhèr dào Běijīng hái yǒu duō yuǎn a?

(6.b) *从北京到这儿还有多远啊？

*Cóng Běijīng dào zhèr hái yǒu duō yuǎn a?

2. The Word for "Self": 自己

自己 *zìjǐ* is a pronoun that can be attached to all personal pronouns and nouns.

(1) 我自己 wǒ zìjǐ "myself"   我们自己 wǒmen zìjǐ "ourselves"
     你自己 nǐ zìjǐ "yourself"   你们自己 nǐmen zìjǐ "yourselves"
     他自己 tā zìjǐ "himself"   他们自己 tāmen zìjǐ "themselves"
     她自己 tā zìjǐ "herself"   她们自己 tāmen zìjǐ "themselves"

(2) 大夫自己   dàifu zìjǐ   "the doctor himself"
     学生们自己   xuéshengmen zìjǐ   "the students themselves"
     帕兰卡自己   Pàlánkǎ zìjǐ   "Palanka herself"

(3) 明天我自己去看他。
     Míngtiān wǒ zìjǐ qù kàn tā.
     I'll go see him myself tomorrow.

(4) 帕兰卡想给（她）自己买一顶帽子。
     Pàlánkǎ xiǎng gěi (tā) zìjǐ mǎi yìdǐng màozi.
     Palanka wants to buy a hat for herself.

(5) 你应该自己去跟他说。
     Nǐ yīnggāi zìjǐ qù gēn tā shuō.
     You should go talk to him yourself.

(6) 大夫不能给自己看病。
     Dàifu bù néng gěi zìjǐ kàn bìng.
     A doctor cannot treat himself.

If the personal reference is clear from the context, as in sentences (4) to (6), 自己 may appear all by itself as an independent unit in a sentence.

The 自己 expression may also take on a genitive function, in which case it may be translated as "(one's) own."

(7) 自己的努力
     zìjǐ de nǔlì
     one's own diligence

(8) 古波自己的朋友
     Gūbō zìjǐ de péngyou
     Gubo's own friends

(9)　她的家就象我自己的家。

　　　Tā de jiā jiù xiàng wǒ zìjǐ de jiā.

　　　Her home is like my own home.

(10)　我们开自己的车去吧。

　　　Wǒmen kāi zìjǐ de chē qù ba.

　　　Let's go in our own car.

(11)　每个人都不愿意离开自己的孩子。

　　　Měi ge rén dōu bú yuànyì líkāi zìjǐ de háizi.

　　　No one wants to leave his/her own children.

1. The Time—Measure Complement

1.1   A time—measure complement is an expression that denotes the duration of an action. Structurally, it is placed *after* a verb. However, a time expression that tells when an action takes place comes *before* a verb. The positional contrast between the expression of time *when* and that of time *spent* is best captured in the following pair of sentences.

(1)   你每天几点休息？

Nǐ měi tiān jǐdiǎn xiūxi?

What time do you rest every day?

(2)   你每天休息几个小时？

Nǐ měi tiān xiūxi jǐge xiǎoshí?

How many hours do you rest every day?

1.2   When we describe a general state of affairs, whether set in the past, present or future time frames, the expression of time-spent always appears post-verbally. If we refer to a specific incident, focusing on its perfective aspect, the durational expression appears after the entire verb—了 unit.

(3)   你昨天休息了几个小时？

Nǐ zuótiān xiūxile jǐge xiǎoshí?

How many hours did you rest yesterday?

(4)   他八点来看我，十二点离开。你说他在我这儿坐了几个小时？

Tā bādiǎn lái kàn wǒ, shí'èrdiǎn líkāi. Nǐ shuō tā zài wǒ zhèr zuòle jǐge xiǎoshí?

He came to see me at eight o'clock. He left at twelve o'clock. How many hours would you say he spent (sitting) in my place?

In the last example, the visit began at eight o'clock and ended at twelve midnight, a four-hour session that seemed to have been a bit too long for the speaker-host. Suppose, in a similar scenario, it is now midnight and the guest who came at eight still shows no intention of leaving. How would the host express his complaint?

（5）　他八点来看我，现在已经十二点了。你说他在我这儿坐了几个小时了？

Tā bādiǎn lái kàn wǒ, xiànzài yǐjīng shí'èrdiǎn le. Nǐ shuō tā zài wǒ zhèr zuòle jǐge xiǎoshí le?

He came to see me at eight o'clock, and it is now already twelve o'clock. How many hours would you say he has been sitting in my house?

The semantic distinction between (4) and (5) is that while the former represents a completed event, the latter refers to an ongoing situation.

Grammatically, sentence (4) contains the verbal 了, and sentence (5) both the verb−了 and the sentence−了. The function of the new situation particle in (5) is to provide a reference point, punctuating the continuous nature of the visit: as of now, this state has been going on for this period of time, and it will go on beyond this point. The adverb 已经 *yǐjīng* "already" is often used in this pattern with both 了's. To recapitulate our discussion on the use of the time−measure complement construction so far, the following are the three patterns and some more examples. Please note the use of "the perfect continuous tense" in English ("have been Verbing") for the double−了 construction with the time−measure complement.

General Action: Subject + Verb + Time

（6）　他每天学习八个小时。
Tā měi tiān xuéxí bāge xiǎoshí.
He studies eight hours a day.

Past Action: Subject + Verb −了 + Time

（7）　他昨天学习了八个小时。
Tā zuótiān xuéxíle bāge xiǎoshí.
He studied for eight hours yesterday.

> Continuing Action: Subject + Verb − 了 + Time + 了

(8)   他已经学习了八个小时了。

Tā yǐjīng xuéxíle bāge xiǎoshí le.

He has already been studying for eight hours.

(9)   去年我在北京住了三个多月。明年我想去上海住几个月。

Qùnián wǒ zài Běijīng zhùle sāngeduō yuè. Míngnián wǒ xiǎng qù
Shànghǎi zhù jǐge yuè.

I lived in Beijing for more than three months last year. Next year, I
want to go to Shanghai and live there for a few months.

(10)   A: 对不起，请你再等一会儿。王老师还在打电话呢。

Duì bu qǐ, qǐng nǐ zài děng yīhuǐr. Wáng lǎoshī hái zài dǎ
diànhuà ne.

Sorry, but can you wait for a few more minutes? Teacher Wang
is still on the phone.

B: 我已经等了二十分钟了。你还要我再等多长时间？

Wǒ yǐjīng děngle èrshí fēnzhōng le. Nǐ hái yào wǒ zài děng duō
cháng shíjiān?

I've already been waiting for twenty minutes. How much longer
do you want me to wait?

1.3 When the verb takes an Object, the above patterns need to be modified. Recall from an earlier lesson that when a verb takes both an Object and a complement, the verb may be repeated to follow the formula: "Verb − Object Verb − Complement." The predicate contains two verbal phrases, each verb governing its own grammatical constituent. The same rule applies here and the following are modifications of the time − measure patterns.

> General Action:
> Subject + [Verb + Object] + [Verb + Time]

(11)   他每天学习中文学习八个小时。

Tā měi tiān xuéxí Zhōngwén xuéxí bāge xiǎoshí.

He studies Chinese eight hours a day.

> Past Action:
>   Subject + ［Verb + Object］ + ［Verb －了 + Time］

(12) 他昨天学习中文学习了八个小时。
      Tā zuótiān xuéxí Zhōngwén xuéxíle bāge xiǎoshí.
      He studied Chinese for eight hours yesterday.

> Continuing Action:
>   Subject + ［Verb + Object］ + ［Verb －了 + Time］ + 了

(13) 他学习中文已经学习了八个小时了。
      Tā xuéxí Zhōngwén yǐjīng xuéxíle bāge xiǎoshí le.
      He has already been studying Chinese for eight hours.

(14) 你们开会已经开了一个星期了。明天还要开吗？
      Nǐmen kāi huì yǐjīng kāile yíge xīngqī le. Míngtiān hái yào kāi ma?
      You've been in meetings for a week now. Is there going to be
      another meeting tomorrow?

(15) 我们坐飞机坐了十几个小时，大家都很辛苦。现在快去睡觉吧。
      Wǒmen zuò fēijī zuòle shíjǐge xiǎoshí, dàjiā dōu hěn xīnkǔ. Xiànzài
      kuài qù shuì jiào ba.
      We were on the plane for more than ten odd hours. It must have
      been very hard on all of us. Let's go catch some sleep now.

(16) A: 机场离学校远不远？开车要开多久？
         Jīchǎng lí xuéxiào yuǎn bu yuǎn? Kāi chē yào kāi duō jiǔ?
         How far is the airport from the school? How long does it take to
         get there by car?
      B: 很远很远，开车要开六个多小时。
         Hěn yuǎn hěn yuǎn, kāi chē yào kāi liùgeduō xiǎoshí.
         Very, very far. You'll have to drive for more than six hours.

(17) A: 你学法文学了多久了？说得真不错。
         Nǐ xué Fǎwén xuéle duō jiǔ le? Shuō de zhēn bú cuò.
         How long have you been studying French? You speak really
         well.
      B: 哪里。我学了两年多了，可是说得还不很流利。
         Nǎli. Wǒ xuéle liǎngniánduō le, kěshì shuō de hái bù hěn liúlì.

It's nothing. I've been studying it for more than two years and I'm still not very fluent.

Please note that the Adverb 已经 appears before the second verb phrase in the Verb–Object Verb–Complement paradigm.

1.4 A variation of the above patterns is to place the time and the Object together, making the former a modifier of the latter. The modification marker, 的 , appears between the two constituents. Though the marker is not obligatory in the construction, its presence is preferred.

> General Action:
>   Subject + Verb + [Time + 的 + Object]

(18)　他每天学八个小时的中文。
　　　　Tā měitiān xué bāge xiǎoshí de Zhōngwén.
　　　　He studies Chinese eight hours a day.

> Past Action:
>   Subject + Verb–了 + [Time + 的 Object]

(19)　他昨天学了八个小时的中文。
　　　　Tā zuótiān xuéle bāge xiǎoshí de Zhōngwén.
　　　　He studied Chinese for eight hours yesterday.

> Continuing Action:
>   Subject + Verb–了 + [Time + 的 + Object] + 了

(20)　他已经学了八个小时的中文了。
　　　　Tā yǐjīng xuéle bāge xiǎoshí de Zhōngwén le.
　　　　He has already been studying Chinese for eight hours.

(21)　这个星期的考试，老师开了两个多小时的会。我们都希望这次的考试
　　　　不会太长。
　　　　Zhè ge xīngqī de kǎoshì, lǎoshī kāile liǎnggeduō xiǎoshí de huì.
　　　　Wǒmen dōu xīwàng zhè cì de kǎoshì bú huì tài cháng.
　　　　For this week's test, the teachers met for more than two hours. We all hope that the test this time won't be too long.

(22) 昨天他看了一个上午的电视，下午又听了两个多小时的音乐。晚上我
      让他整理房间的时候，他说他没有时间，他要准备考试。

      Zuótiān tā kànle yíge shàngwǔ de diànshì, xiàwǔ yòu tīngle liǎng-
      geduō xiǎoshí de yīnyuè. Wǎnshang wǒ ràng tā zhěnglǐ fángjiān de
      shíhòu, tā shuō tā méiyǒu shíjiān, tā yào zhǔnbèi kǎoshì.

      Yesterday, he spent the entire morning watching T.V. and another
      two hours in the afternoon listening to music. When I asked him to
      clean up his room in the evening, he said he didn't have time. He
      had to prepare for the exams.

(23) 她九点多离开学校，九点五十五分到机场。她在路上开了四十多分钟
      的车。

      Tā jiǔdiǎn duō líkāi xuéxiào, jiǔdiǎn wǔshiwǔfēn dào jīchǎng. Tā
      zài lùshang kāile sìshiduō fēn zhōng de chē.

      She left the school after nine o'clock and arrived at the airport at
      nine fifty-five. She spent more than forty minutes (driving) on
      the road.

(24) A: 你学了多长时间的音乐了？
         Nǐ xuéle duō cháng shíjiān de yīnyuè le?
         How long have you been studying music?
      B: 我学了八年了。开始的时候，我学唱民歌。上大学的时候，我开始
         学拉小提琴。我现在已经学了六年多的小提琴了。

         Wǒ xuéle bānián le. Kāishǐ de shíhòu, wǒ xué chàng míngē.
         Shàng dàxué de shíhòu, wǒ kāishǐ xué lā xiǎotíqín. Wǒ xiànzài
         yǐjīng xuéle liùniánduō de xiǎotíqín le.

         It's been eight years. In the beginning, I learned how to sing folk
         songs. In college, I started to learn how to play the violin. I've
         been playing the violin for more than six years now.

One restriction in using this "modification" pattern is that its Object can never be a
personal pronoun. Therefore,

(25.a) 我们等你等了一刻钟。
       Wǒmen děng nǐ děngle yíkè zhōng.
       We waited for you for fifteen minutes.
(25.b) *我们等了一刻钟的你。
       *Wǒmen děngle yíkè zhōng de nǐ.

The modification is used most frequently with non-Q/Q Objects. When a verb takes a generic Object or an Object that carries no modifier of its own, there is a strong tendency for turning the durational segment into a time modifier. If the Object is a complex noun phrase, the preferred pattern is topicalization.

1.5 Topicalization offers another alternative for separating the Object from the verb—complement cluster. The Object to be topicalized has to be definite in reference and is often grammatically complex in structure. The Object phrase may contain a demonstrative, an adjective, and/or a relative clause.

> **General Action: Object, Subject ＋ Verb ＋ Time**

(26) 中文，他每天学习八个小时。
Zhōngwén, tā měi tiān xuéxí bāge xiǎoshí.
He studies Chinese eight hours a day.

> **Past Action: Object, Subject ＋ Verb－了 ＋ Time**

(27) 中文，他昨天学习了八个小时。
Zhōngwén, tā zuótiān xuéxíle bāge xiǎoshí.
He studied Chinese for eight hours yesterday.

> **Continuous Action: Object, Subject ＋ Verb－了＋ Time ＋了**

(28) 中文，他已经学习了八个小时了。
Zhōngwén, tā yǐjīng xuéxíle bāge xiǎoshí le.
He has already been studying Chinese for eight hours.

(29) 第三十一课的语法，老师已经教了三天多了，但是我还不懂。
Dì sānshiyīke de yǔfǎ, lǎoshī yǐjīng jiāole sāntiānduō le, dànshì wǒ hái bù dǒng.
The teacher has already been teaching the grammar in Lesson 31 for more than three days now, but I still don't understand.

(30)   去中国的手续，我已经办了几个星期了。不知道有什么问题？

       Qù Zhōngguó de shǒuxù, wǒ yǐjīng bànle jǐge xīngqī le. Bù zhīdao yǒu shénme wèntí?

       The formalities for going to China — I have already dealt with them for several weeks. I don't know what problems there are.

(31)   A: 这个星期五的考试，你说要准备多长时间？

          Zhè ge xīngqīwǔ de kǎoshì, nǐ shuō yào zhǔnbèi duō cháng shíjiān?

          How much time do you think it'll take to prepare for the test this Friday?

       B: 这个星期的考试不会太难，不用准备太久吧。

          Zhè ge xīngqī de kǎoshì bú huì tài nán, bú yòng zhǔnbèi tài jiǔ ba.

          The test this week is probably not going to be too hard. I don't think it'll take too long to prepare for it.

(32)   这两个很难的问题，我想了一个晚上。

       Zhè liǎngge hěn nán de wèntí, wǒ xiǎngle yíge wǎnshang.

       I spent the entire evening thinking about these two difficult problems.

1.6   The following table sums up the various time—measure patterns that we have described in this lesson.

General Action	Past Action	Continuing Action
Subject Verb Time	Subject Verb 一了 Time	Subject Verb 一了 Time 了
Subject Verb 一Object Verb Time	Subject Verb 一Object Verb 了 Time	Subject Verb 一Object Verb 一了 Time 了
Subject Verb Time 的 Object	Subject Verb 一了 Time 的	Subject Verb 一了 Time 的 Object 了
Object, Subject Verb Time	Object, Subject Verb 一了 Time	Object, Subject Verb 一了 Time 了

2. Approximate Number Indicators

2.1 There are two markers in Chinese to indicate an approximate number: 几 *jǐ* and 多 *duō*. Although both appear with measure words when counting things, their behaviors and implications are not exactly the same.

1 – 9	几个	*多个
11 – 19	十几个	*十多个
21 – 29	二十几个	二十多个
……	……	……
101 – 109	一百零几个	*一百多个
111 – 119	一百一十几个	一百一十多个
121 – 129	一百二十几个	一百二十多个
……	……	……
101 – 199	*一百几个	一百多个
10 – 90	几十个	*多十个
100 – 900	几百个	*多百个

2.2 几 can appear either by itself (for example, 几个 *jǐge* "several") or in combination with any numbers as an approximation indicator (for example, 十几个 *shí-jǐge* "ten odd: 11–19.") It always represents a number range from 1 to 9. When placed before 十, 几十 *jǐshí* it means a round figure between 10 and 90. By the same token, 几百 *jǐbǎi* means a round figure between 100 and 900.

On the other hand, 多 must appear after a multiple of 10, representing the remainder of the figure. *多十 *duōshí* and *多百 *duōbǎi* are incorrect because 多 never appears in the initial position of a numerical expression. 十多个 *shíduōge* is correct and it means the same thing as 十几个: "ten odd items." In 一百一十多个

yībǎiyìshíduōge, 多 comes after 十, hence representing the range of 111−119. Again, as the range of approximation is within the scope of ten, 几 may be used as a substitute: 一百一十几个 *yībǎiyìshíjǐge*. Now, in the expression 一百多个 *yībǎiduōge*, 多 comes after 百 and therefore covers the entire range of 101−199. This range is of course not possible for 几: *一百几个. For the range of 101−109, 多 is not applicable, since the approximation does not represent a digital range immediately after the 百 unit. 几 is qualified but needs 零 to identify the exact digital range: 一百零几个 *yībǎilíngjǐge*.

几 is also one of the two interrogative words for asking "how many," the other one being 多少. Again, the target number for 几 is smaller than ten. The following conversation demonstrates the two uses of 几:

(1)　　A: 你在这儿几年了。你认识了几个中国朋友？

　　　　　Nǐ zài zhèr jǐnián le. Nǐ rènshile jǐge Zhōngguó péngyou?

　　　　　You've been here for several years. How many Chinese friends do you know?

　　　　B: 我在这儿没有几个朋友。星期六星期天，我常常一个人在宿舍看电视。

　　　　　Wǒ zài zhèr méiyǒu jǐge péngyou. Xīngqīliù xīngqītiān, wǒ chángcháng yíge rén zài sùshè kàn diànshì.

　　　　　I don't have many friends here. On Saturdays and Sundays, I often watch T.V. by myself in the dorm.

2.3 多 can also be used to indicate a fraction of a measuring unit. For example, with 月 *yuè* "month" as the referential point, 一个月 is "a month" and 一个多月 is "a month and a fraction of it" or "over a month but not two months." The difference between this fractional use of 多 and the above described approximation 多 is essentially in the positioning of the marker.

Approximation	Fraction
[Number＋多＋Measure＋Noun]	[Number＋Measure＋多＋Noun]
十多个月 *shíduōge yuè* ten to twenty months	十个多月 *shígeduō yuè* over ten but not quite eleven months

One easy rule to remember is that 多 always refers to a fraction of whatever stands immediately before it. If it is a number preceded by it, as in 十多个月, then 多 is a fraction of that numerical unit. Hence, 多 represents an approximation of what comes after ten, namely between eleven and nineteen months. If 多 follows a measure word, it represents a fraction of the noun. In 十个多月, the positioning of 多 tells us that the fraction refers to the measure, which represents 月. Therefore, "ten months plus a fraction of a month." Now compare the following two phrases:

    (2.a) 十多个人
            shíduōge ren
    (2.b) *十个多人
            *shígeduō ren

(2.a) means "more than ten people : under 20." (2.b) is ungrammatical because it would mean "ten plus a fragment of a person." Except in statistics, such a fragmentation is not possible.

    Unlike 多, 几 is never used to indicate fraction.

2.4 The four major time units, 年 *nián* "year," 月 *yuè* "month," 星期 *xīngqī* "week," and 天 *tiān* "day," fall into two categories: 年 and 天 are measure words whereas 月 and 星期 are nouns, both taking 个 as their measures.

一年	*yìnián*	"one year"
一天	*yìtiān*	"one day"
一个月	*yíge yuè*	"one month"
一个星期	*yíge xīngqī*	"one week"

Because of this categorical distinction, the four terms behave quite differently in both patterns of approximation and of fraction, a situation that beginning students often find inconceivable and confusing. "Ten odd months (11−19)" is 十几个月, but "ten odd years" is 十几年 and not *十几个年. 年 is a measure word by itself and does not require another measure when appearing with a numeral: 三年 "three years," 十多年 "ten odd years," 几十年 "tens of years." It also sits immediately before 多 in the fractional pattern, which requires the marker to appear after a measure: 十年多 and not *十个多年 "over ten years." 月, on the other hand, is a noun that takes its own measure 个 as it appears in 十个多月 and not *十月多 "over ten months," and also in 十多个月 and not *十多月 "ten odd months." The following is a table to sum up the differences. 天 and 星期 exhibit the same pattern of dissimilarities.

	Approximation	Fraction
几个月 十几个月 几十个月	十多个月	十个多月
几年 十几年 几十年	十多年	十年多
一百零几个星期 一百一十几个星期 一百几十个星期	一百一十多个星期 一百多个星期	
一百零几天 一百一十几天 一百几十天	一百一十多天 一百多天	

2.5 Below are more examples to illustrate the various uses of 几 and 多. Both will be given when they may be used interchangeably.

(3)　一个多月
　　　yígeduō yuè
　　　1 < X < 2 months

(4)　一年多
　　　yìniánduō
　　　1 < X < 2 years

(5)　十几个大学／十多个大学
　　　shíjǐge dàxué/shíduōge dàxué
　　　10 < X < 20 universities

(6)　两百多个国家
　　　liǎngbǎiduōge guójiā
　　　200 < X < 300 countries

(7)　几个机场
　　　jǐge jīchǎng
　　　1 < X < 10 airports

(8) 九百二十多张照片 / 九百二十几张照片
     jiǔbǎi'èrshiduōzhāng zhàopiàn (/jǐ)
     920 < X < 930 pictures

(9) 三百几十个学生
     sānbǎijǐshige xuésheng
     300 < X < 400 foreign students (in tens)

(10) 三天多
      sāntiānduō
      3 < X < 4 days

(11) 八个多星期
      bāgeduō xīngqī
      8 < X < 9 weeks

(12) 一百二十多本小说 / 一百二十几本小说
      yìbǎi'èrshiduōběn xiǎoshuō (/jǐ)
      120 < X < 130 novels

(13) A: 你坐了十几个小时的飞机，路上一定很辛苦吧。
         Nǐ zuòle shíjǐge xiǎoshí de fēijī, lùshang yídìng hěn xīnkǔ ba.
         You were on the plane for more than ten odd hours. It definitely
         must have been a very tiring trip.
      B: 谁说我坐了十多个小时的飞机？我从北京飞上海，从上海飞日本，
         从日本飞美国，再从美国飞英国。我想我坐了几十个小时的飞机
         吧！
         Shéi shuō wǒ zuòle shíduōge xiǎoshí de fēijī? Wǒ cóng Běijīng
         fēi Shànghǎi, cóng Shànghǎi fēi Rìběn, cóng Rìběn fēi Měiguó,
         zài cóng Měiguó fēi Yīngguó. Wǒ xiǎng wǒ zuòle jǐshige xiǎoshí
         de fēijī ba!
         Who said that I was on the plane for some ten hours? I flew from
         Beijing to Shanghai, from Shanghai to Japan, from Japan to
         America, and then from America to England. I think I must have
         been on the plane for several tens of hours.

(14) 这位老华侨在美国住了三十多年了。他已经不会说中文了。
      Zhè wèi lǎo huáqiáo zài Měiguó zhùle sānshiduōnián le. Tā yǐjīng
      bú huì shuō Zhōngwén le.
      This old overseas Chinese gentleman has been in the United States
      for more than thirty years. He doesn't know how to speak Chinese
      anymore.

(15) 古波自己去商店买了几十条裙子。帕兰卡知道了以后，不知道应该哭
      还是应该笑。

      Gǔbō zìjǐ qù shāngdiàn mǎile jǐshitiáo qúnzi. Pàlánkǎ zhīdaole
      yǐhòu, bù zhīdao yīnggāi kū háishi yīnggāi xiào.

      Gubo went to the store by himself and bought several dozens of
      skirts. When Palanka found out about it, she didn't know if she
      should laugh or cry.

(16) 我在翻译一本小说。这本词典我要用几个晚上。几天以后，你再来借
      吧。

      Wǒ zài fānyì yìběn xiǎoshuō. Zhè běn cídiǎn wǒ yào yòng jǐge wǎn-
      shang. Jǐtiān yǐhòu, nǐ zài lái jiè ba.

      I'm in the middle of translating a novel and I'll need to use this dic-
      tionary for several evenings. Why don't you come back a few days
      later to borrow it?

(17) 我们班有十多个学生。你们班呢？有二十几个吧？

      Wǒmen bān yǒu shíduōge xuésheng. Nǐmen bān ne? Yǒu èrshijǐge
      ba?

      We have more than ten students in our class. What about yours?
      More than twenty, I guess?

(18) A: 你复习课文复习了一个晚上吗？
          Nǐ fùxí kèwén fùxíle yíge wǎnshang ma?
          Did you spend the entire evening reviewing the lesson?
      B: 没有。这课课文不很长，我复习了半个多小时。你呢？
          Méiyou. Zhè kè kèwén bù hěn cháng, wǒ fùxíle bàngeduō
          xiǎoshí. Nǐ ne?
          No. This lesson is not too long. I spent a little over half an hour
          to review it. How about you?

3. 多 as a Question Word

几 may function as an interrogative word as well as an approximation indicator.
Similarly, 多 plays several roles in the language. It is an adjective meaning "many";
it is a marker of both numerical approximation and fraction. It is also the question
word for asking "How Adjective?"

多 + Adjective?

(1) 多大？
Duō dà?
How big? How old?

(2) 多好看？
Duō hǎokàn?
How beautiful?

(3) 多长？
Duō cháng?
How long?

(4) 多长时间？
Duō cháng shíjiān?
How long (time)?

(5) 多久？
Duō jiǔ?
How long (time)?

(6) 你等了我多长时间了？等了很久了吧？
Nǐ děngle wǒ duō cháng shíjiān le? Děngle hěn jiǔ le ba?
How long have you been waiting for me? It must have been very long, right?

(7) 这个问题有多难？你们还要研究多久？
Zhè ge wèntí yǒu duō nán? Nǐmen hái yào yánjiū duō jiǔ?
How difficult is this question? How much longer do you need to study it?

(8) 你今年多大了？我们有多久没见面了？
Nǐ jīnnián duō dà le? Wǒmen yǒu duō jiǔ méi jiàn miàn le?
How old are you now? How long has it been since we last saw each other?

For some speakers, the interrogrative 多 may be pronounced in the second tone. Also, please note that the interrogative compound 多少 *duōshao* "How much? How many?" is not formed with 多 modifying 少 *shǎo*, which would have given the meaning "How few!" 少 is a neutral tone syllable in the question form.

4. The Ordinal Number Prefix 第

The form 第 *dì* may be prefixed to a numeral to form an ordinal number. When the ordinal expression appears before a noun, the proper measure word should also appear in the unit.

$$\boxed{\text{第一 Numeral + Measure}}$$

(1)   第一课
       dìyīkè
       Lesson One

(2)   第二次
       dì'èrcì
       the second time

(3)   第三天
       dìsāntiān
       the third day

(4)   这是你第一次回国。你回国以后，第一件想作的事儿是什么事儿？
       Zhè shì nǐ dìyīcì huí guó. Nǐ huí guó yǐhòu, dìyījiàn xiǎng zuò de
       shìr shì shénme shìr?
       This was your first time returning to your (native) country. What
       was the first thing you wanted to do when you returned?

(5)   上个星期六我第一次去见我女朋友的爸爸妈妈。我走的时候，她妈妈
       说，"我们希望你以后常来玩儿。"
       Shàngge xīngqīliù wǒ dìyīcì qù jiàn wǒ nǚ péngyou de bàba māma.
       Wǒ zǒu de shíhou, tā māma shuō, "Wǒmen xīwàng nǐ yǐhòu cháng
       lái wánr."
       Last Saturday I went to see my girlfriend's parents for the first
       time. When I left, her mother said, "We hope you'll come and visit
       us often in the future."

(6)   这个问题，我问了三个人。第一个人说不懂，第二个说不会，第三个
       说不清楚。
       Zhè ge wèntí, wǒ wènle sānge rén. Dìyīge rén shuō bù dǒng,
       dì'èrge shuō bú huì, dìsānge shuō bù qīngchu.
       I asked three people about this problem. The first one said he didn't
       understand, the second one said he didn't know, and the third one
       said it wasn't clear to him.

(7)　他每天晚上一点睡觉，第二天早上五点半起床。真辛苦。

Tā měi tiān wǎnshang yīdiǎn shuì jiào, dì'èrtiān zǎoshang wǔdiǎn-bàn qǐ chuáng. Zhēn xīnkǔ.

Everyday he goes to bed at one o'clock in the morning and gets up at half past five the next day. Really tough!

In the last sentence, 第二天 is literally "the second day" and, by extension, "the next day." Sometimes, a numeral may function as an ordinal number even without the prefix 第. For example, 二三三号房间 and not *第二三三号房间 "Room 233," 四楼 and not *第四楼 "fourth floor." Cf. the interchangeable use in English between "Fourth floor, please," and "Four, please," in an elevator situation.

5. Point of Time vs. Period of Time

The distinction between 一月 *yīyuè* "January" and 一个月 *yíge yuè* "one month" is that while the former refers to a particular point in time (January as opposed to another month), the latter indicates the duration of an entire month. The following are more phrases demonstrating this contrast.

(1)　（两点零）三分　　　　vs.　　　三分钟
　　　liǎngdiǎn líng sānfēn　　　　　sānfēn zhōng
　　　two o'clock and three　　　　　three minutes
　　　minutes: 2:03

(2)　（两点）一刻　　　　　vs.　　　一刻钟
　　　(liǎngdiǎn) yíkè　　　　　　　yíkè zhōng
　　　two o'clock and a quarter:　　　one quarter (fifteen minutes)
　　　2:15

(3)　两点（钟）　　　　　　vs.　　　两个小时
　　　liǎngdiǎn (zhōng)　　　　　　　liǎngge xiǎoshí
　　　two o'clock　　　　　　　　　　two hours

When it is three minutes after the hour, we are looking at a specific point in time. On the other hand, if we wish to speak of a specific three-minute period within an hour, we are referring to a period of time. Like its counterpart in English, the measure 分 *fēn* may be used for both designations. The noun 钟 *zhōng* "clock" generally follows the measure when 分 is used for a duration of time. 刻 *kè* exhibits the same behavior. On the other hand, the difference between "o'clock" and "hour" is just as pronounced in Chinese as in English. The former is "X 点（钟）"

and the latter "X（个）小时 ." While the noun 钟 is optional in the time－when expression, the optional element in the time-spent unit is the measure 个 .

（4）　我每天晚上十二点睡觉，早上八点起床。我每天睡八个小时的觉。

　　　　Wǒ měi tiān wǎnshang shí'èrdiǎn shuì jiào, zǎoshang bādiǎn qǐ chuáng. Wǒ měi tiān shuì bāge xiǎoshí de jiào.

　　　　I go to bed at twelve midnight and get up at eight in the morning. I have eight hours of sleep every day.

（5）　他说他八点二十分到。现在已经八点五十分了。我们已经等了三十分钟了。

　　　　Tā shuō tā bādiǎn èrshifēn dào. Xiànzài yǐjīng bādiǎn wǔshiwǔfēn le. Wǒmen yǐjīng děngle sānshiduōfēn zhōng le.

　　　　He said he would come at 8:20. It's now 8:55.
　　　　We've been waiting for more than thirty minutes.

（6）　这个会应该九点一刻开始。学校的钟现在九点，所以还有一刻钟就开始开会了。

　　　　Zhè ge huì yīnggāi jiǔdiǎn yíkè kāishǐ. Xuéxiào de zhōng xiànzài jiǔdiǎn, suǒyǐ hái yǒu yíkè zhōng jiù kāishǐ kāi huì le.

　　　　This meeting should begin at a quarter after nine. It's now nine according to the campus clock. So, in another quarter of an hour, the meeting will begin.

Lesson 32

1. 过 as an Experience Marker

1.1 The difference between "Did you go to China?" and "Have you ever been to China?" is that while the former question inquires about a particular trip, the latter relates more of a general experience. In English, the adverb "ever," or its negative counterpart "never," serves to underscore the experiential nature of an action. In Chinese, the most common experiential marker is the verbal suffix 过 *guo*, a form that is derived from the full verb *guò* meaning "to cross, to pass, to traverse, to undergo." As a suffix, 过 is pronounced in the neutral tone, always spelled together with the preceding verb. Syntactically, it follows the verb and precedes the Object, if there is one. Its negative is formed with 没有 and its interrogative forms include both the 吗—question and the affirmative—negative patterns. The following are a few examples of this experiential 过.

Positive:	Verb—过 Object
Negative:	没 (有) Verb—过 Object
Interrogative:	Verb—过 Object 吗？
	Verb—过 Object 没有？

来过	没有来过	来过吗？
láiguo	*méiyou láiguo*	*láiguo ma?*
去过日本	没有去过日本	去过日本没有？
qùguo Rìběn	*méiyou qùguo Rìběn*	*qùguo Rìběn méiyou?*
been to Japan	never been to Japan	ever been to Japan?
写过信	没有写过信	写过信没有？
xiěguo xìn	*méiyou xiěguo xìn*	*xiěguo xìn méiyou?*
wrote a letter	never wrote a letter	ever written a letter?

(1)   A: 你去过哪几个国家？去过意大利没有？

Nǐ qùguo nǎ jǐge guójiā? Qùguo Yìdàlì méiyou?

What countries have you been to? Have you ever been to ltaly?

B: 我去过英国和法国，没有去过意大利。

Wǒ qùguo Yīngguó hé Fǎguó, méiyou qùguo Yìdàlì.

I have been to England and France. I have never been to ltaly.

(2)   A: 你以前得过什么病？

Nǐ yǐqián déguo shénme bìng?

What illnesses have you had before?

B: 没有。——对了，我小时候得过胃病。

Méiyou. —— Duìle, wǒ xiǎo shíhou déguo wèibìng.

No, I haven't had any. —— Oh, yes, when I was little, I had stomach problems.

(3)   他说他自己是一个很有名的作家，可是我们都没听过他的名字。

Tā shuō tā zìjǐ shì yíge hěn yǒumíng de zuòjiā, kěshì wǒmen dōu méi tīngguo tā de míngzi.

He claimed to be a famous writer, but none of us has heard of his name.

(4)   你没到过我们的国家，所以不了解这样的事儿。

Nǐ méi dàoguo wǒmen de guójiā, suǒyǐ bù liǎojiě zhèyàng de shìr.

You have never been to our country and so you don't understand such matters.

1.2 过 is a member of the aspect class, which includes of course the infamously complex 了. Like this perfective marker, 过 connotes completion of an action or end of a state. However, whereas "Verb－了＋ Object" indicates that a specific action has taken place with reference to a specific point in time, "Verb－过 Object" stresses that an event has been experienced at least once in the past. If you ask a tourist if he has ever been to the Great Wall since he came to China, you will use verb－过 to phrase your question. On the other hand, if you want to ask a tourist if he did go to the Great Wall as scheduled, you will use the verbal 了 instead.

(5)   你去过长城没有？

Nǐ qùguo Chángchéng méiyou?

Have you been to the Great Wall?

(6)   你今天去了长城没有？

Nǐ jīntiān qùle Chángchéng méiyou?

Did you go to the Great Wall today?

A drastic, though rather morbid, example to further illustrate this difference between the two aspect markers is that only 了 and not 过 can be used in the following situation.

(7.a) 他死了。
Tā sǐle.
He died.
(7.b) *他死过。
*Tā sǐguo.

As death is a finality that few, if any, can undergo and live again to tell the experience, it is extremely unlikely that we ever use the experiential marker 过 with the verb 死. The following pairs of examples further contrast the two aspect markers.

(8) 我写了汉字，但是我没作翻译。
Wǒ xiěle Hànzì, dànshì wǒ méi zuò fānyì.
I wrote the Chinese characters but I didn't do the translation.

(9) 我写过汉字。汉字真难写。
Wǒ xiěguo Hànzì. Hànzì zhēn nán xiě.
I have had the experience of writing Chinese characters. They are really difficult to write.

(10) 他去了日本。
Tā qùle Rìběn.
He has gone to Japan (and is still there).

(11) 他去过日本。
Tā qùguo Rìběn.
He has been to Japan (but is not necessarily there now).

(12) 我没看电视。我在准备考试呢。
Wǒ méi kàn diànshì. Wǒ zài zhǔnbèi kǎoshì ne.
I didn't watch T.V. I was preparing for a test.

(13) 电视是什么？我没看过电视。
Diànshì shì shénme? Wǒ méi kànguo diànshì.
What is a T.V.? I have never seen one.

(14) 你透视了没有？
Nǐ tòushìle méiyou?
Have you had your X-ray yet?

(15) 你透视过没有？

Nǐ tòushìguo méiyou?

Have you ever had an X-ray?

Although both aspect markers form negatives with 没有, 了 disappears in the negation (没有 Verb) but 过 remains intact (没有 Verb 过), as exemplified in sentences (12) and (13). 过 may also appear in the " 还没有……呢 " pattern, with the meaning "haven't had the experience of doing it *yet*."

(16) 你的男朋友是谁？我还没见过呢。

Nǐ de nánpéngyou shì shéi? Wǒ hái méi jiànguo ne.

Who is your boy friend? I haven't met him yet.

(17) 来中国三年多了，可是还没有参观过北京大学呢。

Lái Zhōngguó sānniánduō le, kěshì hái méiyou cānguānguo Běijīng Dàxué ne.

I have been in Beijing for more than three years now but I have yet to visit Beijing University.

(18) 白先生已经七十多岁了，可是他还没结过婚。

Bái xiānsheng yǐjīng qīshiduōsuì le, kěshì tā hái méi jiéguo hūn.

Mr. Bai is over seventy years of age but he has never been married.

2. The Action—Measure Complement

2.1 When counting the number of times an action is executed or repeated, we use an action measure word together with the numeral to form a numeral—measure unit. The unit appears after the verb and is, therefore, referred to as a complement. The membership of action measures in Chinese is quite limited, the most frequently used ones being 次 *cì* and 遍 *biàn*. While both mark the number of times, 遍 stresses the entire process from beginning to end. Hence, 一次 *yícì* is "once" and 一遍 *yíbiàn* is "once through."

(1) 这本书，我看了两遍。

Zhè běn shū, wǒ kànle liǎngbiàn.

I read through this book twice (from cover to cover).

(2) 这本书，我看了两次。

Zhè běn shū, wǒ kànle liǎngcì.

I read this book twice (perhaps a few pages each time).

(3)　请你再说一遍。

Qǐng nǐ zài shuō yíbiàn.

Could you go over it again?

(4)　请你再说一次。

Qǐng nǐ zài shuō yícì.

Please repeat it.

As a complement, the numeral－measure unit appears post-verbally. When the verb takes an Object, the placement of the action-measure varies according to the nature of the Object. If the Object is a noun, it appears after the measure; if it is a pronoun, it appears before the measure. The advancement of a pronoun Object is a syntactic phenomenon quite common in many languages. Cf. in English: "I gave up *the idea*." vs. "I gave *it* up."

Verb－Aspect ＋ Numeral－Measure ＋ Noun Object

(5)　我们听了一遍新闻。

Wǒmen tīngle yíbiàn xīnwén.

We listened to the news once.

(6)　你去过几次大使馆？

Nǐ qùguo jǐcì dàshǐguǎn?

How many times have you been to the embassy?

(7)　他最近进了两次城。

Tā zuìjìn jìnle liǎngcì chéng.

He recently went to the city twice.

(8)　北京队最近赢过一次上海队。

Běijīng duì zuìjìn yíngguo yícì Shànghǎi duì.

The Beijing team beat the Shanghai team once recently.

(9)　我到北京以后，去医务所检查过一次身体，可是最近两个月没有检查过。

Wǒ dào Běijīng yǐhòu, qù yīwùsuǒ jiǎncháguo yícì shēntǐ, kěshì zuìjìn liǎngge yuè méiyou jiǎncháguo.

I had a physical check-up at the clinic after I came to Beijing, but I haven't had one in the last two months.

Verb－Aspect ＋ Pronoun Object ＋ Numeral－Measure

(10) 老师辅导过我们一次。

Lǎoshī fǔdǎoguo wǒmen yícì.

The teacher tutored us once.

(11) 她们来过这儿多少次？

Tāmen láiguo zhèr duōshaocì?

How many times have they been here?

(12) 帕兰卡来找过你两次，你都不在。

Pàlánkǎ lái zhǎoguo nǐ liǎngcì, nǐ dōu bú zài.

Palanka came to look for you twice, and you weren't here either time.

(13) 我见过他一次，可是没有人给我们介绍。

Wǒ jiànguo tā yícì, kěshì méiyou rén gěi wǒmen jièshào.

I saw him once, but no one introduced me to him.

(14) 他来找过你三次，也给你留过三次条子。你有空儿的时候，请给他打个电话，好吗？

Tā lái zhǎoguo nǐ sāncì, yě gěi nǐ liúguo sāncì tiáozi. Nǐ yǒu kòngr de shíhòu, qǐng gěi tā dǎ ge diànhuà, hǎo ma?

He came to look for you three times and left you three messages. Please call him when you have time, OK?

In the last sentence, since the first clause contains a pronoun Object（你）and the second clause a noun Object（条子）the positioning of 三次 varies accordingly. In some cases, the Object may be preposed as the topic of the sentence.

(15) 这样的表，我已经填过三遍了。别再拿了。

Zhèyàng de biǎo, wǒ yǐjīng tiánguo sānbiàn le. Bié zài ná le.

I have already filled out such forms three times. Don't get any more of them.

(16) "长城"这个电影很有意思，我还想再看一次。

"Chángchéng" zhè ge diànyǐng hěn yǒu yìsi, wǒ hái xiǎng zài kàn yícì.

The movie "The Great Wall" is really good. I want to see it again.

(17) 这样的话，你已经跟我说过几百遍了。我不想再听了。

Zhèyàng de huà, nǐ yǐjīng gēn wǒ shuōguo jǐbǎibiàn le, wǒ bù xiǎng zài tīng le.

You've said these words to me hundreds of times already. I don't want to listen to them again.

2.2 Recall that when a verb takes a time−measure complement (Lesson 31), there is a crucial difference in meaning as to whether it appears with one or two 了's. While the use of a single verb−了 sets the event in the past, the addition of the sentence−了 brings the relevance to the present or to the moment of the speech act with the implication that the action may continue beyond this time. The same distinction is observed in the action−measure complement construction. Only in the double−了 pattern does the frequency expression imply an ongoing situation. Many of the above examples demonstrate this connotative use. The following is another pair of sentences to contrast the two patterns.

(18) 我小时候得过一次肺炎，病了一个星期。

Wǒ xiǎo shíhòu déguo yícì fèiyán, bìngle yíge xīngqī.

I had pneumonia once when I was little. I was sick for a whole week.

(19) 他最近身体很不好，已经得过几次肺炎了。大夫说他应该每个星期去检查一次身体。

Tā zuìjìn shēntǐ hěn bù hǎo, yǐjīng déguo jǐcì fèiyán le. Dàifu shuō tā yīnggāi měi ge xīngqī qù jiǎnchá yícì shēntǐ.

His health is really bad now. He has already had a few bouts of pneumonia. The doctor said that he should go in for check-ups every week.

2.3 一下儿 *yíxiàr* is also an action−measure expression and is positioned, likewise, either before or after the Object depending on its status.

(20) 打他一下儿

dǎ tā yíxiàr

hit him once

(21) 打一下儿门

dǎ yíxiàr mén

knock the door once

The semantic characteristics of 下儿 is that it indicates not only number of times but, more importantly, the quickness or short duration of an action. For example, 打了我三下儿 is "hit me thrice," vs. 打了我三次 "hit me three times: three beatings." By extension, "Verb 一下儿" has become a pattern to indicate an action done in a casual manner or lasting for a very short period of time. In this regard, it functions like the repetition of a verb.

听一下儿	=	听听
tīng yíxiàr		*tīngting*
介绍一下儿	=	介绍介绍
jièshào yíxiàr		*jièshaojièshao*

(22)　对不起，我现在还不能跟你一起回家。我要先去一下儿图书馆，借一些书。你等我一下儿，好吗？

Duì bu qǐ, wǒ xiànzài hái bù néng gēn nǐ yìqǐ huí jiā. Wǒ yào xiān qù yíxiàr túshūguǎn, jiè yìxiē shū. Nǐ děng wǒ yíxiàr, hǎo ma?

Sorry, I can't go home with you right now. I have to go to the library first to check out some books. Can you wait a little bit?

(23)　我以前没听过这张唱片。我想听一下儿。

Wǒ yǐqián méi tīngguo zhè zhāng chàngpiàn. Wǒ xiǎng tīng yíxiàr.

I have never listened to this album before. I'd like to hear it.

3. The Time—Measure Complement

As described in Lesson 23, there are certain verbs that represent, to the Chinese, inherently non-continuative actions, i.e. actions that can be either done or not done, and never in the middle of being done. For example, a person is either "dead" or "not dead"; it is not possible in Chinese to say that a person "is dying." Other verbs of this non-continuative category include 来 "to come," 去 "to go," 到 "to arrive," 离开 "to leave," 下课 "to dismiss class," etc. A non-continuative or non-durative verb is of course incompatible with a durational expression marking the amount of time the action takes. It is therefore incorrect to say the following sentence, using a time—measure complement in the manner as it was introduced in Lesson 31.

(1)　*他离开我已经离开十年了。

*Tā líkāi wǒ yǐjīng líkāi shínián le.

*He has been leaving me for ten years.

However, as it is possible to tell the length of time that has passed since this non-continuative action happened, the time—measure complement construction has another pattern for non-continuative verbs. For example, the following sentence tells the time that has elapsed since his departure; the complement does not mark the duration of the departure process itself.

(2)   他离开我已经十年了。
        Tā líkāi wǒ yǐjīng shínián le.
        It's been ten years since he left me.

Structurally, this new pattern does not require the repetition of the verb to conform to the formula "Verb—Object Verb—Complement." The Object and the Complement are juxtaposed next to each other, without creating any grammatical fuss as it would with continuative verbs.

```
Continuative Verbs:
    [Verb + Object] [Verb—了 + Time] + 了
```

(3)   我们上课已经上了二十分钟了。
        Wǒmen shàng kè yǐjīng shàngle èrshifēn zhōng le.
        We have been in class for twenty minutes now.

```
Non—continuative Verbs:
    Verb + Object + Time + 了
```

(4)   我们下课已经二十分钟了。
        Wǒmen xià kè yǐjīng èrshifēn zhōng le.
        It's been twenty minutes since our class was dismissed.

The two verbal expressions 上课 and 下课 may seem similar in their compositional pattern: Verb—Object, but they actually belong to separate categories of verbs, thereby explaining why they behave differently in the time-measure construction. The following are a few more examples of this new pattern:

(5)   你来美国已经两个多月了，你去过哪些地方？
        Nǐ lái Měiguó yǐjīng liǎnggeduō yuè le, nǐ qùguo nǎ xiē dìfang?
        It's been more than two months since you came to the United States. What places have you been to?

(6)　　他们结婚十多年了，可是还没有孩子。

Tāmen jié hūn shíduōnián le, kěshì hái méiyou háizi.

They have been married for more than ten years now but they still don't have any children.

(7)　　你到这儿多久了？你给家打过电话没有？

Nǐ dào zhèr duō jiǔ le? Nǐ gěi jiā dǎguo diànhuà méiyou?

How long have you been here? Have you called home?

(8)　　我离开中国五年了，我很想家。我希望明年能回北京看看家人。

Wǒ líkāi Zhōngguó wǔnián le, wǒ hěn xiǎng jiā. Wǒ xīwàng míng-nián néng huí Běijīng kànkan jiārén.

It's been five years since I left China. I miss my family very much. I hope I can go back to Beijing next year to see my family.

Lesson 33

1. The New Situation 了

1.1 The primary function of the sentence final particle 了 is to indicate a change in situation. The particle appears frequently in ordinary conversation and may play a variety of roles in different speech situations, most of which can be tied to this basic reading. We have already examined in some detail its behavior in relation to the verbal 了. The following are some examples to illustrate its use solely as a marker of a new situation.

┌───┐
│   〔 Subject + Predicate 〕 + 了   │
└───┘

(1)　现在天气冷了。
　　　Xiànzài tiānqì lěng le.
　　　The weather is cold now.
　　　(It wasn't chilly before but now it is.)

(2)　他现在是大学生了。
　　　Tā xiànzài shì dàxuéshēng le.
　　　He is a college student now.
　　　(He wasn't in college before.)

(3)　以前他不喜欢写汉字，现在他喜欢写汉字了。
　　　Yǐqián tā bù xǐhuan xiě Hànzì, xiànzài tā xǐhuan xiě Hànzì le.
　　　He didn't like writing Chinese characters before, but now he does.

(4)　已经三点了。
　　　Yǐjīng sāndiǎn le.
　　　It's already three o'clock.
　　　(It wasn't three a while ago.)

(5)   他明天要去日本了。

Tā míngtiān yào qù Rìběn le.

He is going to Japan tomorrow.

(This is something new: a new decision on his part, or a piece of new information for me and/or you.)

While the above examples demonstrate a change from "not being the case" to "now being the case," the sentence 一了 may also signify the end of an action. When appearing with a negative verb, it indicates that a situation which was going on before has now stopped.

┌──┐
│   [Subject + Negative Predicate]   +   了   │
└──┘

(6)   他以前喜欢写汉字，现在不喜欢写汉字了。

Tā yǐqián xǐhuan xiě Hànzì, xiànzài bù xǐhuan xiě Hànzì le.

He used to like writing Chinese characters, but now he doesn't like doing it any more.

(7)   他不去了。

Tā bú qù le.

He is not going any more.

(He said he was going, but he has now changed his mind. Or, he used to go there a lot but has now stopped going.)

(8)   他不去。

Tā bú qù.

He's not going.

(9)   我没有时间了。

Wǒ méi yǒu shíjiān le.

I don't have time any more.

(10)   我没有时间。

Wǒ méi yǒu shíjiān.

I don't have time.

The function of 了 as a new situation marker is evident in (7) and (9) when the sentences are compared with their non一了 versions in (8) and (10).

1.2   One way to turn a 了一sentence into a question is to attach the interrogative particle 吗 to the very end of the sentence.

> [[Subject ＋ Predicate] ＋ 了] ＋ 吗？

(11) 天气凉快了吗？

Tiānqì liángkuai le ma?

Has the weather become cool?

(12) 他们现在开始唱歌儿了吗？

Tāmen xiànzài kāishǐ chàng gēr le ma?

Are they going to begin singing now?

Now compare the following two negative sentences, (13) and (14), and speculate which is the "no" answer to (12).

(13) 他们现在不唱歌儿了。

Tāmen xiànzài bú chàng gēr le.

They are going to stop singing now.

(14) 他们现在还没唱歌儿呢。

Tāmen xiànzài hái méi chàng gēr ne.

They haven't started singing yet.

As the English translation indicates, (13) reports the conclusion of a singing act and does not address the question in (12), an inquiry that pertains to the beginning of the performance. Phrased with the sentence 一了, (13) reports a change from "singing" to "not singing," a development that is opposite of what (12) suggests. The correct negative response to (12) is (14), which is formed with the "还没有 Verb 呢" pattern, implying that the singing has yet to begin. For the same reason, it is (14) and not (13) that negates the following statement.

(15) 他们现在唱歌儿了。

Tāmen xiànzài chàng gēr le.

They are going to sing now.

Sentence (15) marks commencement; its negative or denial is of course (14) and not (13), the latter relating the beginning of a different situation. Hence, the negative of the sentence 一了 is not "不……了" but rather the following:

> （还） ＋ 没有 Verb ＋ Object ＋ （呢）

The selection of the 还 option depends on whether there is an implied meaning of a change that may already be on its way. Recall the various ways of marking the imminent aspect of an action, which always include 了 at the end of the sentence and which form the negative by using the 还没有……呢 pattern (Lesson 29). That final particle for imminence is precisely this new situation 了, which together with the preverbal element (要, 快要 or 就要) signals the quick approach of a change. Here are a few more sentences of this new situation 了.

(16)   春天到了，天气暖和了。树上的叶子都绿了，路旁边的花儿也都开
       了。
       Chūntiān dào le, tiānqì nuǎnhuo le. Shùshang de yèzi dōu lǜ le, lù
       pángbiān de huār yě dōu kāi le.
       Spring is here now and the weather has turned warm. The leaves on
       the trees have all turned green and the flowers by the roadside have
       all blossomed.

(17)   大使馆到了，请下车。
       Dàshǐguǎn dào le, qǐng xià chē.
       Here's the embassy. You can get off here.

(18)   我以前有车，天天去城里看朋友。现在没车了，朋友也没有了。
       Wǒ yǐqián yǒu chē, tiāntiān qù chéngli kàn péngyou. Xiànzài méi
       chē le, péngyou yě méiyǒu le.
       When I had a car, I went into the city every day to see my friends.
       Now that I don't have a car, I don't have friends anymore.

(19)   外边下雨了。学校的舞会，我不去了，你自己一个人去吧。
       Wàibiān xià yǔ le. Xuéxiào de wǔhuì, wǒ bú qù le, nǐ zìjǐ yíge rén
       qù ba.
       It's raining (outside) now. I'm not going to the school dance. Why
       don't you go by yourself?

(20)   现在是冬天了，我们可以去山上滑雪了。
       Xiànzài shì dōngtiān le, wǒmen kěyǐ qù shānshang huá xuě le.
       It's winter now. (For a change,) We can go to the mountains to ski.

(21)   A: 现在十一点了，应该睡觉了吧。
          Xiànzài shíyīdiǎn le, yīnggāi shuì jiào le ba.
          It's eleven o'clock now. It's time to go to bed.
       B: 我的表现在还没到十点呢。你再复习一会儿吧。
          Wǒ de biǎo xiànzài hái méi dào shídiǎn ne. Nǐ zài fùxí yìhuǐr ba.
          It's not even ten yet according to my watch. Study a little bit
          more.

(22) A: 你来美国已经一年多了。这儿的天气你习惯了吗？

Nǐ lái Měiguó yǐjing yìniánduō le. Zhèr de tiānqì nǐ xíguàn le ma?

You've been in the States for more than a year. Are you used to the weather here now?

B: 还没有呢。我很怕冷，这儿的冬天常常刮风，有时候还下雪。真不习惯。

Hái méiyou ne. Wǒ hěn pà lěng. Zhèr de dōngtiān chángcháng guā fēng, yǒu shíhòu hái xià xuě. Zhēn bù xíguàn.

No, not yet. I don't like the cold weather. It is always windy in the winter and sometimes it even snows. It's really difficult to get accustomed to such weather.

1.3 This sentence-final 了 is of course to be distinguished from the verb-final 了, which is the marker of the perfective aspect. The following table compares the behaviors of these two homophonous forms. The sentence-final 了 will be spelled as *LE* and the suffix form as *le*.

Completion *le*	New Situation *LE*
我们开始了。 Verb−*le* + *LE*. (We have begun.)	我们开始了。 Verb + *LE*. (We now begin.)
我们吃了饭，就…… Verb−*le* Object, V... After we eat, then... (Projected)	我们吃了饭，就……了。 Verb−*le* Object, Verb... + *LE*. After we ate, then... (Completed)
我们吃(了)饭了。 Verb−(*le*) Object + *LE*. We have eaten.	我们吃饭了。 Verb Object + *LE*. We will be eating.
我们吃了三碗饭。 Verb−*le* Q/Q−Object. We ate three bowls of rice.	我们吃了三碗饭了。 Verb−*le* Q/Q−Object *LE*. We've finished three bowls of rice and are still eating.

1.3.1 The two 了's are distinguishable by the positions they occupy in a sentence: — *le* after the verb and *LE* at the end of a sentence. Because the general meaning of *LE* is to indicate a new situation, it is often used as a reference point for the perfective *le*. In fact as has been pointed out, a *le*—sentence should always be accompanied by *LE*, unless the verb is followed by a Q/Q Object. However, when the two 了's are both present, one of them may disappear. The first section in the above table illustrates this contrast between the particle *LE* and its fusion with *le*. The following sentence may mean either (a) or (b) depending on whether 了 is a fused form.

> (23)　他们出发了。
>
> 　　　Tāmen chūfā le.
>
> 　　　(a) *le* + LE: They already left.
>
> 　　　(b) LE: They are now leaving.

1.3.2 The third section in the table provides another case that may generate ambiguity as a result of truncation. The following sentence (24.a) contains both 了's, the first of which may be optionally deleted, thereby yielding (24.b). On the surface, (24.b) is identical in structure with (25), which carries only one 了.

> (24.a) 我们听了录音了。
>
> 　　　Wǒmen tīngle lùyīn LE.
>
> 　　　We've listened to the recording.
>
> (24.b) 我们听（　　）录音了。
>
> 　　　Wǒmen tīng (　) lùyīn LE.
>
> (25)　我们听录音了。
>
> 　　　Wǒmen tīng lùyīn LE.
>
> 　　　We'll now listen to the recording.

Without a given context, both sentences (24.a) and (25) are unclear as to what the intended messages are. Once properly contextualized, however, the delivery is never ambiguous.

> (26)　A: 你们昨天作什么了？
>
> 　　　　Nǐmen zuótiān zuò shénme le?
>
> 　　　　What did you do yesterday?
>
> 　　　B: 我们听录音了。
>
> 　　　　Wǒmen tīng lùyīn le.
>
> 　　　　We listened to the recording.

（27）　别说话了，我们听录音了。

Bié shuō huà le, wǒmen tīng lùyīn le.

Stop talking. We'll now listen to the recording.

1.3.3　The fourth section contrasts the two 了's in conjunction with the use of a quantifier. In Lesson 31, we noted the distinction between placing a time—measure complement in the "Verb—*le*" pattern and placing it in the "Verb—*le*...*LE*" form. The former represents a past action (他睡了三个小时: "He slept for three hours.") and the latter a continuing situation (他睡了三个小时了:"He's been sleeping for three hours.") This differentiation is observed in all cases of quantified Objects. With two 了's, a sentence like (28) always implies an ongoing action.

（28）　我们已经学了三十三课了。我们下星期学第三十四课。

Wǒmen yǐjīng xuéle sānshisānkè le. Wǒmen xià xīngqī xué dìsānshi-sìkè.

We've already finished thirty-three lessons. We'll be learning Lesson 34 next week.

In contrast, sentence (29) which relates an aborted effort in the past is marked by only one 了, the perfective *le*.

（29）　我以前学汉语的时候，用过这本书。我们学了三十三课。

Wǒ yǐqián xué Hànyǔ de shíhòu, yòngguo zhè běn shū. Wǒmen xuéle sānshisānkè.

I used this book when I studied Chinese before. We finished thirty-three lessons.

1.3.4　The second section in the above table is concerned with the sequential ordering of two actions, one finished before the other begins. The finished action is readily marked by *le*. If the entire scenario is set in the past, then *LE* is called into play to set the present moment as the reference point for the chain of past events. The following are two examples to illustrate this difference.

（30）　你的胃不好，你不应该每天晚上吃了饭就上楼去睡觉。

Nǐ de wèi bù hǎo, nǐ bù yīnggāi měi tiān wǎnshang chīle fàn jiù shàng lóu qù shuì jiào.

You have a stomach problem. You should not go upstairs and sleep immediately after you eat every night.

(31) 我昨天晚上吃了三十多个饺子就上楼去看书了。睡觉的时候，胃很不
      舒服。

Wǒ zuótiān wǎnshang chīle sānshiduōge jiǎozi jiù shàng lóu qù kàn
shū le. Shuì jiào de shíhòu, wèi hěn bù shūfu.

Last night right after I had eaten more than thirty dumplings, I
went upstairs to study. By the time I went to bed, my stomach was
churning.

1.4 Here are some examples that combine the two 了's in various situational contexts.

(32) 今天真冷，零下十度了。明天怎么样？你听天气预报了吗？

Jīntiān zhēn lěng, líng xià shídù le. Míngtiān zěnmeyàng? Nǐ tīng
tiānqì yùbào le ma?

It's really cold today — ten degrees below zero now. What about
tomorrow? Did you hear the weather forecast?

(33) 昨天下午两点，风小了，雪也停了。我和哥哥去公园走了走。我们走
      得很慢，走了一个半小时。

Zuótiān xiàwǔ liǎngdiǎn, fēng xiǎo le, xuě yě tíng le. Wǒ hé gēge qù
gōngyuán zǒule zǒu. Wǒmen zǒu de hěn màn, zǒu le yígebàn
xiǎoshí.

By two o'clock yesterday afternoon, the wind had died down and
the snow had stopped too. My brother and I went to the park for a
walk. We walked very slowly for an hour and a half.

(34) 下了一个多星期的雨了，今天又是阴天。明天会晴了吧。

Xiàle yígeduō xīngqī de yǔ le, jīntiān yòu shì yīntiān. Míngtiān huì
qíng le ba.

It's been raining for more than a week now, and today is again
overcast. Let's hope it'll be clear tomorrow.

(35) A: 时候不早了，我应该走了。

      Shíhòu bù zǎo le, wǒ yīnggāi zǒu le.

      It's getting late. I've got to go now.

      B: 再坐一会儿吧。

      Zài zuò yìhuǐr ba.

      Stay a little longer.

      A: 不，我已经坐了很久了。

      Bù, wǒ yǐjīng zuòle hěn jiǔ le.

      No, I have stayed long enough.

(36) 那首古诗，我以前看过几十遍，可是诗里的意思，我总是不太了解。
他昨天来给跟我谈了一下儿，我就懂了。

Nà shǒu gǔ shī, wǒ yǐqián kànguo jǐshibiàn, kěshì shīli de yìsi, wǒ
zǒngshì bú tài liǎojiě. Tā zuótiān lái gēn wǒ tán le yíxiàr, wǒ jiù
dǒng le.

I had read that old poem many times before but I never could figure
out its meaning. Yesterday he came and went over it with me briefly, and I understood it.

(37) A: 你已经病了十多天了。看过大夫没有？
Nǐ yǐjīng bìngle shíduōtiān le. Kànguo dàifu méiyǒu?
You've been sick for more than ten days now. Have you seen a
doctor?

B: 我今天觉得好点儿了。我想不用去看大夫了。
Wǒ jīntiān juéde hǎo diǎnr le. Wǒ xiǎng bú yòng qù kàn dàifu le.
I feel a bit better today. I don't think I need to go see a doctor.

2. The Subjectless Sentence

It is a common practice in Chinese to leave out the subject if the agent of the action
is clear from the context. For example, in answering the question "你来吗?" one
can simply say "来" and not necessarily "我来." Strictly speaking, "来" is not a
sentence without a subject; the subject is merely omitted in the surface form and
can always resurface if necessary. There are, however, some sentence types that can
truly be described as "subjectless."

(A) Sentences that describe natural phenomena.

(1) 下雨了。
Xià yǔ le.
It's raining now.

(2) 外边刮风了吗？
Wàibiān guā fēng le ma ?
Is it now windy outside?

(3) 现在还没下雪，可是天气已经很冷了。
Xiànzài hái méi xià xuě, kěshì tiānqì yǐjīng hěn lěng le.
It hasn't begun to snow but the weather is already very cold.

Most of the weather terms in Chinese are expressions without subjects. They include 下雨 *xià yǔ* "it rains," 刮风 *guā fēng* "it's windy," 下雪 *xià xuě* "it snows," and 下雾 *xià wù* "It's foggy, the fog is coming in." Please note that meteorological expressions in English are often formed with "it" as in "It's cold," or "It's hailing." There is no actual reference for "it," which is in essence a dummy element, simply to fill the subject slot in a sentence. In other words, "It's raining" is just as much without a referential subject as "下雨了" is without a grammatical subject. It is, in fact, a common practice among languages to utilize the "subjectless" paradigm to describe natural and climatic phenomena. Please compare the following two sentences:

(4)   今天早上刮风了。
      Jīntiān zǎoshang guā fēng le.
      It was windy this morning.

(5)   风刮得很大。
      Fēng guā de hěn dà.
      The wind was strong.

In sentence (4) 风 is the generic Object of 刮. Together with the verb, it forms a general meteorological expression to describe a windy weather condition. In sentence (5), however, 风 is the subject of the same verb, now referring to a specific windstorm. (Notice the use of "the" in the English translation.) All meteorological terms can behave with this split role, as shown in the following sentences.

(6)   昨天晚上下雪了，可是雪下得不很大。
      Zuótiān wǎnshang xià xuě le, kěshì xuě xià de bù hěn dà.
      It snowed last night, but it didn't snow heavily.

(7)   有雾的天，开车最好别开得太快。
      Yǒu wù de tiān, kāi chē zuì hǎo bié kāi de tài kuài.
      When it is foggy, it's best not to drive too fast.

(8)   今天雾很大，我们最好不要开车。
      Jīntiān wù hěn dà, wǒmen zuì hǎo bú yào kāi chē.
      The fog is really heavy today. We'd better not drive.

(9)   雨停了，我们可以去老张家玩儿了。
      Yǔ tíng le, wǒmen kěyǐ qù Lǎo Zhāng jiā wánr le.
      The rain has stopped. We can now go to Old Zhang's place (for fun).

(10) 已经下了几天的雨了。天气预报说什么时候会天晴？

Yǐjīng xiàle jǐtiān de yǔ le. Tiānqì yùbào shuō shénme shíhòu huì tiān qíng?

It's been raining for a few days. Did the weather forecast say when it would become clear?

(11) 明天要刮大风，天气会很冷。你要多穿点儿衣服。

Míngtiān yào guā dà fēng, tiānqì huì hěn lěng. Nǐ yào duō chuān diǎnr yīfu.

It's going to be very windy and cold tomorrow. You should put on more layers of clothing.

In the last sentence, 刮大风, lit. "blow big wind," contains the adjective 大, an intensifier that can modify all weather terms cast in the subjectless mode: 下大雨 "to rain hard," 下大雪 "to snow heavily," 下大雾 "a heavy fog." On the other hand, its antonym, 小, may appear with all terms with the exception of 刮风: 下小雨 "it rains lightly," but *刮小风 "the wind is light." The literal meaning of 刮 "to blast" excludes 小 as a possible attributive candidate, unless the combination is intended to be an oxymoron.

(B) Sentences that indicate existence, corresponding to "there is/are..." in English are cast in the subjectless mode. These sentences all begin with 有 (or 没有 for the negative), followed by the nominal in focus. The pattern may also include a verb specifying the action performed by that someone.

> 有人 ＋ Verb
> Someone/There is someone ＋ Verb

(12) 有人在唱歌儿。

Yǒu rén zài chàng gēr.

Someone is singing.

(13) 有人找你。

Yǒu rén zhǎo nǐ.

There is someone looking for you.

(14) "听，有人在敲门。" 我问："谁啊？" 可是没有人回答。

"Tīng, yǒu rén zài qiāo mén." Wǒ wèn, "Shéi a?" Kěshì méi yǒu rén huídá.

"Listen, someone is knocking at the door." I asked, "Who is there?" But no one answered.

（15） 他说没人喜欢他，所以他常常哭。

Tā shuō méi rén xǐhuan tā, suǒyǐ tā chángcháng kū.

He says no one likes him, and so he cries a lot.

（16） 昨天有人来过吗？

Zuótiān yǒu rén láiguo ma?

Did anyone come yesterday?

（17） 昨天医务所里有人来过吗？

Zuótiān yīwùsuǒli yǒu rén láiguo ma?

Did anyone come to the clinic yesterday?

Although the last two sentences begin with a time word and/or a place expression, they are basically subjectless in structure, following the pattern described above. Now compare the following two sentences:

（18） 有学生来找你了。

Yǒu xuésheng lái zhǎo nǐ le.

There are some students who have come to see you.

（19） 学生来找你了。

Xuésheng lái zhǎo nǐ le.

The students have come to see you.

It is true that 学生 is the subject of 来找你 in both sentences, but only in (19) is it the subject of the entire sentence. In (18) it also serves as the Object of 有, which carries no subject of its own. In other words, sentence (18) is a pivotal sentence, with 学生 functioning as both subject and Object at the same time. Semantically, 学生 in (19) is definite in reference: "the students," whereas the reference of 学生 in (18) is unclear: "some students." Or, to put it in a different way, 学生 represents old information in (19) but a new message in (18). In Chinese, new information is rarely placed in the subject position of a sentence. Hence, we opt for the subjectless construction when we say "There is someone/there isn't anyone..."

3. More about the Weather Terms

3.1 Grammatically, there are four groups of weather terms, including names for the seasons, that we will describe below.

(A) Nominals: 春天 *chūntiān* "spring," 夏天 *xiàtiān* "summer," 秋天 *qiūtiān* "autumn," and 冬天 *dōngtiān* "winter." These seasonal terms may serve as subjects,

Objects, modifiers, and they may also form nominal predicates without 是 .

(1)　　已经五月了，夏天快要到了。
　　　　Yǐjīng wǔyuè le, xiàtiān kuài yào dào le.
　　　　It's already May now, and summer will be here soon.

(2)　　这儿秋天的天气怎么样？
　　　　Zhèr qiūtiān de tiānqì zěnmeyàng?
　　　　What is the fall weather like here?

(3)　　我不习惯这儿的冬天。
　　　　Wǒ bù xíguàn zhèr de dōngtiān.
　　　　I am not used to the winter here.

(4)　　现在（是）春天了，花儿都开了。
　　　　Xiànzài (shì) chūntiān le, huār dōu kāi le.
　　　　It is spring now, and the flowers have come into bloom.

(B) Adjectivals: 冷 *lěng* "cold," 热 *rè* "hot," 凉快 *liángkuai* "cool," and 暖和 *nuǎnhuo* "warm."

(5)　　这儿春天很暖和，秋天不冷也不热。
　　　　Zhèr chūntiān hěn nuǎnhuo, qiūtiān bù lěng yě bú rè.
　　　　It's warm here in the spring; in the fall, it's neither cold nor hot.

(6)　　去年这个时候，天气已经很凉快了。
　　　　Qùnián zhè ge shíhòu, tiānqì yǐjīng hěn liángkuai le.
　　　　By this time last year, the weather was already quite cool.

(C) Verb－Object Expressions: 下雨 *xià yǔ*, 刮风 *guā fēng*, 下雪 *xià xuě*, and 下雾 *xià wù*. As described in Section 2, the Objects in these expressions may be turned into subjects, depending on the context.

(D) Sentential Units: 天晴 *tiān qíng* "clear sky" and 天阴 *tiān yīn* "overcast." Structurally these units consist of a subject and an adjectival predicate. 晴 and 阴 are not versatile in behavior; they appear only with 天 , thereby explaining why (9) is not acceptable.

(7)　　今天天晴。
　　　　Jīntiān tiān qíng.
　　　　The sky is clear today.

(8)   下午天阴了。

Xiàwǔ tiān yīn le.

It became overcast in the afternoon.

(9)   *今天很晴。

Jīntiān hěn qíng.

Both 天晴 and 天阴 may be reversed to create 晴天 and 阴天 , which are also very limited in usage.

(10)   昨天是晴天，今天是阴天。

Zuótiān shì qíngtiān, jīntiān shì yīntiān.

It was a sunny day yesterday, but a cloudy day today.

(E) The measure word for "degree" is 度 *dù*, as in

(11)   八十多度

bāshiduō dù

over eighty degrees

(12)   零下十五度了。

Líng xià shíwǔdù le.

It's now fifteen degrees below zero.

(13)   今天多少度？有七十度吗？

Jīntiān duōshaodù? Yǒu qīshidù ma?

What is the temperature today? Around seventy degrees?

(14)   我们这儿夏天很热，天天都一百多度。

Wǒmen zhèr xiàtiān hěn rè, tiāntiān dōu yìbǎiduōdù.

It's very hot here in the summer. Over a hundred degrees every day.

(15)   这儿最冷的时候，到过零下二十度。

Zhèr zuì lěng de shíhòu, dàoguo líng xià èrshidù.

At the coldest point, it reached twenty degrees below zero here.

3.2 The following table is a summary of the different ways to tell weather. If we want to report a change in the weather conditions, we use the particle 了 . If we wish to emphasize the continuation of a certain condition, we use the adverb 还 . If we are simply describing the situation as is, we use neither.

	Question	Positive	Negative
Descriptive	下雨吗？ 雨大吗？	下雨。 雨很大。	不下雨。 雨不大。
Change of Situation	下雨了吗？ 雨小了吗？	下雨了。 雨小了。	没下雨。 雨还没小。 雨还很大。
Continuation	还下雨吗？ 雨还很大吗？	还下雨。 雨还很大。	不下雨了。 雨不大了。

Please note that while 很 is required in an adjectival predicate（雨很大）, the intensifier is generally dropped when the adjective appears in the new situation pattern（雨大了）.

4. Markers of Adjectival Comparison

It has been noted that when an adjective is used all by itself without 很, it represents an implicit comparison. For example, the difference between the following two sentences is that while (1) is descriptive, (2) is comparative.

(1)　这个学生很好。
　　　Zhè ge xuésheng hěn hǎo.
　　　This student is good.

(2)　这个学生好。
　　　Zhè ge xuésheng hǎo.
　　　(By comparison,) This student is good.
　　　= This student is good (and that one isn't.)

While the student in (1) is unquestionably a good pupil, the one in (2) is not necessarily a model student. Only when he is put in contrast with someone else is he considered 好. Hence, an unmarked adjective carries a contrastive connotation. To explicitly mark a comparison, we can use either specific patterns which we will learn in a later lesson or degree adverbs such as the following two forms: 更 *gèng* and 最 *zuì*.

```
┌─────────────────────────────────────────┐
│              更    +    Adjective         │
│            [ even more Adjective ]        │
└─────────────────────────────────────────┘
```

```
┌─────────────────────────────────────────┐
│              最    +    Adjective         │
│            [ the most Adjective ]         │
└─────────────────────────────────────────┘
```

(3)　他个子高，他哥哥个子更高，他爸爸个子最高。

Tā gèzi gāo, tā gēge gèzi gèng gāo, tā bàba gèzi zuì gāo.

He (his build) is tall, his brother is even taller, and his father the tallest.

(4)　北京的冬天时间最长，从十二月开始，有四个多月。

Běijīng de dōngtiān shíjiān zuì cháng, cóng shí'èryuè kāishǐ, yǒu sìgeduō yuè.

The winter is the longest season in Beijing. It begins in December and lasts for more than four months.

(5)　你说上海冷，北京更冷。我在那儿住过一个冬天，我知道。

Nǐ shuō Shànghǎi lěng, Běijīng gèng lěng. Wǒ zài nàr zhùguo yíge dōngtiān, wǒ zhīdao.

You said that it was cold in Shanghai? It is even more so in Beijing. I spent a winter there. I know.

(6)　他以前上大学的时候，汉语已经说得很不错。现在在中国住了几年，应该说得更流利了吧。

Tā yǐqián shàng dàxué de shíhòu, Hànyǔ yǐjīng shuō de hěn bú cuò. Xiànzài zài Zhōngguó zhùle jǐnián, yīnggāi shuō de gèng liúlì le ba.

When he was in college, his Chinese was already quite good. Now that he has been living in China for a few years, he should be even more fluent.

(7)　你们谁开车开得最快？

Nǐmen shéi kāi chē kāi de zuì kuài?

Which one of you drives the fastest?

In the last two sentences, the degree adverbs appear in the complement construction.

5. The Construction 从⋯⋯到⋯⋯

To indicate the distance between two points, either temporally or spatially, the following pattern is used. X and Y may of course be either place words or time words.

```
从   X   到   Y
[ from X to Y ]
```

(1) 请问，从这儿到学校有多远？

Qǐng wèn, cóng zhèr dào xuéxiào yǒu duō yuǎn?

Excuse me, how far is it from here to the campus?

(2) 他从一九八五年十月到一九八九年一月在中国学习。

Tā cóng 1985 nián shíyuè dào 1989 nián yīyuè zài Zhōngguó xuéxí.

From October 1985 to January 1989, he was studying in China.

(3) 从第一课到第十三课，我们都没有语法问题。

Cóng dìyīkè dào dìshísānkè, wǒmen dōu méi yǒu yǔfǎ wèntí.

We don't have any grammar problems on Lessons 1 through 13.

(4) 你们每天从几点到几点上中文课？

Nǐmen měi tiān cóng jǐdiǎn dào jǐdiǎn shàng Zhōngwén kè?

When is your Chinese class every day? (From what hour to what hour?)

Lesson 34

1. The Continuous Aspect Marker 着

1.1 There are two types of continuous tense in English, both formed with the verb-to-be and an -ing form of the verb:

    (a) He is sitting down in the room.
    (b) He is sitting in the room.

Sentence (a) means he is in the middle of sitting down, i.e. an action is being carried out at the very moment of utterance. Sentence (b), on the other hand, indicates that the person is in the state of being seated, which is the resultative state of his having sat down. Both represent the continuation of an action, but while the former stresses the dynamic nature of the action, the latter depicts it in a static mode. In Chinese, we have two different, but related, patterns to express these two messages.

    First, the active aspect, or the progressive aspect as it is generally known in grammatical studies, is represented by the following pattern:

> 在 ＋ Verb ＋ Object

In addition, we can modify the pattern by placing 正 *zhèng* before the verb, 着 *zhe* after the verb, and/or 呢 *ne* at the end. For details, see Lesson 23.

> Subject ＋ （正）在 ＋ Verb （着） ＋ Object ＋ （呢）

Now, the static aspect, hereafter referred to as the continuous aspect, is solely represented by a post-verbal 着.

> Positive: Verb 一着 Object

Please compare the following two sentences:

(1)　　他在穿衣服呢。

Tā zài chuān yīfu ne.

He is putting on his clothes.

(2)　　他穿着一件红衬衫。

Tā chuānzhe yíjiàn hóng chènshān.

He is wearing a red shirt.

Sentence (1) tells what the person is doing while sentence (2) describes his appearance. They in fact answer different questions, one pertaining to action and the other, description.

(3)　　他在作什么呢？

Tā zài zuò shénme ne?

What is he doing?

(4)　　他穿着什么？

Tā chuānzhe shénme?

What is he wearing?

(= What does he have on?)

They may be used in different contexts, again stressing either the active mode or the descriptive aspect of the situation.

(5)　　请你等一下儿，他在穿衣服呢。

Qǐng nǐ děng yíxiàr, tā zài chuān yīfu ne.

Please wait. He is getting dressed.

(6)　　他穿着一件红衬衫，非常好看。

Tā chuānzhe yíjiàn hóng chènshān, fēicháng hǎokàn.

He is wearing a red shirt, looking extremely handsome.

More examples of this descriptive 着 :

(7)　　他在椅子上坐着。

Tā zài yǐzishang zuòzhe.

He is sitting in a chair.

(8)　　门开着。

Mén kāizhe.

The door is open.

（9）　他手里拿着书。
　　　　Tā shǒuli názhe shū.
　　　　He is holding a book in his hand.

The negative and interrogative are formed in the following manners:

```
          Negative:  没（有）　Verb －着　Object
```

（10）　窗户开着，门没（有）开着。
　　　　Chuānghu kāizhe, mén méi (you) kāizhe.
　　　　The windows are open, the door is not.

（11）　车上没（有）放着行李。
　　　　Chēshang méi (you) fàngzhe xíngli.
　　　　There is no luggage (placed) in the car.

```
      Interrogative:  Verb －着　Object　吗？
                      Verb －着　Object　没有？
```

（12）　电视开着没有？
　　　　Diànshì kāizhe méiyou?
　　　　Is the T.V. on?

（13）　她今天穿着一件黑衬衫吗？
　　　　Tā jīntiān chuānzhe yíjiàn hēi chènshān ma?
　　　　Is she wearing a black blouse today?

1.2　When to use this continuous 着？

1.2.1　We use the pattern to describe the state in which we find a person. Only certain verbs are qualified for this pattern, including 站 *zhàn* "stand," 坐 *zuò* "sit," 穿 *chuān* "wear," 拿 *ná* "hold," etc.

（14）　客人都在客厅里坐着。
　　　　Kèren dōu zài kètīngli zuòzhe.
　　　　The guests are all sitting in the living room.

(15) 照片里坐着的是王老师，站着的是她爱人。

Zhàopiànli zuòzhe de shì Wáng lǎoshī, zhànzhe de shì tā àiren.

In the picture, the one who is sitting is Teacher Wang and the one who is standing is her husband.

(16) 你手里拿着什么？

Nǐ shǒuli názhe shénme?

What are you holding in your hand?

(17) 她昨天来看我的时候，穿着一条白裙子，一件白大衣。

Tā zuótiān lái kàn wǒ de shíhou, chuānzhe yìtiáo bái qúnzi, yíjiàn bái dàyī.

She was wearing a white skirt and a white overcoat when she came to see me yesterday.

1.2.2 We use the pattern to describe the state in which we find an object. This would include cases such as a machine being on or off (T.V., radio, lights, etc.), the opening/closing of a door or a window, etc. Notice, 开 *kāi* is used for both kinds of "opening": "opening a door" and "turning on a switch."

(18) 外边有人敲门，请你去开门。

Wàibiān yǒu rén qiāo mén, qǐng nǐ qù kāi mén.

Someone is knocking on the door outside. Please go open the door.

(19) 门开着，请进来。

Mén kāizhe, qǐng jìnlái.

The door is open. Please come in.

The verb 开 is used as a simple action verb in (18) but with the continuous marker in (19). The following are more examples of this continuous 开 .

(20) 房间里没有人，为什么灯都开着？

Fángjiānli méi yǒu rén, wèishénme dēng dōu kāizhe?

There is nobody in the room. How come all the lights are on?

(21) 收音机开着，可是我没在听。我在跟他们谈话呢。

Shōuyīnjī kāizhe, kěshì wǒ méi zài tīng. Wǒ zài gēn tāmen tán huà ne.

The radio was on but I wasn't listening. I was chatting with them.

（22） 客厅里的灯和电视都没开着，他们一定不在家。

Kètīngli de dēng hé diànshì dōu méi kāizhe, tāmen yídìng bú zài jiā.

Neither the lights nor the T.V. were on in the living room. They must not be home.

1.2.3 We use the pattern to describe the state in which an object is found at a certain place. For example, if we find some pictures on a wall, we may report what we see by saying,

（23） 墙上有几张画儿。

Qiángshang yǒu jǐzhāng huàr.

There are a few pictures on the wall.

Sentence (23) is constructed with the existential 有, a pattern we learned in Lesson 15: Place ＋ 有 ＋ X. If we want to include more information in our report such as the pictures being hung on the wall rather than glued onto it, we can replace 有 with a concrete verb like 挂 *guà* "hang" and set it in the continuous or descriptive mode.

```
Place  ＋  Verb－着  ＋  X
```

（24） 墙上挂着几张画儿。

Qiángshang guàzhe jǐzhāng huàr.

There are several pictures hanging on the wall.

The verb 挂 of course represents the actual action of "hanging," having been accomplished by someone previous to the moment of observation. The emphasis of the sentence is, however, not on "hanging the pictures" but, rather, the resultative state of such an action. It does not matter who hung the pictures there, when it was done, how it was done, or why it was done; the message of the sentence is what one finds on the wall, namely, paintings hanging on it. Sentences (23) and (24) are essentially describing the same observation; by substituting 有 with a substantial action verb, (24) is more descriptive and vivid in its narrative effect. Here are more examples of this pattern to indicate existence or presence of something/someone at a location.

（25）　牌子上写着"请不要吸烟。"
Páizishang xiězhe "Qǐng bú yào xī yān."
On the signboard, it's written "No smoking!"
［signboard ＋ write ＋ "No smoking"］

（26）　信封上没写着名字。
Xìnfēngshang méi xiězhe míngzi.
There is no name written on the envelope.

（27）　楼上住着三个人。
Lóushang zhùzhe sānge rén.
There are three people living upstairs.
［upstairs ＋ live ＋ three persons］

（28）　书房不大，墙上挂着两张照片。窗户下边放着一张桌子和四把椅子。
桌子上放着一些明信片。
Shūfáng bú dà, qiángshang guàzhe liǎngzhāng zhàopiàn. Chuānghu
xiàbiān fàngzhe yìzhāng zhuōzi hé sìbǎ yǐzi. Zhuōzishang fàngzhe
yìxiē míngxìnpiàn.
The study is not big. There are two pictures hanging on the wall.
Under the window, there is a desk with four chairs. On the deak,
there are some postcards.

（29）　桌子上放着一封信，信封上只写着收信人的姓名，没有写着地址。
Zhuōzishang fàngzhe yìfēng xìn, xìnfēngshang zhǐ xiězhe shōuxìn-
rén de xìngmíng, méiyou xiězhe dìzhǐ.
On the desk there is a letter. Only the receiver's name is written on
the envelope; there is no address written on it.

1.2.4　We use the pattern to describe the state or manner in which an action is carried out. More specifically, the pattern involves two verbal units, the first of which
modifies the execution of the following action. 着 appears in the modifying segment.

［Verb －着 (Object)］$_1$　　　［Verb － (Object)］$_2$

（30）　他坐着打电话。
Tā zuòzhe dǎ diànhuà.
He is telephoning while sitting down.

（31） 古波拿着表去看大夫。

Gŭbō názhe biăo qù kàn dàifu.

Gubo went to see the doctor, holding the forms in his hand.

The main action in (30) is 打电话, and the first verb phrase 坐着 describes the physical position of the person while he is making the call. Similarly, (31) is primarily concerned with where Gubo is going. The 着－expression draws a more graphic depiction by telling us what he carries, perhaps the medical charts or the insurance forms, as he goes to the physician's office. The secondary or attributive status of the 拿 expression may be contrasted with the following sentence in which 拿, in its progressive form, functions as a full verb.

（32） 古波在拿表呢。

Gŭbō zài ná biăo ne.

Gubo is getting the forms.

The following are more examples of this pattern:

（33） 他们笑着谈话。

Tāmen xiàozhe tán huà.

They are chatting smilingly.

（34） 他拿着一张照片来找我。

Tā názhe yìzhāng zhàopiàn lái zhăo wŏ.

He came to look for me, holding a picture in his hand.

（35） 他指着椅子问我，“你为什么不坐着听音乐？”

Tā zhĭzhe yĭzi wèn wŏ, "Nĭ wèishénme bú zuòzhe tīng yīnyuè?"

Pointing to the chair, he asked me, "Why don't you listen to the music sitting down?"

（36） 老师站着讲，学生们都坐着听。

Lăoshī zhànzhe jiăng, xuéshengmen dōu zuòzhe tīng.

The teacher lectured standing up, and the students listened sitting down.

（37） 我们都在等着买票。

Wŏmen dōu zài děngzhe măi piào.

We are all waiting to buy tickets.

(38) 我不喜欢开着灯睡觉。

Wǒ bù xǐhuan kāizhe dēng shuì jiào.

I don't like to sleep with the lights on.

1.3 How do we distinguish the continuous from the progressive? Grammatically, the continuous aspect involves only a post-verbal 着, whereas the progressive aspect could involve up to four elements, including 着. Semantically, on the other hand, the continuous aspect relates more to a state whereas the progressive aspect relates more to an activity. As described above, there are four ways in which the continuous 着 can be used. The first two patterns are restricted to certain verbs and expressions, which need to be learned one by one. The last two are more productive in speech, but they are still quite idiomatic in usage. Idiomacy exists in all languages. Cf. the following sentences in which the verb for "to sit" may be used both literally and figuratively in English but not so in Chinese. As is always the case, we have to be careful with what we say and to learn from our errors.

(39) There are a few students sitting in the classroom.

教室里坐着几个学生。

Jiàoshìli zuòzhe jǐge xuésheng.

(40) You can take these chairs. They're just sitting here in the classroom.

*教室里坐着几把椅子。

*Jiàoshìli zuòzhe jǐbǎ yǐzi.

(41) 教室里放着几把椅子。

Jiàoshìli fàngzhe jǐbǎ yǐzi.

2. The Adverbial Modifier Marker 地

2.1 An adverb is a form that modifies a verb. Of the adverbs we have learned, there are adverbs of negation: 不, 没有, 别; adverbs of scope: 也, 都, 还, 只, etc.; adverbs of frequency: 再, 又, 常常, etc.; adverbs of degree: 很, 太, 最, 非常, etc.; adverbs of contingency: 一定, 就, etc. Another important category of adverbs is the manner adverbial, often formed with an adjective and marked by an adverbial ending, 地 *de*.

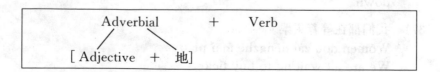

(1)   他很高兴。   (Adjective)
      Tā hěn gāoxìng.
      He is happy.

(2)   他很高兴地告诉我，"我今天不用上课。"   (Adverb)
      Tā hěn gāoxìng de gàosu wǒ, "Wǒ jīntiān bú yòng shàng kè."
      He happily told me, "I don't have to go to school today."

(3)   他说话很大声。   (Adjective)
      Tā shuō huà hěn dàshēng.
      He is very loud when he speaks.

(4)   他大声地问我，"你去不去？"   (Adverb)
      Tā dàshēng de wèn wǒ, "Nǐ qù bu qù?"
      He asked me loudly, "Are you going?"

(5)   他是一个很热情的人。   (Adjective)
      Tā shì yíge hěn rèqíng de rén.
      He is a very warm person.

(6)   他很热情地回答我的问题。   (Adverb)
      Tā hěn rèqíng de huídá wǒ de wèntí.
      He eagerly answered my question.

2.2   Notice that there are three homophonous *de's* in the Chinese language; graphically, however, they are all different.

(A) As marker of the noun modification: 的 *de*:

```
┌──────────────────────────────────────────┐
│        Modifier  ＋  的  ＋  Noun          │
└──────────────────────────────────────────┘
```

(7)   很好看   的 姑娘   (a beautiful girl)
(8)   我们   的 书   (our books)
(9)   去参观   的 同学   (the classmate who has gone on the field trip)
(10) 我送给你 的 书   (the book which I gave you)

(B) As marker of the "degree complement": 得 *de*:

```
┌──────────────────────────────────────────────┐
│   [Verb － Object] [Verb －得－ Complement]    │
└──────────────────────────────────────────────┘
```

(11)　写　汉字　写　得　　很好看　(to write characters well)

(12)　学习　　　　得　　很快　　(to learn fast)

(C) As marker of the verb modification: 地 *de*:

```
[ Adjective  —  地]   +   Verb
```

(13)　很高兴　　　地　说　　　(to speak happily)

(14)　大声　　　　地　唱　　　(to sing loudly)

(15)　注意　　　　地　听　　　(to listen attentively)

The following is a minimal set of sentences contrasting and illustrating the different usages of these three *de*'s:

(16)　他是一个很认真的学生。

　　　Tā shì yíge hěn rènzhēn de xuésheng.

　　　He is a conscientious student.　　　　　　　　(Noun Modification)

(17)　他学习课文学习得很认真。

　　　Tā xuéxí kèwén xuéxí de hěn rènzhēn.

　　　He studies his lessons conscientiously.　　　　(Verb Complement)

(18)　请认真地练习生词。

　　　Qǐng rènzhēn de liànxí shēngcí.

　　　Please practice the new words conscientiously.　(Verb Modification)

2.3　How do we distinguish the use of a complement expression as in (17) from that of an adverbial expression as in (18)? Both can be rendered with an adverbial form in English (as with "conscientiously"). One major difference is that a complement expression is most often used in connection with an action that has already taken place or that frequently occurs, whereas an adverbial modifier may refer to an action that has yet to happen. In other words, the complement expression stresses the result of an accomplished act, but the adverbial expression describes the manner in which an action is to be undertaken.

(19)　你以前学习得不很努力。

　　　Nǐ yǐqián xuéxí de bù hěn nǔlì.

　　　You didn't study diligently before.

（20） 你以后应该很努力地学习。

Nǐ yǐhòu yīnggāi hěn nǔlì de xuéxí.

From now on, you should study diligently.

（21） 昨天放假，我们玩儿得很高兴。

Zuótiān fàng jià. Wǒmen wánr de hěn gāoxìng.

Yesterday was a holiday. We played happily.

(= We had a great time.)

（22） 明天放假，我们要高高兴兴地玩儿。

Míngtiān fàng jià, wǒmen yào gāogāoxìngxìng de wánr.

Tomorrow is a holiday. We shall play happily.

(= We should have great fun.)

（23） 他说得很大声。

Tā shuō de hěn dàshēng.

He spoke loudly.

（24） 他很大声地说。

Tā hěn dàshēng de shuō.

He spoke loudly.

In the last pair of sentences, (23) reports the result of the speech act, namely, the delivery was loud and clear and we can all hear him very well. Sentence (24), however, tells us the way he speaks; it is almost like saying that the speaker makes a specific effort to raise his voice as he talks, but the sentence is not concerned with whether we can hear him or not. Again, the preverbal modifier (Adjective－地 ＋ Verb) simply describes the manner, not necessarily guaranteeing the result; but the post-verbal complement (Verb－得 ＋ Adjective) highlights the consequence. Another pair of sentences for illustration is:

（25） 她说得很快。

Tā shuō de hěn kuài.

She spoke fast.

（26） 她很快地说，……

Tā hěn kuài de shuō, ...

She quickly said, ...

While sentence (25) characterizes the speed with which she speaks (for example, 15 words in a second), (26) emphasizes the timely response she makes. Therefore, 快 in sentence (26) refers not to the consequence of the speech act but rather to the manner in which the speaker begins one.

Because of this semantic difference between the two constructions, there are certain adjectives that may not be used as adverbial modifiers. For example, when we describe someone having neatly cleaned up a room, we are in fact reporting the result of the sprucing effort. Hence, 乾净 *gānjìng* may only appear as a complement and never as an adverbial.

（27） 他整理房间整理得很乾净。

　　　　Tā zhěnglǐ fángjiān zhěnglǐ de hěn gānjìng.

　　　　He straightened out his room neatly.

（28） *他很乾净地整理房间。

　　　　Tā hěn gānjìng de zhěnglǐ fángjiān.

Another example is 累 *lèi*, a word meaning "tired," which again represents a resultative state. We may set it in a complement construction to state the consequence of hard work, but, in order to describe the laborious manner in which the work is done, we need to use another word such as 努力 .

（29） 他每天都很努力地作他的工作。

　　　　Tā měi tiān dōu hěn nǔlì de zuò tā de gōngzuò.

　　　　Everyday he attends to his work diligently.

（30） 他每天都作得非常累。

　　　　Tā měi tiān dōu zuò de fēicháng lèi.

　　　　Everyday, he feels exhausted after work.

Other adjectives that cannot be used in an adverbial position include 整齐 *zhěngqí* "neatly," 有意思 *yǒu yìsi* "interestingly," etc. There are also some adjectives that cannot occur in the complement construction. One is 着急 *zhāojí* "anxious."

（31） 他很着急地问我，……

　　　　Tā hěn zhāojí de wèn wǒ, ...

　　　　He anxiously asked me, ...

（32） *他问我问得很着急。

　　　　*Tā wèn wǒ wèn de hěn zhāojí

（33） 他很注意地听我说话。

　　　　Tā hěn zhùyì de tīng wǒ shuō huà.

　　　　He listened to me attentively as I spoke.

In the last sentence, 注意 *zhùyì* is basically a verb meaning "to pay attention to" and can never be used as a complement. Learning which adjectives may occur as adverbial modifiers and which may not is a very important and demanding task for beginning students. In addition, students must learn to distinguish the different meanings and usages for those adjectives that can appear in both complement and modification patterns.

3. The Attributive 有的

3.1 Placing the expression 有的 *yǒude* before a noun as its modifier gives the reading of "some + Noun."

(1) 有的人喝咖啡，有的人喝茶。
Yǒude rén hē kāfēi, yǒude rén hē chá.
Some drink coffee and some drink tea.

(2) 有的学生很努力，有的不努力。
Yǒude xuésheng hěn nǔlì, yǒu de bù nǔlì.
Some students are diligent, and some aren't.

Please notice that in sentence (2), the second 有的 clause does not carry a noun. As its reference is the same as that for the first unit, the noun may be optionally deleted in the repeated segment. The following are more examples:

(3) 邮局里人很多，有的坐着写信，有的等着寄东西。
Yóujúli rén hěn duō, yǒude zuòzhe xiě xìn, yǒude děngzhe jì dōngxi.
There are many people in the post office. Some are sitting, writing letters, and some are waiting to mail things.

(4) 他生病了。朋友知道了都很着急。有的给他写信，有的给他打电话，有的还买了花儿来看他。
Tā shēng bìng le. Péngyou zhīdaole dōu hěn zhāojí. Yǒude gěi tā xiě xìn, yǒu de gěi tā dǎ diànhuà, yǒude hái mǎile huār lái kàn tā.
He became ill. His friends all felt concerned when they learned about it. Some wrote to him, some telephoned, and some even bought flowers to come see him.

(5) 有的纸上写着汉字，有的纸上写着英文。
Yǒude zhǐshang xiězhe Hànzì, yǒude zhǐshang xiězhe Yīngwén.
Some sheets have Chinese characters written on them, some have English written on them.

(6)   我看过很多小说，有的非常有意思，有的写得不太好。

Wǒ kànguo hěn duō xiǎoshuō, yǒude fēicháng yǒu yìsi, yǒude xiě de bú tài hǎo.

I have read a great many novels. Some are extremely interesting, and some are not very well-written.

3.1   The "有的 (Noun)" expression can never appear after a verb in a sentence. If it is the Object that the expression modifies, then the entire unit will have to be topicalized.

(7)   有的字我还不认识。

Yǒude zì wǒ hái bú rènshi.

There are still characters that I don't know.

(8)   这些电影，我都看过。有的我很不喜欢，有的我还想再看一遍。

Zhè xiē diànyǐng, wǒ dōu kànguo. Yǒude wǒ hěn bù xǐhuan, yǒude wǒ hái xiǎng zài kàn yíbiàn.

I have seen all these movies. Some I dislike very much, but some I would like to see again.

3.2   The "有的 Noun" always refers to a segment of an entire entity or to members of a group. As such, the expressions are often used in succession, indicating variations within the total picture.

(9)   我们班的学生，有的人喜欢看京剧，有的喜欢看电影，有的喜欢听音乐。

Wǒmen bān de xuésheng, yǒude rén xǐhuan kàn Jīngjù, yǒude xǐhuan kàn diànyǐng, yǒude xǐhuan tīng yīnyuè.

Among the students in our class, some like the Beijing Opera, some like movies, and some like listening to music.

(10)   他的邮票很多，有的是中国的，有的是外国的，有的是最新的，有的是一九三几年的。

Tā de yóupiào hěn duō, yǒude shì Zhōngguó de, yǒude shì wàiguó de, yǒude shì zuì xīn de, yǒude shì yījiǔsānjǐ nián de.

He has a lot of stamps. Some are Chinese stamps, some are from foreign countries. Some are the most recent ones, and some are from the 1930s.

In this regard the following two patterns are quite different in usage, the second of which was introduced in the last lesson.

有的人 ＋ Verb

有人 ＋ Verb

Although both patterns may be translated with "some...," the first pattern points to members of a known group, while the second refers to an unspecified person or persons. Therefore, when noting that someone is singing in the park, we have to use 有人 to refer to this certain singer.

(11) 公园里有人在唱歌儿。
Gōngyuánli yǒu rén zài chàng gēr.
Someone is singing in the park.

On the other hand, if we find the park-goers engaged in different activities, some singing and others reading, we may describe the bustling scene by using 有的人.

(12) 公园里人很多，有的在唱歌儿，有的在看书。
Gōngyuánli rén hěn duō, yǒude zài chàng gēr, yǒude zài kàn shū.
There are a lot of people in the park. Some are singing songs and some are reading books.

The expression for "sometimes" is 有时候 *yǒu shíhou*, a shortened version of 有的时候 *yǒude shíhòu*, used in the same manner.

(13) 他们有（的）时候上午开会，有（的）时候下午开会。
Tāmen yǒu (de) shíhòu shàngwǔ kāi huì, yǒu (de) shíhòu xiàwǔ kāi huì.
They hold their meetings sometimes in the morning and sometimes in the afternoon.

Lesson 35

1. The Adverb 再 (continued)

The basic function of the adverb 再 *zài,* as previously described, is to indicate a projected "repeated action," a repetition that has yet to take place. An extended use of 再 is to mark the postponement of an action to a later time. In other words, it is not the physical act that is to be repeated but rather the idea of implementing it that will be entertained again. Hence, the repetition in thought or intention justifies the use of 再. For example, if I plan to visit the library in the morning（上午去图书馆）, but, because of poor weather conditions, I have to wait until the afternoon, I can use 再 to characterize this change in itinerary.

(1)   我下午再去图书馆。
Wǒ xiàwǔ zài qù túshūguǎn.
I'll go to the library in the afternoon.

Out of context, the sentence may of course mean "I'll go to the library again in the afternoon." But, given the situation as stated above, it is not a matter of actual repetition but in fact a delay in carrying out the plan. The delay may be until a specific time (like 下午 in the above sentence) or the action may occur after the conclusion of another action or event, as in the following sentences:

(2)   我吃了饭再去图书馆。
Wǒ chīle fàn zài qù túshūguǎn.
I'll go to the library after I eat.

(3)   雨停了，我再去图书馆。
Yǔ tíngle, wǒ zài qù túshūguǎn.
I won't go to the library until the rain has stopped.

(4)   我先去食堂再去图书馆。
Wǒ xiān qù shítáng zài qù túshūguǎn.
I'll go to the cafeteria first and then the library.

In sentence (4), when two actions are juxtaposed according to a temporal ordering, they are marked by 先 *xiān* and 再 *zài* respectively.

> 先 Action₁, 再 Action₂
> *now   Later*
> first...,   then ···

The following are more examples of this use of 再 :

(5)   今天没有时间了，明天再回答大家的问题吧。
        Jīntiān méi yǒu shíjiān le, míngtiān zài huídá dàjiā de wèntí ba.
        We're out of time today. I'll answer your questions tomorrow.

(6)   现在还早，我们八点再去。
        Xiànzài hái zǎo, wǒmen bādiǎn zài qù.
        It's still too early now. We'll go at eight.

(7)   我们上午先准备准备，下午再开会。
        Wǒmen shàngwǔ xiān zhǔnbeizhǔnbei, xiàwǔ zài kāi huì.
        We'll first do some preparation in the morning and then we will have the meeting in the afternoon.

(8)   *we   drink wine   eat food*
        我们先喝点儿酒再吃饭。
        Wǒmen xiān hē diǎnr jiǔ zài chī fàn.
        We'll have some wine first before the meal.

(9)   我们今天先学生词，以后有时间再谈语法的问题。
        Wǒmen jīntiān xiān xué shēngcí, yǐhòu yǒu shíjiān zài tán yǔfǎ de wèntí.
        We'll study the new words today and we'll address the grammar problems in the future when we have time.

Lesson 36

1. Degrees of Comparison

An unmarked adjective in Chinese implies a contrast or comparison between objects, as in sentence (1). Some adverbs, including those in sentences (2) to (4), may explicitly label the different degrees of comparison.

(1)　我的自行车好。（你的不好。）
　　　Wǒ de zìxíngchē hǎo. (nǐ de bù hǎo.)
　　　My bike is good. (yours isn't.)

(2)　我的自行车比较好。
　　　Wǒ de zìxíngchē bǐjiào hǎo.
　　　My bike is comparatively better.

(3)　他的自行车更好。
　　　Tā de zìxíngchē gèng hǎo.
　　　His bike is even better.

(4)　帕兰卡的自行车最好。
　　　Pàlánkǎ de zìxíngchē zuì hǎo.
　　　Palanka's bike is the best.

In none of the above examples, however, do we find an object being set side by side with another for comparison. To do so, we need to use the verb 比 *bǐ* "to compare" to construct a comparative sentence. There are different types of comparative sentences, some of which we will be examining in this lesson.

1.1 The Superior Degree: A > B

```
                    Pattern:  A 比 B X
```

This pattern means that "A is more X than B." Grammatically, X may be an adjective or a verb. The pattern may also be set in a complement construction.

1.1.1 When the X element in the formula is an adjective, the pattern requires little modification.

A 比 B Adjective

[A is more Adjective than B]

(5)   我比你高。
       Wǒ bǐ nǐ gāo.
       I am taller than you.

There are several factors to remember about this simple pattern. First, as the adjective is now set in the comparative mode, it automatically excludes the use of descriptive or intensive adverbs such as 很, 太, 非常, etc.

(6)   *我比你很高。
       *Wǒ bǐ nǐ hěn gāo.

Second, sentence (5) makes no explicit mention as to whether either one of the candidates is tall. Both can be under five feet, but as long as one is a bit taller than the other, the pattern may be utilized to characterize the comparison. If both are over six feet, we may qualify the pattern by using the adverb 更 *gèng* "even more so."

A 比 B 更 Adjective

[A is even more Adjective than B]

(7)   我比你更高。
       Wǒ bǐ nǐ gèng gāo.
       I am even taller than you.

Like its counterpart in English, the superlative 最 *zuì* "the most" never appears in this pattern.

(8)　*我比你们最高。

　　　*Wǒ bǐ nǐmen zuì gāo.

(9)　　我最高。

　　　Wǒ zuì gāo.

　　　I am the tallest.

Third, the negative is formed by placing 不 before 比, and the interrogative has only one form: 吗 .

(10)　帕兰卡比丁云高吗？

　　　Pàlánkǎ bǐ Dīng Yún gāo ma?

　　　Is Palanka taller than Ding Yun?

(11)　帕兰卡不比丁云高。

　　　Pàlánkǎ bù bǐ Dīng Yún gāo.

　　　Palanka is not taller than Ding Yun.

A few more examples:

(12)　这个问题比那个问题难。

　　　Zhè ge wèntí bǐ nà ge wèntí nán.

　　　This question is more difficult than that one.

(13)　这套历史书比那套贵，为什么你不买那套？

　　　Zhè tào lìshǐ shū bǐ nà tào guì, wèishénme nǐ bù mǎi nà tào?

　　　This set of history books is more expensive than that set. Why don't you get that set?

(14)　弟弟的脚比我们的都大，很难买鞋。

　　　Dìdi de jiǎo bǐ wǒmen de dōu dà, hěn nán mǎi xié.

　　　My younger brother has bigger feet than all of us. It's difficult for him to buy shoes.

(15)　他考试的成绩总比我好。

　　　Tā kǎoshì de chéngjì zǒng bǐ wǒ hǎo.

　　　His exam results are always better than mine.

In the last sentence, the literal translation would be "His exam results are better than *me*." While it is possible to rephrase (15) as (16) or (17), it is not necessary to repeat 考试成绩 or even to include 的 in the second unit. The comparison is made between two people in terms of their test performances. As long as this reference is clearly established in the beginning of the sentence, it is linguistically expedient and economical to omit the repetition when the subject matter recurs in the conversation.

（16） 他考试的成绩总比我考试的成绩好。

Tā kǎoshì de chéngjī zǒng bǐ wǒ kǎoshì de chéngjī hǎo.

（17） 他考试的成绩总比我的好。

Tā kǎoshì de chéngjī zǒng bǐ wǒ de hǎo.

1.1.2   As we know, certain transitive quality verbs in Chinese are descriptive in nature and, therefore, allow comparison. One such example is 喜欢 *xǐhuan* "to like, be fond of." Of the following two sentences, the first one is descriptive and the second is contrastive.

（18） 我很喜欢帕兰卡。

Wǒ hěn xǐhuan Pàlánkǎ.

I like Palanka.

（19） 我喜欢帕兰卡。

Wǒ xǐhuan Pàlánkǎ.

I like Palanka.

(Implying: "I don't like Gubo." or "You don't like Palanka.")

Transitive quality verbs may, of course, appear in a comparative construction.

> A 比 B Verb
>
> [A is more so than B in doing Verb]

（20） 我比你喜欢看电影。

Wǒ bǐ nǐ xǐhuan kàn diànyǐng.

I like movies more than you do.

（21） 你爱说话，他比你更爱说话。

Nǐ ài shuō huà, tā bǐ nǐ gèng ài shuō huà.

You love to talk. He loves to talk even more than you do.

（22） 没有人比他更了解中国的情况。

Méi yǒu rén bǐ tā gèng liǎojiě Zhōngguó de qíngkuàng.

No one understands the situation in China better than he.

(23) 帕兰卡比古波更想家吗？

Pàlánkǎ bǐ Gǔbō gèng xiǎng jiā ma?

Is Palanka more homesick than Gubo?

It is interesting to note that in cases like (22) and (23), the comparative pattern often takes 更. Unlike 高, for example, which is in fact neutral in terms of height (either tall or short) when it enters a comparative construction, a Verb–Object expression such as 想家 "homesick" carries only one reading, namely "homesick," and therefore requires 更 to highlight the comparison.

1.1.3 In a complement of degree construction, the complement itself is made up of a descriptive element, which may readily occur in a comparison scheme. The complete schema is as follows:

> A (Verb – Object) Verb –得 比 B Verb –得 Complement

As two occurrences of verb–得 appear in the sequence, one of them may be deleted, thereby producing the following two variations which are the patterns we use in speech:

> A (Verb – Object) Verb –得 比 B   Complement
> A (Verb – Object)   比 B Verb –得 Complement

(24.a) 我走得比你快。

Wǒ zǒu de bǐ nǐ kuài.

I walk faster than you.

(24.b) 我比你走得快。

Wǒ bǐ nǐ zǒu de kuài.

(25.a) 我吃饭吃得比你多。

Wǒ chī fàn chī de bǐ nǐ duō.

I eat more (rice) than you do.

(25.b) 我吃饭比你吃得多。

Wǒ chī fàn bǐ nǐ chī de duō.

As the negative marker 不 always appears before the comparative verb 比, there are again two possible negative patterns:

```
A (Verb－Object) Verb －得 不比  B              Complement
A (Verb－Object)           不比  B Verb －得 Complement
```

(26.a) 我作菜作得不比你好。

Wǒ zuò cài zuò de bù bǐ nǐ hǎo.

I don't cook better than you do.

(26.b) 我作菜不比你作得好。

Wǒ zuò cài bù bǐ nǐ zuò de hǎo.

The interrogative is formed by placing 吗 at the end of the sentence. Here are some more sentences of this complement form in comparison.

(27)   我爸爸是一个大学教授，可是他挣钱挣得不比一个售货员多。

Wǒ bàba shì yíge dàxué jiàoshòu, kěshì tā zhèng qián zhèng de bù bǐ yíge shòuhuòyuán duō.

My father is a college professor, and yet he doesn't earn any more than a sales clerk.

(28)   我说汉语说得比她好，作中国菜也比她作得好，可是她比我喜欢中国。

Wǒ shuō Hànyǔ shuō de bǐ tā hǎo, zuò Zhōngguó cài yě bǐ tā zuò de hǎo, kěshì tā bǐ wǒ xǐhuan Zhōngguó.

I speak Chinese better than she does, and I cook Chinese food better than she too. But she likes China more than I do.

(29)   我姐姐比我漂亮，念书也比我念得好，可是我挣钱比她挣得多。

Wǒ jiějie bǐ wǒ piàoliang, niàn shū yě bǐ wǒ niàn de hǎo, kěshì wǒ zhèng qián bǐ tā zhèng de duō.

My elder sister is prettier than I and she also did better in school than I. But I make more money than she does.

(30)   你昨天走得比他晚吗？为什么他比你先到家？

Nǐ zuótiān zǒu de bǐ tā wǎn ma? Wèishénme tā bǐ nǐ xiān dào jiā?

Did you leave later than he did yesterday? Why did he get home earlier than you?

1.2 The Equaling Degree: A = B: To say that "A is as X as Y," the pattern in Chinese is :

```
┌─────────────────────────────────────────────────┐
│            A  有  B  那么  X                      │
└─────────────────────────────────────────────────┘
```

As in English, B is pre-set as the standard and A is measured against B. In the positive pattern, A is approaching or equal to B in terms of the measurement or achievement of X. Variations of the pattern are given below:

```
┌─────────────────────────────────────────────────┐
│          A  有  B  那么  Adjective                │
└─────────────────────────────────────────────────┘
```

(31) 我有你那么高。
　　　Wǒ yǒu nǐ nàme gāo.
　　　I am as tall as you are.

```
┌─────────────────────────────────────────────────┐
│           A  有  B  那么  Verb                    │
└─────────────────────────────────────────────────┘
```

(32) 我有他那么喜欢看电视。
　　　Wǒ yǒu tā nàme xǐhuan kàn diànshì.
　　　I like to watch T.V. as much as he does.

```
┌─────────────────────────────────────────────────┐
│ A Verb－Object Verb－得 有 B        那么 Complement │
│ A Verb－Object          有 B Verb－得 那么 Complement │
└─────────────────────────────────────────────────┘
```

(33.a) 我看电视看得有他那么多。
　　　　Wǒ kàn diànshì kàn de yǒu tā nàme duō.
　　　　I watch T.V. as much as he does.
(33.b) 我看电视有他看得那么多。
　　　　Wǒ kàn diànshì yǒu tā kàn de nàme duō.

Several things to note about this pattern. First, the word 那么 *nàme*, literally "in that manner," may be substituted by 那样 *nàyàng*, with the same meaning. As 那么 and 那样 both contain 那 "that," it would be inappropriate to use either when the pre-set standard item, namely B in the pattern, is a first person pronoun or modified by 这 "this." To avoid such incongruity between, say, 这个 and 那样, the pattern may opt for 这么, pronounced either as *zhème* or *zème* or 这样 *zhèyàng* as replacement.

（34） 那件衬衫有这件这样厚。
　　　Nà jiàn chènshān yǒu zhè jiàn zhèyàng hòu.
　　　That shirt is as thick/heavy as this one.

（35） 弟弟快有我这么高了。
　　　Dìdi kuài yǒu wǒ zhème/zème gāo le.
　　　My younger brother will soon be as tall as I.

（36） 那儿有这儿这么热吗？
　　　Nàr yǒu zhèr zhème rè ma?
　　　Is it as hot there as here?

Second, this pattern is used more frequently in its negative and interrogative versions than its positive counterpart. In the interrogative pattern, the adverbial modifier, 那么 etc., may be omitted.

（37） 他有你（这么）会说话吗？
　　　Tā yǒu nǐ (zhème) huì shuō huà ma?
　　　Is he as articulate as you are?

（38） 妈妈，我什么时候会有你高？
　　　Māma, wǒ shénme shíhòu huì yǒu nǐ gāo?
　　　Mom, when will I be as tall as you?

（39） 你考试有他考得好吗？
　　　Nǐ kǎoshì yǒu tā kǎo de hǎo ma?
　　　Did you do as well as he did in the test?

Third, for the negative pattern, see the next section.

1.3 The Inferior Degree: A < B: The negative of the equaling degree is a case of "inferior degree," represented by the following pattern:

A 没有 B （那么） X

If A is not as X as B, then A is of course less X than, or inferior to, B.

（40） 帕兰卡没有古波（那么）忙。
　　　Pàlánkǎ méiyou Gǔbō (nàme) máng.
　　　Palanka is not as busy as Gubo.

How is sentence (40) different from the following, which is the negative of a 比一 sentence?

（41） 帕兰卡不比古波忙。
Pàlánkǎ bù bǐ Gǔbō máng.
Palanka is not busier than Gubo.

Sentence (41) carries two possible readings:

(a) Palanka may not be busier than Gubo, but she can be just as busy as he.
(b) Palanka is not busier than Gubo and, in fact, she is less busy than Gubo.

In other words, the negative of A > B implies either A = B or A < B. The first reading is a case of the "equaling degree" and the second an example of the "inferior degree." The two interpretations can be paraphrased as the following:

（42） 帕兰卡不比古波忙，但是她也有古波那么忙。
Pàlánkǎ bù bǐ Gǔbō máng, dànshì tā yě yǒu Gǔbō nàme máng.

（43） 帕兰卡不比古波忙，她也没有古波那么忙。
Pàlánkǎ bù bǐ Gǔbō máng, tā yě méiyou Gǔbō nàme máng.

More examples of the inferior degree pattern:

A 没有 B （那么） Adjective

（44） 这种自行车价钱没有那种便宜，样子也没有那种好看。你最好买那种吧。
Zhè zhǒng zìxíngchē jiàqián méiyou nà zhǒng piányi, yàngzi yě méiyou nà zhǒng hǎokàn. Nǐ zuì hǎo mǎi nà zhǒng ba.
The price of this kind of bicycle is not as cheap as that of that kind, and its style is not as nice looking either. You'd better buy that kind.

（45） 这儿天气，夏天没有你们那儿那么热，冬天也没有你们那儿那么冷。所以我们都不愿意去你们那儿工作。
Zhèr tiānqi, xiàtiān méiyou nǐmen nàr nàme rè, dōngtiān yě méiyou nǐmen nàr nàme lěng. Suǒyǐ wǒmen dōu bú yuànyì qù nǐmen nàr gōngzuò.

Compared with where you are, it is not as hot here in the summer, nor as cold in the winter. So, none of us is willing to go work there.

(46) 我比你吃得多，可是身体没有你好。
       Wǒ bǐ nǐ chī de duō, kěshì shēntǐ méiyou nǐ hǎo.
       I eat more than you do, but my health is not as good as yours.

| A   没有   B   （那么）   Verb |
---

(47) 我没有你那么会说话，也没有你那么爱说话。
       Wǒ méiyou nǐ nàme huì shuō huà, yě méiyou nǐ nàme ài shuō huà.
       I am not as articulate as you are, nor am I as talkative as you.

(48) 我没有你这么会学外语。
       Wǒ méiyou nǐ zhème huì xué wàiyǔ.
       I am not as capable as you are in learning a foreign language.

| A Verb－Object Verb－得 没有B   （那么）Complement |
| A Verb－Object   没有B Verb－得 （那么）Complement |

(49.a) 我朋友订报订得没有我多。
       Wǒ péngyou dìng bào dìng de méiyou wǒ duō.
       My friend does not subscribe to as many papers as I.
(49.b) 我朋友订报没有我订得多。
       Wǒ péngyou dìng bào méiyou wǒ dìng de duō.

(50) 我说中文没有你说得流利，也没有你说得清楚。
       Wǒ shuō Zhōngwén méiyou nǐ shuō de liúlì, yě méiyou nǐ shuō de qīngchu.
       I don't speak Chinese as fluently or as clearly as you.

(51) 我又没有他考得好，真奇怪！他不比我努力，可是他的成绩总是比我好。
       Wǒ yòu méiyou tā kǎo de hǎo, zhēn qíguài! Tā bù bǐ wǒ nǔlì, kěshì tā de chéngjī zǒngshì bǐ wǒ hǎo.
       Again I didn't test as well as he. It's really strange. He is not any more diligent than I, but his scores are always better than mine.

（52） 他比他妹妹喜欢画画儿，可是没有他妹妹画得那么好。

Tā bǐ tā mèimei xǐhuan huà huàr, kěshì méiyou tā mèimei huà de nàme hǎo.

He likes to draw more than his sister, but he doesn't draw as well.

1.4 Summary:

	Positive	Negative	Interrogative
A > B	A 比 B X A Verb—Object Verb 得比 B Complement A Verb—Object 比 B Verb 得 Complement	A 不比 B X A Verb—Object Verb 得不比 B Complement A Verb—Object 不比 B Verb 得 Complement	A 比 B X 吗？ A Verb—Object Verb 得 比 B Complement 吗？ A Verb—Object 比 B Verb 得 Complement 吗？
A = B	A 有 B 那么 X A Verb—Object Verb 得 有 B 那么 Complement A Verb—Object 有 B Verb 得 那么 Complement		A 有 B（那么）X 吗？ A Verb—Object Verb 得有 B（那么）Complement 吗？ A Verb—Object 有 B Verb 得（那么）Complement 吗？
A < B		A 没有 B（那么）X A Verb—Object Verb 得没有 B（那么）Complement A Verb—Object 没有 B Verb 得（那么）Complement	

2. Counting Money

2.1
The basic monetary units in Chinese are 块 *kuài* "dollar," 毛 *máo* "dime, ten cents," and 分 *fēn* "cent." Each of these units is grammatically a measure word, its

noun being, of course, 钱 *qián* "money." In sequential ordering, they appear like this:

		块 *kuài*	毛 *máo*	分 *fēn*	（钱 *qián*）
(1)	$ 2.00	两块			钱
(2)	$ 5.20	五块	两毛		（钱）
(3)	$32.22	三十二块	两毛	二分	（钱）
(4)	$ 0.55		五毛	五分	（钱）
(5)	$ 0.60		六毛		钱
(6)	$ 0.05			五分	钱

Compared with the American system, there is an additional monetary unit in Chinese, namely 毛 for ten cents. Twenty cents is therefore 两毛钱. As in the case of counting numbers, whenever it is possible we always go to the next higher unit. While 1,200 may be either "twelve hundred" or "a thousand and two hundred" in English, it is always 一千二百 in Chinese. Similarly, twelve cents is always 一毛二分 and never 十二分.

2.2   When the monetary figure involves only one monetary unit, 钱 *qián* usually appears at the end of the expression. If there is more than one unit, the use of 钱 becomes optional.

(7)	$3.00	三块钱
(8)	$3.30	三块三毛（钱）
(9)	$3.33	三块三毛三分（钱）

2.3   When a figure involves more than one monetary unit in successive ordering, the last unit may be unnamed in speech. If so, the noun 钱 is also omitted.

(10)	$26.37	二十六块三毛七（分）
(11)	$ 8.20	八块二（毛）
(12)	$ 0.54	五毛四（分）

2.4   二 vs. 两: In a string of numbers and units that involves "two" we always start the counting with 两 and end with 二, and use either 两 or 二 in between.

| (13) | $ 2.20 | 两块二毛 |
| (14) | $ 2.22 | 两块二毛二   or   两块两毛二 |

(15) $ 222.22   两百二十二块两毛二   or   两百二十二块二毛二

(16) $ 2,222.20   两千二百二十二块二   or   两千两百二十二块二

There is however only one way of saying the number "twenty-two," namely "二十二." Hence, in (15) and (16), a third variation is not possible.

2.5 The use of 零 *líng* "zero" in counting money:

(17) $ 100.50   一百块零五毛
(18) $ 100.05   一百块零五分
(19) $ 3.02   三块零二分
(20) $ 3.20   三块二
(21) $ 10.50   十块零五毛
(22) $ 10.05   十块零五分
(23) $ 108.05   一百零八块零五分

Each time a unit or a digit is skipped, 零 has to be inserted to indicate a gap in the figure. However, when two omissions occur in a row, as in (18) and (22), only one 零 is needed.

2.6 The word 半 *bàn* "half" may occur in a monetary expression. A dollar fifty may be either 一块五（毛（钱））or 一块半（钱）. Similarly, fifteen cents may be either 一毛五（分）or 一毛半; it is, however, never *十五分. With other measure words, 半 may stand in the initial position in a "Numeral ＋ Measure" expression, as in 半个小时 *bànge xiǎoshí* "half an hour." With monetary terms, however, 半 never occupies the initial position. Therefore, "half a dollar" is 五毛钱 and never * 半块钱. In Beijing, 半 is not preferred in counting money. Hence, 一块五 "a dollar fifty" sounds more idiomatic than 一块半.

2.7 The question word for asking for a price is 多少钱 *duōshao qián*. If we wish to be specific about the cost per item, we may put "一 ＋ Measure" either before or after the cost. The following are a few examples of the use of monetary terms in various buying and selling scenarios.

(24)   这种帽子六块两毛五一顶。您要四顶，一共二十五块钱。
        Zhè zhǒng màozi liùkuài liǎngmáo wǔ yìdǐng. Nín yào sìdǐng, yígòng èrshiwǔkuài.
        These hats are six twenty-five each. You want four of them. The total is twenty-five dollars.

(25) 这种自行车一辆多少钱？我买两辆，可以便宜一点儿吗？

Zhè zhǒng zìxíngchē yíliàng duōshaoqián? Wǒ mǎi liǎngliàng, kěyǐ piányi yìdiǎnr ma?

How much do these bicycles cost? If I buy two, can it be any cheaper?

(26) A: 十个信封一块五，五套明信片六块二。一共是七块七。您给了我七块钱，还差七毛钱。

Shíge xìnfēng yíkuài wǔ, wǔtào míngxìnpiàn liùkuài èr. Yígòng shì qīkuài qī. Nín gěile wǒ qīkuài qián, hái chà qīmáo qián.

Ten envelopes are a dollar fifty, five sets of postcards are six twenty. The total is seven seventy. You gave me seven dollars, and it is still seventy cents short.

B: 对不起，我没零钱了。我给你一块钱，好吗？

Duì bu qǐ, wǒ méi língqián le. Wǒ gěi nǐ yíkuài qián, hǎo ma?

Sorry, I don't have any small change. Will it be alright if I give you a dollar?

A: 没关系。我找您三毛钱。

Méi guānxi. Wǒ zhǎo nín sānmáo qián.

No problem. I'll give you thirty cents as your change.

(27) 一张京剧票十五块五，一张电影票也是十五块五。京剧票不比电影票贵。

Yìzhāng jīngjù piào shíwǔkuài wǔ, yìzhāng diànyǐng piào yě shì shíwǔkuài wǔ. Jīngjù piào bù bǐ diànyǐng piào guì.

Beijing Opera tickets are fifteen fifty each and movie tickets are also fifteen fifty each. Opera tickets are not any more expensive than movie tickets.

(28) 你们那儿东西太贵了。喝一杯咖啡要三块钱，坐一次车要两块五毛。有机会你来我们这儿看看，这儿东西便宜。

Nǐmen nàr dōngxi tài guì le. Hē yìbēi kāfēi yào sānkuài qián, zuò yícì chē yào liǎngkuài wǔmáo. Yǒu jīhuì nǐ lái wǒmen zhèr kànkan, zhèr dōngxi piányi.

Things are too expensive where you are. It costs three dollars to have a cup of coffee and two fifty to ride a bus. When there is a chance, you should come to our place and take a look. Things are cheaper here.

Lesson 37

1. Degrees of Comparison (continued)

1.1 The Identical Degree: A = B

1.1.1 To indicate that two things are identical, the following pattern is used:

> A 跟 B 一样
>
> A is the same as B.

The negative and the interrogative patterns are as follows:

> A 不跟 B 一样
>
> A 跟 B 不一样

> ……吗？
>
> A 跟 B 一样不一样？

The predicate is constituted of only one word: 一样 *yíyàng*. Literally meaning "the same," 一样 requires more than one entity as its subject. The subject could be in the form of "A 跟 B" or it can simply be a plural noun phrase. In the latter case, 都 needs to appear before 一样 to underscore the plurality.

(1)　这本书跟那本书一样。
　　　Zhè běn shū gēn nà běn shū yíyàng.
　　　This book and that one are the same.

(2)　这些书都一样。

Zhè xiē shū dōu yíyàng.

These books are all the same.

(3)　他们用的书都一样。

Tāmen yòng de shū dōu yíyàng.

The books they use are all the same.

(4)　古波穿了棉袄就跟中国人一样。

Gūbō chuānle mián'ǎo jiù gēn Zhōngguó rén yíyàng.

When Gubo puts on a Chinese jacket, he looks just like a Chinese.

(5)　你这件毛衣跟我上次买的那件一样，都是灰的。

Nǐ zhè jiàn máoyī gēn wǒ shàng cì mǎi de nà jiàn yíyàng, dōu shì huī de.

Your sweater is similar to the one I bought last time. They are both grey in color.

In sentence (5), the identical feature, namely the color "grey," is noted in the second clause. Another way of specifying the identical feature is to place it as the second subject immediately before the predicate. The following are some examples.

(6)　这两个碗大小厚薄都一样，但是价钱不一样。

Zhè liǎngge wǎn dàxiǎo hòubáo dōu yíyàng, dànshì jiàqián bù yíyàng.

These two bowls are the same in size and thickness, but their prices are different.

(7)　这两件雨衣一样不一样？大小长短都一样，但是颜色不一样。一件是蓝的，一件是绿的。

Zhè liǎngjiàn yǔyī yíyàng bù yíyàng? Dàxiǎo chángduǎn dōu yíyàng, dànshì yánsè bù yíyàng. Yíjiàn shì lán de, yíjiàn shì lǜ de.

Are these two raincoats the same? They are identical in size and length, but not so in color. One is blue and one is green.

(8)　我想买一辆跟你那辆颜色一样的汽车，可是我不想花太多钱。

Wǒ xiǎng mǎi yíliàng gēn nǐ nà liàng yánsè yíyàng de qìchē, kěshì wǒ bù xiǎng huā tài duō qián.

I want to buy a car that is exactly like yours in color, and yet I don't want to spend too much money on it.

(9)　有人说男人结婚以前跟结婚以后很不一样。你说呢？

Yǒu rén shuō nánrén jié hūn yǐqián gēn jié hūn yǐhòu hěn bù yíyàng. Nǐ shuō ne?

It is said that men, after marriage, are quite different from what they used to be before marriage. What do you say?

1.1.2 Another way of stating the feature or quality that the items share is to adopt the following pattern, placing the pertinent adjective after 一样.

```
         Positive：A  跟  B  一样  Adjective
```

(10)　他跟我一样忙。

Tā gēn wǒ yíyàng máng.

He is just as busy as I am.

(11)　很长时间没见了。你还跟以前一样年轻。

Hěn cháng shíjiān méi jiàn le. Nǐ hái gēn yǐqián yíyàng niánqīng.

I haven't seen you for a long time, but you still look just as young as before.

The negative and interrogative patterns are:

```
         A  不跟  B      一样  Adjective
         A    跟  B    不一样  Adjective
```

```
              ……吗？
         A  跟  B  一样不一样  Adjective?
```

(12)　你的毛衣跟我的毛衣不一样大，也不一样长。

Nǐ de máoyī gēn wǒ de máoyī bù yíyàng dà, yě bù yíyàng cháng.

Your sweater and mine are not the same size or length.

(13)　我朋友跟我不一样高，可是跟我一样胖。

Wǒ péngyou gēn wǒ bù yíyàng gāo, kěshì gēn wǒ yíyàng pàng.

My friend and I are not the same height, but he is just as plump as I am.

（14）陈先生跟陈太太年纪一样大吗？不，陈太太比陈先生大两岁。

Chén xiānsheng gēn Chén tàitai niánjì yíyàng dà ma? Bù, Chén tàitai bǐ Chén xiānsheng dà liǎngsuì.

Are Mr. and Mrs. Chen the same age? No, Mrs. Chen is older than Mr. Chen by two years.

（15）你看，这束用布作的花儿跟真花儿一样好看。

Nǐ kàn, zhè shù yòng bù zuò de huār gēn zhēn huār yíyàng hǎokàn.

Look, this bunch of flowers made of cloth looks just as pretty as real flowers.

What is the distinction between the identical degree (A 跟 B 一样 Adjective) and the equaling degree introduced in the previous lesson (A 有 B 那么 Adjective)? The two patterns are very close in meaning and may often be translated the same way in English. However, while the equaling degree implies that the B element is used as the standard against which the A element is measured, there is no such pre-set standard in the identical degree comparison. Therefore, in the following sentence, "我" is put in comparison with "他" and equals the latter insofar as height is concerned.

（16）我有他那么高。

Wǒ yǒu tā nàme gāo.

I am just as tall as he is.

On the other hand, as the identical degree is more neutral in this regard and does not specify that A or B is pre-set as the standard, the following sentence is simply saying that the two are equally tall.

（17）我跟他一样高。

Wǒ gēn tā yíyàng gāo.

He and I are the same height.

1.1.3 The identical degree construction can, again, appear with verbs and also in the complement sentence.

```
A   跟   B   一样   Verb
```

| A Verb－Object Verb－得 跟 B　　　　　一样 Complement |
| A Verb－Object　　　　　　　　跟 B Verb－得 一样 Complement |

(18)　我跟以前一样爱你。
　　　Wǒ gēn yǐqián yíyàng ài nǐ.
　　　I love you just the same as before.

(19)　他说汉语说得跟中国人一样好。
　　　Tā shuō Hànyǔ shuō de gēn Zhōngguó rén yíyàng hǎo.
　　　He speaks Chinese as well as a Chinese person.

(20)　白先生已经七十多岁了，可是他骑自行车骑得跟年轻人一样快。
　　　Bái xiānsheng yǐjīng qīshiduōsuì le, kěshì tā qí zìxíngchē qí de gēn niánqīng rén yíyàng kuài.
　　　Mr. Bai is over seventy years old, but he still rides a bike as fast as a youngster.

(21)　我的工作跟小王一样忙，可是我们挣钱挣得不一样多。
　　　Wǒ de gōngzuò gēn Xiǎo Wáng yíyàng máng, kěshì wǒmen zhèng qián zhèng de bù yíyàng duō.
　　　My work is just as busy as Little Wang's, but we don't earn the same amount of money.

1.2　All comparative expressions, including the ones introduced in the last lesson, can appear as modifiers as illustrated in the following sentences.

(22)　我要买一辆 [跟你那辆一样] 的自行车。
　　　Wǒ yào mǎi yíliàng　[gēn nǐ nà liàng yíyàng]　de zìxíngchē.
　　　I want to buy a bicycle that is identical to yours.

(23)　我要买一辆 [跟你那辆一样好] 的自行车。
　　　Wǒ yào mǎi yíliàng　[gēn nǐ nà liàng yíyàng hǎo]　de zìxíngchē.
　　　I want to buy a bicycle that is just as good as yours.

(24)　我要买一辆 [比你那辆更好] 的自行车。
　　　Wǒ yào mǎi yíliàng　[bǐ nǐ nà liàng gèng hǎo]　de zìxíngchē.
　　　I want to buy a bicycle that is even better than yours.

(25)　我要买一辆 [没有你那辆那么贵] 的自行车。
　　　Wǒ yào mǎi yíliàng　[méiyou nǐ nà liàng nàme guì]　de zìxíngchē.
　　　I want to buy a bicycle that is not as expensive as yours.

2. The Quantity Complement

2.1   In a comparison construction, the exact difference between two elements may be specified in the sentence. It usually appears in the form of a numeral—measure complement placed at the end of the predicate.

A 比 B Adjective Quantity

（1）　他比我小<u>三岁</u>。

Tā bǐ wǒ xiǎo sānsuì.

He is younger than I by three years.

（2）　这个班比那个班多<u>五个学生</u>。

Zhè ge bān bǐ nà ge bān duō wǔge xuésheng.

This class has five students more than that class.

（3）　这件衬衫比你穿的大<u>一号</u>。

Zhè jiàn chènshān bǐ nǐ chuān de dà yíhào.

This shirt is larger than the one you are wearing by one size.

（4）　航空信比平信贵<u>多少钱</u>？

Hángkōngxìn bǐ píngxìn guì duōshao qián?

How much more expensive is airmail than surface mail?

（5）　为什么你的表比我们的都快<u>三个小时</u>？你一定还在用纽约的时间。

Wèishénme nǐ de biǎo bǐ wǒmen de dōu kuài sānge xiǎoshí? Nǐ yídìng hái zài yòng Niǔyuē de shíjiān.

Why is it that your watch is three hours ahead of ours? You must be still on New York time.

2.2   The difference between two items under comparison may be phrased in impressionistic or imprecise terms. They may be very different or just slightly dissimilar. To express such a rough estimation, we may use the following patterns:

(A) "a little bit more so":

... Adjective ＋ 一点儿	or	... Adjective ＋ 一些

(6) 这张桌子比那张大一些。

Zhè zhāng zhuōzi bǐ nà zhāng dà yìxiē.

This table is a little bigger than that one.

(7) 这课比那课难一点儿。

Zhè kè bǐ nà kè nán yìdiǎnr.

This lesson is a little harder than that one.

(8) 我这件蓝衣服比你那件旧一点儿，料子也没有你的好。

Wǒ zhè jiàn lán yīfu bǐ nǐ nà jiàn jiù yìdiǎnr, liàozi yě méiyou nǐ de hǎo.

This blue garment of mine is a bit older than (that one of) yours. The material is not as good as yours either.

(B) "much more so":

...Adjective ＋ 得多	or	...Adjective ＋ 多了

(9) 他比我年轻得多。

Tā bǐ wǒ niánqīng de duō.

He is much younger than I.

(10) 真奇怪，我跟他吃得一样多，可是我比他胖多了。

Zhēn qíguài, wǒ gēn tā chī de yíyàng duō, kěshì wǒ bǐ tā pàng duō le.

It's really strange. I eat just as much as he does, but I am much fatter than he.

(11) A: 好久不见，你比以前瘦一点儿。

　　　Hǎo jiǔ bú jiàn, nǐ bǐ yǐqián shòu yìdiǎnr.

　　　Haven't seen you for a long time. You look a little bit thinner than before.

　　B: 是吗？你还跟五年以前一样年轻。

　　　Shì ma? Nǐ hái gēn wǔnián yǐqián yíyàng niánqīng.

　　　Is that right? You still look just as young as five years ago.

　　A: 哪里，我比以前老多了。

　　　Nǎli, wǒ bǐ yǐqián lǎo duō le.

　　　Not really. I look much older than before.

(12) 你定作的那件棉袄比我这件漂亮一些，料子也比我的好得多。

Nǐ dìng zuò de nà jiàn mián'ǎo bǐ wǒ zhè jiàn piàoliang yìxiē, liàozi yě bǐ wǒ de hǎo de duō.

The Chinese jacket you have had custom-made is (a little bit) prettier than mine, and the material is a lot better too.

2.3 The quantity complement may also be used in conjunction with the 得－pattern set in a comparative mode. The quantity specification follows the 得－expression, describing the difference in degree between achievements.

| | A 比 B Verb－得 Complement + Quantity |
---

(13) 我比你跑得快得多。

Wǒ bǐ nǐ pǎo de kuài de duō.

I ran much faster than you did.

(14) 你笑得比我好看一点儿。

Nǐ xiào de bǐ wǒ hǎokàn yìdiǎnr.

You smile more charmingly than I.

(15) 他考试考得比你好多了。

Tā kǎo shì kǎo de bǐ nǐ hǎo duō le.

He does much better than you on exams.

However, when 多*duō,* 少*shǎo,* 早*zǎo* and 晚*wǎn* appear in a comparison construction with a quantity complement, the word order does not follow the usual pattern. Instead of functioning as complements, these four words occur before the verb, serving as adverbial modifiers.

	A 比 B + Adverb + Verb + Quantity
	多
	少
	早
	晚
---

(16) 他比我早来十分钟。

Tā bǐ wǒ zǎo lái shífēn zhōng.

He came ten minutes earlier than I.

(17)　你先走吧，我想晚走十分钟。

Nǐ xiān zǒu ba, wǒ xiǎng wǎn zǒu shífēn zhōng.

You go first, I want to leave ten minutes later (than planned).

(18)　我比你多买了三本书。

Wǒ bǐ nǐ duō mǎile sānběn shū.

I bought three more books than you.

(19)　他比我少回答了一个问题。

Tā bǐ wǒ shǎo huídále yíge wèntí.

He answered one less question than I.

(20)　他少买了一张电影票，我不去了。

Tā shǎo mǎile yìzhāng diànyǐng piào, wǒ bú qù le.

He bought one ticket less than needed. I'm not going.

(21)　骑车比走路快，所以他比你早到了十五分钟。

Qí chē bǐ zǒu lù kuài, suǒyǐ tā bǐ nǐ zǎo dàole shíwǔfēn zhōng.

Riding a bike is faster than walking. So he arrived fifteen minutes earlier than you.

(22)　在我们学校，外国学生跟美国学生交钱交得不一样多。外国学生要比美国学生多交两千八百块钱。

Zài wǒmen xuéxiào, wàiguó xuésheng gēn Měiguó xuésheng jiāo qián jiāo de bù yíyàng duō. Wàiguó xuésheng yào bǐ Měiguó xuésheng duō jiāo liǎngqiān bābǎikuài qián.

At our school, foreign students do not pay the same amount of fees as the American students. Foreign students have to pay two thousand and eight hundred dollars more than the American students.

In (17) and (20), even though the explicit marking of 比 is lacking, the sentences nonetheless connote comparison. In (22), the verb 交 is a transitive verb and takes 钱 as its Object. When set in a comparison pattern with one of the above four adverbs, the Object must be omitted, and it may not occur in a "Verb−Object Verb−得" pattern. Hence, in the following sentence, both verbs 睡 and 起 would have to forego their regular Objects (睡觉 and 起床) in order to qualify for the use of the adverbs 晚 and 早 in a comparison pattern.

(23.a)　他每天都比我晚睡一个小时，早起一个小时。你说我每天晚上比他多睡多少个小时？

Tā měi tiān dōu bǐ wǒ wǎn shuì yíge xiǎoshí, zǎo qǐ yíge xiǎoshí. Nǐ shuō wǒ měi tiān wǎnshang bǐ tā duō shuì duōshao ge xiǎoshí?

Every day he goes to bed later than I by one hour and gets up earlier by one hour. How many more hours of sleep do you say I have over him every night?

(23.b) *他每天都比我晚睡觉一个小时，早起床一个小时，……

       *Tā měi tiān dōu bǐ wǒ wǎn shuì jiào yíge xiǎoshí, zǎo qǐ chuáng yíge xiǎoshí...

3. Compounds of Antonyms

When adjectives of opposite qualities are juxtaposed, the combinations form new compounds that represent general concepts of measurement.

(1)   大 dà   +   小 xiǎo   →   大小 dàxiǎo
      "big"   "small"   "size"

(2)   快 kuài   +   慢 màn   →   快慢 kuàimàn
      "fast"   "slow"   "speed"

(3)   高 gāo   +   矮 ǎi   →   高矮 gāo'ǎi
      "tall"   "short"   "height, stature"

(4)   长 cháng   +   短 duǎn   →   长短 chángduǎn
      "long"   "short"   "length"

(5)   厚 hòu   +   薄 báo   →   厚薄 hòubáo
      "thick"   "thin"   "thickness (of surfaces)"

(6)   肥 féi   +   瘦 shòu   →   肥瘦 féishòu
      "fat"   "thin"   "girth, size of clothes"

(7)   这件蓝的长短合适，可是太瘦了；这件灰的肥瘦合适，可是太长了。这件长短肥瘦都合适，可是我不喜欢这个颜色。

      Zhè jiàn lán de chángduǎn héshì, kěshì tài shòu le; zhè jiàn huī de féishòu héshì, kěshì tài cháng le. Zhè jiàn chángduǎn féishòu dōu héshì, kěshì wǒ bù xǐhuan zhè ge yánsè.

      This blue one is right in length, but it is too tight. This grey one is right in size, but it is too long. This one is right in both size and length, but I don't like the color.

Antonymous compounding is not a process to be applied to any pair of opposite words at will. The products are idiomatic in nature and need to be learned one by one. For example, although 胖 *pàng* "fat" and 瘦 *shòu* "thin" are direct opposites of each other, they do not pair together naturally to form a new compound *胖瘦

meaning "weight." Another case is 大小 which only means "size" even though both 大 and 小 may be individually used to refer to age. 多少 *duōshao* is used mostly as an interrogative word meaning "how many? how much?" There are many other examples of antonymous compounds, which are not necessarily limited to adjectives. Even verbs may be combined in like manner. For instance, 买 *mǎi* "to buy" ＋ 卖 *mài* "to sell" →买卖 *mǎimai* "business, trade."

4. The Conjunctive Expression 要不

The conjunctive expression 要不 *yào bù*, literally meaning "if not," is often used to join two sentences together, marking a semantic relationship of "if not A, then B."

(1)　应该写信了。要不，妈妈会很不放心。
　　　Yīnggāi xiě xìn le; yào bù, māma huì hěn bú fàngxīn.
　　　It's time to write home. Or else, mom will get worried.

(2)　可以打电话去问他。要不，你就自己去找他。
　　　Kěyǐ dǎ diànhuà qù wèn tā. Yào bù, nǐ jiù zìjǐ qù zhǎo tā.
　　　You can call him on the phone. Or else, you can go and ask him (in person).

(3)　这双袜子一定是蓝的。要不，就是黑的。
　　　Zhè shuāng wàzi yídìng shì lán de. Yào bù, jiù shì hēi de.
　　　This pair of socks must be blue. If not, they are black.

(4)　你下午三点一定要到这儿。要不，我就走了。
　　　Nǐ xiàwǔ sāndiǎn yídìng yào dào zhèr. Yào bù, wǒ jiù zǒu le.
　　　You have to be here by three in the afternoon. If not, I'll be gone.

(5)　你一定是不爱我了。要不，你怎么忘了我的生日？
　　　Nǐ yídìng shì bú ài wǒ le. Yào bù, nǐ zěnme wàngle wǒ de shēngri?
　　　You must have stopped loving me. Or else, how could you have forgotten my birthday?

(6)　对不起，您要的袜子，现在没有了。您下星期再来看看，好吗？要不，您先打个电话来问问。
　　　Duì bu qǐ, nín yào de wàzi, xiànzài méi yǒu le. Nín xià xīngqī zài lái kànkan, hǎo ma? Yào bù, nín xiān dǎ ge diànhuà lái wènwen.
　　　Sorry, the socks you want — we don't have them any more (we are out of them). Would you want to come back next week and see? Or, you can call first to ask about it.

5. More on the Use of 还是

As described in Lesson 19, 还是 *háishì* may serve as an alternative question marker, indicating a selection between two or more choices. When used in a statement, 还是 underscores a selected choice or a preferable suggestion in the sense that "it'd be better to..."

(1)　今天太冷，你还是多穿点儿衣服吧。

Jīntiān tài lěng, nǐ háishì duō chuān diǎnr yīfu ba.

It is very cold today. You'd better put on more clothes.

(2)　还是你来吧。我在家等你。

Háishì nǐ lái ba. Wǒ zài jiā děng nǐ.

It'd be better if you come. I'll wait for you at home.

(3)　定作比买合适多了，还是定作吧。

Dìngzuò bǐ mǎi héshì duō le, háishì dìngzuò ba.

One that is made to order will fit much better than one that is bought. You'd better have one made.

(4)　A: 你想给你儿子买一辆什么车？买日本车还是买美国车？

Nǐ xiǎng gěi nǐ érzǐ mǎi yíliàng shénme chē? Mǎi Rìběn chē háishì mǎi Měiguó chē?

What kind of a car do you want to get for your son? Do you want to buy a Japanese car or an American car?

B: 给年轻人买车，还是别买太好的车。

Gěi niánqīng rén mǎi chē, háishì bié mǎi tài hǎo de chē.

Buying a car for a youngster — it's better not to buy too good a car.

(5)　我看了很久，我想还是买红的好。我穿红的比较好看。

Wǒ kànle hěn jiǔ, wǒ xiǎng háishì mǎi hóng de hǎo. Wǒ chuān hóng de bǐjiào hǎokàn.

I've looked for a long time. I think I'd better buy the red one. I look better in red.

There are two cases of 还是 in sentence (4), the first marking a choice type question and the second a decision that is made after some deliberation. There is still another use of 还是, which is to indicate "still the case," as in the following sentence.

(6) 我们已经分开很久了，但是我还是跟以前一样爱你。

Wǒmen yǐjīng fēnkāi hěn jiǔ le, dànshì wǒ háishì gēn yǐqián yíyàng ài nǐ.

We've been separated for a long time but I still love you the same way as before.

The following sentence illustrates a combination of all three uses of 还是.

(7) 我上哪个学校好呢？上 Berkeley 还是上 Harvard？我很想上 Harvard，因为这个学校比 Berkeley 更有名。我爸爸说 Berkeley 比较便宜，还是上 Berkeley 吧。我想了很久，我还是要去 Harvard。我的女朋友在 Boston 工作。

Wǒ shàng nǎ ge xuéxiào hǎo ne? Shàng Berkeley háishì shàng Harvard? Wǒ hěn xiǎng shàng Harvard, yīnwèi zhè ge xuéxiào bǐ Berkeley gèng yǒumíng. Wǒ bàba shuō Berkeley bǐjiào piányi, háishì shàng Berkeley ba. Wǒ xiǎngle hěn jiǔ, wǒ háishì yào qù Harvard. Wǒ de nǚ péngyou zài Boston gōngzuò.

Which school should I go to? Berkeley or Harvard? I really want to go to Harvard, because it is even more famous than Berkeley. My father said that since Berkeley is cheaper, it'd be better to go there. I've thought about it for a long time, and I still insist on going to Harvard. My girl friend works in Boston.

6. The Sequential Use of 上 and 下

6.1 We have learned in an earlier lesson that 上 *shàng* and 下 *xià* may be used to indicate "last" and "next," as in 上个月 *shàng ge yuè* "last month" and 下个星期 *xià ge xīngqī* "next week." This sequential use of 上 and 下 is quite common in the language and has a widespread application to many nouns. And, as such, both behave like demonstratives and have to be followed by a measure word.

(1)	上次	shàng cì	"last time"
(2)	上一课	shàng yíkè	"last lesson"
(3)	上一封信	shàng yìfēng xìn	"previous letter"
(4)	下次	xià cì	"next time"
(5)	下一个学期	xià yíge xuéqī	"next semester"
(6)	下半年	xià bànnián	"the second half year"

(7) 我上次在这儿看过。

Wǒ shàng cì zài zhèr kànguo.

I saw it here last time.

(8) 这一课难，下一课比这课更难。

Zhè yíkè nán, xià yíkè bǐ zhè kè gèng nán.

This lesson is difficult——the next one will be even more difficult.

(9) 他上一封信里说些什么？

Tā shàng yìfēng xìnli shuō xiē shénme?

What did he say in his last letter?

(10) 这是古波，下一个是帕兰卡，再下一个是丁云。

Zhè shì Gǔbō, xià yíge shì Pàlánkǎ, zài xià yíge shì Dīng Yún.

This is Gubo, the next one is Palanka, and the one after that is Ding Yun.

The following are a few facts to note about this use. First, the number that appears in this pattern is generally "one." The numeral 一 may be omitted in some cases, as in 下一次 *xià yícì*: 下次 *xià cì* "next time." Also, the measure word in the pattern may become omissible with certain calendar terms: 上个星期五 *shàng ge xīngqīwǔ*: 上星期五 *shàng xīngqīwǔ* "Friday of last week," 下个月 *xià ge yuè*: 下月 *xià yuè* "next month." Finally, when 半 *bàn* "half" appears in the pattern, as in 下半年, the expression usually refers to the second half of a cycle, hence "the second half of the year (July to December)" and not "the next half year (which could be any six months)."

6.2 上 and 下 are spatial terms, which are here borrowed for temporal usage. The extension from spatial to temporal references is a common linguistic phenomenon that can be found in many languages. Cf. the use of "before" in English: "He is standing before you," and "What happened before..." The extension is achieved of course through metaphorical association. 上 points to what is above us and 下 what lies under us. As humans are able to see what flies in the sky and not what hides beneath the ground, the spatial dichotomy takes on a cognitive connotation of what is known and unknown, an abstraction that may be transferred and applied to the temporal realm. As the past constitutes what we have experienced and the future represents the unknown, the 上/下 distinction readily takes charge of this temporal differentiation: 上 referring to the past and 下 the future. A similar case of this metaphorical extension is the pair 前/后, as in 以前 *yǐqián* "before, ago" and 以后 *yǐhòu* "afterwards, after." 前 and 后 mark the same distinction in perceptibility: what is in front of us is what we can clearly see, therefore representing the "known" or the past, whereas what is physically behind us, 后, is what we are unable to see and, hence, the unknown future. Though not without exceptions, the Chinese language is in general quite consistent with this metaphorical application. For example, predecessors and successors may be referred to as 前人 *qiánrén* and 后人 *hòurén,* or 上一代 *shàng yídài* "the previous generation" and 下一代 *xià yídài* "the next generation." English does not fare as neatly in this regard. As noted, the word "before" carries the same spatial and temporal readings as 前: "front" and "past." However, there is another English word, "ahead," that denotes "what is in the front" and connotes "what is coming in the *future*." In other words, the same spatial concept of frontness may be diversely associated with the past (as in "before") and the future (as in "ahead"), an anomaly that has yet to be further studied. Language is a highly complex form of conceptual creativity. It is replete with metaphors, which by their very associative nature, make the learning an interesting and thought-provoking experience. Yet, at the same time, as the association is often culture-bound and idiosyncratic in usage, beginners have to make a special effort to remember how to make the correct link between images and ideas.

---

1. The Resultative Complements

1.1   The Chinese language employs different types of complement constructions; thus far, we have learned three:

> Complement of Degree (Verb Object   Verb 得 Complement): Lesson 25
> Complement of Time (Verb Object   Verb Time): Lesson 31
> Complement of Quantity (A 比 B Adjective Quantity) : Lesson 37

In this lesson, we shall learn a fourth kind: a complement that indicates the resultative aspect of an action. Hence, the term "Resultative Complement."

In English, when we say "kill," we are describing not only an action such as picking up a gun and shooting, we are also reporting the result of this action, namely, the victim's death. In other words, the word "kill" contains two semantic units: the action and the result, and the resultative aspect of the action (i.e. "death") is built into the word. Or, let us look at the line "looking without seeing, listening without hearing." "Look" or "listen" designates an intentional sensory action, directing the eyes or ears to gain awareness of something, but the verb itself does not tell about the success in perception. On the other hand, "see" and "hear" represent not only the sensory actions but also the perception aspect as well. Thus, "see" and "hear" are semantically more composite in nature than "look" and "listen." The former pair denotes "action" whereas the latter pair "action" plus "result." In Chinese, most verbs are like "look" in English; they don't necessarily tell us the results. To do so, we need to introduce another word that explicitly states the consequence. That resultative word, which could be either a verb or an adjective, is placed immediately after the action verb and functions as its complement.

> Verb   +   Resultative Complement

(1)   看见
(2)   听见

看 *kàn* "to look" and 见 *jiàn* "to perceive" combine to stand for the concept of "looking and seeing." Likewise, 听 *tīng* "to listen" combines with 见 *jiàn* to form the compound word 听见 *tīngjiàn* meaning "to hear." In this regard, Chinese is more analytical than English, each semantic unit being represented by one single word in word formation. Here are a few more examples:

Verb + Resultative Complement

(3)   听 tīng   + 懂 dǒng   → 听懂 tīngdǒng
      "listen"   "understand"   "comprehend through listening"
(4)   说 shuō   + 清楚 qīngchu   → 说清楚 shuōqīngchu
      "speak"   "clearly"   "speak clearly"
(5)   回答 huídá   + 对 duì   → 回答对 huídáduì
      "answer"   "correctly"   "answer correctly"
(6)   学 xué   + 会 huì   → 学会 xuéhuì
      "learn"   "know how to"   "master through learning"
(7)   拿 ná   + 住 zhù   → 拿住 názhù
      "hold"   "stay"   "hold firmly"

1.2 A verb—resultative complement combination (V—RC) is a compound word functioning as one verbal unit. Therefore, the perfective aspect marker 了 comes after the entire unit. So does the Object.

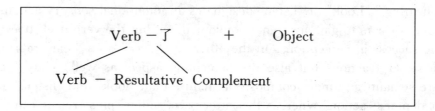

(8)   我写完了一封信。
       Wǒ xiěwánle yìfēng xìn.
       I finished writing a letter.

(9)   我听懂了他的话。
       Wǒ tīngdǒngle tā de huà.
       I (heard and) understood his words.

（10） 我学会了骑自行车了。
Wǒ xuéhuìle qí zìxíngchē le.
I have learned how to ride a bike.

（11） 张老师总是叫错我的名字，真气人。
Zhāng lǎoshī zǒngshì jiàocuò wǒ de míngzi, zhēn qì rén.
Teacher Zhang always calls me by the wrong name. That really makes me mad.

（12） 下车的时候，别忘了带好自己的东西。
Xià chē de shíhòu, bié wàngle dàihǎo zìjǐ de dōngxi.
When you get off, don't forget to take all your things with you.

The V－RC unit may appear with the aspectual 了 as well as the sentence 了, and the conditions are the same as those with a regular verb. Certain V－RC combinations prefer the final 了, as illustrated in the following sentence:

（13） 我昨天在学校看见王老师了。
Wǒ zuótiān zài xuéxiào kànjiàn Wáng lǎoshī le.
I saw Teacher Wang in school yesterday.

1.3 The negative of a V－RC unit is formed with 没(有). As always the aspectual 了 is automatically dropped in this pattern.

没（有） Verb － Resultative Complement ＋ Object

（14） 我没有看见他。
Wǒ méiyou kànjiàn tā.
I didn't see him.

（15） 他还没学会开车。
Tā hái méi xuéhuì kāi chē.
He still hasn't mastered (through learning) driving.

（16） 我看错问题了，所以我没有回答对。
Wǒ kàncuò wèntí le, suǒyǐ wǒ méiyou huídáduì.
I misunderstood the question, therefore I answered wrongly.

(17) 他说中文说得很流利，可是故事没讲清楚，所以我们都没听懂。

Tā shuō Zhōngwén shuō de hěn liúlì, kěshì gùshì méi jiǎngqīngchu, suǒyǐ wǒmen dōu méi tīngdǒng.

He speaks Chinese fluently, but he didn't tell the story clearly. So, none of us understood.

1.4   There are two interrogative patterns for the V—RC compound:

Verb — Resultative Complement … + 吗？
Verb — Resultative Complement … + 没有？

(18) 请问，我的表修好了没有？

Qǐng wèn, wǒ de biǎo xiūhǎole méiyou?

Excuse me, has my watch been fixed?

(19) A: 你看见丁大夫了吗？

Nǐ kànjiàn Dīng dàifu le ma?

Have you seen Dr. Ding?

B: 看见了。他就在那儿。

Kànjiàn le. Tā jiù zài nàr.

Yes, I have. He is right there.

(20) A: 听，有人在外边唱歌儿。你听见了吗？

Tīng, yǒu rén zài wàibiān chàng gēr. Nǐ tīngjiànle ma?

Listen, someone is singing outside. Did you hear it?

B: 没有，我没听见，我在听收音机呢。

Méiyou, wǒ méi tīngjiàn, wǒ zài tīng shōuyīnjī ne.

No, I didn't hear it. I was listening to the radio.

1.5   The resultative complement could, of course, represent a result that is deliberately sought or something unintentional or accidental. One can make a conscious act of looking and then see something as a result, or one may just happen to sight something without making any deliberate attempt. In either case, 看见 would be the verbal compound to use. But, in the case of 说错 *shuōcuò* "speak-wrong: to make a mistake in speaking, to say incorrectly") one doesn't usually err intentionally, unless the slip is to achieve a certain purpose. We should also be aware that English often differs from Chinese in the linguistic format it chooses to express the idea of "doing something wrong." While Chinese prefers the complement construction and includes 错 in the verbal unit, English generally opts for the adjectival modification and places the word "wrong" before the pertinent Object. The following sentences illustrate this contrast in linguistic operation.

(21)　你拿错帽子了。这顶帽子不是我的，是别人的。

Nǐ nácuò màozi le. Zhè dǐng màozi bú shì wǒ de, shì bié rén de.

You took the wrong hat. This hat is not mine, it belongs to someone else.

(22)　A: 你怎么来得这么晚？

Nǐ zěnme lái de zhème wǎn?

How come you got here so late?

B: 我坐错车了。

Wǒ zuòcuò chē le.

I took the wrong bus.

1.6　The resultative complement construction is a very useful pattern in Chinese. Certain words are frequently used as resultative complement and can be combined with almost all verbs. One such example is 完 *wán* "to finish."

```
┌──────────────────────────────────────────────────┐
│        Verb一完：to finish doing the action         │
└──────────────────────────────────────────────────┘
```

(23)　看完

kànwán

"finish looking"

(24)　吃完

chīwán

"finish eating"

(25)　跑完

pǎowán

"finish running"

(26)　这个电影真没意思。我没看完就离开了。

Zhè ge diànyǐng zhēn méi yìsi. Wǒ méi kànwán jiù líkāi le.

This movie is truly boring. I left without finishing seeing the entire show.

（27） 你说完了没有？

Nǐ shuōwánle méiyou?

Are you finished (speaking, yet)?

On the other hand, there are some resultative complement forms that appear only with certain verbs. For example, 见 is restricted to verbs like 看 and 听：看见，听见. Another non-versatile case is 会 *huì*, a verb meaning "to know how to; to master." As a resultative complement, it appears with only one verb: 学 *xué* "to learn."

（28） 我学会游泳了。

Wǒ xuéhuì yóu yǒng le.

I have learned how to swim.

（29） A: 你学过骑自行车吗？

Nǐ xuéguo qí zìxíngchē ma?

Did you ever learn how to ride a bike?

B: 学过，可是没学会。

Xuéguo, kěshì méi xuéhuì.

Yes, I did, but I didn't succeed.

Some resultative compounds may mean different things in different contexts. One example is 好, the basic meaning of which is "good."

In a verb－resultative complement combination, 好 may refer to the performance result or it may refer to the completion of a job.

Verb－好: to achieve adequate results

（30） 学好中文

xuéhǎo Zhōngwén

to learn Chinese well, to master Chinese

（31） 坐好

zuòhǎo

sit well, sit properly

（32） 放好杂志

fànghǎo zázhì

put the magazine in its proper place

(33) 拿好你的行李快跑，公共汽车就要开了。
      Náhǎo nǐ de xíngli kuài pǎo, gōnggòng qìchē jiù yào kāi le.
      Take along your luggage and run fast. The bus is about to leave.

> Verb—好: to achieve completion

---

(34) 画好一幅画儿
      huàhǎo yífù huàr
      finish drawing a picture

(35) 作好
      zuòhǎo
      finish doing

(36) 先穿好袜子再去。
      Xiān chuānhǎo wàzi zài qù.
      First finish putting on the socks and then go.

(37) 我办护照已经办了一个多星期了，不知道什么时候能办好。
      Wǒ bàn hùzhào yǐjīng bànle yígeduō xīngqī le, bù zhīdao shénme
      shíhòu néng bànhǎo.
      It's been already more than a week since I applied for a passport. I
      don't know when it will be ready.

In its second meaning, verb—好 seems interchangeable with verb—完. However, as satisfactory completion often pertains to not only the finishing of a job but also the quality of the performance, there are cases where verb—好 cannot be replaced by verb—完. When we call the garage to ask if our car is repaired and ready for pickup, we are concerned not only with whether the job is done but also how well it is done. In this case, 修好 conveniently incorporates both concerns into one linguistic expression, as in the following sentence.

(38) 请问，我的车修好了没有？
      Qǐng wèn, wǒ de chē xiūhǎole méiyou?
      Excuse me, has my car been fixed?

1.7 Differences between the Complement of Result and the Complement of Degree: As you may recall, a complement of degree describes the manner in which an action is carried out. And, as such, the pattern may be used to report the result, or what is being observed, of an action. Then, how does this complement of degree differ from the verb 一 resultative complement, which by definition pertains to "result"?

Structurally, the two types of complements are quite different in composition. A complement of degree can be a word, a phrase, or even a whole sentence, as in sentences (39) to (42), whereas a resultative complement is usually only one word, as in (43). In fact, a resultative compound forms a closely-bound unit that does not usually allow the intrusion of another word such as 很，又，etc.

(39) 这些字，我写得很快。
     Zhè xiē zì, wǒ xiě de hěn kuài.
     I wrote these characters fast.

(40) 这些字，我写得又快又好。
     Zhè xiē zì, wǒ xiě de yòu kuài yòu hǎo.
     I wrote these characters both fast and beautifully.

(41) 这些字，我写得比谁都快。
     Zhè xiē zì, wǒ xiě de bǐ shéi dōu kuài.
     I wrote these characters faster than anyone else.

(42) 这些字，我写得每个人都说很漂亮。
     Zhè xiē zì, wǒ xiě de měi ge rén dōu shuō hěn piàoliang.
     I wrote these characters (in such a way) that everyone says they are beautiful.

(43) 这些字，我写错了。
     Zhè xiē zì, wǒ xiěcuòle.
     I wrote these characters wrong.

In sentence (43), the resultative complement unit 写错 constitutes a compound verb and behaves like a single linguistic unit here taking the aspectual marker 了 at the end. Some of these resultative compounds, such as 看见 and 听见, are listed in dictionaries as separate entries.

Semantically, the complement of result represents the absolute result of an action or event whereas the complement of degree describes the consequence often in relative terms. As its name indicates, a complement of degree allows various degrees of comparison in the description: 作得很好 "to have done something very well": 作得非常好 "to have done something extremely well": 作得不太好 to have done something not too well," etc. But, a resultative complement tells an absolute state: either done or not done (作好了 or 没作好) and nothing in between. Please compare the following pair of sentences:

(44) 我的车修好了，现在能开了。

Wǒ de chē xiūhǎole, xiànzài néng kāi le.

My car has been fixed. I can drive it now.

(45) 我的车修得不太好，现在能开，但是不能开得太快。

Wǒ de chē xiū de bú tài hǎo, xiànzài néng kāi, dànshì bù néng kāi de tài kuài.

My car was not fixed too well. I can drive it now, but not too fast.

In the first sentence, the compound 修好 reports the successful completion of a car repair job: the car is now restored to its working condition. As there are different degrees of success, the second sentence is a qualified statement, assessing the success of the auto service. Another pair of contrasts is sentences (46) and (47).

(46) 听清楚。

Tīng qīngchu.

(47) 听得很清楚。

Tīng de hěn qīngchu.

As (46) is a case of the complement of result, the emphasis is on the consequence of the action: "to listen and understand clearly." It may be used as a command or a warning: "You'd better hear every word I say." Or, when cast in the perfective mode, 我听清楚了, it means "full comprehension of what is being said, down to the last detail." (47), on the other hand, describes a different scenario. For instance, someone may have put on a hearing aid and is able to hear clearly. Remember, there are always different degrees of clarity as one turns the volume up or down. Also, acoustically, the aid could be working fine, enabling the user to hear every sound, but it does not necessarily guarantee that the hearer will understand every word. In other words, the emphasis in (47) is more on audible clarity than informational comprehension. There are certain words that may function only as resultative complements and never as complements of degree. 完 is one such example: a job is either "finished" or "incomplete."

(48) 我吃完饭了。

Wǒ chīwán fàn le.

I finished eating.

(49)   *我吃饭吃得很完。

       *Wǒ chī fàn chī de hěn wán.

Be assured, it is not an easy matter for a beginning student to decide when a word can function as what kind of a complement. It is necessary to become familiar with the construction by remembering the individual items one by one and using the more productive words as often as possible. You will make mistakes, but only through erring "说错" will you be able to learn "学会" the pattern.

2. The Adverb 刚

The adverb 刚 *gāng* "just, a short while ago" sets the verb it modifies in the immediate past.

(1)   他刚走。

       Tā gāng zǒu.

       He just left.

(2)   我们刚吃完晚饭，现在不想再吃。

       Wǒmen gāng chīwán wǎnfàn, xiànzài bù xiǎng zài chī.

       We just finished our dinner; we don't want to eat again.

(3)   她刚来几天。

       Tā gāng lái jǐtiān.

       She has been here for just a few days.

(4)   我刚上大学没多久。

       Wǒ gāng shàng dàxué méi duō jiǔ.

       It hasn't been long since I began my studies at college.

(5)   刚上车的人，请买票。

       Gāng shàng chē de rén, qǐng mǎi piào.

       Those who have just boarded, please buy tickets.

Please note that as a monosyllabic adverb 刚 never appears before the subject. Also, it generally does not co-occur with 了.

(6)   *他刚走了。

       *Tā gāng zǒu le.

3. The Directional 往

The basic meaning of 往 is "moving towards" or "in the direction of." It may be used as a verb or as a preposition, and is pronounced with a different tone as it assumes a different status.

3.1 As a preposition, 往 is pronounced in the fourth tone: *wàng*. The prepositional unit always comes before a verb.

$$[往 \ + \ \text{direction/location}] \ + \ \text{Verb}$$

(1)　往东跑
　　　wàng dōng pǎo
　　　to run eastward

(2)　往城里开
　　　wàng chéngli kāi
　　　to drive toward the town

(3)　你出了门，先往南走，过了咖啡馆，再往西拐，一会儿就到了。
　　　Nǐ chūle mén, xiān wàng nán zǒu, guòle kāfēiguǎn, zài wàng xī
　　　guǎi, yìhuǐr jiù dào le.
　　　When you leave, go south first. Turn west after you have passed the
　　　coffee shop. You will be there in no time.

(4)　去银行，你应该在邮局前边换往北走的十五路公共汽车。
　　　Qù yínháng, nǐ yīnggāi zài yóujú qiánbiān huàn wàng běi zǒu de
　　　shíwǔlù gōnggòng qìchē.
　　　To go to the bank, you should transfer to No. 15 bus, north bound,
　　　in front of the post office.

Most of the directional words, including those for the four basic directions: 东边 *dōngbiān*, 南边 *nánbiān*, 西边 *xībiān,* and 北边 *běibiān*, contain the suffix 边. However, when used in this 往 pattern, the suffix 边 is often omitted, as shown in the above examples.

3.2 When pronounced in the third tone *wǎng*, 往 is a verb, meaning "to go in the direction of." The verbal form is rarely used in speech, and is most commonly found in contexts such as (5).

> | Verb   +   [往   +   direction/location] |

(5)   飞机飞往北京。
        Fēijī fēi wǎng Běijīng.
        The plane is flying to Beijing.

4. The Interrogative Word 怎么

怎么 *zěnme* is an interrogative word that may be used to pose different kinds of questions. It may be used to ask "How?" or "Why?" As a question word for "How?" it has a variant form 怎么样 *zěnmeyàng*.

4.1   怎么 may be used as an interrogative adverb to ask "How to carry out an action?" Structurally, it appears between the subject and its predicate in a sentence.

> | 怎么   +   Verb? |

(1)   这个表怎么填？
        Zhè ge biǎo zěnme tián?
        How do I fill out this form?

(2)   他怎么来？
        Tā zěnme lái?
        How is he coming? (By bus?)

(3)   请问，到银行怎么走？
        Qǐng wèn, dào yínháng zěnme zǒu?
        Excuse me, how do I get to the bank?

(4)   去机场坐出租汽车太贵，走路又太远。你说怎么办？
        Qù jīchǎng zuò chūzū qìchē tài guì, zǒu lù yòu tài yuǎn. Nǐ shuō
        zěnme bàn?
        It's too expensive to go to the airport by taxi, and it is too far to get
        there on foot. Tell me, what should I do?

怎么办 in the last sentence is an idiomatic expression often used when one is at one's wit's end: "How should I deal with the situation? What should I do?"

Please remember that in this use as "how?" and in this use only, 怎么 is interchangeable with 怎么样.

(5.a) 王老师，这个汉字怎么写？
       Wáng lǎoshī, zhè ge Hànzì zěnme xiě?
       Teacher Wang, how do we write this Chinese character?

(5.b) 王老师，这个汉字怎么样写？
       Wáng lǎoshī, zhè ge Hànzì zěnmeyàng xiě?

4.2 怎么 may also be used to ask for a reason: "How come?" Structurally, it may appear either before or after the subject, as shown in the following sentences. 怎么样 is not a variant form of 怎么 when used in this sense.

怎么 + Verb?

(6) 他怎么没来？
     Tā zěnme méi lái?
     How come he didn't come?

(7) 他怎么胖了很多？
     Tā zěnme pàngle hěn duō?
     How is it that he has gained so much weight?

(8) 怎么你又回答错了？
     Zěnme nǐ yòu huídá cuò le?
     How come you answered wrongly again?

The following sentence could have two meanings, depending on how it is said and where the stress falls.

(9) 他怎么去中国？
     Tā zěnme qù Zhōngguó?

If the stress is placed on "怎么," the sentence means "How is he going to China?" It is a question about the means of transportation. However, if the stress is on "去中国," it means "How come he is going to China (and not somewhere else)?"

4.3 怎么 and 怎么样 may also be used as predicates, carrying specific idiomatic meanings.

> Noun 怎么了？
>
> [What has happened to Noun? What became of Noun?]

> Noun　怎么样？
>
> [What about/how about Noun?]

If you came to class wearing a cast on your right arm, your teacher and fellow students may express their concern by asking:

(10)　你怎么了？

　　　Nǐ zěnme le?

　　　What has happened to you? What happened?

On the other hand, because of the injury you may want to reschedule your test with the teacher. You can ask the following question to find out if the new date is acceptable:

(11)　明天怎么样？

　　　Míngtiān zěnmeyàng?

　　　How about tomorrow?

As we learned in Lesson 25, 怎么样 may also be used as a complement of degree, posing a question on the manner or result of an action.

(12)　你考试考得怎么样？

　　　Nǐ kǎo shì kǎo de zěnmeyàng?

　　　How did you do in the test?

Lesson 39

1. The Resultative Complement (continued)

1.1 The resultative complements introduced in the previous lesson are:

> Verb 一见： as in 看见，听见
> Verb 一懂： as in 看懂，听懂
> Verb 一对： as in 写对（write correctly），说对（speak correctly）
> Verb 一错： as in 拿错（take by mistake），回答错（answer wrongly）
> Verb 一会： as in 学会（to have learned）
> Verb 一好（finish doing）： as in 写好字（finish writing characters）
> Verb 一好（do something satisfactorily）： as in 坐好（sit properly）
> Verb 一完： as in 吃完饭（finish eating）
> Verb 一清楚： as in 说清楚（speak clearly）

In this lesson, we will learn two more resultative complement forms.

1.2 Verb一到： 到 *dào*, literally "to arrive," may function as a resultative complement to indicate the successful conclusion of an action. This use of 到 is very much like that of 见, which is limited to a few compound verbs like 看见 and 听见. As explained earlier, 看 and 听 describe the actions or attempts and 见 marks the success. A more general success marker is 到, which may in fact appear with a wide range of verbs including 看 and 听.

> (1) 我去找张老师了，可是没找到他。
> Wǒ qù zhǎo Zhāng lǎoshī le, kěshì méi zhǎodào tā.
> I went to look for Teacher Zhang, but did not find him.

Sentence (1) demonstrates a difference between 找 and 找到, a distinction that is also found between "to look for" and "to find" in English. 找 "to look for" is the attempt of searching for something/someone, and the resultative complement 到 in 找到 "to find" tells the success of the effort. The following are a few more examples.

(2)　你买到今天的报了没有？

Nǐ mǎidào jīntiān de bào le méiyou?

Have you bought (with success) today's newspaper?

(3)　我给你写的信，你接到了没有？

Wǒ gěi nǐ xiě de xìn, nǐ jiēdàole méiyou?

Have you received the letter I wrote you?

(4)　我听收音机了，可是没听到这个新闻。

Wǒ tīng shōuyīnjī le, kěshì méi tīngdào zhè gè xīnwén.

I did listen to the radio but I didn't hear this news.

(5)　妈妈说，"你上完大学，找到工作以后，我就可以退休了。"

Māma shuō, "Nǐ shàngwán dàxué, zhǎodào gōngzuò yǐhòu, wǒ jiù kěyǐ tuìxiū le."

Mother said, "After you graduate from college and find a job, then I can retire."

(6)　我没想到会在儿看到你。

Wǒ méi xiǎngdào huì zài zhèr kàndào nǐ.

I didn't think that I would run into you here.

The last sentence contains two resultative complement compounds, both with 到. 看到 is of course interchangeable with 看见. 想到 tells the result of 想: 想 describes the soul-searching effort of "to think," and 想到 the actual result: "to think of/about."

1.3　Verb一住: The meaning of 住 *zhù* as a resultative complement is derived from its basic verbal meaning "to live, to stay." When attached to a verb, it indicates that something stays at a certain place or is fixed in a certain position as a result of the action.

(7)　那个球，你怎么没接住？

Nà ge qiú, nǐ zěnme méi jiēzhù?

How come that you didn't catch (and hold) the ball?

接 in (7) represents the action of trying to catch the ball, the success or failure of which is indicated by the use of the resultative complement: 接住 or its negative 没接住.

(8) 我妈妈想留客人在家住几天，可是他一定要走。妈妈没能留住他，心里很不高兴。

Wǒ māma xiǎng liú kèren zài jiā zhù jǐtiān, kěshi tā yídìng yào zǒu. Māma méi néng liúzhù tā, xīnli hěn bù gāoxìng.

My mother wanted to ask the guest to stay at our house for a few days. He insisted on leaving. My mother couldn't get him to stay and she was very upset.

Sentence (8) illustrates both uses of 住: as a verb in 在家住几天 and as a resultative complement in 没能留住他. In its second use, 住 serves as the success marker for the verb 留, which means "to make someone stay, to keep someone where he/she is." The causative use of 留 is derived from its primary reading "to stay, to remain." (For example, 我在北京留了几天. *Wǒ zài Běijīng liúle jǐtiān*. "I stayed in Beijing for a few days.")

(9) 站住！

Zhànzhù!

Stand still!

(= Freeze!)

(10) 上星期学的汉字，我记住了十八个，两个没记住。

Shàng xīngqī xué de Hànzì, wǒ jìzhùle shíbāge, liǎngge méi jìzhù.

Of the Chinese characters we learned last week, there are eighteen that I remember and two that I don't remember.

In the last example, we have a compound verb 记住, which means "to make an effort to remember something and that something now stays firmly in mind." Hence, 记住 is the word for "to remember, to bear in mind, to learn by heart." In a similar fashion, its antonym 忘了 *wàngle* "to forget" is a compound made up of two parts, the verb 忘 and the aspectual 了 which marks perfection or completion. It is obvious from the above examples that the use of the resultative complement 住 is an idiomatic operation, which requires individual memorization. Therefore, please 记住 the compounds as they are introduced.

2. The Locative Complement

There are two locative complements that we shall learn is this lesson.

2.1   Verb＋［在 Place］：As we have repeatedly noted, a locative 在－expression usually appears before a verb.

```
┌─────────────────────────────────────────────┐
│            ［在 Place］   +   Verb            │
└─────────────────────────────────────────────┘
```

(1)   我们在北京大学学习。
        Wǒmen zài Běijīng dàxué xuéxí.
        We're studying at Beijing University.

(1.a)＊我们学习在北京大学。
        Wǒmen xuéxí zài Běijíng dàxué.

There are, however, a number of verbs that take the 在－expression after them as a complement.

```
┌─────────────────────────────────────────────┐
│            Verb  +  ［在   Place］            │
└─────────────────────────────────────────────┘
```

(2)   站：我站在桌子前边。
            Wǒ zhàn zài zhuōzi qiánbiān.
            I stand in front of the desk.

(3)   坐：我坐在椅子上。
            Wǒ zuò zài yǐzishang.
            I am sitting in a chair.

(4)   住：我住在北京。
            Wǒ zhù zài Běijīng.
            I live in Beijing.

The verb 住 can take the place expression either before or after it with little difference in meaning, but the post-verbal locative is preferred. Also when other grammatical elements are added to the sentence, then one form may be preferable to the other. For example, if the verb is also followed by a complememt of time, then the sentence would select the pre－verbal 在 so as to avoid a confusing cluttering of different complements.

(5)   我在北京住了三年多。
        Wǒ zài Běijīng zhùle sānnián duō.
        I lived in Beijing for more than three years.

A few more examples of these Verb–在 forms:

(6) 我在北京学习中文的时候，我住在北大学生宿舍。

Wǒ zài Běijīng xuéxí Zhōngwén de shíhòu, wǒ zhù zài Běidà xuéshēng sùshè.

When I was studying Chinese in Beijing, I lived in the students dorm at Beijing University.

(7) 这些书，看完以后，请放在书架上。

Zhè xiē shū, kànwán yǐhòu, qǐng fàng zài shūjiàshang.

Please put the books on the shelves when you have finished reading them.

(8) 电影票，他们找到了没有？放在哪儿了？

Diànyǐngpiào, tāmen zhǎodàole méiyou? Fàng zài nǎr le?

Have they found the movie tickets? Where did they put them?

(9) 坐在你前边的人是谁？

Zuò zài nǐ qiánbiān de rén shì shéi?

Who is the person sitting in front of you?

(10) 我还没买到床。这几天，我的邻居让我睡在他们客厅里，我觉得很不好意思。

Wǒ hái méi mǎidào chuáng. Zhè jǐtiān, wǒ de línjū ràng wǒ shuì zài tāmen kètīngli, wǒ juéde hěn bù hǎo yìsi.

I still haven't bought a bed. In the last few days, my neighbors let me sleep in their living room. I really felt bad.

2.2 Verb + [到 Place] : The complement 到–expression indicates the arrival at a certain point, either in place or in time, as result of the action verb that precedes it.

> Verb + [到 Place]

(11) 他回到家就睡了。

Tā huí dào jiā jiù shuì le.

He fell asleep as soon as he returned home.

(12) 昨天晚上我看书看到了十二点。

Zuótiān wǎnshang wǒ kàn shū kàn dào le shí'èrdiǎn.

Last night I read till twelve o'clock.

In sentence (12), the verb 看 takes both an Object, which is "book," and a complement, which is "till twelve o'clock." The arrangement observes the golden rule of "Verb—Object Verb—Complement." Here are some more examples:

(13)　你们上学期学到了第几课？

Nǐmen shàng xuéqī xué dàole dìjǐkè?

Which lesson did you study up to last term?

(14)　我的好朋友住在城里。昨天我去看他。他留我吃饭。晚上我们谈到了十二点。回到家已经很晚了。

Wǒ de hǎo péngyou zhù zài chéngli. Zuótiān wǒ qù kàn tā. Tā liú wǒ chī fàn. Wǎnshang wǒmen tán dàole shí'èrdiǎn. Huí dào jiā yǐjīng hěn wǎn le.

My good friend lives in the city. I went to see him yesterday. He asked me to stay for dinner. We talked till twelve midnight. When I got home, it was very late.

(15)　我等了很久。等到今天才等到了这个机会。

Wǒ děngle hěn jiǔ. Děng dào jīntiān cái děngdào zhè ge jīhuì.

I'd been waiting very long. It wasn't till today that I (waited and) got this chance.

Sentence (14) contains the 到—complement in both usages: the temporal 到（谈到十二点）and the spatial 到（回到家）. In sentence (18), we have two kinds of 到: 等到今天 is a case of the locative complement and 等到这个机会 is an example of the resultative complement: the success of 等.

2.3　These two complements, "Verb ＋ 在" and "Verb ＋ 到," are sometimes described as resultative complements in other grammatical studies. While semantically they do resemble a regular resultative complement in that they also connote some kind of resultative state following an action, syntactically they behave somewhat differently. Hence, we choose to place them in a different category. For one thing, they do not co-occur with an Object as do the regular resultative complements, a distinction that is self-evident in the following pair of examples.

(16)　我等他等到十二点钟。　　　　　　　　　　(Locative Complement)

Wǒ děng tā děng dào shí'èrdiǎn zhōng.

I waited for him till twelve o'clock.

（17） 我等了很久，可是没有等到他。　　　　(Resultative Complement)
Wǒ děngle hěn jiǔ, kěshì méiyou děngdào tā.
I waited for a long time, but he didn't show up.
(= I didn't succeed in my effort of waiting for him.)

There are other syntactic differences between these two types of complements, which we will examine in a later lesson.

3. Sentence Conjoining

Beginning with this lesson, we will learn how to join clauses and sentences by means of a variety of rhetorical patterns. These patterns not only produce sentences that are more sophisticated in style, they also mark in explicit terms the semantic and/or logical relationship that exists between the clauses. The grammatical mechanism involved in these patterns is actually very simple: they require the use of paired words to bind the clauses together. One member of the pair appears in the first clause and the other in the second clause, and, as a pair, the markers serve to characterize the relationship. There are many such sets of correlatives in Chinese that we may use to signal various types of semantic relationships, including cause/ effect, contradiction, concession, immediacy, etc. In this lesson, we will learn two conjoining patterns.

3.1 The Pattern for Concession: The English word for marking concession is "although, though," a conjunction that accompanies the concessive clause. The Chinese equivalent is 虽然 *suīrán*, to be followed by either 但是 *dànshì* or 可是 *kěshì* "but" in the other clause of the conjoined sentence. While it is grammatically incorrect to use "although" and "but" together in the same English sentence, such redundancy is never considered problematic in Chinese. In fact, it is stylistically preferable to qualify each clause with its own appropriate marker.

虽然……，但是（or 可是）……

[Although..., (but)...]

（1）　他虽然不是北京人，可是北京话说得很好。
Tā suīrán bú shì Běijīng rén, kěshì Běijīng huà shuō de hěn hǎo.
Even though he is not a native of Beijing, he speaks very good Pekingese.

(2)　那儿春天虽然很暖和，但是风很大。你们还是秋天再去吧。

Nàr chūntiān suīrán hěn nuǎnhuo, dànshì fēng hěn dà. Nǐmen háishì qiūtiān zài qù ba.

Although it is warm there in the spring, it is still quite windy. Why don't you go in the fall?

(3)　王教授以前在这个大学工作。他现在虽然退休了，但是他还很关心中文系的学生。

Wáng jiàoshòu yǐqián zài zhè ge dàxué gōngzuò. Tā xiànzài suīrán tuìxiū le, dànshì tā hái hěn guānxīn Zhōngwén xì de xuésheng.

Professor Wang used to work at this university. Even though he is now retired, he is still very concerned about the students in the Chinese Department.

If both clauses share the same subject, then the subject generally comes at the beginning of the entire sentence, as in the following pattern:

> Subject　虽然　Clause ₁，但是 / 可是　Clause ₂

(4)　他虽然是美国人，但是不会说英文。

Tā suīrán shì Měiguó rén, dànshì bú huì shuō Yīngwén.

Although he is American, he doesn't speak English.

(5)　这件毛衣虽然很便宜，可是有点儿旧。还是别买吧。

Zhè jiàn máoyī suīrán hěn piányi, kěshì yǒu diǎnr jiù. Háishì bié mǎi ba.

This sweater is cheap but it looks a little bit old. You'd better not buy it.

If, on the other hand, the two clauses do not have a common subject, markers usually appear before the subjects.

> 虽然[Subject Predicate] ₁，但是 / 可是[Subject Predicate] ₂

(6)　虽然外边下着大雨，但是他还要开车来看我。

Suīrán wàibiān xiàzhe dà yǔ, dànshì tā hái yào kāi chē lái kàn wǒ.

Even though it was raining hard outside, he insisted on driving over to see me.

(7) 虽然他很聪明，可是我比他更聪明。

Suīrán tā hěn cōngming, kěshì wǒ bǐ tā gèng cōngming.

He is smart, but I am smarter than he.

(8) 虽然学生写错了，可是老师没看见。

Suīrán xuésheng xiěcuò le, kěshì lǎoshī méi kànjiàn.

Even though the students wrote it wrong, the teacher didn't spot it.

(9) 虽然他对我很好，但是我不喜欢他。

Suīrán tā duì wǒ hěn hǎo, dànshì wǒ bù xǐhuan tā.

Although he is good to me, I don't like him.

但是 and 可是 are exactly the same in meaning and are interchangeable in most cases. The only restriction is that 但是 always comes before the subject of a clause, while 可是 may appear either before or after it. Hence,

(10a) 我虽然住在美国，但是心还留在中国。

Wǒ suīrán zhù zài Měiguó, dànshì xīn hái liú zài Zhōngguó.

Even though I live in the States, I've left my heart in China.

(10b) *我虽然住在美国，心但是还留在中国。

*Wǒ suīrán zhù zài Měiguó, xīn dànshì hái liú zài Zhōngguó.

(11a) 我虽然住在美国，可是心还留在中国。

(11b) 我虽然住在美国，心可是还留在中国。

3.2 The Pattern for Immediacy: The following pattern is used to connect two actions or events that closely follow one another.

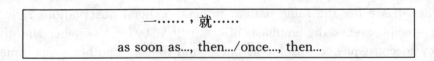

一……，就……

as soon as..., then.../once..., then...

Structurally, both 一 and 就 are monosyllabic adverbs, and both always come <u>after</u> the subjects. In terms of usage, the pattern may be employed to underscore the immediacy in time "as soon as..." or, by extension, the unfailing consequence of a condition "once...then.../whenever..." The use of 一 resembles that of "once" in English, which means both "for one time" and "immediately." The adverb 就 indicates consequence: "then."

Examples of the primary use of this pattern to signal immediacy are:

（12） 他们一到，我们就开始吃饭了。

Tāmen yí dào, wǒmen jiù kāishǐ chī fàn le.

As soon as they arrived, we began eating.

（13） 老师讲得很清楚，我们一听就懂了。

Lǎoshī jiǎng de hěn qīngchu, wǒmen yì tīng jiù dǒng le.

The teacher explained it clearly. As soon as we heard it, we understood.

（14） 他很聪明。他一听就知道爸爸的意思是什么。

Tā hěn cōngming. Tā yì tīng jiù zhīdao bàba de yìsi shì shénme.

He was smart. He knew what his father meant as soon as he heard him speak.

（15） 请你一接到我信就给我打电话。

Qǐng nǐ yì jiēdào wǒ de xìn jiù gěi wǒ dǎ diànhuà.

Please call me as soon as you receive my letter.

（16） 那本小说，我一看完就放在你的桌子上。怎么你没找到呢？真奇怪。

Nà běn xiǎoshuō, wǒ yí kànwán jiù fàng zài nǐ de zhuōzishang. Zěnme nǐ méi zhǎodào ne? Zhēn qíguài.

As soon as I finished reading that novel I put it on your desk. How come you weren't able to find it? It's really strange.

（17） 他一看见我就问，"今天的翻译，你作完了没有？"

Tā yí kànjiàn wǒ jiù wèn, "Jīntiān de fānyì, nǐ zuòwánle méiyou?"

As soon as he saw me, he asked, "Have you finished the translation exercises for today?"

In all of the above sentences, we are concerned primarily with particular incidents. Each scenario involves two actions that are sequentially ordered but immediate to one another. If we use the same pattern to make general observations rather than reporting specific events, the emphasis of " 一……，就…… " switches slightly from immediacy to consequence. Insofar as one action follows another every time without fail, then the former becomes almost like the conditioning factor responsible for the latter. Hence, the first clause represents the condition, the second clause the result. The following are examples of this use.

（18） 我一不注意，就会念错。

Wǒ yì bú zhùyì, jiù huì niàncuò.

Whenever I don't pay attention, I make mistakes right away.

(19) 天气一冷，我们就可以去滑冰。
       Tiānqì yì lěng, wǒmen jiù kěyǐ qù huá bīng.
       As soon as it turns cold, we can go ice skating.

(20) 在这儿工作，一到七十岁就可以退休。
       Zài zhèr gōngzuò, yí dào qīshisuì jiù kěyǐ tuì xiū.
       Working here, one can retire as soon as one reaches the age of
       seventy.

(21) 我每次一接到家里的信，心里就很高兴。
       Wǒ měi cì yì jiēdào jiāli de xìn, xīnli jiù hěn gāoxìng.
       Every time I receive a letter from home, I feel very happy.

(22) 记住，一接到球就跑。
       Jìzhù, yì jiēdào qiú jiù pǎo.
       Remember, once you get the ball, run.

4. The Preposition 对

Like their counterparts in English, prepositions in Chinese are idiosyncratic in behavior and need to be memorized one by one. The use of 对 *duì* can be summarized as below:

X 对 Y 很 关 心

X duì Y hěn guānxīn
X is concerned with Y.

X 对 Y 有 帮 助

X duì Y yǒu bāngzhù
X is helpful to Y

X 对 Y 说

X duì Y shuō
X says to Y

```
┌─────────────────────────────────────────┐
│              X  对  Y  笑                 │
└─────────────────────────────────────────┘
```

X duì Y xiào
X smiles at Y

```
┌─────────────────────────────────────────┐
│            X  对  Y  很  好               │
└─────────────────────────────────────────┘
```

X duì Y hěn hǎo
X is good to Y

对 can, of course, appear with other verbs and adjectives and take part in other constructions. But, for the time being, please remember the usages listed above. The following are some sample sentences:

(1) 学习汉语对以后找工作有什么帮助？请你给我们说说。

Xuéxí Hànyǔ duì yǐhòu zhǎo gōngzuò yǒu shénme bāngzhù? Qǐng nǐ gěi wǒmen shuōshuo.

What good would learning Chinese do to help us find a job later? Please explain to us.

(2) 关老师对学生很关心。他常常对学生说，"你们应该学好中文，但是也要注意身体。"

Guān lǎoshī duì xuésheng hěn guānxīn. Tā chángcháng duì xuésheng shuō, "Nǐmen yīnggāi xuéhǎo Zhōngwén, dànshì yě yào zhùyì shēntī."

Teacher Guan is very concerned about his students. He often says to them, "You should learn your Chinese well, but you should also take care of your health."

(3) 他每次一看见我，就对我笑。

Tā měi cì yí kànjiàn wǒ, jiù duì wǒ xiào.

Every time he sees me, he smiles at me.

(4) 他以前对我很好。可是他认识你以后，就不很关心我了。

Tā yǐqián duì wǒ hěn hǎo. Kěshì tā rènshi nǐ yǐhòu, jiù bù hěn guānxīn wǒ le.

He used to be very good to me. But since he met you, he hasn't cared for me as much.

Please notice that in the last sentence 关心 is not cast in the 对 pattern. There are certain verbs that may appear with or without 对, without any difference in meaning. The following is another pair of sentences with 关心 to illustrate this optional use of the 对 pattern.

(5)　　我对今年的选举很关心。

Wǒ duì jīnnián de xuǎnjǔ hěn guānxīn.

I am greatly concerned about the election this year.

(6)　　我很关心今年的选举。

Wǒ hěn guānxīn jīnnián de xuǎnjǔ.

To review, 对 may function as an adjective or as a complement, as in the following sentences. 对了 in sentence (9) and 对不起 in sentence (10) are both idiomatic expressions.

(7)　　对，你说得很对。

Duì, nǐ shuō de hěn duì.

Right. What you have said is absolutely correct.

(8)　　你写对了。

Nǐ xiě duì le.

Now, you wrote it right.

(9)　　对了，上个月的选举，谁当了学生代表？

Duì le, shàng ge yuè de xuǎnjǔ, shéi dāngle xuésheng dàibiǎo?

By the way, who became the student representative in the election last month?

(10)　　你的信我接到了。但是我没有你的地址，所以不能给你回信。真对不起。

Nǐ de xìn wǒ jiēdào le. Dànshì wǒ méi yǒu nǐ de dìzhǐ, suǒyǐ bùnéng gěi nǐ huí xìn. Zhēn duì bu qǐ.

I got your letter. But, as I did not have your address, I wasn't able to write back. I am truly sorry.

Lesson 40

1. Adjective—极了

极了 *jíle* is an exclamatory form that may be attached to the end of an adjective to express the meaning "extremely/awfully Adjective." The entire adjectival unit may of course function as a complement as illustrated in sentences (4) and (5).

Adjective — 极了

(1)　我听见你来，高兴极了。
　　　Wǒ tīngjiàn nǐ lái, gāoxìng jíle.
　　　I was extremely happy to hear that you were coming.

(2)　Madonna 好看极了，对吗？
　　　Madonna hǎokàn jíle, duì ma?
　　　Madonna is awfully pretty, isn't she?

(3)　这儿的东西，价钱便宜极了。你怎么不多买一些？
　　　Zhèr de dōngxi, jiàqián piányi jíle. Nǐ zěnme bù duō mǎi yìxiē?
　　　Things here are extremely inexpensive. Why don't you buy more?

(4)　他跑得快极了。
　　　Tā pǎo de kuài jíle.
　　　He runs extremely fast.

(5)　你这句话说得好极了。我们听了都很高兴。
　　　Nǐ zhè jù huà shuō de hǎo jíle. Wǒmen tīngle dōu hěn gāoxìng.
　　　What you said was extremely well put. We were all very pleased when we heard it.

2. How to Read a Fraction

To read a figure that contains a fraction, follow these steps:

(A) What comes before the decimal point is to be read like a whole number. If it is a zero, then say 零 *líng*.

(B) The decimal point is to be read as 点（儿）*diǎnr*, literally meaning "point, dot."

(C) What comes after the decimal point is to be read like separate numbers.

(1)	0.1	:	零点一	líng diǎnr yī
(2)	0.02	:	零点零二	líng diǎnr líng èr
(3)	0.12	:	零点一二	líng diǎnr yī èr
(4)	0.29	:	零点二九	líng diǎnr èr jiǔ
(5)	0.204	:	零点二零四	líng diǎnr èr líng sì
(6)	1.1	:	一点一	yī diǎnr yī
(7)	1.2	:	一点二	yī diǎnr èr
(8)	2.22	:	二点二二	èr diǎnr èr èr
(9)	12.02	:	十二点零二	shí'èr diǎnr líng èr
(10)	20.202	:	二十点二零二	èrshi diǎnr èr líng èr
(11)	22.44	:	二十二点四四	èrshi'èr diǎnr sì sì

(12)   他比我快零点儿五秒，打破了我以前的记录。

Tā bǐ wǒ kuài líng diǎnr wǔ miǎo, dǎpòle wǒ yǐqián de jìlù.

He was faster than I by 0.5 seconds. He broke my previous record.

Lesson 41

1. The Simple Directional Complement

1.1 To indicate whether an action is moving towards the speaker or away from the speaker, a "Directional Complement" is attached to the verb. If the motion is towards the speaker, the complement is 来 *lái* "come"; if it is away from the speaker, it is 去 *qù* "go."

Verb—来 vs. Verb—去
上来 vs. 上去
shànglái   *shàngqù*
[come up]   [go up]

In English, the distinction between "to come up" and "to go up" also lies in the direction of the movements. The former represents an upward motion towards the speaker and the latter an upward motion away from the speaker. The adverb "up" remains the same in both phrases, but the difference in directionality is indicated by the verbs, namely, "come" vs. "go." In Chinese, likewise, we use 来 / 去 to take care of this difference, but they do not function as main verbs like their English counterparts; rather, they behave like complements.

1.2 The directional complements (DC) can appear with the following motion verbs:

上 *shàng*	"upward"		
下 *xià*	"downward"		
进 *jìn*	"inward"	来 *lái*	"toward the speaker"
出 *chū*	"outward"	去 *qù*	"away from the speaker"
回 *huí*	"return"		
过 *guò*	"cross"		

(1)   你们都进来吧。
       Nǐmen dōu jìnlái ba.
       Please come in, all of you.

(2)   他出去了，一会儿就回来。请进来等吧。
       Tā chūqù le, yìhuǐr jiù huílái. Qǐng jìnlái děng ba.
       He went out, but will be back soon. Please come in and wait.

(3)   那边就是天安门广场。我们过去看看，好吗？
       Nà biān jiù shì Tiān'ānmén Guǎngchǎng. Wǒmen guòqù kànkan,
       hǎo ma?
       That is Tian'anmen Square over there. Shall we go over and take a
       look?

(4)   你忙吧，我应该回去了。你不要出来了。
       Nǐ máng ba, wǒ yīnggāi huíqù le. Nǐ bú yào chūlái le.
       You go ahead with your work. I should be going back. Don't come
       out.

(5)   他不下来，那你上去吧。
       Tā bú xiàlái, nà nǐ shàngqù ba.
       He is not coming down. In that case, why don't you go up?

(6)   这个地方，进去容易出来难。
       Zhè ge dìfang, jìnqù róngyi chūlái nán.
       This place is easy to get in but difficult to get out.

1.3 To indicate where the movement originates, the 从······ pattern may be used, as illustrated in the following sentences.

$$\boxed{[\text{从 Place}] \quad + \quad [\text{Verb} - \text{Directional Complement}]}$$

(7)   外边的门都关了，我们应该从哪儿进去呢？
       Wàibiān de mén dōu guānle, wǒmen yīnggāi cóng nǎr jìnqù ne?
       All the outside doors are locked. Where should we go in from?

(8)   刚从外边进来的那个男学生是谁？
       Gāng cóng wàibiān jìnlái de nà ge nán xuésheng shì shéi?
       Who is that male student that just came in from outside?

To specify the destination of the movement, the place word appears between the verb and the directional complement.

Verb + [Place] + Directional Complement
上 下 进 回 + [Place] + 来 去

(9)　我们进教室去吧。

Wǒmen jìn jiàoshì qù ba.

Let's go into the classroom.

(10)　他们上楼来了。

Tāmen shàng lóu lái le.

They are coming upstairs.

(11)　他没有回宿舍去。

Tā méiyou huí sùshè qù.

He didn't return to the dorm.

(12)　天气好的时候，我们常常上山去玩儿。

Tiānqì hǎo de shíhòu, wǒmen chángcháng shàng shān qù wánr.

When the weather is good, we often go up to the mountains to play.

(13)　听说住你楼上的那位小姐很漂亮。她常常下楼来洗衣服。你给我介绍介绍，好不好？

Tīng shuō zhù nǐ lóushàng de nà wèi xiǎojiě hěn piàoliang. Tā chángcháng xià lóu lái xǐ yīfu. Nǐ gěi wǒ jièshao jièshao, hǎo bu hǎo?

I've heard that the young woman who lives upstairs from you is very beautiful. She often comes down to do her laundry. Would you introduce me to her?

Please notice that of the six motion verbs listed in Section 1.2, only 上 , 下 , 进 and 回 may appear in this pattern. Also, only certain place words can appear in the pattern, an idiosyncracy that requires memorization. The other two motion verbs, 出 and 过 , do not participate in this construction.

1.4   Aside from motion verbs, the directional complement can appear with other types of action verbs:

（14） 跑来：他跑来告诉我……
                  Tā pǎolái gàosu wǒ...
                  He ran over to tell me...

（15） 送去：这封信等着要，请你现在就送去。
                  Zhè fēng xìn děngzhe yào, qǐng nǐ xiànzài jiù sòngqù.
                  They are waiting for the letter. Please take it over right away.

（16） 带来：书，我忘了放在哪儿了。所以今天没带来。
                  Shū, wǒ wàngle fàng zài nǎr le. Suǒyǐ jīntiān méi dàilái.
                  I forgot where I put the book. So, I didn't bring it with me today.

（17） 带去：这些点心是他爱吃的。请你都给他带去。
                  Zhè xiē diǎnxīn shì tā ài chī de. Qǐng nǐ dōu gěi tā dàiqù.
                  These pastries are what he likes to eat. Please take all of them along for him.

As the English translation indicates, 带来 in (16) is "to bring" and 带去 in (17) is "to take." The distinction between "bring" (toward the speaker) and "take" (away from the speaker) is a built-in directional differentiation in English, a distinction that is explicitly stated in the choice of an appropriate directional complement in Chinese for the same action verb 带. The verbs in sentences (15) to (17), 送 and 带, are both action verbs, whereas 跑 in (14) is actually a motion verb. However, unlike 上, 下, etc.; which are exclusively directional, 跑 "to run" represents a specific form of motion (for example, "run" vs. "walk"). In other words, it is more a manner/action verb than a directional verb. The significance of this distinction will become evident in our discussion of the directional complement in a later lesson.

1.5   In the last few examples in Section 1.4, the verbs are transitive verbs but the Objects are either preposed or understood, thereby leaving the verb－directional complement closely bound to each other. But, should the verb take an Object in its normal post-verbal position, the ordering of the constituents would become quite complicated. The following is a basic rule, of which there are many variations.

Verb   +   Object   +   Directional Complement

1.5.1   In a sentence where the action is yet to be completed, we follow the word order given above.

（18）　拿书来。
　　　　Ná shū lái.
　　　　Bring the book.

（19）　拿三本书来。
　　　　Ná sānběn shū lái.
　　　　Bring three books.

（20）　你还是带钱去吧。
　　　　Nǐ háishì dài qián qù ba.
　　　　It's better for you to take along some money.

（21）　请他明天送东西来。
　　　　Qǐng tā míngtiān sòng dōngxi lái.
　　　　Please ask him to deliver the things (here) tomorrow.

（22）　我想寄一封信去。
　　　　Wǒ xiǎng jì yìfēng xìn qù.
　　　　I want to send (them) a letter.

（23）　今天客人很多。请你去拿几把椅子来。
　　　　Jīntiān kèren hěn duō. Qǐng nǐ qù ná jǐbǎ yǐzi lái.
　　　　There are many guests today. Go and get (i.e. bring back) some chairs.

（24）　本子，我带来了。我没有忘。我每天都带本子来。
　　　　Běnzi, wǒ dài lái le. Wǒ méiyou wàng. Wǒ měi tiān dōu dài běnzi lái.
　　　　I did bring my notebook. I didn't forget. I bring my notebook every day.

1.5.2   In a sentence where a completed action is involved, 了 is added to the verb. The negative pattern is formed with 没有 .

Verb–了 + Object + Directional Complement

没（有）+ Verb + Object + Directional Complement

（25）　我们都带了钱来。

Wǒmen dōu dàile qián lái.

We have all brought money with us.

（26）　我们已经寄了几封信去。

Wǒmen yǐjīng jìle jǐfēng xìn qù.

We have already sent a few letters.

（27）　我们都没买东西来。

Wǒmen dōu méi mǎi dōngxi lái.

None of us (bought and) brought anything with us.

（28）　听说小张丢了钱，爸爸就给他寄了两百块钱来了。

Tīng shuō xiǎo Zhāng diūle qián, bàba jiù gěi tā jìle liǎngbǎikuài qián lái le.

Upon hearing that Little Zhang had lost his money, his father immediately sent him two hundred dollars.

（29）　他想得真周到。你看，他给我们带了一个司机来。

Tā xiǎng de zhēn zhōudào. Nǐ kàn, tā gěi wǒmen dàile yíge sījī lái.

He's really thoughtful. Look, he has brought us a driver.

A variation of this pattern is to have (a) the Object placed at the end and (b) the aspect 了 coming after the "Verb–Directional Complement" combination.

Verb + Directional Complement + 了 + Object

没（有） + Verb + Directional Complement + Object

（30）　他们拿来了三块钱。

Tāmen náláile sānkuài qián.

They have brought three dollars with them.

（31）　我已经寄去了一封信。

Wǒ yǐjīng jìqùle yìfēng xìn.

I have already sent off a letter.

（32）　我给他带去了一些点心。

Wǒ gěi tā dàiqùle yìxiē diǎnxīn.

I've taken to him some snacks.

（33） 我们找来了一个会说中国话的人。

Wǒmen zhǎoláile yíge huì shuō Zhōngguóhuà de rén.

We've found (and brought) a person who can speak Chinese.

（34） 我没给你买来长城的明信片。

Wǒ méi gěi nǐ mǎilái Chángchéng de míngxìnpiàn.

I didn't buy (and bring) you postcards of the Great Wall.

（35） A: 对不起，我忘了带照相机来。我回旅馆去拿吧。

Duì bu qǐ, wǒ wàngle dài zhàoxiàngjī lái. Wǒ huí lǚguǎn qù ná ba.

Sorry, I've forgotten to bring my camera. I'll go back to the hotel to get it.

B: 没关系，我带来了我的照相机。你可以用我的。

Méi guānxi, wǒ dàiláile wǒ de zhàoxiàngjī. Nǐ kěyǐ yòng wǒ de.

It's all right. I have brought my camera. You can use mine.

1.6 In the preceding few pages, we have described in some detail the use of the simple directional complement construction. The COMPLEX directional complements will be introduced in a later lesson.

2. The Destination Expression with 到

We learned from early on that the destination expression would appear after the motion verb 来 and 去，as in "来 / 去 Place." A variation of this pattern which is just as common in speech is to introduce the destination with 到. In fact, a complete pattern with both ORIGIN and DESTINATION involves the use of two coverbial units, sequentially ordered, one marked with 从 and the other 到.

来 / 去 PLACE

[到 PLACE] + 来 / 去

[从 PLACE] + [到 PLACE] + 来 / 去

（1） 你什么时候到中国去？

Nǐ shénme shíhòu dào Zhōngguó qù?

When are you going to China?

（2）　我每天都到图书馆去念书。

Wǒ měi tiān dōu dào túshūguǎn qù niàn shū.

I go to the library to study every day.

（3）　从这儿开车到学校去，要多少时间？

Cóng zhèr kāi chē dào xuéxiào qù, yào duōshao shíjiān?

How long does it take to go from here to school by car?

（4）　我们走路到邮局去。

Wǒmen zǒu lù dào yóujú qù.

We will walk to the post office.

In sentences (3) and (4), the 到－expressions are preceded by 开车 and 走路, both Verb－Object units representing means of transportation.

（5）　她很快地跑到楼下来，请我们上楼去坐坐。

Tā hěn kuài de pǎo dào lóuxià lái, qǐng wǒmen shàng lóu qù zuòzuo.

She hurriedly ran down from upstairs and invited us to go up and sit for a while.

（6）　她很快地跑到楼下来，请我们到楼上去坐坐。

Tā hěn kuài de pǎo dào lóuxià lái, qǐng wǒmen dào lóushang qù zuòzuo.

Please note that sentences (5) and (6) are essentially the same in meaning, even though they employ different locative patterns in the second half. 上楼去 is "Verb + PLACE + Directional Complement" whereas 到楼上去 is "到 + PLACE + Verb."

3. Reduplication of Adjectives

Certain adjectives can be repeated and used as modifiers for both nouns (marked by 的) and verbs (marked by 地). They may also function as complements, marked by 得 . Semantically, a reduplicated form carries the same meaning as that of " 很 / 非常 Adjective." In addition, it generates a lively and poetic effect, which the corresponding version does not have. For example, 一束很红的花儿 *yíshù hěn hóng de huār* is simply "a bunch of red flowers" but 一束红红的花儿 *yíshù hónghóng de huār* is "a bouquet of attractively red flowers." Hence, the form of reduplication is often referred to as the vivid reduplication. A reduplicated adjective may not take on another degree adverb such as 很, 非常, etc., since vivid reduplication is in itself already a form of intensification: *很红红的花儿 **hěn hónghóng de huār.*

The reduplication patterns are slightly different for one-syllable adjectives and two-syllable adjectives.

3.1 Monosyllabic Adjectives

```
┌──────────────────────────────────────────────┐
│                 Pattern:  X X                 │
└──────────────────────────────────────────────┘
```

The repeated syllable, i.e. the second X in the pattern, may be pronounced in the first tone and it may also take on a retroflex ending (-r). For example, 好→好好 儿 *hǎohāor.* Please note that not all adjectives can be repeated for a vivid rhetorical effect. For example, while 好好儿的 is acceptable, *错错的 *cuòcuò de is not.

3.1.1 As illustrated in the following sentences, an XX unit may function in a variety of grammatical roles. In (1), 好好儿的 is an adjectival unit modifying the noun 人; in (2), it is an adverbial modifier for the verb 玩儿; and, in (3), it is a complement of degree for 睡觉. When used as a complement, the XX unit generally keeps its suffix 的.

(1)   好好儿的一个人，怎么会得了心脏病？
      Hǎohāor de yíge rén, zěnme huì déle xīnzàngbìng?
      How could such a healthy person have gotten a heart attack?

(2)   你们好好儿地玩儿。
      Nǐmen hǎohāor de wánr.
      Play well. (Don't fight.)

(3)   他睡觉睡得好好儿的，我们别叫他。
      Tā shuì jiào shuì de hǎohāor de, wǒmen bié jiào tā.
      He's sleeping so soundly. Let's not call (wake) him.

A few more examples:

(4)   慢：你慢慢儿地说，别着急。
           Nǐ mànmānr de shuō, bié zhāojí.
           Please speak slowly. Don't be anxious.

(5)   高：那个高高的男学生是古波吗？
           Nà ge gāogāo de nán xuésheng shì Gǔbō ma?
           That male student who is kind of tall, —— is he Gubo?

(6) 短：她穿了一件短短的白毛衣，非常好看。

　　　Tā chuānle yíjiàn duǎnduǎn de bái máoyī, fēicháng hǎokàn.

　　　She wore a short white sweater and looked extremely attractive.

(7) 远：我要走得远远的。我不愿意再看见你。

　　　Wǒ yào zǒu de yuǎnyuǎnde. Wǒ bú yuànyì zài kànjiàn nǐ.

　　　I want to go somewhere really far away. I don't want to see you again.

3.2 Disyllabic Adjectives

Pattern:　X X Y Y

The main stress in XXYY is on the last syllable. A neutral tone syllable in an XY compound may therefore regain its original pitch. For example, 清楚 *qīngchu* → 清清楚楚 *qīngqīngchǔchǔ*. With regard to membership, again, only certain adjectives can undergo this form of reduplication. While 高兴 and 愉快 both mean "happy," only the former can be reduplicated 高高兴兴 *gāogāoxìngxìng*, and not the latter,*愉愉快快 **yúyúkuàikuài*. Some of the other non-expandable adjectives are 聪明 *cōngming*, 容易 *róngyi*, 热情 *rèqíng*, etc. As in the case with the monosyllabic adjectives, no general rules explain why certain adjectives may participate in the reduplication and why others cannot. It is simply a matter of idiomacy and a task for memorization.

3.2.1 An XXYY unit may serve as an adjectival modifier as in (8), an adverbial modifier as in (9), or a complement as in (10).

(8) 漂亮：这个漂漂亮亮的小姑娘是谁的孩子？

　　　Zhè ge piàopiàoliàngliàng de xiǎo gūniang shì shéi de háizi?

　　　Whose child is this pretty young girl?

(9) 高兴：他高高兴兴地跑来对我说，"这个地方美极了。"

　　　Tā gāogāoxìngxìng de pǎolái duì wǒ shuō, "Zhè ge dìfang měi jíle."

　　　Happily he ran over and said to me, "This place is extremely beautiful."

(10) 整齐：孩子们穿得整整齐齐（的）。

　　　Háizimen chuān de zhěngzhěngqíqí de.

　　　The children were all dressed neatly.

Please note that, in the case of a complement, 的 is optional with an XXYY unit as in sentence (10), but obligatory with XX, as in (3) and (7). The following are more examples of the XXYY pattern.

(11)　清楚：在山上可以清清楚楚地看到山下的风景。

Zài shānshang kěyǐ qīngqīngchǔchǔ de kàndào shānxià de fēngjǐng.

On the mountain, one can have a clear and distinct view of the scenery below.

(12)　客气：他每次看见我，总是客客气气地对我说，"对不起，我又没有给你写信。"

Tā měi cì kànjiàn wǒ, zǒng shì kèkèqìqì de duì wǒ shuō, "Duì bu qǐ, wǒ yòu méiyou gěi nǐ xiě xìn."

Every time he sees me, he always says to me very politely, "Sorry, once again I didn't write to you ."

(13)　舒服：我们在这儿住得舒舒服服的，我不想搬。

Wǒmen zài zhèr zhù de shūshūfúfú de, wǒ bù xiǎng bān.

We've been living here comfortably. I don't want to move.

(14)　乾净：这是一间乾乾净净的房间，你可以来住

Zhè shì yìjiān gāngānjìngjìng de fángjiān. Nǐ kěyǐ lái zhù.

This room is neat and tidy. You can come and stay in it.

The following is a partial list of the common disyllabic adjectives that may be repeated in the form of XXYY: 乾净 *gānjìng* "clean." 高兴 *gāoxìng* "happy," 客气 *kèqi* "polite," 漂亮 *piàoliang* "pretty," 清楚 *qīngchu* "clear," 认真 *rènzhēn* "conscientious," 舒服 *shūfu* "comfortable," 整齐 *zhěngqí* "tidy," and 辛苦 *xīnkǔ* "toilsome." Even in this list, not all members may function in all the capacities described above. Beginners should be cautious when using this pattern.

3.3 To review, verbs can also be repeated, but in the sense of "to do it a little bit." The reduplication patterns are XX（看看）for monosyllabic verbs and XYXY (and not XXYY) for disyllabic forms （休息休息）.

4. The Conditional Sentence

To join two clauses together that bear the relationship of "if...then...," we use the following pair of correlatives:

要是……，就……

yàoshi..., jiù...

[if...then...]

要是, the marker for the conditional clause, may stand either before or after the subject, but the corresponding adverb 就 always appears after the subject in the consequence clause.

(1)   要是有时间，我就来看你。
        Yàoshi yǒu shíjiān, wǒ jiù lái kàn nǐ.
        If I have time, I'll come to see you.

(2)   你要是今天没空儿，我就明天再来找你。
        Nǐ yàoshi jīntiān méi kòngr, wǒ jiù míngtiān zài lái zhǎo nǐ.
        If you don't have time today, I'll come to look for you again tomorrow.

(3)   要是放春假的时候天气好，我们就上山去玩儿。
        Yàoshi fàng chūnjià de shíhòu tiānqì hǎo, wǒmen jiù shàng shān qù wánr.
        If the weather is nice during the spring break, we will go up to the hills and have a good time.

(4)   要是那个门口太挤了，我们就从西边的门出去吧。
        Yàoshi nà ge ménkǒu tài jǐ le, wǒmen jiù cóng xībiān de mén chū-qu ba.
        If it is too crowded at that exit, then let's get out from the door on the west side.

(5)   这儿风景美极了。要是我带了照相机来，我就一定会照很多相。
        Zhèr fēngjǐng měi jíle. Yàoshì wǒ dàile zhàoxiàngjī lái, wǒ jiù yídìng huì zhào hěn duō xiàng.
        The scenery here is extremely beautiful. If I had brought my camera with me, I would have taken a lot of pictures.

(6)   我要是有钱，就会给你买一辆摩托车。
        Wǒ yàoshì yǒu qián, jiù huì gěi nǐ mǎi yíliàng mótuōchē.
        If I had money, I would buy you a motorcycle.

(7)   要是没坐错车，我们早就到了。
        Yàoshì méi zuòcuò chē, wǒmen zǎo jiù dào le.
        If we hadn't taken the wrong bus, we would have arrived much earlier.

(8)   要是我是你，我就不接电话。
        Yàoshì wǒ shì nǐ, wǒ jiù bù jiē diànhuà.
        If I were you, I wouldn't answer the phone

You may have noticed that examples (5) to (8) are all subjunctive sentences in English, requiring a different marking format for the verbs. In Chinese, however, the same pattern "要是……，就……" is used for all conditional sentences, factual as well as hypothetical.

5. The Differences between 就 and 才

Both 就 *jiù* and 才 *cái* are monosyllabic adverbs, and as such they are always placed between the subject and the predicate in a sentence. Semantically, they both relate an event (as represented by the verb) to one's expectation of it. 就 is used when the action takes place earlier than expected, requires shorter time to carry out than expected, or costs less money than expected. On the other hand, if the event takes place later than expected, is more time-consuming or more expensive than expected, then the adverb to use is 才. Structurally, the 就 sentence often ends with 了; 才 is incompatible with this final particle. To illustrate this contrast between what is expected and what actually occurs, the examples below are preceded by scenarios which include both the expectations and the actual occurrences.

(1)   Expected time of arrival: 9:00 p.m.
        Actual time of arrival: 8:00 p.m.
        Sentence: 八点就到了。
                  Bādiǎn jiù dào le.
(2)   Expected time of arrival: 9:00 p.m.
        Actual time of arrival: 10:00 p.m.
        Sentence: 十点才到。
                  Shídiǎn cái dào.

Please note that English uses different constructions to render this difference:

(3)   The plane had already arrived by eight o'clock.
        飞机八点就到了。
        Fēijī bādiǎn jiù dào le.

(4) The plane didn't arrive till ten.
(= The plane finally arrived at ten o'clock)
飞机十点才到。
Fēijī shídiǎn cái dào.

(5) Expected amount of time studying: 3 years
Actual amount of time spent: 1 year
Sentence: 他很聪明，学习了一年就学会了。
Tā hěn cōngming, xuéxíle yìnián jiù xuéhuì le.
He is smart. He learned it in only one year.

(6) Expected amount of time studying: 3 years
Actual amount of time spent: 10 years
Sentence: 中文很难，他学习了十年才学会。
Zhōngwén hěn nán, tā xuéxíle shínián cái xuéhuì.
Chinese is difficult to learn. He spent ten years to master the language.

(7) Expected number of repetitions: 3 times
Actual number of repetitions: 1 time
Sentence: 这个句子很容易，我听了一遍就听懂了。
Zhè ge jùzi hěn róngyi, wǒ tīngle yíbiàn jiù tīngdǒng le.
This sentence is easy. I got it after listening to it only once.

(8) Expected number of repetitions: 3 times
Actual number of repetitions: 5 times
Sentence: 这个句子虽然很短，可是我听了五遍才听懂。
Zhè ge jùzi suīrán hěn duǎn, kěshì wǒ tīngle wǔbiàn cái tīngdǒng.
Although the sentence is short, I didn't understand it until I had heard it five times.

(9) Expected price: $5.00
Actual amount paid: $2.00
Sentence: 这本书，我花了两块钱就买到了。
Zhè běn shū, wǒ huāle liǎngkuài qián jiù mǎidào le.
I bought this book for as little as two dollars.

(10) Expected price: $5.00
Actual amount paid: $10.00
Sentence: 我用了十块钱才买到这本书，真贵。
Wǒ yòngle shíkuài qián cái mǎidào zhè běn shū, zhēn guì.

> I spent as much as ten dollars to buy this book. How expensive!

(11) 这本小说我看了一天就看完了。

  Zhè běn xiǎoshuō, wǒ kànle yìtiān jiù kànwán le.

  (The novel is short, or I am smart, or for other some reasons,) I have managed to finish reading the novel in only one day.

(12) 这本小说我看了一天才看完。

  Zhè běn xiǎoshuō wǒ kànle yìtiān cái kànwán.

  (The novel is too long, too difficult, or I am a slow reader, or, for whatever reasons,) I spent as much as one whole day to finally finish reading this novel.

(13.a) 他七点半就离开了。

  Tā qīdiǎnbàn jiù líkāi le.

(13.b) 他七点半才离开。

  Tā qīdiǎnbàn cái líkāi.

  (What is the difference in meaning?)

(14) 你说从北京开车到这儿来，半个小时就能到了。我怎么开了一个半小时才到呢？

  Nǐ shuō cóng Běijīng kāi chē dào zhèr lái, bànge xiǎoshí jiù néng dào le. Wǒ zěnme kāile yígebàn xiǎoshí cái dào ne?

  You said it'd take only half an hour to get here from Beijing by car. How come it took me an hour and a half?

(15) 昨天电影院门口真挤。我等了三个小时才买到票。

  Zuótiān diànyǐngyuàn ménkǒu zhēn jǐ. Wǒ děngle sānge xiǎoshí cái mǎidào piào.

  It was really crowded outside of the movie theater yesterday. I had to wait for three hours before I could get my tickets.

(16) A: 你怎么现在才来啊？

    Nǐ zěnme xiànzài cái lái a?

    How come that you didn't get here till now?

  B: 我八点钟就到了。我已经等了很久了。

    Wǒ bādiǎn zhōng jiù dàole. Wǒ yǐjīng děngle hěn jiǔ le.

    I was already here by eight o'clock. I have been waiting for a long time.

(17) 今天天气不太好，我们走到山脚才能看见山上的建筑。要是不是阴天，我们在城里就能清清楚楚地看到山上的房子了。

  Jīntiān tiānqì bú tài hǎo, wǒmen zǒu dào shānjiǎo cái néng kànjiàn

shānshang de jiànzhù. Yàoshì búshì yīntiān, wǒmen zài chéngli jiù néng qīngqīngchǔchǔde kàndào shānshang de fángzi le.
The weather is not too good today. We weren't able to see the buildings on the mountain until we reached the foot of the mountain. If it weren't overcast, we would have been able to see the houses on the mountains clearly from the city.

Lesson 42

1. The Potential Complement

A "Potential Complement" construction (PC) is a special grammatical device in the Chinese language to indicate the possibility or impossibility of achieving a desired result through an action. It is formed by inserting a particle between a verb (i.e. the action) and its resultative or directional complement. The particle always remains as an unstressed syllable.

1.1 The particle for the positive potential form is 得 *de*.

> Positive Form: Verb－得－Complement

For example, if the verbal unit is 听懂 (Verb－Resultative Complement) "to figure out from listening," the potential form is 听得懂 "to be able to figure out from listening." If the complement is a directional form, the formation follows the same pattern: 进来→进得来 .

(A) Resultative Complement: 听懂→听得懂

　　(1)　　我想他听得懂这个故事。
　　　　　Wǒ xiǎng tā tīng de dǒng zhè ge gùshì.
　　　　　I think he is able to understand this story.

(B) Resultative Complement: 找到→找得到

　　(2)　　今天下午你找得到王老师吗？
　　　　　Jīntiān xiàwǔ nǐ zhǎo de dào Wāng lǎoshī ma?
　　　　　Are you able to find Teacher Wang this afternoon?

(C) Directional Complement: 回来→回得来

(3)　十二点以前我回得来。

Shí'èrdiǎn yǐqián wǒ huí de lái.

I am able to return before twelve o'clock.

(4)　今天的练习不难，我半个小时作得完。

Jīntiān de liànxí bù nán, wǒ bànge xiǎoshí zuò de wán.

The exercises today are not difficult. I will be able to finish them in half an hour.

(5)　虽然汉语不容易学，但是你这么聪明，你一定学得会。

Suīrán Hànyǔ bù róngyi xué, dànshì nǐ zhème cōngming, nǐ yídìng xué de huì.

Although Chinese is not easy to learn, you will be able to master it since you are so very smart.

1.2　The negative pattern places 不 between the verb and the complement. 得 and 不 are mutually exclusive in the potential complement construction.

```
            Negative Form:   Verb－不－Complement
```

(6)　记得住 → 记不住

我记不住这些生词的意思。

Wǒ jì bu zhù zhè xiē shēngcí de yìsi.

I can't remember the meanings of these new words.

(7)　听得清楚 → 听不清楚

你说什么？我听不清楚。请你说得慢一点儿。

Nǐ shuō shénme? Wǒ tīng bu qīngchu. Qǐng nǐ shuō de màn yìdiǎnr.

What did you say? I can't hear you very well. Please speak a little more slowly.

(8)　回得去 → 回不去

太晚了，没有公共汽车了。我们今天回不去了。

Tài wǎn le, méi you gōnggòng qìchē le. Wǒmen jīntiān huí bu qù le.

It's too late and there aren't any more buses. We can't go home today.

(9)　门太小了，车进不去。

Mén tài xiǎo le, chē jìn bu qù.

The gate is too small. It's impossible for the car to get through.

(10)　我才学了几个月汉语，我还看不懂中文报。

Wǒ cái xuéle jǐge yuè Hànyǔ, wǒ hái kàn bu dǒng Zhōngwén bào.

I have only studied Chinese for a few months. I still can't read a Chinese newspaper.

(11)　天太黑了，我看不见墙上的字。

Tiān tài hēi le, wǒ kàn bu jiàn qiángshang de zì.

It's too dark. I can't see clearly the characters on the wall.

1.3 The interrogative is formed by either using the 吗－particle or adopting the affirmative－negative pattern. In the latter case, as illustrated below, the juxtaposition requires the use of the entire positive and negative units and not just a part of either unit.

$$[\text{Verb}-得-\text{Complement}] \quad + \quad [\text{Verb}-不-\text{Complement}]$$

(12)　讲完：这课语法，你一个小时讲得完讲不完？

Zhè kè yǔfǎ, nǐ yíge xiǎoshí jiǎng de wán jiǎng bu wán?

Are you able to finish the grammar of this lesson in an hour?

(13)　看懂：这个艺术家的画儿，你看得懂看不懂？

Zhè ge yìshùjiā de huàr, nǐ kàn de dǒng kàn bu dǒng?

Can you understand the paintings by this artist?

(14)　带来：那些书，你明天带得来带不来？

Nà xiē shū, nǐ míngtiān dài de lái dài bu lái?

Will you be able to bring those books tomorrow?

(15)　这些照片，今天洗得好洗不好？

Zhè xiē zhàopiàn, jīntiān xǐ de hǎo xǐ bu hǎo?

Will these pictures be ready today?

(16)　我在这儿说话，你们在那儿听得见听不见？

Wǒ zài zhèr shuō huà, nǐmen zài nàr tīng de jiàn tīng bu jiàn?

I'm talking over here. Can you hear me from over there?

(17)　你要去这么多地方，你说你吃饭以前回得来吗？

Nǐ yào qù zhème duō dìfang, nǐ shuō nǐ chī fàn yǐqián huí de lái ma?

You have to go to all these places. Do you think you will be able to get back before lunch?

1.4　A simple Object may appear after the potential complement, but a complex Object is usually preposed.

(18)　我找不到他。

Wǒ zhǎo bu dào tā.

I wasn't able to find him.

(19.a)　你看得见看不见山上的亭子？

Nǐ kàn de jiàn kàn bu jiàn shānshang de tíngzi?

Are you able to see the pavilion on the mountain?

(19.b)　山上的亭子，你看得见看不见？

Shānshang de tíngzi, nǐ kàn de jiàn kàn bu jiàn?

(20)　我新买的那辆自行车，明天修得好吗？

Wǒ xīn mǎi de nà liàng zìxíngchē, míngtiān xiū de hǎo ma?

Will you be able to fix by tomorrow the bike that I newly bought?

(21)　寄到上海的航空信，下星期一一定收得到。

Jì dào Shànghǎi de hángkōngxìn, xià xīngqīyī yídìng shōu de dào.

It is possible (for the receiver) to receive by next Monday the letter sent to Shanghai by airmail.

Sentence (18) contains a very simple Object 他, which comes after the potential complement unit. On the other hand, the Objects in sentences (20) and (21) are both long nominal expressions, each modified by a relative clause, and, for this reason, it is stylistically preferable to place them at the very beginning of the sentences as topics. In sentences (19.a) and (19.b), however, topicalization is an option since the Object 亭子 carries an attribute（山上的）that is relatively short and simple.

1.5　For emphasis, a potential complement may sometimes be used together with an optative auxiliary that expresses possibility or ability. Semantic redundancy is never considered a linguistic flaw in Chinese so long as it does not involve grammatical repetition. For example, the messages of the following sentences are reinforced through the combined use of (a) either 能 or 可以 as the preverbal auxiliary and (b) the 得 units as potential complements.

(22)　虽然他写字写得不很清楚，但是我都能看得懂。
　　　Suīrán tā xiě zì xiě de bù hěn qīngchu, dànshì wǒ dōu néng kàn de dǒng.
　　　Even though he doesn't write very clearly, I can figure out all of it.

(23)　一个星期的练习，我一天怎么可以作得完呢？
　　　Yíge xīngqī de liànxí, wǒ yìtiān zěnme kěyǐ zuò de wán ne?
　　　How can I finish one week's exercises in one day?

However, in a request form, we must use the auxiliary, and not the potential complement. In other words, the potential complement expresses potentiality and not permissibility.

(24)　我可以进来吗？
　　　Wǒ kěyǐ jìnlái ma?
　　　May I come in?

(25)　*我进得来吗？
　　　*Wǒ jìn de lái ma?

In a different situational context, such as when referring to someone who is trying to squeeze his/her way through a very narrow doorway, (25) is a perfectly acceptable sentence. The following are some more examples to illustrate the use of the optative, and not the potential complement, in making a request.

(26.a)　我们能进来打个电话吗？
　　　　Wǒmen néng jìnlái dǎ ge diànhuà ma?
　　　　Can we come in to make a call?

(26.b)　*我们进得来打个电话吗？
　　　　*Wǒmen jìn de lái dǎ ge diànhuà ma?

(27.a)　我们可以带他去吗？
　　　　Wǒmen kěyǐ dài tā qù ma?
　　　　Can we take him along?

(27.b)　*我们带得他去吗？
　　　　*Wǒmen dài de tā qù ma?

1.6 Distinctions between the Potential Complement and the Complement of Degree: The complement of degree, as introduced in Lesson 25, is formed by attaching the complement expression to the end of the verb with the marker 得 sitting in between: "Verb ＋ 得 ＋ Complement." Hence, it is identical to the potential complement in form, at least on the surface. For example, sentence (28) could mean either "He writes clearly," or "He is able to write clearly," a distinction that would become obvious when the proper contexts are given.

（28）　他写得清楚。

Tā xiě de qīngchu.

（29）　A: 那些字很难。他写得清楚写不清楚？

Nà xiē zì hěn nán. Tā xiě de qīngchu xiě bu qīngchu?

Those Chinese characters are difficult. Is he able to write them clearly?

B: 他写得清楚。　　　　　　　　　　　　　(Potential Complement)

Tā xiě de qīngchu.

He is able to write them clearly.

（30）　A: 那些字他写得清楚不清楚？

Nà xiē zì tā xiě de qīngchu bu qīngchu?

Did he write those characters clearly?

B: 他写得（很）清楚。　　　　　　　　　　(Complement of Degree)

Tā xiě de (hěn) qīngchu.

He wrote them clearly.

There are, however, more formal ways to distinguish the two complement constructions.

(A) A potential complement never takes an adverbial modifier (such as 很), but a degree complement generally appears with some kind of a degree adverbial.

（31）　Potential Complement: 这些汉字，她写得清楚。

Zhè xiē Hànzì, tā xiě de qīngchu.

She is able to write these Chinese characters clearly.

（32）　Degree Complement: 这些汉字，她写得非常清楚。

Zhè xiē Hànzì, tā xiě de fēicháng qīngchu.

She wrote these Chinese characters extremely clearly.

(B) A potential complement construction can take an Object directly after it, but a degree complement requires that either the Object be preposed or the verb be repeated.

(33)　Potential Complement:　她写得清楚这些汉字。
　　　　　　　　　　　　　　　Tā xiě de qīngchu zhè xiē Hànzì.
　　　　　　　　　　　　　　　She is able to write these Chinese characters clearly.

(34.a) Degree Complement:　这些汉字，她写得很清楚。
　　　　　　　　　　　　　　　Zhè xiē Hànzì, tā xiě de hěn qīngchu.

(34.b) Degree Complement:　她写这些汉字写得很清楚。
　　　　　　　　　　　　　　　Tā xiě zhè xiē Hànzì xiě de hěn qīngchu.
　　　　　　　　　　　　　　　She wrote these Chinese characters clearly.

(C) A potential complement forms its negative by replacing 得 with 不, but a degree complement forms its negative by putting 不 after 得.

(35)　Potential Complement:　这些汉字，她写不清楚。
　　　　　　　　　　　　　　　Zhè xiē Hànzì, tā xiě bu qīngchu.
　　　　　　　　　　　　　　　She isn't able to write these Chinese characters clearly.

(36)　Degree Complement:　这些汉字，她写得不清楚。
　　　　　　　　　　　　　　　Zhè xiē Hànzì, tā xiě de bù qīngchu.
　　　　　　　　　　　　　　　She didn't write these Chinese characters clearly.

(D) Interrogative: Study the following pairs of sentences.

(37)　Potential Complement:　她写得清楚吗？
　　　　　　　　　　　　　　　Tā xiě de qīngchu ma?
　　　　　　　　　　　　　　　Is she able to write clearly?

(38)　Degree Complement:　她写得（很）清楚吗？
　　　　　　　　　　　　　　　Tā xiě de (hěn) qīngchu ma?
　　　　　　　　　　　　　　　Did she write clearly?

(39) Potential Complement: 她写不清楚吗？

                                          Tā xiě bu qīngchu ma?

                                          She isn't able to write clearly, is she?

(40) Degree Complement: 她写得不清楚吗？

                                          Tā xiě de bù qīngchu ma?

                                          She didn't write clearly, did she?

(41) Potential Complement: 她写得清楚写不清楚？

                                          Tā xiě de qīngchu xiě bu qīngchu?

                                          Is she able to write clearly (or not)?

(42) Degree Complement: 她写得清楚不清楚？

                                          Tā xiě de qīngchu bu qīngchu?

                                          Did she write clearly (or not)?

Notice that only in the first pair do we have a possible complete identity between the two complement constructions. In the other two pairs where the negative pattern is involved, the differentiation is very 清楚. In the affirmative－negative question form, the potential complement juxtaposes the entire potential units (Verb 得 Complement ＋ Verb 不 Complement), whereas the pattern for the degree complement takes only the complement and its negative after the verb (Verb 得 Complement－不 Complement). The following is a table to sum up the distinctions between the two types of complements. A few more examples are given at the end of this section to further demonstrate a mixed use of various complement patterns.

	Degree Complement	Potential Complement
Positive	Verb 得 很 Complement	Verb 得 Complement
Negative	Verb 得 不 Complement	Verb 不 Complement
Interrogative	Verb 得 Complement 不 Complement? Verb 得 Complement 吗? Verb 得 不 Complement 吗?	Verb 得 Complement Verb 不 Complement Verb 得 Complement 吗? Verb 不 Complement 吗?
Verb＋Object	Verb Object Verb 得 Complement	Verb 得 Complement Object

(43) A: 别走，你故事还没讲完呢。

Bié zǒu, nǐ gùshì hái méi jiǎngwán ne.

Don't go! You haven't finished telling the story yet.

B: 时间不早了，我今天讲不完了。明天再讲吧。

Shíjiān bù zǎo le, wǒ jīntiān jiǎng bù wán le. Míngtiān zài jiǎng ba.

It's getting late and I won't be able to finish telling it today. I'll continue telling it tomorrow.

A: 明天一定讲得完吗？

Míngtiān yídìng jiǎng de wán ma?

Are you sure you will be able to finish telling it tomorrow?

(44) A: 今天的菜太多了。

Jīntiān de cài tài duō le.

There are too many dishes today.

B: 不多，不多。我们这么多人，一定吃得完。你尝尝这个菜吧。

Bù duō, bù duō. Wǒmen zhème duō rén, yídìng chī de wán. Nǐ chángcháng zhè ge cài ba.

Not really. With all of us here, we will definitely be able to finish them. Please try this dish.

A: 是鱼！对不起，大夫说我不能吃鱼。

Shì yú! Duì bu qǐ, dàifu shuō wǒ bù néng chī yú.

It's fish! Sorry, the doctor said that I can't eat fish.

B: 是吗？太可惜了。我们今天要的这个鱼作得非常好吃。

Shì ma? Tài kěxī le. Wǒmen jīntiān yào de zhè ge yú zuò de fēicháng hǎochī.

Really? That's too bad. The fish that we ordered today is really delicious.

(45) A: 我想拿照片去那儿洗。不知道他们一天洗得好洗不好？

Wǒ xiǎng ná zhàopiàn qù nàr xǐ. Bù zhīdao tāmen yìtiān xǐ de hǎo xǐ bu hǎo?

I want to take my film there for development. I wonder if they will be able to do it in one day.

B: 那个商店，我以前去过。他们洗照片洗得不太好。你还是去别的地方洗吧。

Nà ge shāngdiàn, wǒ yǐqián qùguo. Tāmen xǐ zhàopiàn xǐ de bú tài hǎo. Nǐ háishì qù biéde dìfang xǐ ba.

I've been to that store before. They don't develop film well. You'd better go somewhere else to do it.

1.7 In our previous discussion of the resultative complement, we made a distinction between the resultative and the locative complements. One important reason for the differentiation is that they exhibit different degrees of compatibility with the potential form. As demonstrated above, resultative units are always ready to be expanded into a potential form: "Verb－得/不－Resultative Complement." In contrast, a locative complement is seldom placed in the potential pattern. Please compare the following sentences:

(A) Resultative Complement:

（46）那本语法书，你找得到找不到？

Nà běn yǔfǎ shū, nǐ zhǎo de dào zhǎo bu dào?

Are you able to find that grammar book?

(B) Locative Complement:

（47.a）我们下星期可以学到第五十课吗？

Wǒmen xià xīngqī kěyǐ xué dào dìwǔshíkè ma?

Are we able to learn up to Lesson 50 by next week?

（47.b）*我们下星期学得到学不到第五十课？

*Wǒmen xià xīngqī xué de dào xué bu dào dìwǔshíkè?

(C) Directional Complement:

（48）上边没有路，我们上不去。

Shàngbiān méi yǒu lù, wǒmen shàng bu qù.

There is no trail up there. We can't go up.

Both sentences (46) and (48) are cast in the potential mode; the former contains a resultative complement and the latter a directional complement. The resultative complement in (46) is 到, which is identical in form to the locative complement in (47.a). Yet, the 到－complement in (47.b) is not expandable in the potential pattern. To indicate ability or possibility, we need to use an optative verb, as phrased in (47.a). Hence, even though this 到 bears some semantic resemblance to a resultative or directional complement in marking the consequential state of an action, its syntactic behavior is quite different.

2. Idiomatic Potential Complement Expressions

Some special potential complement expressions carry idiomatic readings and have, therefore, to be memorized individually. A few of these idiomatic potential complement expressions may not be converted back to regular resultative complement units. For example, while 看得见 is derived from 看见, none of the following "Verb 一得／不一Complement" has a corresponding "Verb一Complement" in modern Mandarin.

2.1 Verb 一得下: The expression verb 得下 "Verb *de xià*" indicates capacity or ability to contain or hold.

(1)   这个停车场很大，停得下七百辆汽车。
Zhè ge tíngchēchǎng hěn dà, tíng de xià qībǎiliàng qìchē.
This parking lot is big; it can hold 700 cars.
(= It has room for 700 cars to park there.)

(2)   这个房间住不下四个人。
Zhè ge fángjiān zhù bu xià sìge rén.
This room is not big enough for four people (to live in it).

(3)   没想到这个礼堂这么大。有八十米宽，一百米长吧？坐得下一万人吗？
Méi xiǎngdào zhè ge lǐtáng zhème dà. Yǒu bāshimǐ kuān, yìbǎimǐ cháng ba? Zuò de xià yíwàn rén ma?
I never thought that this auditorium would be so huge. It must be eighty meters wide and one hundred meters long. Can it hold ten thousand people?

(4)   万太太的孩子病了。这几天，她吃不下东西，睡不好觉。
Wàn tàitai de háizi bìngle. Zhè jītiān, tā chī bu xià dōngxi, shuì bu hǎo jiào.
Mrs. Wan's child is sick. For the last few days, she hasn't been able to eat or sleep well.

Sentences (1) to (3) refer to the size or accommodation of a room or building. The verb in each case is not a word meaning "to contain" but rather a verb that refers to the way in which one makes use of the structure, for example, 停 in relation to a

parking lot, 住 in relation to a room, and 坐 in relation to an auditorium. The verb may change depending on the scenario, as illustrated in the following sentence.

（5） 一辆 Volkswagen 坐得下四个人。可是我们有六个人，你说挤得下挤
不下？
Yíliàng Volkswagen zuò de xià sìge rén. Kěshì wǒmen yǒu liùge rén, nǐ shuō jǐ de xià jǐ bu xià?
A Volkswagen can hold four people. But there are six of us. Do you think we can all squeeze in?

It is interesting to note that, among the examples given above, only (4) demonstrates an actor-action relationship between its subject and verbs. Both actions, 吃不下 and 睡不好, are what the subject, 万太太, experiences. In all the other sentences, however, the subject nominals represent not the agents but rather the places where the actions are carried out. The agents appear in the Object slots instead. A simple rule to remember in this seemingly complicated "Verb－得／不－下" pattern is that, regardless of what appears in the subject position, the choice of the verb is contingent upon what the agent does or undergoes. The agent may actually be the subject of the sentence as in (4); or, when the subject slot is occupied by a place expression, the agent may take up the Object position, as in the other examples. The verb remains constant in its relationship with the agent of the action.

2.2 Verb－得－了: 了 *liǎo*, a verb meaning "to complete," is seldom used as a predicate or a resultative complement by itself. But, it often functions as a potential complement with the following meanings.

2.2.1 Verb 得了 "able to finish Verb": The first use of the pattern is built upon the literal reading of 了 "to complete." In this sense, "Verb 得了" is similar to "Verb 得完" in meaning as well as in usage. The two patterns are often interchangeable, except for certain idiomatic expressions.

（6） 你们两个人吃得了六个菜吗？
Nǐmen liǎngge rén chī de liǎo liùge cài ma?
Are the two of you able to finish eating six dishes?

（7） 我一个人花不了这么多钱。
Wǒ yíge rén huā bu liǎo zhème duō qián.
I can't spend (use up) so much money all by myself.

(8) 我作这些练习，用不了两个小时。
     Wǒ zuò zhè xiē liànxí, yòng bu liǎo liǎngge xiǎoshí.
     I don't need (to use) two hours to do these exercises.

(9) 买这种旧车，用不了一万块钱。
     Mǎi zhè zhǒng jiù chē, yòng bu liǎo yíwànkuài qián.
     It won't cost ten thousand dollars to buy an old car like this.

While "Verb 得完" may be used to replace "Verb 得了" in sentences (6) and (7), the substitution is not possible for 用不了 in sentences (8) and (9). 吃得了 in sentence (6) indicates the ability to eat, and insofar as gastronomic appetite is concerned, it seems very close in meaning to 吃得下 *chī de xià*. In usage, however, the two forms are not interchangeable. 吃得了 refers more to the quantity of food that one is able to consume, whereas 吃得下 is more concerned with one's appetite, which may be conditioned by a host of factors such as one's culinary taste. The following examples illustrates this difference.

(10) 你今天叫的菜太多了，我真的吃不了。
     Nǐ jīntiān jiào de cài tài duō le, wǒ zhēn de chī bu liǎo.
     You've ordered too many dishes. I really can't eat all of them.

(11) 你今天叫的菜都是肉，我真的吃不下。
     Nǐ jīntiān jiào de cài dōu shì ròu, wǒ zhēn de chī bu xià.
     All the dishes you've ordered are meat dishes. I really can't eat them.

(12) 我刚吃过饭。我现在真的吃不下。
     Wǒ gāng chīguo fàn. Wǒ xiànzài zhēn de chī bu xià.
     I just had my meal. I really can't eat any more now.

2.2.2 Verb 得了 "possible/able to Verb": The second use of the pattern is simply to indicate possibility or ability.

(13) 明天早上七点，你来得了吗？
     Míngtiān zǎoshang qīdiǎn, nǐ lái de liǎo ma?
     Are you able to come at seven o'clock tomorrow morning?

(14) 这种翻译工作，他作得了作不了？
     Zhè zhǒng fānyì gōngzuò, tā zuò de liǎo zuò bu liǎo?
     Is he able to carry out such a translation assignment?

(15) 他昨天病了，今天来不了了。
     Tā zuótiān bìngle, jīntiān lái bu liǎo le.
     He fell ill yesterday. He won't be able to come today.

（16）　我永远忘不了你在信里说的话。

Wǒ yǒngyuǎn wàng bu liǎo nǐ zài xìnli shuō de huà.

I shall never (be able to) forget what you said in the letter.

In none of the above sentences does the word 了 *liǎo* denote "completion." In fact, it does not carry any meaning of its own, except for the reading of "possibility/ability" as part of the potential pattern. Its function may be likened to that of a dummy constituent that is included in a pattern for lack of a better choice. The potential construction requires the presence of a complement, but as there are no appropriate complement words for the verbs in the above sentences, the dummy 了 is selected to fill the slot.

The graph 了 represents several different words in Chinese, most of which are related by the basic semantic feature of "completion." Its use as a full verb is no longer productive in the modern language, but its completive reading is still prominent in its appearance as a complement. The perfective use of 了 as an aspect marker also betrays its origin as a linguistic form denoting completion or conclusion.

2.3　Verb 得动 : This potential unit indicates the ability or inability to make something or some person move 动 *dòng*. As a verb, means "to move, to get moving." As a complement, it describes movement as a result of an action.

（17）　这么远，你走得动吗？

Zhème yuǎn, nǐ zǒu de dòng ma?

It is so far! Are you able to walk there?

（18）　你一个人拿不动这些东西吧。

Nǐ yíge rén ná bu dòng zhè xiē dōngxi ba.

You can't carry these things all by yourself.

(= It is not possible for you to pick up the things and hold them yourself.)

In the first example, 动 refers back to the subject or actor of 走 , whereas in the second sentence it refers to the Object 东西 , to which the actor applies the action 拿. In other words, the "Verb－得/不－动" unit may be either inward or outward in terms of the direction of the action: it may revert back to the actor or it may act upon something/someone else. The following are a few more examples:

(19) 这个电视机太重了，我一个人搬不动。请你帮我搬到客厅去。

Zhè ge diànshìjī tài zhòng le, wǒ yíge rén bān bu dòng. Qǐng nǐ bāng wǒ bān dào kètīng qù.

This TV set is too heavy. I can't move it all by myself. Can you help me move it into the living room?

(20) 虽然我老了，干不了重活儿了，但是我还走得动路。

Suīrán wǒ lǎo le, gàn bu liǎo zhòng huór le, dànshì wǒ hái zǒu de dòng lù.

Although I am old and can no longer do heavy work, yet I still can walk.

(21) 我已经跑了三个多小时了，我真的跑不动了。

Wǒ yǐjīng pǎole sānge duō xiǎoshí le, wǒ zhēnde pǎo bu dòng le.

I've been running for more than three hours now; I really can't run any more.

(22) 这个车已经几个月没开了。你看现在还开得动开不动？

Zhè ge chē yǐjīng jǐge yuè méi kāi le. Nǐ kàn xiànzài hái kāi de dòng kāi bu dòng?

This car hasn't been driven for months. See if you can still make it run?

3. 开 as a Resultative Complement

开 *kāi* generally functions as a full verb, meaning "to open, to turn on (a switch)." As a complement, it marks the result of an action that moves an object away from its original position. In this sense, its use is similar to that of "away" is English.

(1) 跑开
     pǎokāi
     to run away

(2) 拿开椅子
     nákāi yǐzi
     to take away the chair

(3) 开开门
     kāikāi mén
     to open the door
     (the action of opening causes the door to move away from its original position of being shut)

(4)   打开书
dǎkāi shū
to open the book
(literally, to strike open the book)

(5)   桌子上的东西，请你搬开一下儿，好吗？我们现在要用桌子吃饭。
Zhuōzishang de dōngxi, qǐng nǐ bānkāi yíxiàr, hǎo ma? Wǒmen
xiànzài yào yòng zhuōzi chī fàn.
Can you move away the things on the table? We need to use the
table for eating.

开 as an resultative complement may also appear in the potential complement pattern. Examples are:

(6)   我今天很忙，一定走不开。
Wǒ jīntiān hěn máng, yídìng zǒu bu kāi.
I am very busy today. For sure, I won't be able to get away from
work.

(7)   教室的门坏了，打不开。学生都在里边，出不来了。
Jiàoshì de mén huài le, dǎ bu kāi. Xuésheng dōu zài lǐbiān, chū bu
lái le.
The classroom door is broken. It can't be opened. The students are
all inside, unable to get out.

(8)   A: 今天这么热，你怎么不开窗户？
Jīntiān zhème rè, nǐ zěnme bù kāi chuānghu?
It's so hot today. How come you didn't open the window?
B: 我开不开。
Wǒ kāi bu kāi.
I can't open it.
A: 开得开！你看，我一开就开开了。
Kāi de kāi! Nǐ kàn, wǒ yì kāi jiù kāikāi le.
It sure can be opened. See, all I did was to turn the handle and
it's now opened. (See, as soon as I opened it, it opened.)

4. Numbers (continued)

We have learned how to say numbers up to 九百九十九 "999." The next number
goes to a higher digit, which is 千 *qiān* "thousand." The digit beyond 千, namely

"ten thousand," has its own designation in Chinese: 万 *wàn*. Therefore, in contrast with English which basically uses four numerical units, Chinese operates on a five unit system.

	万 wàn	千 qiān	百 bǎi	十 shí	一一
900			九百		
990			九百	九十	
1,000		一千			
1,001		一千			零一
1,019		一千		零一十	九
1,122		一千	一百	二十	二
1,801		一千	八百		零一
2,000		二千			
3,644		三千	六百	四十	
9,890		九千	八百	九十	四
10,000	一万				
10,001	一万				零一
99,803	九万	九千	八百		零三
100,000	十万				
100,001	十万				零一
825,179	八十二万	五千	一百	七十	九
1,000,000	一百万				

When counting, it is obligatory in Chinese to go to the next higher numerical unit whenever possible. For example, 1,500 could be either "one thousand and five hundred" or "fifteen hundred" in English; in Chinese it is always 一千五百 *yìqiān wǔbǎi*, and never *十五百. Similarly, 10,000 is 一万 *yíwàn* and never *十千. Thirty-eight thousand is 三万八千 *sānwàn bāqiān* and not *三十八千. The following are some sample sentences with large numerical expressions:

(1)　　这个广场真大，站得下十几万人吧？
　　　　Zhè ge guǎngchǎng zhēn dà, zhàn de xià shíjǐwàn rén ba?
　　　　This is really a huge square. It probably can hold more than a hundred thousand people.

(2)　　你的房子只有两间卧室，一个厕所。我看卖不了二十多万。
　　　　Nǐ de fángzi zhǐ yǒu liǎngjiān wòshì, yíge cèsuǒ. Wǒ kàn mài bu liǎo èrshiduōwàn.
　　　　Your house has only two bedrooms and one bath room. I don't think it can sell for two hundred and some thousand dollars.

5. The Use of 这么

这么 *zhème* may be used with both adjectives and verbs, carrying the same meaning "so..., in such a manner."

(1)　　天气这么冷，我不想出去了。
　　　　Tiānqì zhème lěng, wǒ bù xiǎng chūqù le.
　　　　The weather is so cold. I don't want to go out.

(2)　　来，来，我们一起吃吧。我一个人吃不了这么多菜。
　　　　Lái, lái, wǒmen yìqǐ chī ba. Wǒ yíge rén chī bu liǎo zhème duō cài.
　　　　Come, come. Let's eat together. I can't possibly finish this food all by myself.

(3)　　雨下得这么大，我怕我叔叔来不了了。
　　　　Yǔ xià de zhème dà, wǒ pà wǒ shūshu lái bu liǎo le.
　　　　It's raining so hard. I'm afraid my uncle won't be able to make it.

(4)　　这个汉字应该这么写。
　　　　Zhè ge Hànzì yīnggāi zhème xiě.
　　　　This Chinese character should be written like this.

(5)　这个箱子要这么拿才拿得动。

Zhè ge xiāngzi yào zhème ná cái ná de dòng.

Only by holding the box this way can you carry it.

(6)　这么走，什么时候才可以走到？

Zhème zǒu, shénme shíhòu cái kěyǐ zǒu dào?

Walking like this, when will we be able to get there?

The first three sentences illustrate the use of "这么 ＋Adjective," and the last three, "这么 ＋Verb." In sentence (3), the unit 这么大 serves as the complement of the verbal expression 下雨.

In conversation, *zhème* is often pronounced as *zème*.

6. The Use of 对

The following is another idiomatic expression that requires the use of 对 :

> 对……很有研究
>
> duì...hěn yǒu yánjiū
>
> "to be knowledgeable in"

研究 *yánjiū* is in itself a verb, meaning "to study, to research." 有研究 *yǒu yánjiū* is a compound expression that behaves like an adjective: "knowledgeable, conversant." Hence, it is always modified by some kind of an adverb, such as 很 . To indicate the subject matter in which one is knowledgeable, we use the coverb 对 to introduce the nominal. The following are a few examples.

(1)　他对小说很有研究。

Tā duì xiǎoshuō hěn yǒu yánjiū.

He knows a lot about fiction.

(2)　你对哪种艺术最有研究？

Nǐ duì nǎ zhǒng yìshù zuì yǒu yánjiū?

What type of art are you most knowledgeable about?

(3)　他学建筑，可是对中国诗也很有研究。

Tā xué jiànzhù, kěshì duì Zhōngguó shī yě hěn yǒu yánjiū.

His speciality is architecture, but he is quite knowledgeable about Chinese poetry too.

1. The Complex Directional Complement

1.1 A complex directional complement refers to the juxtaposition of two indicators of direction in a verbal expression, the last being 来 or 去. The first member of the complex directional complement is from a very small set of seven motion verbs, all of which have already been introduced as main verbs: 上, 下, 进, 出, 回, 过, and 起. While the second member of the complement (DC$_2$) tells whether the movement is coming towards or going away from the speaker, the first one (DC$_1$) characterizes the movement in terms of its spatial relation with the location: for example, 进 *jìn* marks a motion entering a destination point and 出 *chū* indicates exit from an origin point. The verb itself specifies the manner in which the motion (for example, 跑 *pǎo* "running," 走 *zǒu* "walking," 飞 *fēi* "flying," etc.) or action (for example, 拿 *ná* "carrying," 寄 *jì* "mailing," 送 *sòng* "escorting," etc.) is carried out.

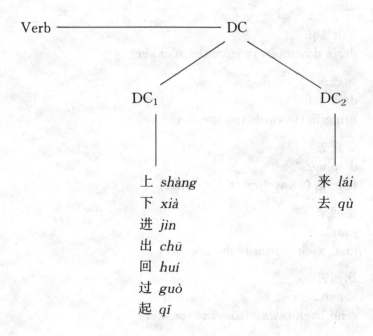

Or,

Verb +	上来　下来　进来　出来　回来　过来　起来
	上去　下去　进去　出去　回去　过去

Please note that, of all the possible combinations, 起去 is not acceptable in modern Mandarin. The complex directional complements are generally pronounced as unstressed syllables even though they are here marked with their original tones. The following are some examples of the complex directional complement combinations:

(1)　走上来
　　　zǒushànglái
　　　walk up (towards the speaker)

(2)　飞上去
　　　fēishàngqù
　　　fly up (away from the speaker)

(3)　跑下来
　　　pǎoxiàlái
　　　run down (towards the speaker)

(4)　开下去
　　　kāixiàqù
　　　drive down (away from the speaker)

(5)　带进来
　　　dàijìnlái
　　　bring in (towards the speaker)

(6)　带进去
　　　dàijìnqù
　　　take in (away from the speaker)

(7)　寄回来
　　　jìhuílái
　　　mail back (towards the speaker)

(8)　送回去
　　　sònghuíqù
　　　send back (away from the speaker)

(9)　拿过来
náguòlái
carry over (towards the speaker)

(10)　游过去
yóuguòqù
swim over (away from the speaker)

(11)　站起来
zhànqǐlái
stand up

(12)　下雨了，等他的车开过来，我们再走出去。
Xià yǔ le, děng tā de chē kāiguòlái, wǒmen zài zǒuchūqù.
It's raining. Wait till his car is driven over and then we'll go out.

(13)　他一看见顾客走进来，就站起来，走过去问，"你们几位？"
Tā yí kànjiàn gùkè zǒujìnlái, jiù zhànqǐlái, zǒuguòqù wèn, "Nǐmen jǐwèi?"
As soon as he saw customers walk in, he got up and went over to ask, "How many are there in your party?"

(14)　这个饭馆的服务真快，我在门口要了菜，还没坐下来，菜就送上来了。我吃完了，筷子还没放下来，东西就都拿走了。
Zhè gè fànguǎn de fúwù zhēn kuài, wǒ zài ménkǒu yàole cài, hái méi zuòxiàlái, cài jiù sòngshànglái le. Wǒ chīwánle, kuàizi hái méi fàngxiàlái, dōngxi jiù dōu názǒu le.
The service at this restaurant is really fast. I ordered food at the entrance, and I had not yet sat down when the food was brought to me. After I finished eating, I had hardly put down the chopsticks when everything was taken away.

The complex directional complement is a very useful and productive construction in the Chinese language, but there are cases where some verbs do not appear with certain complex directional complements. 起来, for example, has a rather restricted appearance: it occurs mostly with 站 *zhàn* "stand," 坐 *zuò* "sit," 跳 *tiào* "jump," 拿 *ná* "carry, grab," and a few other verbs.

1.2　When a complex directional complement construction explicitly states a location, the place word appears between DC₁ and DC₂.

$$\boxed{\text{Verb} - \text{DC}_1 - \text{Place} - \text{DC}_2}$$

(15) 走进教室来

zǒujìn jiàoshì lái

Walk into the classroom (towards the speaker)

(16) 开进城去

kāijìn chéng qù

drive into the city (away from the speaker)

(17) 跑上楼去

pǎoshàng lóu qù

run upstairs (away from the speaker)

The place word in the pattern normally represents the destination point, as shown in (15) to (17). In some special situations, however, as in the next few examples, the place word may stand for the distance travelled or even the place of origin.

(18) 游过河去

yóuguò hé qù

swim across the river (away from the speaker)

(19) 跑下山来

pǎoxià shān lái

run down the hill (toward the speaker)

(20) 走出礼堂来

zǒuchū lǐtáng lái

walk out from the auditorium (toward the speaker)

In general, the place of origin appears in the form of 从……, while the place of destination occurs between the two directional complement elements.

$$\boxed{[\text{从 ORIGIN}] \quad + \quad [\text{Verb DC}_1 - \text{DESTINATION} - \text{DC}_2]}$$

(21) 你想从哪儿飞过去？

Nǐ xiǎng cóng nǎr fēi guòqù?

From where do you want to fly across?

（22） 你想从哪个门开进公园去？

Nǐ xiǎng cóng nǎ ge mén kāijìn gōngyuán qù?

From which gate do you want to drive into the park?

（23） 他一看见王老师从前门走进来，就从后门跑出去了。

Tā yí kànjiàn Wáng lǎoshī cóng qiánmén zǒujìnlái, jiù cóng hòumén pǎochūqù le.

As soon as he saw Teacher Wang walk in from the front door, he ran out from the back door.

（24） 张老师很高兴地从厨房里走出客厅来，欢迎大家。

Zhāng lǎoshī hěn gāoxìng de cóng chúfángli zǒuchū kètīng lái, huānyíng dàjiā.

Teacher Zhang came out happily from the kitchen into the living room to welcome everyone.

1.3 There are several slots in which an Object may appear in a complex directional complement construction:

a.	Verb	Object	DC$_1$		DC$_2$	
b.	Verb		DC$_1$	Object	DC$_2$	
c.	Verb		DC$_1$		DC$_2$	Object

（25.a） 他每星期寄一封信回去。

Tā měi xīngqī jì yìfēng xìn huí qù.

He writes home once a week.

（25.b） 他每星期寄回一封信去。

Tā měi xīngqī jìhuí yìfēng xìn qù.

（25.c） 他每星期寄回去一封信。

Tā měi xīngqī jìhuíqù yìfēng xìn.

The positioning of an Object in a directional complement construction is a rather complex matter, and the choice is often based on factors such as whether the Object is definite in reference, or whether the verb represents a completed action. Some of the general rules are:

(A) If the Object is definite in reference, it is preferable to move the Object to the front as the topic of the sentence.

(26)　　这本书，请你拿回去。

　　　　Zhè běn shū, qǐng nǐ ná huíqù.

　　　　Please take this book back.

Another possible placement of this Object involves the use of a coverb 把, a pattern we will learn in Lesson 47.

(B) If the Object is not definite in reference, the preferable word order is to position the Object after the complex directional complement: "Verb－DC_1－DC_2－Object." The preference becomes even more prevalent when the verb represents a completed action and the Object is preceded by "一　＋　Measure."

(27)　　我明年回中国的时候，很想带回去一个照相机。

　　　　Wǒ míngnián huí Zhōngguó de shíhòu, hěn xiǎng dàihuíqù yíge zhàoxiàngjī.

　　　　When I return to China next year, I'd really like to take a camera back with me.

(28)　　他从家里带出来了一张旧照片。

　　　　Tā cóng jiāli dàichūláile yìzhāng jiù zhàopiàn.

　　　　He has brought from home an old photo.

(29)　　他拿出来一条红裙子对我说，"你穿这条比较好看。"

　　　　Tā náchūlái yìtiáo hóng qúnzi duì wǒ shuō, "Nǐ chuān zhè tiáo bǐjiào hǎokàn."

　　　　He took out a red skirt and said to me, "You'll look better in this skirt."

(30)　　他从非洲寄回来很多好吃的东西。

　　　　Tā cóng Fēizhōu jìhuílái hěn duō hǎochī de dōngxi.

　　　　He sent back a lot of delicious things from Africa.

(31)　　最近有点儿冷，我的衣服不够，所以我妈妈给我买回来了一件毛衣。

　　　　Zuìjìn yǒu diǎnr lěng, wǒ de yīfu bú gòu, suǒyǐ wǒ māma gěi wǒ mǎihuíláile yíjiàn máoyī.

　　　　It's getting a bit chilly lately and I don't have enough clothes. So, my mother bought (and brought back for) me a sweater.

(C) If the Object is a pronoun, we always place the Object before the complex directional complement: Verb－Object－DC_1－DC_2.

(32) 我现在没空儿。请你送他回去，好吗？
Wǒ xiànzài méi kòngr. Qǐng nǐ sòng tā huíqù, hǎo ma?
I don't have time now. Can you take him home?

(33) 我进来的时候，带了他一起进来。
Wǒ jìnlái de shíhòu, dàile tā yìqǐ jìnlái.
I brought him in when I came in.

(D) If ever in doubt as to what is the correct way to phrase a complex directional complement with an Object, it is generally (but not always) safe to adopt the order "Verb－Object－DC_1－DC_2". Most complex directional complement units can accommodate Objects in the pre-complemental position.

(E) Some idiomatic usages favor certain arrangements. For example, 拿起来 prefers the order in either (34.b) or (34.c), but not (34.a).

(34.a) *他从桌子上拿一本书起来。
*Tā cóng zhuōzishang ná yìběn shū qǐlái.
(34.b) 他从桌子上拿起一本书来。
Tā cóng zhuōzishang ná qǐ yìběn shū lái.
He picked up a book from the desk.
(34.c) 他从桌子上拿起来一本书。
Tā cóng zhuōzishang náqǐlái yìběn shū.

Or, when 出来 is used with certain verbs denoting the act of speaking or expressing an idea, the directional complement prefers the split arrangement, as in the following examples.

(35) 有的人说出话来，让人高兴，有的人说出话来，真不好听。
Yǒu de rén shuōchū huà lái, ràng rén gāoxìng, yǒu de rén shuōchū huà lái, zhēn bù hǎotīng.
There are those who say things that will make others feel happy, and there are those who say things that others will find difficult to accept.

(36) 你觉得我的话不对，请提出你的意见来。
Nǐ juéde wǒ de huà bú duì, qǐng tíchū nǐ de yìjiàn lái.
If you think what I said is wrong, please express your opinion.

In both cases, 说出来 and 提出来 place the Objects between the two directional complement elements. As always is the case, idomatic usages and preferences will have to be learned individually.

1.4   The perfective 了 usually appears after the verb in a "Verb—DC_1—DC"$_2$ combination, as in sentence (37).

(37)   他走了进去。
       Tā zǒule jìnqù.
       He walked in.

However, when a complex directional complement construction involves the use of an Object, the placement of 了 becomes a challenge, particularly for beginning students. As noted above, there are several possible patterns of ordering the Object with the verb and the two directional complements. Each pattern dictates its own positioning of 了. In other words, each time we want to mark a complex directional complement with 了, we have first to decide where to put the Object before we can place the perfective marker. The following table schematizes the complexity of the complex directional complement construction.

a.	Verb—了	Object	DC_1		DC_2

b.	Verb		DC_1	Object	DC_2 了

c.	Verb		DC_1		DC_2 了 Object

(38.a) 他带了东西回来。
        Tā dàile dōngxi huílái.
        He brought back something.

(38.b) 他带回东西来了。
        Tā dàihuí dōngxi lái le.

(38.c) 他带回来了东西。
        Tā dàihuíláile dōngxi.

(39)   他今天不想作饭，所以从食堂买了几个菜回来。
        Tā jīntiān bù xiǎng zuò fàn, suǒyǐ cóng shítáng mǎile jǐge cài huílái.
        He didn't want to cook, so he bought (and brought back) a few dishes from the cafeteria.

(40)   我从邮局拿回那封信来了。

Wǒ cóng yóujú náhuí nà fēng xìn lái le.

I brought back the letter from the post office.

(41)   他从房间里拿出来了一张照片。他对我说，"这张照片,请你寄回北京去。"

Tā cóng fángjiānli náchūláile yìzhāng zhàopiàn. Tā duì wǒ shuō,
"Zhè zhāng zhàopiàn, qǐng nǐ jìhuí Běijīng qù."

He brought out a photo from his room and said to me, "Please send this picture back to Beijing."

In sentence (40), when the split complement pattern is used, 了 is placed at the end of the sentence to indicate a completed action. If the two DC elements are bound together, 了 generally comes before the Object, as shown in (39) and (41). There are again exceptions to all these rules, as you will tell from examples you will encounter in either conversation or reading. The use of the double directional complement construction is a highly flexible and complicated process even for native speakers, who do not often agree on their preferences. Only through continuous exposure and repetitive practice will students be able to overcome their initial shock at these seemingly irregular or even capricious phenomena. The directional complement is one of the most common constructions in the Chinese language and it is important that we should 学好 in order to 说得好.

2. The Rhetorical Question (continued)

One way to form a rhetorical question in Chinese is to put the statement in the following interrogative pattern:

不是……吗？
bú shì...ma?

(1)   你不是很想看这个电影吗？为什么不去呢？

Nǐ bú shì hěn xiǎng kàn zhè ge diànyǐng ma? Wèishénme bú qù ne?

Didn't you want to see this movie very much? Why aren't you going?

Sentence (1) contains two questions. The first one, in the form of "不是……吗？", is not really intended to be a question; the speaker is perfectly sure of the fact that "you want to see the movie." The question is posed not to seek information but rather to produce certain special rhetorical effects, such as lending weight to the actual query, "Why aren't you going?"

      (2)   这不是你的表吗？

                  Zhè bú shì nǐ de biǎo ma?

                  Isn't this your watch?

                  (Scenario: The watch is right here. How come you didn't see it?)

Notice that when the main verb is 是 , as in (2), the pattern yields 不是（是……）吗？One of the two consecutive forms of 是 will be deleted.

      (3)   不是他来吗？怎么你来了？

                  Bú shì tā lái ma? Zěnme nǐ lái le?

                  Wasn't he supposed to come? How is it that you came (instead)?

Notice that the contrast in (3) now lies between the subjects, 他 vs. 你 . Therefore, the pattern envelopes the whole sentence（他来）and not just the predicate（来）.

      (4)   你不是有一点儿累了吗？怎么还不回家休息呢？

                  Nǐ bú shì yǒu yìdiǎnr lèi le ma? Zěnme hái bù huí jiā xiūxi ne?

                  Aren't you a little tired? Why haven't you gone home to rest?

      (5)   你不是有意见吗？请站起来告诉大家。

                  Nǐ bú shì yǒu yìjiàn ma? Qǐng zhànqǐlái gàosu dàjiā.

                  Don't you have a suggestion? Please stand up and tell everyone.

Compare sentence (4) with the following sentence, which is constructed with the confirmation particle 吧 .

      (6)   你有点儿累了吧？怎么还不回家休息？

                  Nǐ yǒu diǎnr lèi le ba? Zěnme hái bù huí jiā xiūxi?

                  You are a bit tired, aren't you? Why haven't you gone home to rest?

Although the main advice（回家休息）remains the same as in (4), sentence (6) begins not with a query but with a confirmation. The speaker could see signs of weariness on his friend's face, which prompts him to ask the question in (6) so as to confirm his impression. The situation in (4) is, however, somewhat different. The speaker may have heard his friend complain about exhaustion from work and finds it strange that he is still working in the office. Therefore, he poses the rhetorical question first before he gives his advice.

3. The Construction 又⋯⋯又⋯⋯

The pattern 又⋯⋯又⋯⋯ *yòu...yòu...* "both...and..." is used to join together two parallel verbal expressions that share some kind of a semantic relationship. The relationship may be a matter of situational similarity or contrast between the two clauses, but the emphasis is always on the coexistence of these situations or qualities. For example, the verbs in sentence (1) represent simultaneous actions while the adjectives in (2) describe similar physical characteristics.

(1) 他们又说又笑，非常高兴。

Tāmen yòu shuō yòu xiào, fēicháng gāoxìng.

They talked and laughed, and were very happy.

(2) 这个孩子又高又胖，大家都很喜欢他。

Zhè ge háizi yòu gāo yòu pàng, dàjiā dōu hěn xǐhuan tā.

This child is both tall and big. Everyone likes him.

(3) 他小时候又瘦又小。他妈妈让他每天喝牛奶。所以他现在又高又大。

Tā xiǎo shíhòu yòu shòu yòu xiǎo. Tā māma ràng tā měi tiān hē niúnǎi. Suǒyǐ tā xiànzài yòu gāo yòu dà.

He was small and skinny when he was little. His mother made him drink milk every day. So he is both big and tall now.

(4) 他说话说得又快又清楚。

Tā shuō huà shuō de yòu kuài yòu qīngchu.

He speaks both fast and clearly.

(5) 她心里觉得又高兴又难过。

Tā xīnli juéde yòu gāoxìng yòu nánguò.

She feels both happy and sad in her heart.

(6) 帕兰卡又会唱歌儿，又会跳舞。

Pàlánkǎ yòu huì chàng gēr, yòu huì tiào wǔ.

Palanka can sing and she can dance as well.

Please note that in sentences (1) to (3), the 又⋯⋯又⋯⋯ construction appears in the main predicates, whereas it is used with the complement（说得⋯⋯）in sentence (4). In sentence (6), the pattern connects two 会 expressions to stress the musical talents of Palanka. In sentence (5), the adjectives set in the pattern, 高兴 and 难过, are antonyms, and therefore describe a mixture of feelings or a state of emotional confusion.

When there are more than two parallel elements in a sentence, we may use 又 before each of the elements.

（7）　坐火车又快，又舒服，又便宜。

　　　　Zuò huǒchē yòu kuài, yòu shūfu, yòu piányi.

　　　　Going by train is fast, comfortable, and cheap.

Unlike its counterpart "both...and..." in English which may be used to join nouns, the Chinese pattern applies only to verbs and adjectives. Hence, it is incorrect to render "Both Gubo and Palanka are going to Beijing." with the 又……又…… construction.

4. 有点儿 Adjective

4.1　The expression 有一点儿 *yǒu yìdiǎnr*, often shortened to 有点儿 in speech, may be used with an adjective to indicate a slight degree of dissatisfaction with the situation: "a bit too Adjective."

```
有（一）点儿  Adjective
yǒu  (yì) diǎnr  Adjective
```

（1）　这儿有点儿冷。

　　　　Zhèr yǒu diǎnr lěng.

　　　　It's a bit too cold here.

（2）　他有点儿累。

　　　　Tā yǒu diǎnr lèi.

　　　　He is a little tired.

（3）　这件衣服有点儿贵。

　　　　Zhè jiàn yīfu yǒu diǎnr guì.

　　　　This outfit is a little too expensive.

As this pattern generally carries a negative connotation, it is not used with adjectives that represent desirable qualities. Therefore, in contrast with (3) which complains about the high price, the following sentence is incorrect since the positive messege of the sentence, namely the attractiveness of the clothes, automatically excludes the use of the pattern.

（4）　*这件衣服有点儿好看。

　　　　*Zhè jiàn yīfu yǒu diǎnr hǎokàn.

　　　　*This outfit is a little pretty.

Here are a few more examples:

(5) 我来晚了，他心里有点儿不高兴。

Wǒ lái wǎn le, tā xīnli yǒu diǎnr bù gāoxìng.

I came late. He was a bit unhappy in his heart.

(6) 我有一点儿渴。我们先喝一点儿啤酒，好吗？

Wǒ yǒu yìdiǎnr kě. Wǒmen xiān hē yìdiǎnr píjiǔ, hǎo ma?

I'm a little thirsty. Let's have some beer first, OK?

(7) 我姐姐从楼上跑下来对我说，"今天有点儿冷，你穿得够不够？"

Wǒ jiějie cóng lóushang pǎoxiàlái duì wǒ shuō, "Jīntiān yǒu diǎnr lěng. Nǐ chuān de gòu bu gòu?"

My elder sister came running down from upstairs and said to me, "It's a little cold today. Are you wearing enough?"

4.2 Please note that this pattern is very different, both in form and in meaning, from a pattern first introduced in Lesson 29.

Adjective 一点儿

Adjective *yìdiǎnr*

[a little more Adjective]

This old pattern indicates a request for more of the quality represented by the Adjective, whereas the new pattern, 有点儿 Adjective, complains about that quality. Compare the following examples.

(8) 你说得有点儿快。

Nǐ shuō de yǒu diǎnr kuài.

You spoke a little too fast.

(9) 请说得慢一点儿。

Qǐng shuō de màn yìdiǎnr.

Please speak a bit more slowly.

If the request in (9) is based upon the dissatisfaction in (8), the two patterns are used accordingly in that order. A similar contrast is shown in the following sentence.

（10）　这件大衣有一点儿长，还是买一件短一点儿的吧。

Zhè jiàn dàyī yǒu yìdiǎnr cháng, háishì mǎi yíjiàn duǎn yìdiǎnr de ba.

This coat is a bit too long. Why don't you get one that is a bit shorter?

4.3　The pattern 有点儿…… may also be used to qualify some verbs, such as 象 *xiàng* "to resemble." These verbs are essentially quality transitive verbs, which allow degree comparisons and may be modified by degree adverbs such as 很：很象. Also, when set in this pattern, the verbal expression does not necessarily carry a negative connotation, a semantic neutrality that sets it apart from the reading of "有点儿 Adjective."

（11）　帕兰卡跟她妈妈有点儿象。

Pàlánkǎ gēn tā māma yǒu diǎnr xiàng.

Palanka looks a bit like her mother.

5. Two Different Uses of 别

The character 别 *bié* actually represents two different words that have very little in common semantically or in terms of usage. As described earlier, when used with a verb 别 marks a negative imperative. When it appears with a noun, it functions like a demonstrative, meaning "other."

5.1　别 as a Negative Imperative Marker: When 别 stands before a verb, it is a negative particle meaning "Don't!"

别　＋　Verb!
Bié　＋　Verb!

（1）　别动！

Bié dòng!

Don't move!

（2）　请别说话。

Qǐng bié shuō huà.

Please don't talk!

(3)   请别叫太多的菜。我真的吃不下。

Qǐng bié jiào tài duō de cài. Wǒ zhēn de chī bu xià.

Please don't order too many dishes. I really can't eat much.

(4)   我家又小，又挤，又不方便。我真想搬进宿舍去。可是我妈妈说，
"要是你搬出去，就别想再搬回来了。"

Wǒ jiā yòu xiǎo, yòu jǐ, yòu bù fāngbiàn. Wǒ zhēn xiǎng bānjìn
sùshè qù. Kěshì wǒ māma shuō, "Yàoshì nǐ bānchūqù, jiù bié xiǎng
zài bānhuílái le."

My home is small, crowded and inconvenient. I'd really like to move
into the dorm. But my mother said, "If you move out, then don't
you ever think about moving back again."

5.2   As a demonstrative, 别 generally appears in combination with 的, as in the
following pattern. Only in some special compounds do we find 别 standing directly
before a noun, as in (8).

别的   +   Noun

biéde Noun

other Noun

---

(5)   别的学生都来了。
Biéde xuésheng dōu lái le.
All the other students came.

(6)   这个字还有别的意思。
Zhè ge zì hái yǒu biéde yìsi.
This character has other meanings as well.

(7)   我看这样吧。自行车你先推进去。书架和别的东西，你明天再来拿
吧。
Wǒ kàn zhèyàng ba. Zìxíngchē nǐ xiān tuījìnqù. Shūjià hé biéde
dōngxi, nǐ míngtiān zài lái ná ba.
Let's do it this way. You push the bicycle in first. As for the book
case and the other stuff, you can come to get them tomorrow.

(8)   别人的事，别多说。
Biérén de shì, bié duō shuō.
Don't say too much about other people's business.

In the last sentence, the first 别 stands directly before 人 to form a special compound 别人 *biéren* "other people, others." The second 别 is the negative marker qualifying the verb phrase 多说.

6. A Special Use of 来

The verbs we have learned for ordering food in a restaurant are 要 *yào* and 叫 *jiào*. The verb 来 may also be used in the same capacity, but usually with a more casual and colloquial flavor.

(1)　　来一杯咖啡，两杯牛奶。

Lái yìbēi kāfēi, liǎngbēi niúnǎi.

Bring me one coffee and two milks.

(2)　　二位要来点儿什么？

Èrwèi yào lái diǎnr shénme?

What do (the two of) you want to order?

(3)　　顾客从桌子上拿起菜单来说，"我有点儿饿了。先给我来一碗粥吧。"

Gùkè cóng zhuōzishang náqǐ càidān lái shuō, "Wǒ yǒu diǎnr è le. Xiān gěi wǒ lái yìwǎn zhōu ba."

The customer picked up the menu from the table and said, "I'm a bit hungry. Why don't you bring me a bowl of porridge first?"

Lesson 44

1. The Construction 是……的

1.1 To report a past action or event with specific emphasis on its time, place, manner or other circumstantial aspects related to the action, we have to use a special sentence pattern in Chinese: 是……的 . Structurally, 是 appears before the emphasized element and 的 appears at the end of the sentence. 是 may sometimes be omitted. The pattern can be schematically represented as,

> Subject （是） Predicate 的

The following are examples to illustrate the various types of circumstantial elements that the pattern may highlight in relation to the action.

(A) With emphasis on Time:

> (1) 我是昨天来的。
> Wǒ shì zuótiān lái de.
> I came yesterday.

> (2) 客人是十点走的。
> Kèren shì shídiǎn zǒu de.
> The guests left at ten o'clock.

(B) With emphasis on Place:

> (3) 我是从北京来的。
> Wǒ shì cóng Běijīng lái de.
> I came from Beijing.

> (4) 你是在哪儿出生的？
> Nǐ shì zài nǎr chūshēng de?
> Where were you born?

(C) With emphasis on Company:

    （5）   我是跟她母亲一起来的。

            Wǒ shì gēn tā mǔqīn yìqǐ lái de.

            I came with her mother.

    （6）   你是跟谁一起去看电影的？

            Nǐ shì gēn shéi yìqǐ qù kàn diànyǐng de?

            Whom did you go see the movie with?

(D) With emphasis on Conveyance:

    （7）   他是骑自行车去的。

            Tā shì qí zìxíngchē qù de.

            He went by bike.

    （8）   他是怎么来的？

            Tā shì zěnme lái de?

            How did he get here?

(E) With emphasis on Purpose:

    （9）   我是来看朋友的。

            Wǒ shì lái kàn péngyou de.

            I came to see friends.

    （10）   他们是来旅行的。

            Tāmen shì lái lǚxíng de.

            They came for sightseeing.

As the emphasis in each of the above sentences falls on an expression other than the verb itself, a more accurate rendition in English would be either to place a stress on the pertinent expression in speech or to employ a different grammatical construction to reflect such an emphasis.

    (11)   他是去年毕业的。

            Tā shì qùnián bìyè de.

            He graduated *last year*.

            It was last year that he graduated.

1.2 This pattern is, of course, to be distinguished from the use of 了, which stresses the perfective aspect of an action. For comparison, let's first look at the following two English sentences:

(12)　He went swimming yesterday. (Said with a normal stress pattern)

(13)　It was yesterday that he went swimming.

Both relate the same past event of a person dipping himself into the water. But, whereas sentence (12) is a simple statement of what happened in the past, sentence (13) stresses the temporal circumstances, the date of the event. In other words, sentence (13) carries a different emphasis from that in sentence (12). Sentence (12) answers the question "What did he do yesterday?" but sentence (13) is a response to the question "When did he do it?" Sentence (12) identifies a past event, but, in sentence (13), we know what happened and we want to find out when it happened. Therefore, sentence (12) focuses on the verb whereas sentence (13) focuses on the time word. The same kind of distinction can be found in Chinese as represented by the following two Chinese sentences:

(14)　他昨天去游泳了。

　　　Tā zuótiān qù yóu yǒng le.

　　　He went swimming yesterday.

(15)　他是昨天去游泳的。

　　　Tā shì zuótiān qù yóu yǒng de.

　　　It was yesterday that he went swimming.

The use of the particle 了 is to indicate a simple completed action; but the use of 是……的 highlights the pertinent time element. Like their counterparts in English, they answer different questions as given below:

(16)　A: 他昨天作什么了？

　　　　Tā zuótiān zuò shénme le?

　　　　What did he do yesterday?

　　　B: 他昨天游泳了。

　　　　Tā zuótiān yóu yǒng le.

　　　　He swam yesterday.

(17)　A: 他是什么时候游泳的？

　　　　Tā shì shénme shíhòu yóu yǒng de?

　　　　When did he swim?

B: 他是昨天游泳的。

　　Tā shì zuótiān yóu yǒng de.

　　He swam *yesterday*.

Whenever we wish to ask for specific information relating to a past action (such as *when, where, why, how, with whom*, etc.), we always use this 是……的 pattern to phrase our question as well as to answer it. As noted above, 是 may be omitted from the pattern, and when it is, the final 的 becomes the only characteristic marker of such a sentence type. Since an unstressed 的 sounds very much like 了, we indeed need to prick up our ears so as not to misunderstand the message of the utterance.

(18)　他昨天来的。

　　　Tā zuótiān lái de.

　　　It was yesterday that he came.

(19)　他昨天来了。

　　　Tā zuótiān lái le.

　　　He came yesterday.

The following is a scenario set in the past. The sentence is phrased with 了, as the emphasis is on the core action of 去法国 itself. There are several phrases surrounding the main verb, adding more information to the narration. Each of these additional or peripheral elements may be brought into focus by restructuring the sentence with the 是……的 construction.

(20)　他　上星期二　从中国　坐船　去法国　渡假　了。
　　　　　Time　　Place　　Means　　　Purpose
　　　Tā shàng xīngqī'èr cóng Zhōngguó zuò chuán qù Fǎguó dù jià le.
　　　Last Tuesday he went from China to France by boat for vacation.

(21)　When: 他是上星期二去法国的。
　　　　　　Tā shì shàng xīngqī'èr qù Fǎguó de.
　　　　　　It was last Tuesday that he went to France.

(22)　From Where: 他是从中国去法国的。
　　　　　　Tā shì cóng Zhōngguó qù Fǎguó de.
　　　　　　It was from China that he went to France.

(23)　By Means of What: 他是坐船去法国的。
　　　　　　Tā shì zuò chuán qù Fǎguó de.
　　　　　　It was by ship that he went to France.

(24) For What Purpose: 他是去法国渡假的。

Tā shì qù Fǎguó dù jià de.

It was for vacation that he went to France.

(25) 他是上星期二从中国坐船去法国渡假的。

Tā shì shàng xīngqī'èr cóng Zhōngguó zuò chuán qù Fǎguó dù jià de.

In the last sentence where all the information is put together in the 是……的 construction, the emphasis may be on any one of the peripheral elements depending on where the stress falls. Under normal circumstances, a 是……的 sentence would not contain more than one or two pieces of such peripheral information, so as not to confuse the communication with competing messages.

The following are a few more examples of the pattern:

(26) 你们去年去哪儿旅行了？坐船去的还是坐飞机去的？

Nǐmen qùnián qù nǎr lǚxíng le? Zuò chuán qù de háishì zuò fēijī qù de?

Where did you go for vacation last year? Did you go by boat or did you fly?

(27) A: 你是来北京探亲的吗？

Nǐ shì lái Běijīng tàn qīn de ma?

Did you come to Beijing to visit your relatives?

B: 不，我是来出差的。

Bù, wǒ shì lái chū chāi de.

No, I am here on business.

(28) A: 昨天晚上他是什么时候离开的？

Zuótiān wǎnshang tā shì shénme shíhòu líkāi de?

When did he leave last night?

B: 他是吃了晚饭以后才离开的。

Tā shì chīle wǎnfàn yǐhòu cái líkāi de.

He didn't leave until after dinner.

A: 他是跟谁一起坐车回家的？你知道吗？

Tā shì gēn shéi yìqǐ zuò chē huí jiā de? Nǐ zhīdao ma?

Whom did he ride with when he went home? Do you know?

B: 我想他是一个人开车走的。

Wǒ xiǎng tā shì yíge rén kāi chē zǒu de.

I think he was alone when he drove away.

(29) 你去过广州没有？是最近去的吗？自己一个人去的还是跟朋友一起去的？好玩儿吗？

Nǐ qùguo Guǎngzhōu méiyou? Shì zuìjìn qù de ma? Zìjǐ yíge rén qù de háishì gēn péngyou yìqǐ qù de? Hǎowánr ma?

Have you been to Guangzhou? Did you go there recently? All by yourself or with friends? Was it fun?

In the last example, the first question tries to establish whether the core action 去广州 ever took place. Once beyond that, the next two questions that ask for specific details are phrased with the 是……的 pattern. The last question does not follow the same pattern simply because 好玩儿 itself constitutes the entire predicate and there is no other message that needs to be foregrounded for emphasis.

1.3 As described above, the 是……的 pattern embraces the predicate in a sentence. If the sentence contains an Object in its regular post-verbal position, the final particle appears after the Object, as in the following scheme, with X representing the unit that is being highlighted.

```
Subject  +  是  ［X + Verb + Object］  的
```

A variation of this scheme is to reverse the order of the Object and the final particle 的, yielding the following new pattern:

```
Subject  +  是  ［X  +  Verb］  的  Object
```

(30.a) 你是在哪儿看电影的？
Nǐ shì zài nǎr kàn diànyǐng de?
Where did you see the movie?

(30.b) 你是在哪儿看的电影？
Nǐ shì zài nǎr kàn de diànyǐng?

Sentences (30.a) and (30.b) demonstrate the two different orders of word arrangement, and yet they are exactly the same in meaning. There are, however, certain conditions for the use or non-use of the variation pattern:

(A) If the Object is a noun, 的 may come either before or after the noun.

（31.a）你是在哪儿上车的？

Nǐ shì zài nǎr shàng chē de?

Where did you board the bus?

（31.b）你是在哪儿上的车？

Nǐ shì zài nǎr shàng de chē?

（32.a）他是在教室里找到铅笔的。

Tā shì zài jiàoshìli zhǎodào qiānbǐ de.

He found the pencil in the classroom.

（32.b）他是在教室里找到的铅笔。

Tā shì zài jiàoshìli zhǎodào de qiānbǐ.

(B) If the Object is a pronoun, 的 always comes at the end.

（33.a）   我是写信告诉他的。

Wǒ shì xiě xìn gàosu tā de.

I told him by writing him a letter.

（33.b）＊我是写信告诉的他。

＊Wǒ shì xiě xìn gàosu de tā.

（34.a）   他是五点钟来接我的。

Tā shì wǔdiǎn zhōng lái jiē wǒ de.

He came to pick me up at five o'clock.

（34.b）＊他是五点钟来接的我。

＊Tā shì wǔdiǎn zhōng lái jiē de wǒ.

(C) If the verb is followed by a directional complement or a locative expression, 的 comes at the end.

（35）   你是从哪儿借来这些书的？

Nǐ shì cóng nǎr jièlái zhè xiē shū de?

Where did you check out these books?

（36）   我是坐飞机到上海去的。

Wǒ shì zuò fēijī dào Shànghǎi qù de.

I went to Shanghai by plane.

In general, 是……的 functions as an embracing frame, situating the predicate in between. If you are not sure whether 的 should come before or after the verb, always put it at the end of the sentence.

1.4 If the emphasis of a 是……的 sentence is placed upon the subject rather than other elements in the predicate, the markers embrace the entire sentence.

```
            是  〔Subject  +  Predicate〕  的
```

(37) 是我跟他一起去看朋友的。

Shì wǒ gēn tā yìqǐ qù kàn péngyou de.

It was I who went with him to see a friend.

(38) 是他买这张票的。

Shì tā mǎi zhè zhāng piào de.

It was he who bought this ticket.

In the last sentence, the Object may be preposed as the topic, thereby yielding a form that is actually more idiomatic in style than (38).

(39) 这张票是他买的。

Zhè zhāng piào shì tā mǎi de.

1.5 The negative formation of the 是……的 pattern is as follows:

```
            Subject  不  是  Predicate  的
```

In the negative form, 是 can never be omitted.

(40) 我不是一个人来的。我是跟朋友一起来的。

Wǒ bú shì yíge rén lái de. Wǒ shì gēn péngyou yìqǐ lái de.

I didn't come all by myself. I came with friends.

(41) 我不是走去的，我是坐公共汽车去的。

Wǒ bú shì zǒuqù de, wǒ shì zuò gōnggòng qìchē qù de.

I didn't go there on foot. I went by bus.

1.6 When forming an interrogative, we may choose either the 吗－type or the affirmative－negative pattern, each of which is illustrated below.

> Subject 是 Predicate 的 吗？

(42) 你是在北京出生的吗？
Nǐ shì zài Běijīng chūshēng de ma?
Were you born in Beijing?

(43) 你的老朋友是到美国来工作的吗？
Nǐ de lǎo péngyou shì dào Měiguó lái gōngzuò de ma?
Did your old friend come to America to work?

> Subject 是 不 是 Predicate 的？

(44) 你爷爷是不是坐船来美国的？
Nǐ yéye shì bu shì zuò chuán lái Měiguó de?
Did your grandpa come to the States by boat?

(45) 那个机场是不是今年才修建好的？
Nà ge jīchǎng shì bu shì jīnnián cái xiūjiànhǎo de?
Was the construction of the airport completed just this year?

In addition to these two kinds of questions, there is also the interrogative-word question, as we have seen earlier. The following are a few more examples:

> 是 ... Question Word ... 的？

(46) 你是从哪儿买来这些小吃的？
Nǐ shì cóng nǎr mǎilái zhè xiē xiǎochī de?
Where did you get these snacks?

(47) 长城是哪个皇帝修建的？你知道吗？
Chángchéng shì nǎ ge huángdì xiūjiàn de? Nǐ zhīdao ma?
Which Emperor built the Great Wall? Do you know?

(48) 这个句子你是怎么翻译的？
Zhè ge jùzi nǐ shì zěnme fānyì de?
How did you translate this sentence?

(49)　是谁告诉你的？

　　　　Shì shéi gàosu nǐ de?

　　　　Who told you?

In sentence (49), 是……的 frames the entire sentence since the question falls on the subject 谁. In sentence (48), 怎么 is the interrogative word for "How?" Recall that 怎么 could also be used to ask "How come?" A clear distinction is made between the two uses with regard to the 是……的 pattern. Only the former ("How?") may be set in the construction; the latter ("How come?") appears with 了. The following dialogue illustrates this difference in behavior.

(50)　A: 他怎么去上海了？

　　　　　　Tā zěnme qù Shànghǎi le?

　　　　　　How come he went to Shanghai?

　　　　B: 他母亲病了，所以他去上海了。

　　　　　　Tā mǔqīn bìngle, suǒyǐ tā qù Shànghǎi le.

　　　　　　His mother became ill and so he went to Shanghai.

　　　　A: 他是怎么去上海的？

　　　　　　Tā shì zěnme qù Shànghǎi de?

　　　　　　How did he go to Shanghai?

　　　　B: 他坐飞机去的。

　　　　　　Tā zuò fēijī qù de.

　　　　　　He went by plane.

2. The Existence Sentence (continued)

In Lesson 34 we introduced the following 着－pattern, which is more descriptive and vivid in effect than a regular 有－sentence.

PLACE ＋ Verb－着 ＋ X

(1)　墙上挂着几张画儿。

　　　Qiángshang guàzhe jǐzhāng huàr.

　　　There are several pictures hanging on the wall.

PLACE ＋ 有 ＋ X

(2)　　墙上有几张画儿。
　　　　Qiángshang yǒu jǐzhāng huàr.
　　　　There are several pictures on the wall.

Both patterns indicate the existence or presence of something/someone at a location, but the pattern with 着 provides more concrete information, describing how that something/someone is situated at the location. The pattern may be further revised to include a complement or the perfective 了 in the verb phrase, as represented below. The new pattern may also be used to describe appearance as well as disappearance, with the same effect of enhancing the message almost as if to surprise the addressee with the new information.

$$\boxed{\text{PLACE} + [\text{Verb} + 着／了／\text{Complement}] + \text{Noun}}$$

(3)　　楼上放着很多桌子　　　　　　　　　　　　　(Existence)
　　　　Lóushàng fàngzhe hěn duō zhuōzi.
　　　　There are many tables upstairs.

(4)　　楼下来了一个客人。　　　　　　　　　　　　(Appearance)
　　　　Lóuxià láile yíge kèren.
　　　　There came a guest downstairs.
　　　　(= A guest appeared/arrived downstairs.)

(5)　　宿舍里搬走了两个同学。　　　　　　　　　　(Disappearance)
　　　　Sùshèli bānzǒule liǎngge tóngxué.
　　　　There were two students who moved out of the dorm.

Because of the special narrative effect that the pattern generates, it is a desirable rhetorical device to use in telling a story or describing what one witnesses, adding vivacity to the narration. There are, however, certain conditions that restrict its use.

(A) As already noted, the verb unit has to contain, in addition to the verb itself, another element such as a complement (Resultative Complement or Directional Complement) and/or an aspectual particle (了 or 着).

(6)　　对面来了几个小孩儿。
　　　　Duìmiàn láile jǐge xiǎoháir.
　　　　From across the other side there came a few kids.

(7)   对面跑来了几个小孩儿。

Duìmiàn pǎoláile jǐge xiǎoháir.

A few kids ran over from the other side.

(8)   桥下边爬出来了一只小动物，样子真可爱。

Qiáo xiàbiān páchūláile yìzhī xiǎo dòngwù, yàngzi zhēn kě'ài.

From beneath the bridge there crawled out a small creature. Its looks were really cute.

(9)   湖边坐着两个小姑娘，很高兴地在谈话。

Húbiān zuòzhe liǎngge xiǎo gūniang, hěn gāoxìng de zài tán huà.

By the side of the lake, there sat two young girls happily engaged in conversation.

(B) The noun, which represents the new information in the sentence, has to be indefinite in reference. Very often, the noun is introduced by the indefinite phrase "一 Measure," such as 一个, if it is singular in number.

(10)   从楼上走下来了一位老先生。

Cóng lóushàng zǒuxiàláile yíwèi lǎo xiānsheng.

An old gentleman came down from upstairs.

(11)   广场那边刚开走了一辆公共汽车，这边又开过来了几辆摩托车。

Guǎngchǎng nàbiān gāng kāizǒule yíliàng gōnggòng qìchē, zhè biān yòu kāiguòláile jǐliàng mótuōchē.

While a bus just left from that side of the square, a few motorcycles came in on this side.

(12)   墙上挂着一张很大的画儿。画儿上画着山水花草，象真的一样。

Qiángshang guàzhe yìzhāng hěn dà de huàr. Huàrshang huàzhe shān shuǐ huā cǎo, xiàng zhēn de yíyàng.

On the wall there hangs a huge painting. In the painting, there are mountains and water, flowers and grass, all of which look real.

(C) If the noun refers to a specific person or thing, and hence is definite in reference, the pattern may not be used. In the case of a pronoun, the pattern is not applicable either.

(13) *那边走来了张老师。

*Nàbiān zǒuláile Zhāng lǎoshī.

There came Teacher Zhang from over there.

（14）＊楼下坐着他。

　　　　＊Lóuxià zuòzhe tā.

　　　　He sat there downstairs.

3. The Exclamatory Pattern

The following exclamatory pattern may be used to express a strong emotive response to a situation or experience.

> 多么……啊！
>
> *duōme...a!*
>
> [How very/much...!]

The constituent that may appear in this pattern is either an adjective that represents the particular quality the speaker finds impressive in what he sees, or it may be a predicate with a verb that expresses a strong emotional desire or intense likes and dislikes.

（1）　姐姐新买的衣服多么漂亮啊！

　　　Jiějie xīn mǎi de yīfu duōme piàoliang a!

　　　The clothes that sister just bought are so beautiful.

（2）　我多么喜欢中国的山水画儿啊！

　　　Wǒ duōme xǐhuan Zhōngguó de shānshuǐ huàr a!

　　　I like Chinese landscape paintings so much!

（3）　我多么想去日本玩儿啊！

　　　Wǒ duōme xiǎng qù Rìběn wánr a!

　　　I want to go to Japan so much!

As the pattern is charged with strong feelings often to the degree of hyperbole, use it only when you are truly touched by what you see or when you find the experience so spiritually uplifting that you feel exclamation or exaggeration is justifiable. Even then, use 多么 with caution and restraint. Excessive use would not only weaken the intended effect of enhancement, it may in fact project an undesirable impression of being overly sentimental, sensational, or even insincere.

4. The Conditional Sentence (continued)

In Lesson 41, we learned the following pattern for stating a condition:

```
要是  Condition,  就  Result
Yàoshì...,  jiù ……
[ If...,   then... ]
```

(1)   要是天气不好，我就坐公共汽车去学校。
       Yàoshì tiānqì bù hǎo, wǒ jiù zuò gōnggòng qìchē qù xuéxiào.
       If the weather is not good, then I will go to school by bus.

Sentence (1) describes the weather conditions under which one chooses public transportation for going to school. It does not, however, preclude other conditions for such a choice. For example, when one's car breaks down or when one gets up too late and has to catch an early class, taking a bus becomes a practical alternative. Yet, if the weather is the only condition that decides whether one rides a bus, then the sentence should be rephrased with a different pattern.

```
只有  Condition,  才  Result
zhǐyǒu ...,  cái ...
[ Only if/when ..., then... ]
```

(2)   只有天气不好，我才坐公共汽车去学校。
       Zhǐyǒu tiānqì bù hǎo wǒ cái zuò gōnggòng qìchē qù xuéxiào.
       Only when the weather is not good do I go to school by bus.

The pattern contains two units, the second one representing the result that arises only under the condition as set out in the first unit. The conditional unit is marked by 只有, literally "there is only (this condition)," and the consequence clause is introduced by the monosyllabic adverb 才, meaning "then and only then." The conditional unit may be simply a word specifying the condition or it may be a full sentence describing the restrictive situation.

(3) 爸爸说，从今天起，只有星期天我才可以出来跳舞。

Bàba shuō, cóng jīntiān qǐ, zhǐyǒu xīngqītiān wǒ cái kěyǐ chūlái tiào wǔ.

Father said that beginning today, only on Sundays can I come out to dance.

(4) 只有去中国才有机会吃到好的中国菜。

Zhǐyǒu qù Zhōngguó cái yǒu jīhuì chīdào hǎo de Zhōngguó cài.

Only if one goes to China will one have the chance to eat good Chinese food.

(5) 只有努力学习才能学好汉语。

Zhǐyǒu nǔlì xuéxí cái néng xuéhǎo Hànyǔ.

Only if one studies hard can one learn Chinese well.

(6) 你只有自己去看一看，才能了解那儿的情况。

Nǐ zhǐyǒu zìjǐ qù kànyikàn, cái néng liǎojiě nàr de qíngkuàng.

Only by going there and looking around for yourself will you be able to understand the situation there.

(7) 只有去过长城的人才知道长城有多么长。

Zhǐyǒu qùguo Chángchéng de rén cái zhīdao Chángchéng yǒu duōme cháng.

Only those who have been to the Great Wall know how long the Great Wall is.

(8) 只有爬上这座山才看得见那条河。要是不爬，就看不见了。

Zhǐyǒu páshàng zhè zuò shān cái kàn de jiàn nà tiáo hé. Yàoshì bù pá, jiù kàn bu jiàn le.

Only by climbing up this hill will we be able to see that river. If we do not do so, we won't be able to see it.

To underscore the possibility of achieving the result under the restrictive condition, the result clause in the pattern often contains an optative element like 能 or 可以 as in examples (3), (5) and (6), or the potential form "Verb － 得 － Complement" as in example (8).

5. Special Time Expressions

The following is a special pattern for expressing a progressive development of a situation along a time span.

```
┌─────────────────────────────────────────────┐
│              一  Time  比  一  Time           │
└─────────────────────────────────────────────┘
```

(1)   天气一天比一天热了。
       Tiānqì yìtiān bǐ yìtiān rè le.
       The weather is getting warmer day by day.

(2)   学中文的学生一年比一年多了。
       Xué Zhōngwén de xuésheng yìnián bǐ yìnián duō le.
       The number of students studying Chinese grows by the year.

This special comparative pattern is generally placed before an adjective that characterizes a change of situation. The most common time words that appear in the
pattern are 天 *tiān* "day" and 年 *nián* "year." Here are a few more examples:

(3)   春天到了，草一天比一天绿了。
       Chūntiān dào le, cǎo yìtiān bǐ yìtiān lǜ le.
       Spring is here and the grass is getting greener day by day.

(4)   我很久没看见小谢了。我听说他的生活一年比一年好了。
       Wǒ hěn jiǔ méi kànjiàn xiǎo Xiè le. Wǒ tīng shuō tā de shēnghuó
       yìnián bǐ yìnián hǎo le.
       I haven't seen Little Xie for a long time. I've heard that he is doing
       better each year.

(5)   现在去外国旅行真不便宜，飞机票一年比一年贵。
       Xiànzài qù wàiguó lǚxíng zhēn bù piányi, fēijī piào yìnián bǐ yìnián
       guì.
       It is quite expensive to take a trip abroad nowadays. The airfare is
       getting higher each year.

(6)   现在天亮得一天比一天早，太阳六点就出来了。
       Xiànzài tiān liàng de yìtiān bǐ yìtiān zǎo, tàiyang liùdiǎn jiù chūlai
       le.
       It's getting light earlier and earlier every day, and the sun comes out
       at six o'clock.

(7)   她对着镜子说，"我的头发一天比一天白，真象个八十岁的老太太一
       样。"
       Tā duìzhe jìngzi shuō, "Wǒ de tóufa yìtiān bǐ yìtiān bái, zhēn xiàng
       ge bāshisuì de lǎo tàitai yíyàng."
       Facing the mirror she said, "My hair is turning whiter and whiter
       each day. I am really like an eighty-year old woman."

Lesson 45

1. The Potential Complement (continued)

Like all complements, a directional complement may appear in the "Verb 一得 / 不 一 Complement" construction to mark the (in)ability or (im)possibility of achieving the specified result. Both simple and complex directional complements observe the same formation rules.

Positive	Verb 一得一 DC
Negative	Verb 一不一 DC
Interrogative	Verb 一得一 DC 吗？ Verb 一得一 DC Verb 一不一 DC?

Here are some examples:

(1)　现在太晚了，已经没车了。所以我回不来。
　　　Xiànzài tài wǎn le, yǐjīng méi chē le. Suǒyǐ wǒ huí bu lái.
　　　It's too late now; there are no more buses. So, I can't come back.

(2)　这儿人很多，我们挤不进去。
　　　Zhèr rén hěn duō, wǒmen jǐ bu jìnqù.
　　　It's so crowded here; we can't squeeze our way in.

(3)　这个广场里的人太多，我们开不过去。
　　　Zhè ge guǎngchǎngli de rén tài duō, wǒmen kāi bu guòqù.
　　　There are too many people in the square. There is no way that we can drive across the square.

(4)   这个东西不太重。你拿得起来拿不起来？

Zhè ge dōngxi bú tài zhòng. Nǐ ná de qǐlái ná bu qǐlái?

This thing isn't too heavy. Are you able to lift it up?

(5)   这座山不容易爬。你想你爬得上去吗？

Zhè zuò shān bù róngyi pá. Nǐ xiǎng nǐ pá de shàngqù ma?

This mountain is not easy to climb. Do you think you will be able to climb up?

2. 后来 VS. 以后

Both 后来 *hòulái* and 以后 *yǐhòu* are often translated as "afterwards." They are, however, not always interchangeable in use. The following are some of the major distinctions between the two forms.

(A) In terms of time frame, 以后 can be used to refer to both past and future events whereas 后来 is restricted to the past only.

(1.a) 这件事等以后再谈吧。   (Future)

Zhè jiàn shì děng yǐhòu zài tán ba.

We will discuss this matter later.

(1.b)＊这件事等后来再谈吧。

＊Zhè jiàn shì děng hòulái zài tán ba.

(2)   以后怎么样我就不知道了。

Yǐhòu zěnmeyàng wǒ jiù bù zhīdao le.

(a) As for what happened afterwards, I don't know.   (Past)

(b) As for what will happen afterwards, I don't know.   (Future)

(3)   后来怎么样我就不知道了。

Hòulái zěnmeyàng wǒ jiù bù zhīdao le.

As for what happened afterwards, I don't know.   (Past)

(B) Semantically, while both forms may be used in a past time frame, 后来 is more like "then, subsequently" in English whereas 以后 is more like "since then, ever since then."

(4.a) 他以前学法语，后来学英语，都没学好。他一九八五年开始学汉语，
学了这么多年，他现在说得很流利。

Tā yǐqián xué Fǎyǔ, hòulái xué Yīngyǔ, dōu méi xué hǎo. Tā 1985 nián kāishǐ xué Hànyǔ. Xuéle zhème duō nián, tā xiànzài shuō de hěn liúlì.

Before, he studied French, and then he studied English. He didn't succeed with either language. In 1985, he began to study Chinese. He has been working on it for all these years and he can now speak very fluently.

(4.b) *他以前学法语，以后学英语，都没学好。他一九八五年开始学汉语……

*Tā yǐqiān xué Fǎyǔ, yǐhòu xué Yīngyǔ, dōu méi xué hǎo. Tā 1985 nián kāishī xué Hànyǔ…

The reason why (4.b) is incorrect is that the sentence implies he stopped studying English and later, in 1985, began pursuing Chinese; hence, the use of 以后 which means "ever since then (i.e. his studying of English till the present moment)" would create a contradiction in the temporal sequence.

(C) Grammatically, while both 以后 and 后来 can appear initially in a sentence, only 以后 can be used after a clause to express the meaning "after…"

(5.a) 我吃饭以后来看你。
Wǒ chī fàn yǐhòu lái kàn nǐ.
I'll come to see you after dinner.

(5.b) *我吃饭后来来看你。
*Wǒ chī fàn hòulái lái kàn nǐ.

3. Another Use of the Adverb 又

The adverb 又 may also be used as a modal to highlight a noticeable change or contradiction between two actions. It may co-occur with 可是 or 但是 in a sentence.

> [Verb－Object]，（可是／但是）又……

(1) 我心里有很多话，但是又说不出来。
Wǒ xīnli yǒu hěn duō huà, dànshì yòu shuō bù chūlái.
I have a lot of things that I want to say, but I don't know how to say them.

(2) 他刚才很高兴，怎么现在又哭了？

Tā gāngcái hěn gāoxìng, zěnme xiànzài yòu kū le?

He was very happy just a short while ago; how come he is crying now?

(3) 我很想请他去看电影，可是又怕他不肯。所以我现在还没问他。

Wǒ hěn xiǎng qǐng tā qù kàn diànyǐng, kěshì yòu pà tā bù kěn. Suǒyǐ wǒ xiànzài hái méi wèn tā.

I really would like to ask him to a movie, but on the other hand I'm afraid he will say no. So, I still haven't asked him.

As previously described, the basic function of 又 is to mark repetition. In its extended usage as illustrated here, 又 again joins two verbal units, marking their relevance to each other. The connection, however, is characterized not by similarity or recurrence of an action but rather by the disagreement or contradiction in the development of the state of affairs.

Lesson 46

1. The 把—Construction

1.1   You have probably realized by now that it is a common practice in Chinese to move the Object of a verb to the front of the sentence, a transformation commonly known as "topicalization." An Object noun may be topicalized only when it is definite in reference. In other words, a topicalized Object represents something already known to both the speaker and the addressee, and not something introduced for the first time in the discourse. A definite noun corresponds to a "the/this/that Noun" (as opposed to "a Noun") in English. One reason for preposing, or topicalizing, an Object noun is to reserve room in the predicate for the complement or other elements which constitute the main message of the sentence. The speaker is interested in informing the addressee not about the Object itself but, rather, about what has happened to the Object.

The 把—construction, according to some linguists, is a kind of topicalization process in the language. But instead of moving the Object to the very front of the sentence, the construction places the Object right before the verbal complex and marks the Object with 把 *bǎ*. The construction can be schematized as below:

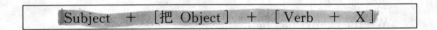

Subject   +   [把 Object]   +   [Verb   +   X]

X in the above scheme represents that extra element in the verb phrase, more of which we will address in a later section. Via this process of transformation, a regular sentence like (1) may be adapted to a new form as in (2).

(1)   他写完汉字了。
       Tā xiěwán Hànzì le.

(2)   他把汉字写完了。
       Tā bǎ Hànzì xiěwán le.
       He finished writing the Chinese characters.

The negative is formed by placing the negative marker before 把:

> Subject + NEG + [把 Object] + [Verb + X]

(3.a)   他没把汉字写完。

Tā méi bǎ Hànzì xiěwán.

He did not finish writing the Chinese characters.

(3.b)   他还没有把汉字写完呢。

Tā hái méiyou bǎ Hànzì xiěwán ne.

He hasn't finished writing the Chinese characters yet.

Although both 不 and 没有 may appear with 把, the latter is more often used to negate a 把－sentence. Since the emphasis of a 把－sentence is on what happens to the Object noun, hence often representing the resultative state of the action, its negative essentially reports that such a state has not been achieved. Therefore, the choice of 没有 over 不.

When an optative verb, like 想 etc., appears in a 把－sentence, it comes before the 把－unit, encompassing the entire action within its optative scope.

(4)   你们要把电视机关上。

Nǐmen yào bǎ diànshìjī guānshang.

You have to turn off the T.V.

(5)   我想把门开了。

Wǒ xiǎng bǎ mén kāile.

I want to open the door.

(6)   我不愿意把车卖了。

Wǒ bú yuànyì bǎ chē màile.

I am not willing to sell the car.

In the last sentence where the negation is on the intention, the negative marker 不 stands in front of the optative and not directly before the 把－unit.

1.2   Grammarians have described the 把－construction as a "disposal" form. That is, its grammatical meaning is to indicate "what has happend to the Object" or "how the Object is disposed of." For example, in the following pair of sentences,

(7)   他作完练习了。

Tā zuòwán liànxí le.

（8）　他把练习作完了。
　　　　Tā bǎ liànxí zuòwán le.
　　　　He finished doing the exercises.

Sentence (7) is a simple report of what happened or what he did (i.e. he finished the exercises, as opposed to something else he did), but (8) tells what he did to his exercises (i.e. he finished doing them, as opposed to handing them in). In other words, 练习 in (7) is part of the information message "作完练习了，" whereas in (8) 练习 represents a known object, the disposal of which is brought out in the predicate "作完了。"

1.3　There are two major conditions for using this construction:

(A) The verb has to be followed by an extra element as represented by X in the schema.

(B) The Object noun has to be definite in reference.

Each of these two conditions will be discussed in detail below.

1.3.1　In terms of the first condition, the X in the verbal complex may be any one of the following types of grammatical elements.

(A) The Resultative Complement:

（9）　他把自行车修好了。
　　　　Tā bǎ zìxíngchē xiūhǎo le.
　　　　He finished repairing the bike.

（10）　他把昨天教的生词都记住了。
　　　　Tā bǎ zuótiān jiāo de shēngcí dōu jìzhù le.
　　　　He has memorized all the words taught yesterday.

(B) The Complement of Degree:

（11）　请把收音机开得大声点儿。
　　　　Qǐng bǎ shōuyīnjī kāi de dàshēng diǎnr.
　　　　Please turn the radio on a little louder.

(12)   你看，我把手洗得多么乾净。
        Nǐ kàn, wǒ bǎ shǒu xǐ de duōme gānjing.
        Look, how clean I have washed my hands.

(C) The Directional Complement:

(13)   他把自行车买来了。
        Tā bǎ zìxíngchē mǎilái le.
        He bought [and brought back] the bike.

(14)   我已经把钱寄去了。
        Wǒ yǐjīng bǎ qián jìqù le.
        I have already sent off the money.

(D) The Complex Directional Complement:

(15)   他把自行车推进去了。
        Tā bǎ zìxíngchē tuījìnqù le.
        He pushed the bike inside.

(16)   她明天会把照相机带回来。
        Tā míngtiān huì bǎ zhàoxiàngjī dàihuílái.
        She will bring back the camera tomorrow.

(E) The Perfective - 了：

(17)   他把自行车卖了。
        Tā bǎ zìxíngchē màile.
        He sold the bike.

(18)   对不起，我把这件事儿忘了。
        Duì bu qǐ, wǒ bǎ zhè jiàn shìr wàngle.
        Sorry, I forgot this matter.

(F) The Indirect Object:

(19)   我把新的杂志给他了。
        Wǒ bǎ xīn de zázhì gěi tā le.
        I gave him the new magazine.

(20)　请把这儿的情况告诉他。
　　　Qǐng bǎ zhèr de qíngkuàng gàosu tā.
　　　Please tell him the situation here.

(G) Reduplication of the Verb:

(21)　你应该把房间整理整理。
　　　Nǐ yīnggāi bǎ fángjiān zhěngli zhěngli.
　　　You should clean up your room.

(22)　请把你的意思给大家说（一）说。
　　　Qǐng bǎ nǐ de yìsi gěi dàjiā shuō(yi)shuo.
　　　Please tell us a little about your idea.

(H) Addition of 一下儿 *yíxiàr*:

(23)　你把自行车洗一下儿，好吗？
　　　Nǐ bǎ zìxíngchē xǐ yíxiàr, hǎo ma?
　　　Wash the bike a bit, would you?

(24)　我们先把课文看一下儿再问问题。
　　　Wǒmen xiān bǎ kèwén kàn yíxiàr zài wèn wèntí.
　　　Let's first look at the text before asking questions.

It is incorrect to use a 把－form if the predicate contains only a simple verb.

(25.a) 他复习课文。
　　　　Tā fùxí kèwén.
　　　　He reviewed the text.
(25.b)*他把课文复习。
　　　　*Tā bǎ kèwén fùxí.

We only have to add an aspectual marker to (25.b), thereby expanding the verbal
unit to include an X element, to produce a grammatical sentence.

(25.c) 他把课文复习了。
　　　　Tā bǎ kèwén fùxí le.
　　　　He reviewed the text.

1.3.2   The Object in a 把 — sentence has to be definite in reference. The definite-ness of the noun may be explicitly marked with words like 这个 / 那个 "this / that" or implicitly inferred from the context.

> (26)   他怎么把这件事儿忘了？
>   Tā zěnme bǎ zhè jiàn shìr wàngle?
>   How come he has forgotten about this thing?

> (27)   他怎么把事儿忘了？
>   Tā zěnme bǎ shìr wàngle?
>   How come he has forgotten about the thing?

Even though the demonstrative marker 这件 is not present in sentence (27), the re-ference of 事儿 is just as clear as it is in (26). The speaker is evidently aware of the specific problem as he/she poses the rhetorical question.

    If the Object is overtly marked with " 一 Measure," the reference is generally indefinite. Hence, it would be incorrect to rephrase the sentence with the 把 — pattern. The following examples illustrate this distinction in application vis-à-vis the referential feature of the Object noun.

> (28.a) 他买来了一本书。   (Indefinite)
>   Tā mǎiláile yìběn shū.
>   He bought a book.
> (28.b)*他把一本书买来了。   (Definite)
>   *Tā bǎ yìběn shū mǎilái le.

> (29)   他把那本书买来了。
>   Tā bǎ nà běn shū mǎilái le.
>   He bought that book.

1.4   As the basic meaning of the 把 — construction is to describe disposal of a known object (which, by the way, can be a thing or a person), we adopt the pattern whenever possible to move the Object to the front, thus saving the predicate exclu-sively for the verb and that extra element, a combination that constitutes the mes-sage of disposal. For example, when the verb takes on a directional complement and when its Object is also definite in reference, then the 把 — form is stylistically much more preferable than a plain sentence without 把.

(30.a) 他推了那辆自行车进去。

Tā tuīle nàliàng zìxíngchē jìnqù.

He pushed that bike in.

(30.b) 他把那辆自行车推了进去。

Tā bǎ nà liàng zìxíngchē tuīlejìnqù.

(31.a) 你带来了包饺子要用的东西没有？

Nǐ dàiláile bāo jiǎozi yào yòng de dōngxi méiyǒu?

Have you brought all the things we need for making the dumplings?

(31.b) 你把包饺子要用的东西都带来了没有？

Nǐ bǎ bāo jiǎozi yào yòng de dōngxi dōu dàiláile méiyǒu?

In our discussion of the complex directional complement in Lesson 43, we mentioned that one of the preferable positions for a definite Object in the pattern would be as topic of the sentence. Another preferable arrangement is to use the 把—construction, as shown in the above sentences. In fact, even though both (a) and (b) forms in each pair are grammatical sentences, the latter sounds much more natural and idiomatic to a native ear. The same stylistic distinction and choice may be applied to the following pairs of sentences, which are constructed with other kinds of post-verbal elements.

(32.a) 别丢了她的地址。快放好它。

Bié diūle tā de dìzhǐ. Kuài fànghǎo tā.

Don't lose her address. Put it in a safe place.

(32.b) 别把她的地址丢了。快把它放好。

Bié bǎ tā de dìzhǐ diūle. Kuài bǎ tā fànghǎo.

(33.a) 你怎么一天就吃完了三天的药？

Nǐ zěnme yìtiān jiù chīwánle sāntiān de yào?

How come you finished the medicine for three days within a day?

(33.b) 你怎么一天就把三天的药都吃完了？

Nǐ zěnme yìtiān jiù bǎ sāntiān de yào dōu chīwán le?

(34.a) 是谁给他我的录音机的？

Shì shéi gěi tā wǒ de lùyīnjī de?

Who gave him my tape recorder?

(34.b) 是谁把我的录音机给他的？

Shì shéi bǎ wǒ de lùyīnjī gěi tā de?

Please note that in (33.b), the 把—version contains the adverb 都, which is absent in (33.a). As 都 refers to 三天的药, the latter has to appear before the former in order to satisfy the word order required by the adverb, namely the referent standing before 都. The 把－transformation provides a ready means to prepose the Object 三天的药, thereby making it possible to incorporate the adverb and produce a sentence stylistically preferable to the unmodified version. The surprise at the improper intake of medicine is emphatically brought out by the disposal construction in conjunction with the all-inclusive 都.

There are certain verbs that do not appear in a 把－construction, primarily because they do not allow a disposal interpretation. For example, the verb－resultative complement unit 看见 *kànjiàn* represents a visual perception, which is something one cannot do at will. One may try to look at something, but as to whether one can actually see it depends on a host of factors beyond one's control or even understanding. In other words, it is semantically very different from a disposal unit like 看完 *kànwán* "to finish reading," an action that one can accomplish if one chooses. Grammatically, the disposal 看完 may readily appear in a 把－pattern, but the involuntary or non-disposal 看见 cannot be so transformed. Hence,

> (35)　　我把那本书看完了。
> 　　　　Wǒ bǎ nà běn shū kànwán le.
> 　　　　I finished reading that book.

> (36)　　*我把那个人看见了。
> 　　　　*Wǒ bǎ nà ge rén kànjiàn le.
> 　　　　I saw that person.

The following is a list of non-disposal verbs incompatible with the 把－construction:

Special verbs:	是 (to be), 有 (to have), 在 (to be at...)
Motion verbs:	来 (to come), 去 (to go), 进 (to enter), 出 (to exit), 上 (to ascend), 下 (to descend), 回 (to return), 过 (to cross), 走 (to leave), 离开 (to depart)
Emotion verbs:	喜欢 (to like), 怕 (to be afraid of), 爱 (to love)
Cognition verbs:	知道 (to know), 认识 (to know, recognize), 觉得 (to feel), 会 (to be able), 看见 (to see), 听见 (to hear)
Others:	访问 (to visit), 欢迎 (to welcome)

1.5 The 把－construction is one of the most difficult grammatical features in the Chinese language. In fact, 把 and 了 are two linguistic phenomena that seem to defy any attempt of systematic characterization. They continue to bewilder scholars and language students with a plentiful supply of multifarious behavioral patterns and anomalous examples. We will learn more about the complexity of the 把一construction in the future, but for the time being please remember

(a) Semantically, the construction indicates "disposal," and
(b) Syntactically: (i) the Object noun has to be definite in reference,
   (ii) the Verbal complex should contain one extra element, such as 了, a complement, etc.

We shall conclude this section on 把 with a few more examples:

(37) 母亲对孩子说，"只有你把练习作完，我才会带你去动物园。要不，你只能留在家里。"

Mǔqīn duì háizi shuō, "Zhǐ yǒu nǐ bǎ liànxí zuòwán, wǒ cái huì dài nǐ qù dòngwùyuán. Yào bù, nǐ zhǐ néng liú zài jiāli."

The mother said to the child, "Only when you have finished your exercises will I take you to the zoo. Otherwise, you will have to stay home."

(38) 大夫小声地对护士说，"请你立刻把这瓶药送到二〇一号病房去，把我刚给病人的药拿回来。"

Dàifu xiǎoshēng de duì hùshì shuō, "Qǐng nǐ lìkè bǎ zhè píng yào sòng dào èrlíngyīhào bìngfáng qù, bǎ wǒ gāng gěi bìngrén de yào náhuílái."

The doctor said to the nurse in a low voice, "Please take this bottle of medicine to Ward 201 immediately and bring back the medicine that I just gave to the patient."

(39) 请先把窗户关上。等我把衣服穿好再开开。

Qǐng xiān bǎ chuānghu guānshang. Děng wǒ bǎ yīfu chuānhǎo zài kāikāi.

Please close the window for now. Wait till I have put on my clothes and then you can open it.

(40) 等你把这课的录音听完以后，就应该把录音机还回录音室去。

Děng nǐ bǎ zhè kè de lùyīn tīngwán yǐhòu, jiù yīnggāi bǎ lùyīnjī huánhuí lùyīnshì qù.

When you have finished listening to the recording of this lesson, you should return the tape recorder to the recording room.

(41)　古波住院了。帕兰卡来电话说，"你觉得怎么样？我已经把你的情况
　　　告诉王老师了。请放心。我明天会把你的汉字练习本带来。"

Gǔbō zhù yuàn le. Pàlánkǎ lái diànhuà shuō, "Nǐ juéde zěnmeyàng?
Wǒ yǐjīng bǎ nǐ de qíngkuàng gàosu Wáng lǎoshī le. Qǐng fàng xīn.
Wǒ míngtiān huì bǎ nǐ de Hànzì liànxíběn dàilái."

Gubo was hospitalized. Palanka called and said, "How are you
doing? I have already explained to Teacher Wang about your situation. Don't worry. I will bring you the character exercise book
tomorrow."

2. 上 as a Resultative Complement

As discussed in a previous lesson, the motion verb 上 *shàng* "to ascend" may function as a directional complement, as in (1).

(1)　别让小孩儿爬上树去玩儿。

Bié ràng xiǎoháir páshàng shù qù wánr.
Don't let the kids crawl up the trees and play.

上 may also serve as a resultative complement with the general meaning of "returning something to the position where it normally is" or "bringing things together."

(2)　请把门关上。

Qǐng bǎ mén guānshàng.
Please close the door.

(3)　收音机，我们现在不听，请关上吧。

Shōuyīnjī, wǒmen xiànzài bù tīng, qǐng guānshàng ba.
We are not listening to the radio. Please turn it off.

In sentence (2) where the main verb is 关 "to close," the complement 上 specifies
the result of returning the door to its normal shut position, making the door and the
frame meet. You may recall that the expression for "to open" a door is 开开, where
the second 开 serves as a complement marking the moving away (or being moved
away) from the original position.

　　The presence of 上 in sentence (3) may be similarly accounted for. Until one
presses the button or turns the knob, a radio is a silent sound box. Thus, the action
of turning off the broadcasting is to bring the radio back to its normal soundless
state. Hence, the use of 上 as the resultative complement.

Both sentences (2) and (3) contain the verb 关 and, if based on this association alone, it would be quite easy and logical to construe 上 as an resultative complement marking the success of "shutting" or "turning off." However, when other sentences such as (4) to (6) are taken into consideration, the function of 上 becomes apparent: it highlights the success of bringing something to a position or state where it should be.

(4)　外边儿有点儿冷，你还是穿上这件毛衣吧。

　　　Wàibiānr yǒu diǎnr lěng, nǐ háishì chuānshàng zhè jiàn máoyī ba.

　　　It's a bit cold outside, You'd better put on this sweater.

(5)　我们说的话你都录上了没有？

　　　Wǒmen shuō de huà nǐ dōu lùshàngle méiyou?

　　　Has everything we said been recorded?

(6)　请你在这儿写上你的名字。

　　　Qǐng nǐ zài zhèr xiěshàng nǐ de míngzi.

　　　Please write your name here.

In sentence (4), clothes are made to be worn; 穿 is the action that brings clothes to the body, and 上 marks the result. In sentence (5), the purpose of 录音 is to bring sounds into the recording machine and 上 indicates the success. In sentence (6), 写上 emphasizes the attachment of words to paper through the action of writing. In all three examples, we see the presence of 上 in association with the semantic notion of "bringing together" rather than that of "closing" as it might appear to be in sentences (2) and (3). The use of 上 as an resultative complement is a highly idiomatic matter, requiring therefore careful observation and imitation of the native speaker's habits. The explanations provided above may help you to anticipate and comprehend its use in other situations.

The following are a few more examples of the resultative 上.

(7)　今天可能会下雨。你出去以前别忘了把窗户关上。

　　　Jīntiān kěnéng huì xià yǔ. Nǐ chūqù yǐqián bié wàngle bǎ chuānghu guānshàng.

　　　It probably will rain today. Please don't forget to close the windows before you leave.

(8)　我一定要戴上眼镜才看得见书里的小字。

　　　Wǒ yídìng yào dàishàng yǎnjìng cái kàn de jiàn shūli de xiǎo zì.

　　　I have to put on my glasses before I can read the small prints in the book.

(9)　　要是能在花园里种上一些花儿，就一定会更好看了。

　　　　Yàoshì néng zài huāyuánli zhòngshàng yìxiē huār, jiù yídìng huì gèng hǎokàn le.

　　　　If you can grow some flowers in the garden, it will definitely look even more beautiful.

(10)　　这个门不知道为什么总是关不上。

　　　　Zhè ge mén bù zhīdao wèishénme zǒng shì guān bu shàng.

　　　　I don't know why this door can never be closed.

Lesson 47

---

1. Special Types of the 把–Construction

The two major conditions for using the disposal construction are (i) the definite-ness of the Object noun phrase, and (ii) the complexity of the verb phrase. This lesson concentrates on the second condition and presents certain sentence types which, because of their verbal complexities, require the use of the 把–form. In other words, unlike the sentences presented in Lesson 46 where for each 把–sent-ence there is always a non-把 version, the use of 把 is obligatory in the following sentence types.

1.1 The 把–pattern is compulsory when the verb is followed by a locative com-plement, indicating placement or relocation of a thing or a person as a result of the disposal action. As described in Lesson 39, a locative complement is made up of 在 or 到, followed by a place word. When a disposal verb takes both an Object and a locative complement, the Object must be preposed, leaving the verb and the comple-ment to form one closed verbal unit, as represented by the following pattern. The locative complement tells where the Object is moved via the disposal verb.

把　Object　＋　Verb　在／到　Place

(1)　　我把那些树种在院子里了。

　　　　Wǒ bǎ nà xiē shù zhòng zài yuànzili le.

　　　　I have planted those trees in the yard.

Please compare sentence (1) with the following sentence:

(2)　　我在院子里种了一些树。

　　　　Wǒ zài yuànzili zhòngle yìxiē shù.

　　　　I have planted some trees in the yard.

Grammatically, (1) is a 把－sentence with a locative complement (i.e. Verb + Place), whereas in (2) the locative appears before the verb and the Object remains in its regular position after the verb (i.e. Place + Verb). More importantly, there is a semantic difference between the two sentences that necessitates such a structural differentiation. Sentence (2) describes what the speaker did in the backyard, namely planting some trees, perhaps in a planter. The preverbal locative specifies where the action takes place and the indefinite marker 一些 "some" prevents the Object from being topicalized. Sentence (1), on the other hand, tells what the speaker did to the trees, namely planting them in the backyard. 院子 is where he actually put the trees into the soil, hence a new location for the trees, and not the site where he worked as in (2). 在院子里 is a locative complement in (1), and for this reason the Object has to be moved out of the verbal scope via the 把－construction.

The following are more examples of the use of 把 in sentences with locative complements.

(3)   你把自行车放在哪儿了？
       Nǐ bǎ zìxíngchē fàng zài nǎr le?
       Where did you put the bike?

(4)   她把老师说的话都写在这个本子上。
       Tā bǎ lǎoshī shuō de huà dōu xiě zài zhè ge běnzishang.
       She wrote down everything that the teacher said in this notebook.

(5)   老师说鲁迅是一位伟大的文学家。所以下课以后，我去买了一本鲁迅写的书。我把它放在书架上，准备以后有空儿的时候看。
       Lǎoshī shuō Lǔ Xùn shì yíwèi wěidà de wénxuéjiā. Suǒyǐ xià kè yǐhòu, wǒ qù mǎile yìběn Lǔ Xùn xiě de xiǎoshuō. Wǒ bǎ tā fàng zài shūjiàshàng, zhǔnbèi yǐhòu yǒu kòngr de shíhou kàn.
       The teacher said that Lu Xun was a great writer. So, after class I went and bought a book that Lu Xun wrote. I put it on the bookshelf and I plan to read it in the future when I have time.

(6)   我已经把那把椅子搬到楼上去了。
       Wǒ yǐjīng bǎ nà bǎ yǐzi bān dào lóushàng qù le.
       I have already moved that chair upstairs.

(7)   我们快把这个病人送到医院去吧。
       Wǒmen kuài bǎ zhè ge bìngrén sòng dào yīyuàn qù ba.
       Let's quickly send this patient to the hospital.

(8)   飞机是八点半起飞的。是我七点十分开车把他们送到机场的。
       Fēijī shì bādiǎnbàn qǐfēi de. Shì wǒ qīdiǎn shífēn kāi chē bǎ tāmen sòng dào jīchǎng de.

The plane left at 8:30. It was I who drove them to the airport at ten (minutes) past seven.

1.2 The 把—construction is compulsory when the verb is followed by a complement expression describing the transformation of the Object via the disposal verb. The complement in this case is marked by 成 *chéng* or 作 *zuò*, both meaning "to become," followed by the noun representing what the Object has been changed into.

> 把　Object　＋　Verb　成／作　Noun

(9)　他想把这本书翻译成英文。
　　　Tā xiǎng bǎ zhè běn shū fānyì chéng Yīngwén.
　　　He wants to translate this book into English.

(10)　他把 "大夫" 两个字念成了 "dafu"。
　　　Tā bǎ "dàifu" liǎngge zì niàn chéng le "dàfu".
　　　He read the word "大夫" as "dàfu."

(11)　你写错了，你把 "北边" 写成 "比边"。
　　　Nǐ xiěcuò le, nǐ bǎ "běibiān" xiě chéng "bǐbiān."
　　　You wrote incorrectly. You wrote 北边 as 比边.

(12)　我想请人把我的花园设计成日本花园。你觉得怎么样？
　　　Wǒ xiǎng qǐng rén bǎ wǒ de huāyuán shèjì chéng Rìběn huāyuán.
　　　Nǐ juéde zěnmeyàng?
　　　I want to hire someone to redesign my garden into a Japanese garden. What do you think?

(13)　他们把她看作家里人。
　　　Tāmen bǎ tā kàn zuò jiāli rén.
　　　They treated her as a member of the family.

(14)　上海人把 "喝茶" 叫作 "吃茶"。
　　　Shànghǎi rén bǎ "hē chá" jiào zuò "chī chá."
　　　The Shanghai people refer to "tea-drinking" as "tea-eating."

1.3 The 把—construction is compusory when the verb is followed by a complement expression which contains an indirect Object, representing the recipient of something or someone, through the disposal action. Please recall from the previous lesson that when used with the verb 给, the 把－construction is an option as illustrated in the following pair of examples:

(15.a) 我给了王老师这本书。

Wǒ gěile Wáng lǎoshī zhè běn shū.

I gave Teacher Wang this book.

(15.b) 我把这本书给了王老师。

Wǒ bǎ zhè běn shū gěile Wáng lǎoshī.

The main verb in both sentences is 给, which takes two Objects: the direct Object 书 and the indirect Object 王老师. The two Objects may be arranged either as "给 + Indirect Object － Direct Object" or "把 Direct Object + 给 Indirect Object." However, when other verbs take two Objects, the indirect Object generally appears as a complement carrying 给 as the marker: "Verb ＋给 Indirect Object" The direct Object, on the other hand, is preposed through the help of 把. Verbs that require the use of the 把－construction include 交 *jiāo* "to hand in, submit," 留 *liú* "to save, reserve," 送 *sòng* "to give as a present," 还 *huán* "to return," 拿 *ná* "to hold," 介绍 *jièshào* "to introduce," etc.

把 Direct Object ＋ Verb 给 Indirect Object

---

(16) 我把钱交给我母亲了。

Wǒ bǎ qián jiāo gěi wǒ mǔqīn le.

I have given (handed over) the money to my mother.

(17) 你说, 你把我的照片送给谁了?

Nǐ shuō, nǐ bǎ wǒ de zhàopiàn sòng gěi shéi le?

Tell me, to whom have you given my picture?

(18) 请你把桌子上的那篇文章拿给我看看。

Qǐng nǐ bǎ zhuōzishàng de nà piān wénzhāng ná gěi wǒ kànkan.

Please hand me that article on the desk so that I can take a look at it.

(19) 你明天去医院看古波的时候，能不能请你把这封信带给他?

Nǐ míngtiān qù yīyuàn kàn Gǔbō de shíhou, néng bu néng qǐng nǐ bǎ zhè fēng xìn dài gěi tā?

When you go to see Gubo at the hospital tomorrow, can you take this letter to him?

(20)　几个月以前，我把小红介绍给张先生张太太。他们非常喜欢她，把她看作自己的女儿。

Jǐge yuè yǐqián, wǒ bǎ xiǎo Hóng jièshào gěi Zhāng xiānsheng Zhāng tàitai. Tāmen fēicháng xǐhuan tā, bǎ tā kàn zuò zìjǐ de nǚ'ér.

Several months ago, I introduced Little Hong to Mr. and Mrs. Zhang. They liked her very much. They treated her as their own daughter.

2. The Construction 除了……以外

The basic meaning of the verb 除 *chú* is "to eliminate, exclude." Its inflected form, 除了 *chúle*, may appear in the following construction and projects two possible readings:

$$\text{除了……以外，……}$$
$$\textit{chúle...yǐwài, ...}$$

The pattern can mean either "with the exception of..." or "in addition to...," a difference that may be readily resolved by selecting an appropriate adverb for the ensuing clause. In either reading, 以外 is optional to the pattern.

2.1 When the accompanying adverb is 都, as in the following pattern, 除了 indicates "with the exception of..."

$$\text{除了 X（以外），都 Verb}$$
$$\textit{chúle X yǐwài, dōu Verb}$$

This pattern expresses an explicit exclusion of X before making a general statement. In other words, the verb represents a general truth with the exception of X. The general truth is highlighted by 都, and the exception is marked by 除了……（以外）. Examples of this exclusive use of 除了 are:

(1)　除了翻译（以外），别的练习他都作了。

Chúle fānyì (yǐwài), biéde liànxí tā dōu zuòle.

Except for the translation, he did all the (other) exercises.

Cf. (2)   他没作翻译。别的练习他都作了。

Tā méi zuò fānyì. Biéde liànxí tā dōu zuò le.

He didn't do the translation. He did all the other exercises.

The two utterances are essentially the same in meaning, but (2) describes the situation in two separate sentences whereas (1) joins the two statements together in a more condensed or concise form.

(3)   除了晚上（以外），别的时候他都不在家。

Chúle wǎnshang (yǐwài), biéde shíhou tā dōu bú zài jiā.

He is not home at any time with the exception of evenings. (Except for evenings, he is never at home.)

(4)   除了他骑自行车去（以外），我们都坐公共汽车去。

Chúle tā qí zìxíngchē qù (yǐwài), wǒmen dōu zuò gōnggòng qìchē qù.

We are all going by bus, except for him who is going by bike.

(5)   除了他们两个人，同学们都把帕兰卡当作自己的妹妹。

Chúle tāmen liǎngge rén, tóngxuémen dōu bǎ Pàlánkǎ dāng zuò zìjǐ de mèimei.

Except for those two, all the classmates look upon Palanka as their own sister.

2.2   When the accompanying adverb is 也 or 还, as in the following pattern, 除了 means "in addition to..."

> 除了 X （以外），也 / 还 Verb
>
> *chúle* X *(yǐwài), yě/hái* Verb

This pattern shows that, even after the exclusion of X, the general truth still （也 / 还）holds. Both X and the other elements are all covered by the same truth. Therefore, this is the "inclusive" use of 除了.

(6)   除了翻译（以外），别的练习他也作了。

Chúle fānyì yǐwài, biéde liànxí tā yě zuòle.

Besides the translation, he also did the other exercises.

If we compare (6) with (1), the distinction between the inclusive and exclusive uses of 除了 is self-evident. The semantic differentiation depends primarily on the appropriate adverbial marking: (6) is marked by 也 and (1) by 都 . Now, compare (6) with the following sentence.

(7)　　翻译和别的练习，他都作了。
　　　　Fānyì hé biéde liànxí, tā dōu zuòle.
　　　　He did the translation and the other exercises.

Again, sentences (6) and (7) are reporting the same event, with a slight difference in emphasis. While (7) describes the diligence in terms of what the student did (namely, both 翻译 and 别的练习), (6) puts more emphasis on 别的练习 , almost as if saying "Besides the translation which everyone was expected to do, he also did the other exercises, which was truly remarkable." Here are a few more examples of the inclusive use of 除了 :

(8)　　除了晚上（以外），下午他也在家。
　　　　Chúle wǎnshang (yǐwài), xiàwǔ tā yě zài jiā.
　　　　Besides evenings, he is also at home in the afternoons.

(9)　　除了他（以外），那两个同学也觉得不舒服。
　　　　Chúle tā (yǐwài), nà liǎngge tóngxué yě juéde bù shūfu.
　　　　Besides him, those two students also felt sick.

(10)　　校园里除了一座小山（以外），还有一个小湖。
　　　　Xiàoyuánli chúle yízuò xiǎo shān (yǐwài), hái yǒu yíge xiǎo hú.
　　　　Aside from a small hill, there is also a small lake on the campus.

(11)　　昨天下午除了游泳（以外），他还钓鱼了。
　　　　Zuótiān xiàwǔ chúle yóu yǒng yǐwài, tā hái diào yú le.
　　　　Besides swimming, he also did some fishing yesterday afternoon.

(12)　　这位护士除了工作认真（以外），生活也很俭朴。
　　　　Zhè wèi hùshi chúle gōngzuò rènzhēn (yǐwài), shēnghuó yě hěn jiǎnpǔ.
　　　　This nurse, aside from being conscientious at work, also leads a simple life.

The following sentences further contrast the two 除了 patterns:

(13.a)　除了 Aspirin 以外，别的药他都吃了。　　　　　(Exclusive)
　　　　Chúle Aspirin yǐwài, biéde yào tā dōu chīle.

(13.b) 除了 Aspirin 以外，别的药他也吃了。   (Inclusive)
　　　　Chúle Aspirin yǐwài, biéde yào tā yě chīle.

(14.a) 除了他以外，我们都会说中国话。   (Exclusive)
　　　　Chúle tā yǐwài, wǒmen dōu huì shuō Zhōngguó huà.

(14.b) 除了他以外，我们也会说中国话。   (Inclusive)
　　　　Chúle tā yǐwài, wǒmen yě huì shuō Zhōngguó huà.

(15)　　A: 这个孩子，除了 Hamburger 以外，还吃什么？
　　　　　　Zhè ge háizi, chúle Hamburger yǐwài, hái chī shénme?
　　　　　　Besides Hamburger, what else does this kid eat?
　　　　B: 除了 Hamburger 以外，别的东西他都不吃。
　　　　　　Chúle Hamburger yǐwài, biéde dōngxi tā dōu bù chī.
　　　　　　Besides Hamburger, he doesn't eat anything.

(16)　　昨天老师对我说，"除了你，别的同学都知道鲁迅是中国一位伟大的
　　　　文学家。"我听了以后，觉得很不好意思。所以下课以后，我就去书店
　　　　买书。除了鲁迅的小说和诗以外，我还买了一本写他在日本生活的
　　　　书。非常有意思。

Zuótiān lǎoshī duì wǒ shuō, "Chúle nǐ, biéde tóngxué dōu zhīdao Lǔ
Xùn shì Zhōngguó yíwèi wěidà de wénxuéjiā." Wǒ tīngle yǐhòu,
juéde hěn bù hǎo yìsi. Suǒyǐ xià kè yǐhòu, wǒ jiù qù shūdiàn mǎi
shū. Chúle Lǔ Xùn de xiǎoshuō hé shī yǐwài, wǒ hái mǎile yìběn xiě
tā zài Rìběn shēnghuó de shū. Fēicháng yǒu yìsi.

The teacher said to me yesterday, "Except for you, everyone else in
the class knows that Lu Xun was a great Chinese writer." I felt
embarrassed when I heard this. So, after class, I went to the bookstore to buy books. Aside from Lu Xun's stories and poetry, I also
bought a book about his life in Japan. It was very interesting.

1. The Passive Sentence

If a verb represents an action that involves two participants, an actor and a recipient, the linguistic representation of such an event often appears in the following order:

> Actor + Action + Recipient
> | | |
> Subject   Verb   Object

(1)   I hit him.
      我打他。
      Wǒ dǎ tā.

The actor unit occupies the place of subject in the sentence and the recipient occupies the Object slot, an arrangement commonly referred to in linguistics as the active construction. Like English and many other languages, Chinese relies heavily on the use of the active construction, with the direction of the action extending from the subject to the Object. In fact, most of the sentences we have examined so far in this book are cast in the active mode. A passive sentence is a sentence in which the direction of the action is reversed and the recipient of the action occurs in the subject position. The following demonstrates how the passive is constructed in English.

> Recipient + Action + Actor
> | | |
> Subject   +   Verb   Object

(2)   He was hit by me.

Now consider the following Chinese sentence:

(3)　　鱼吃了。
　　　　Yú chī le.

The sentence contains only one nominal element, namely 鱼 *yú* "fish," in the subject position. As an active sentence, 鱼 is clearly the actor, and the direction of the action extends outward from the subject. Hence, an equivalent sentence in English is (3.a).

(3.a)　The fish has eaten.

In a different context, however, the Chinese sentence may also mean

(3.b)　The fish has been eaten.

In this second reading, 鱼 is no longer the actor but rather the object of consumption, even though it still occupies the subject position. Such a reversal of semantic roles, from active to passive, is grammatically marked in English by the use of the passive construction. Hence, there is the paradigmatic distinction between "has eaten" and "has been eaten." Unlike English, such grammatical marking is absent in Chinese: the verb remains intact as 吃. The ambiguity of the sentence may, of course, be readily resolved once the proper context is given, as in the following situations:

(4)　　鱼吃了，你不用再喂了。
　　　　Yú chī le, nǐ bú yòng zài wèi le.
　　　　The fish has eaten. You don't have to feed it again.

(5)　　鱼吃了，菜还没吃。
　　　　Yú chī le, cài hái méi chī.
　　　　The fish has been eaten, but not the vegetable.

It is quite clear from the last sentence (5) that 鱼 is put in contrast with 菜 in terms of, say, dietary preference. As noted in earlier lessons, the subject in a Chinese sentence often functions as the topic of the discourse; and in such topical capacity, the subject may be the actor or the recipient of an action depending solely on contextual interpretation. Sentence (3) may either be an active or a passive sentence with no overt specification. As we will learn in the next lesson, overt marking for the passive construction is available in Chinese, but its use is quite infrequent as compared with the employment of the *by*-construction in English. When a sentence stands passive in meaning but unmarked in structure, it may be described as "notionally passive." The following are a few more examples of this passive usage. The passive subjects are all underlined.

(6) 饭菜都准备好了。

Fàncài dōu zhǔnbèihǎo le.

The meal has been prepared.

(7) 电视机还没关上呢。

Diànshìjī hái méi guānshàng ne.

The T.V. hasn't been turned off.

(8) 太晚了，过年要用的东西都买不到了。

Tài wǎn le, guò nián yào yòng de dōngxi dōu mǎi bu dào le.

It's too late now. None of the things needed for the New Year can be purchased (are available).

(9) 桌子摆好了，外边的朋友现在都可以请进来了。

Zhuōzi bǎihǎo le, wàibiān de péngyou xiànzài dōu kěyǐ qǐngjìnlái le.

The table has been set; and the friends outside can all be asked to come in now.

(10) 鲁迅写的小说都翻译成英文了。

Lǔ Xùn xiě de xiǎoshuō dōu fānyì chéng Yīngwén le.

All of Lu Xun's stories have been translated into English.

(11) 我已经找了他们来帮忙了。所以你们就不麻烦了。

Wǒ yǐjīngzhǎole tāmen lái bāngmáng le. Suǒyǐ nǐmen jiù bù máfán le.

I have already asked them to come and help. So, I don't need to bother you.

(12) 兔子准备好了。

Tùzi zhǔnbèihǎo le.

The rabbit has been properly prepared.

Or: The rabbit has properly prepared itself.

It is interesting to note that while sentences (6) and (12) share the same verbal predicate（准备好）, only the latter may have two readings, the second of which is an active interpretation we might find in a fable. The reason for this dissimilarity is actually very simple. The nominal subject in (12), 兔子, is an animate being, thereby qualifying it to be either the preparing agent or the prepared object. On the other hand, by virtue of its inanimateness, 饭菜 in (6) can only be what is prepared. In fact, most of the notional passive sentences in the above examples are of this second type. You should, however, be prepared to encounter the full range of application in the future.

   Please note that since the passive subject is essentially a discursive topic of the comment that follows, it has to be something of which both the speaker and the addressee are aware. In other words, it has to be definite in reference. Unlike its equivalent in English, the following Chinese sentence is incorrect since its subject is marked with 一个 and is an indefinite nominal.

（13）   *一个礼物给你了。

          *Yíge lǐwù gěi nǐ le.

          A present was given to you.

Cf.(14)   那件礼物给你了。

          Nà jiàn lǐwù gěi nǐ le.

          That present was given to you.

2. The Use of the Interrogative for Indefinite Reference

2.1   Interrogative words such as 谁 *shéi* "who," 什么 *shénme* "what," 哪儿 *nǎr* "where," etc., are primarily used for forming questions.

（1）   谁会作灯笼？

          Shéi huì zuò dēnglóng?

          Who knows how to make a lantern?

（2）   哪儿有爆竹卖？

          Nǎr yǒu bàozhu mài?

          Where do you find firecrackers for sale?

（3）   你买了些什么东西？

          Nǐ mǎile xiē shénme dōngxi?

          What (things) have you purchased?

In answering the above sentences, one can provide either very specific information, like (4) in response to (1), or a reply that pertains to an all-inclusive but indefinite reference as in (5).

（4）   李老师的儿子会作灯笼。

          Lǐ lǎoshī de érzi huì zuò dēnglóng.

          Teacher Li's son knows how to make a lantern.

(5) 谁都会作灯笼。

Shéi dōu huì zuò dēnglóng.

Everyone knows how to make a lantern.

Grammatically speaking, the all-inclusive sentence (5) is very similar to the question from (1) in that it also carries the interrogative word 谁. The only difference is that (5) contains the adverb 都, a lexical marker of all-inclusiveness. Similarly, an all-inclusive answer to (2) may also be phrased in the following pattern.

```
                    Interrogative Word  +  都
```

(6) 哪儿都有爆竹卖。

Nǎr dōu yǒu bàozhu mài.

Every place carries firecrackers.

A negative answer may use the same pattern with a negative verb, as in (7)

(7) 哪儿都没有爆竹卖。

Nǎr dōu méiyou bàozhu mài.

No place carries firecrackers.

To answer the question in (3), the word order is somewhat different from that in the question form.

(8) 我什么都买了。

Wǒ shénme dōu mǎi le.

I have bought everything.

As a question word functioning as the Object of the verb 买 in (3), 什么 occurs in its regular Object position; however, its role as an all-inclusive term in the answer (8) demands a new placement right before the verb. The forward movement from a post-verbal to a pre-verbal position is triggered by the presence of 都, an adverbial that marks the general reference of the noun that appears before it. Since an all-inclusive term is by nature plural in reference, it has to occur before the reinforcing 都. The following are a few more sentences to illustrate this inclusive or indefinite use of the interrogative.

(9) 那个挂在公园门口的大灯笼，谁见了都会喜欢。

Nà ge guà zài gōngyuán ménkǒu de dà dēnglóng, shéi jiànle dōu huì xǐhuan.

That big lantern that's hanging by the park entrance, anyone who sees it will like it.

(10) 哪个国家都有自己的节日。

Nǎ ge guójiā dōu yǒu zìjǐ de jiérì.

Every country has its own festivals.

(11) 除了圣诞节那天以外，我哪天都可以来看你。

Chúle Shèngdànjié nà tiān yǐwài, wǒ nǎ tiān dōu kěyǐ lái kàn nǐ.

Except for Christmas day, I can come to see you any day.

(12) 你什么时候去找他，他都在写文章。

Nǐ shénme shíhòu qù zhǎo tā, tā dōu zài xiě wénzhāng.

Whenever you go to see him, he is always writing (articles).

(13) 阳阳哭了，因为他的小兔子不见了。他找了三天，可是哪儿都找不到。

Yángyang kū le, yīnwèi tā de xiǎo tùzi bú jiànle. Tā zhǎole sāntiān, kěshì nǎr dōu zhǎo bu dào.

Yangyang began to cry, as his rabbit had disappeared. He looked for three days, but couldn't find it anywhere.

(14) 因为他刚刚吃完年夜饭，所以他现在什么都吃不下了。

Yīnwèi tā gānggāng chīwán niányè fàn, suǒyǐ tā xiànzài shénme dōu chī bu xià le.

As he has just finished the New Year's Eve dinner, he can't eat anything now.

(15) 你送我什么礼物，我都很高兴。

Nǐ sòng wǒ shénme lǐwù, wǒ dōu hěn gāoxìng.

Whatever present you give me, I'll be very happy.

(16) A: 你想把房间设计成什么样子？

Nǐ xiǎng bǎ fángjiān shèjì chéng shénme yàngzi?

How do you want to design your room?

B: 什么样子都可以。

Shénme yàngzi dōu kěyǐ.

Any design will do.

As a point for comparison, English exhibits a similar use of the interrogative in its formation of an indefinite expression. For example, "who: whoever," "what: whatever," "when: whenever," "where: wherever," etc.

2.2   A variation of the indefinite use of the interrogative is to have 也 instead of 都 as the accompanying adverb. For example, the second half of sentence (14) can be rephrased as:

> (14.a)……所以他现在什么也吃不下了。
>
> ...suǒyǐ tā xiànzài shénme yě chī bu xià le.

While there is no distinction in meaning or in style between (14) and (14.a), the use of 也 in this capacity is generally restricted to negative sentences. Hence, rephrasing the answer portion in sentence (16) with 也 will yield an unacceptable if not utterly ungrammatical sentence.

> (16.a)……什么样子也可以。
>
> ...shénme yàngzi yě kěyǐ.

As always is the case, there are exceptions to this general rule. Yet, until you have acquired the skill to determine which sounds better, you may wish to abide by this restriction.

2.3   With the exception of 为什么, all Chinese interrogatives may readily participate in this indefinite pattern. Likewise, the English parallel "why" has no corresponding "-ever" form for the indefinite usage.

2.4   Insofar as English translation is concerned, the use of 怎么 may pose difficulty for beginning students. While the indefinite use of other interrogative words may be quite easily rendered as "anyone/everyone/whoever," "anywhere/everywhere/wherever," "any time/every time/whenever," etc., the usage of 怎么 sometimes requires paraphrasing in English.

> (17)   我怎么也打不开那个箱子。
>
> Wǒ zěnme yě dǎ bu kāi nà ge xiāngzi.
>
> No matter how hard I tried, I wasn't able to open that box.

怎么, as a question word, asks for the manner in which or by means of which an action is carried out. Hence, the indefinite use of 怎么 amounts to saying "by whatever means" or "however" one attempts the action. But as English lacks a ready equivalent for the indefinite 怎么, students cannot always rely on intuitive knowledge of English to predict its use in Chinese. The following are more examples:

(18)   因为他没作过灯笼，所以怎么也作不好。
       Yīnwèi tā méi zuòguo dēnglóng, suǒyǐ zěnme yě zuò bu hǎo.
       As he had never made a lantern before, he couldn't do a good job no matter what.
       (= No matter how he tried, he couldn't do a good job...)

(19)   明天的会，我怎么忙都要去开。
       Míngtiān de huì, wǒ zěnme máng dōu yào qù kāi.
       No matter how busy I am, I will for sure attend the meeting tomorrow.

3. The Construction 因为……所以……

To mark the cause and effect relationship between two events, we use the paired correlatives 因为 and 所以, each sitting before its appropriate clause. As in the case of other correlatives introduced earlier, even though one of the two connectors may be omitted, the paired usage is always preferred.

(1)   她因为身体不舒服，所以今天晚上不出去玩儿了。
       Tā yīnwèi shēntǐ bù shūfu, suǒyǐ jīntiān wǎnshang bù chūqù wánr le.
       Because she is not feeling well, she is not going out tonight.

(2)   过年的时候，他因为病了，所以哪儿都没去拜年。
       Guò nián de shíhòu, tā yīnwèi bìngle, suǒyǐ nǎr dōu méi qù bài nián.
       Because he was sick during the New Year, he didn't go anywhere to make New Year calls.

(3)   A: 你为什么决定不去旅行了？
          Nǐ wèi shénme juédìng bú qù lǚxíng le?
          Why have you decided not to go on the trip?
       B: 因为快考试了，所以我想还是留在家里多准备准备。
          Yīnwèi kuài kǎo shì le, suǒyǐ wǒ xiǎng háishì liú zài jiāli duō zhǔnbei zhǔnbei.
          Because exams are coming, I think I'd better stay home and prepare.

(4)   因为春节快到了，她还没收拾屋子，所以她想这几天不去工作，在家整理。

Yīnwèi chūnjié kuài dào le, tā hái méi shōushi wūzi, suǒyǐ tā xiǎng zhè jǐtiān bú qù gōngzuò, zài jiā zhěnglǐ.

Because the New Year is almost here and she still hasn't started cleaning her house, she has decided to take a few days off to do the cleanup.

(5)   (因为)他没学过汉语，所以他听不懂你说的话。

(Yīnwèi) Tā méi xuéguo Hànyǔ, suǒyǐ tā tīng bu dǒng nǐ shuō de huà.

He has never studied Chinese, and so he can't understand what you're saying.

(6)   因为你说过没有问题，（所以）我们才决定不去。

Yīnwèi nǐ shuōguo méiyou wèntí, (suǒyǐ) wǒmen cái juédìng bú qù.

As you said it would be alright, we have decided not to go.

The ordering of the 因为 clause before the 所以 clause is a reflection of the natural sequence from cause/reason to result. Sometimes, the 因为 segment may appear at the end of a sentence, almost as if it is an afterthought. In this case, the consequence clause is never marked with 所以.

(7)   我把全家人的圣诞礼物都寄到妹妹家去了——因为今年大家都在妹妹家过节。

Wǒ bǎ quán jiā rén de Shèngdàn lǐwù dōu jì dào mèimei jiā qù le —— yīnwèi jīnnián dàjiā dōu zài mèimei jiā guò jié.

I have sent the Christmas presents for the entire family to my younger sister's house —— since they will all be celebrating the holiday at her home.

Like 虽然……但是…… introduced in Lesson 39, the paired usage of 因为 and 所以 may seem redundant when translated literally into English: "because...therefore..." Remember, however, it is the norm in Chinese to use the correlatives in pairs. Also, when the two clauses share the same subject, the subject may appear before either the first or the second clause, but not before both, as in (8.a) and (8.b). If the subjects are different, the correlatives appear at the beginning of their own clauses, as in (9).

(8.a) 她因为打了一天的球，所以觉得很累。

Tā yīnwèi dǎle yìtiān de qiú, suǒyǐ juéde hěn lèi.

As she played ball for the whole day, she felt very tired.

(8.b)　因为打了一天的球，所以她觉得很累。

Yīnwèi dǎle yìtiān de qiú, suǒyǐ tā juéde hěn lèi.

(9)　　　因为熊猫很可爱，所以去看的人很多。

Yīnwèi xióngmāo hěn kě'ài, suǒyǐ qù kàn de rén hěn duō.

Because the pandas are cute, many people go to see them.

In all cases, 所以 has to appear before the subject of the consequence clause, a requirement that explains why the following sentence seems less acceptable than its corresponding version in (8.b).

(8.c)　打了一天的球，她所以觉得很累。

Dǎle yìtiān de qiú, tā suǒyǐ juéde hěn lèi.

4. The All-Inclusive 全

4.1 Like the adverb 都 which marks the scope of action "all, in all cases," 全 *quán* is another form that directs the all-inclusiveness of the action to the preceding noun. 全 is more emphatic in connotation than 都, and the two may sometimes double up (全 + 都) to further enhance the idea of totality.

(1)　　　这些礼物全是她带来给孩子的。

Zhè xiē lǐwù quán shì tā dàilái gěi háizi de.

She brought all of these gifts for the children.

(2)　　　还没过年，你怎么把爆竹全放了？

Hái méi guò nián, nǐ zěnme bǎ bàozhu quán fàng le?

The New Year is not here yet. How come you have fired off all the firecrackers?

(3)　　　我把他说的话全都记下来了。

Wǒ bǎ tā shuō de huà quán dōu jìxiàlái le.

I jotted down every word he said.

Unlike 都, however, 全 is seldom used in the pattern of the interrogative word for indefinite reference.

(4.a)　中国饭，谁都爱吃。

Zhōngguó fàn, shéi dōu ài chī.

Everyone is fond of the Chinese food.

(4.b) *中国饭，谁全爱吃。

　　　*Zhōngguó fàn, shéi quán ài chī.

4.2　Another difference between 都 and 全 is that only the latter may function as an adjective. It may appear directly before the noun phrase it modifies, as in sentences (5) and (6). Or, though less frequently, it may be used as a predicate, as in (7).

(5)　　春节是全家人团聚的节日。

　　　Chūnjié shì quán jiā rén tuánjù de jiérì.

　　　The Spring Festival is the occasion for the entire family to get together.

(6)　　请你把全篇文章都翻译成日文。

　　　Qǐng nǐ bǎ quán piān wénzhāng dōu fānyì chéng Rìwén.

　　　Please translate the entire article into Japanese.

(7)　　你想研究鲁迅的小说——我们图书馆的书不很全。

　　　Nǐ xiǎng yánjiū Lǔ Xùn de xiǎoshuō —— wǒmen túshūguǎn de shū bù hěn quán.

　　　You want to work on Lu Xun's fiction —— our library collection (on the topic) is not very complete.

(8)　　今年我们全家都没有生病。

　　　Jīnnián wǒmen quán jiā dōu méiyou shēng bìng.

　　　No one in our entire family fell sick this year.

Sentence (8) displays the contrast in status between 全 and 都, the former as an adjectival modifier for 家 and the latter the adverbial modifier for 没有生病. As an adjective, 全 may appear directly before a noun, or preferably before the measure word of the noun. In fact, rephrasing (6) without the intervening measure will yield an ungrammatical sentence.

(6.a) *请你把全文章都翻译成日文。

　　　*Qǐng nǐ bǎ quán wénzhāng dōu fānyì chéng Rìwén.

Only in some special combinations do we find a "全 + Noun" sequence, and these we will have to learn one by one.

(9)　　今天是 Dr. King 的生日，全国都放假吗？

　　　Jīntiān shì Dr. King de shēngri, quán guó dōu fàng jià ma?

　　　Today is Dr. King's birthday. Is it a holiday for the entire country?

5. The Assertive Particle 的

Chinese contains a host of sentence final particles that speakers may use to modify statements with some kind of personal, emotional or modal overtone. For example, the following three sentences all express the expectation that someone will come the next day.

（1）　他明天会来。
　　　　Tā míngtiān huì lái.
　　　　He's coming tomorrow.

（2）　他明天会来吧。
　　　　Tā míngtiān huì lái ba.
　　　　He's coming tomorrow, I guess.

（3）　他明天会来的。
　　　　Tā míngtiān huì lái de.
　　　　He's coming tomorrow, I know.

The sentences differ, however, in the degree of certainty displayed. The differences are marked by the absence or presence of a sentence particle. Sentence (1), not qualified by any modal particle, is simply a projection. It becomes more speculative and less commital in (2) when the suggestion particle 吧 is added to the end. And, when the particle changes to 的 in (3), the statement implies a sense of assertion. The following are a few more sentences to illustrate this assertive use of 的.

（4）　熊猫真可爱，谁见了都会喜欢的。
　　　　Xióngmāo zhēn kě'ài, shéi jiànle dōu huì xǐhuan de.
　　　　The panda is really cute. Anyone who sees it will definitely like it.

（5）　这么要紧的事儿，你应该先问问她的。
　　　　Zhème yàojǐn de shìr, nǐ yīnggāi xiān wènwen tā de.
　　　　For such an important affair, you should have consulted her first.

（6）　你常常帮助他母亲，他一定会非常感谢你的。
　　　　Nǐ chángcháng bāngzhù tā mǔqīn, tā yídìng huì fēicháng gǎnxiè nǐ de.
　　　　You always help his mother. He certainly is very grateful.

As you may have already noticed, the neutral tone word 的 can serve a variety of grammatical functions. The assertive use is just another addition to that list.

Lesson 49

1. The Passive Sentence (continued)

1.1 A passive sentence in English has two formal markers. First, the verb phrase contains the auxiliary verb-to-be. Second, the "actor nominal" appears in the Object position and carries a prepositional marker *by*. An example is :

(1)   He was hit by me.

We have learned from the previous lesson that a passive sentence in Chinese requires no modification of the verb form. We have, however, made no mention of the marking of the actor status of the Object nominal. In fact, we made a deliberate effort to avoid including any passive sentence that would contain an actor nominal. The primary concern in this lesson is how to mark the passive Object in Chinese. The following is the Chinese equivalent to the above sentence (1) :

(2)   他被我打了。
       Tā bèi wǒ dǎle.
       He was hit by me.

被 *bèi* is a preposition whose primary function is to indicate a passive construction. It is placed directly before the actor Object, and the entire Object expression appears between the subject and the verb. The reversal of word order between the active and the passive is demonstrated as follows.

Active	Subject + Verb + Object [Actor] [Recipient]
Passive	Subject + 被－Object + Verb [Recipient] [Actor]

Now, recall the ambiguity of the following sentence:

(3)　鱼吃了。

Yú chī le.

Active: The fish has eaten.

Passive: The fish has been eaten.

The passive reading is termed as "notionally passive," since grammatically it shares the same structure as the active form. The grammatical subject 鱼 is the actor in the active reading and the recipient in the passive sentence. Context determines which message is the intended reading. However, the ambiguity is readily resolved once the 被－segment is introduced. Sentence (4) is unequivocally passive in form as well as in meaning.

(4)　鱼被邻居的孩子吃了。

Yú bèi línjū de háizi chīle.

The fish has been eaten by the neighbor's child.

Hence, in contrast with the notional passive which is grammatically unmarked, the passive proper, which we address in this lesson, is often referred to as simply the 被－sentence. The following are a few more examples to illustrate the transformation between the active and the passive sentences and the different word orders required therein. Only the active version is given an English translation.

(5) 　A: 报上说那个坏人杀了茶馆的掌柜。

Bàoshang shuō nà ge huài rén shāle cháguǎn de zhǎngguì.

The paper says that scoundrel killed the teahouse keeper.

P: 报上说茶馆的掌柜被那个坏人杀了。

Bàoshang shuō cháguǎn de zhǎngguì bèi nà ge huài rén shāle.

(6) 　A: 她把我的汽车开走了。

Tā bǎ wǒ de qìchē kāizǒule.

She drove my car away.

(＝She drove away in my car.)

P: 我的汽车被她开走了。

Wǒ de qìchē bèi tā kāizǒule.

(7) 　A: 他没把那个镜子打破。

Tā méi bǎ nà ge jìngzi dǎpò.

He didn't break that mirror.

P: 那个镜子没被他打破。

Nà ge jìngzi méi bèi tā dǎpò.

(8)   A: 她把我的照片送给别人了吗？

Tā bǎ wǒ de zhàopiàn sòng gěi biérén le ma?

Did she give my picture to someone else?

P: 我的照片被她送给别人了吗？

Wǒ de zhàopiàn bèi tā sòng gěi biérén le ma?

It is evident from sentences (7) and (8) that the negative marker precedes 被 and that the interrogative is formed with 吗.

Affirmative	Recipient + 被－Object + Action
Negative	Recipient + Negative + 被－Object + Action
Interrogative	Recipient + 被－Object + Action + 吗?

1.2   Like the 把－sentence we learned in Lessons 46 and 47, the 被－pattern requires its verb phrase to contain some extra element in addition to the verb itself. The extra element may be as simple as the perfective marker 了, or it may involve a complement or another Object. Neither a 把－sentence or a 被－sentence ends with a verb all by itself. Generally speaking, this additional information indicates the result or extent of the action and represents the focus of the message.

(A) The perfective 了:

(9)   你被谁踢了？

Nǐ bèi shéi tile?

You got kicked by whom?

(B) The indirect Object:

(10)   老师被学生问了三个问题，他都不会回答。

Lǎoshī bèi xuésheng wènle sānge wèntí, tā dōu bú huì huídá.

The teacher was asked three questions by the students, none of which he could answer.

(C) The resultative complement:

（11） 自行车被他修坏了。

Zìxíngchē bèi tā xiūhuàile.

The bike was broken by him while he tried to fix it.

(D) The directional complement:

（12） 我要的书被他借去了。

Wǒ yào de shū bèi tā jièqùle.

The book I want was checked out by him,

(E) The complex directional complement:

（13） 墙上的画儿被风刮下来了。

Qiángshang de huàr bèi fēng guāxiàlái le.

The picture on the wall was blown down by the wind.

(F) The complement of extent:

（14） 他被坏人打得站不起来。

Tā bèi huài rén dǎ de zhàn bu qǐlái.

He got so badly beaten by the scoundrels that he couldn't get up.

Sentence (14) involves the use of a special type of complement which we will discuss later in this lesson.

1.3   Unlike its equivalent passive in English where there is only one prepositional marker *by*, the Chinese 被－sentence has four functioning candidates: 被 *bèi*, 让 *ràng*, 叫 *jiào*, and 给 *gěi*.

（15.a) 买来的冰棍儿都被孩子们吃完了。

Mǎilái de bīnggùnr dōu bèi háizimen chīwán le.

All the popsicles that we had bought were eaten by the children.

（15.b) 买来的冰棍儿都让孩子们吃完了。

Mǎilái de bīnggùnr dōu ràng háizimen chīwán le.

（15.c) 买来的冰棍儿都叫孩子们吃完了。

Mǎilái de bīnggùnr dōu jiào háizimen chīwán le.

（15.d) 买来的冰棍儿都给孩子们吃完了。

Mǎilái de bīnggùnr dōu gěi háizimen chīwán le.

Of the four markers, 被 is the only one used exclusively for the passive construction. The remaining three serve other grammatical functions as well. For example, the following sentence is ambiguous as 让 may signify either passive as in (16.a) or permission as in (16.c).

(16.a)　我让他踢了一脚。

　　　　Wǒ ràng tā tīle yìjiǎo.

　　　　(i) I was kicked by him.

　　　　(ii) I let him (give a) kick.

(16.b)　他真利害。我被他骂了几句，还让他踢了一脚。

　　　　Tā zhēn lìhai. Wǒ bèi tā màle jǐjù, hái ràng tā tīle yìjiǎo.

　　　　He is really fierce. I was yelled at and also got kicked by him.

(16.c)　他不会踢球，但是我还是让他踢了一脚。

　　　　Tā bú huì tī qiú, dànshì wǒ háishì ràng tā tīle yìjiǎo.

　　　　He doesn't know how to play ball, yet I still let him give the ball a kick.

Stylistically 被 is the proper and formal marker most preferred in writing, though others are often used interchangeably with 被 in conversation. 给, on the other hand, is a very common passive marker in colloquial speech. The following are more sentences to illustrate the use of these variants in the passive construction.

(17)　那本旧杂志没让人拿走。

　　　　Nà běn jiù zázhì méi ràng rén názǒu.

　　　　That old magazine wasn't taken away by anyone.

(18)　王掌柜的孩子教他逼死了。

　　　　Wáng zhǎngguì de háizi jiào tā bīsǐ le.

　　　　Storekeeper Wang's son was driven to death by him.

(19)　我的花瓶给谁打破了？

　　　　Wǒ de huāpíng gěi shéi dǎpòle?

　　　　By whom was my vase broken?

To further enhance the marking of the passive, some speakers may opt for the following pattern with an additional 给 before the verb, even when the preposition itself is 给. Sentences (20) and (21) are illustrations of this optional variation.

> Recipient ＋ 被/让/叫/给—Actor ＋（给）—Verb

(20)   我借给他的自行车叫他（给）卖了。
       Wǒ jiè gěi tā de zìxíngchē jiào tā (gěi) màile.
       The bike that I had lent him, ——he sold it.

(21)   在这个话剧里，那个伟大的艺术家让坏人（给）杀死了。
       Zài zhè ge huàjùli, nà ge wěidà de yìshùjiā ràng huàirén (gěi) shā-
       sǐle.
       In this play, that great artist was murdered by the villains.

1.4   Other than stylistic distinctions, 被 differs from 叫 and 让 in that 被 may be used directly with the verb without the Object. When there is no need to specify the performer of the action, the actor nominal may be omitted as in the following schema:

+---+
| Passive: Subject   +   被－Verb |
| [Recipient] |
+---+

The preposition 给 may also participate in this truncated form of passive, but not 叫 or 让.

(22.a)   他被踢了一脚。
         Tā bèi tīle yìjiǎo.
         He got kicked once.
(22.b)   他给踢了一脚。
         Tā gěi tīle yìjiǎo.
(22.c) *他让踢了一脚。
         *Tā ràng tīle yìjiǎo.
(22.d) *他叫踢了一脚。
         *Tā jiào tīle yìjiǎo.

(23)   箱子给打开了，可是里边的东西没被拿走。
       Xiāngzi gěi dǎkāile, kěshì lǐbiān de dōngxi méi bèi názǒu.
       The suitcase was opened, but the things inside were not taken away.

Another grammatical idiosyncracy of the preposition 被 is that it may form special expressions with certain verbs that are not allowed for the other passive markers. For example, 被抓 *bèi zhuā* "to be arrested." If the marker is 给, the verb phrase has to contain an extra element such as an aspect marker: 给抓了. If the marker is 叫 or 让, the verb phrase has to have both the extra element and the Object: 叫/让人抓了. The following table sums up the differences among these four markers:

Subject + Preposition Object + Verb + X	Subject + Preposition + Verb − X	Subject + Preposition + Verb
被 给 叫 让	被 给	被

1.5 As you may have noticed by now, many of the passive sentences given above sounded very strange in English when rendered with the *by*-construction. In other words, even though both languages have a passive construction, the usage is not always the same. English language teachers frequently tell their students to refrain from using the passive when the same sentence can be phrased in the active mode. The employment of the English passive sometimes serves a specific purpose, such as shifting the focus of the sentence to the recipient of the action. For example, compare the following two sentences which relate the same historical event.

(24.a) The king sent Ann Bolyn to the execution ground.
(24.b) Ann Bolyn was sent to the execution ground (by the king).

While the emphasis of (24.a) is on King Henry VIII and what he did, the attention in the passive form (24.b) is drawn to Ann Bolyn and her unfortunate death. Therefore, even though the sentences basically say the same thing, the emphasis is quite different. It is perhaps because of this characteristic shift of focus in a passive sentence that we would say "The glass got broken," instead of "I broke the glass," when we want to avoid responsibility. By opting for the passive pattern, we have not only reported what has happened but have also, in fact, disassociated ourselves from a potentially incriminating incident.

In Chinese, the use of the 被 − sentence serves a particular semantic function, namely reporting something unfavorable, undesirable or unfortunate. This pejorative reading of the 被 − construction should be evident from most of the above examples. Even a seemingly "innocuous" sentence like (4), reproduced below, also carries such a negative undertone.

(4)　　鱼被邻居的孩子吃了。

The sentence is not merely a report of what has happened to the fish; more importantly, it connotes a sense of disappointment or even disgust on the part of the speaker and amounts to saying something like "That naughty child, he ate my fish!" If we compare the following two sentences, one notional passive and the other 被一passive with the Object omitted, the negative tone is distinctly present in the 被一sentence.

> (25.a) 鱼吃了
>   Yú chī le.
> (25.b) 鱼被吃了。
>   Yú bèi chīle.

Having made this "pejorative" characterization of the 被一construction, we should hurry to point out that sentences such as the following seem to debunk such a claim.

> 26) 我们都被这个话剧感动了。
>   Wǒmen dōu bèi zhè ge huàjù gǎndòng le.
>   We have all been touched by this play.

The sentence evidently praises the dramatic achievement of the presentation rather than finding fault with it. Its use of 被 carries no obvious indication of a pejorative reading. This anomaly has long been noted by linguists and language teachers, who agree that the non-pejorative use of the passive construction is a rather late development in the language, probably within the last few decades and as a result of translating foreign passive verbs. Only 被 may readily apply to verbs of favorable meanings; all the other three prepositions seldom take part in non-pejorative use. Hence, rephrasing (26) with 给, 叫, or 让 will generate something that a native speaker may find odd or unacceptable.

> (26.a)?我们都给这个话剧感动了。
>   Wǒmen dōu gěi zhè ge huàjù gǎndòng le.
> (26.b)?我们都叫这个话剧感动了。
>   Wǒmen dōu jiào zhè ge huàjù gǎndòng le.
> (26.c)?我们都让这个话剧感动了。
>   Wǒmen dōu ràng zhè ge huàjù gǎndòng le.

The following are the most common situations where 被 is used non-pejoratively. Invariably, the verbs are followed by some sort of a complex complement:

(A) To be elected, selected, or considered as:

被... Verb ＋ 作...

(27)　他被（大家）选作工人代表了。

　　　　Tā bèi (dàjiā) xuǎn zuò gōngrén dàibiǎo le.

　　　　He was elected (by everyone) to be the workers' representative.

(28)　老舍被大家叫做人民艺术家。

　　　　Lǎo Shě bèi dàjiā jiào zuò rénmín yìshùjiā.

　　　　Lao She was called by everyone the artist of the people.

(B) To be relocated or assigned to:

被... Verb ＋ Location...

(29)　她被（人）请去中国讲学了。

　　　　Tā bèi (rén) qǐngqù Zhōngguó jiǎng xué le.

　　　　She has been invited to China to give lectures.

(30)　他被送到农村去工作了。

　　　　Tā bèi sòng dào nóngcūn qù gōngzuò le.

　　　　He was sent to work in the village.

(C) To be turned or transformed into:

被... Verb ＋ 成...

(31)　这个话剧被翻译成法文和日文了。

　　　　Zhè ge huàjù bèi fānyì chéng Fǎwén hé Rìwén le.

　　　　This play has been translated into French and Japanese.

(D) With certain specific verbs:

(32)　大家都被他们的演出吸引住了。

　　　　Dàjiā dōu bèi tāmen de yǎnchū xīyǐnzhù le.

　　　　Everyone was mesmerized by their performance.

(33)　我们都被他的话感动了。

　　　　Wǒmen dōu bèi tā de huà gǎndòng le.

　　　　We're all touched by his words.

Again, none of the above sentences may be rephrased with another passive marker. Nevertheless, the pejorative use remains the dominant feature of the 被－construction. And, for this reason, often times an English passive should not translate into a 被－sentence in Mandarin.

（34） Your letter has been received.
（34.a)*你的信已经被收到了。

　　　*Nǐ de xìn yǐjīng bèi shōudào le.
（34.b) 你的信已经收到了。

　　　Nǐ de xìn yǐjīng shōudào le.

（35） The skirt was made for you.
（35.a)*这条裙子被给你作了。

　　　*Zhè tiáo qúnzi bèi gěi nǐ zuò le.
（35.b) 这条裙子是给你作的。

　　　Zhè tiáo qúnzi shì gěi nǐ zuò de.

Since neither of the sentences carries any message of adversity, the use of the 被－passive is incorrect. The appropriate rendering is to topicalize the direct Object. In (34.b), the result is a notional passive sentence; in (35.b), since the emphasis is more on the benefactor than the action of sewing, the 是……的 construction is selected.

　　Our discussion of the passive construction in Chinese has been both detailed and replete with examples. Yet, in spite of all the grammatical explanation, you will surely find it difficult to master. The rule to go by in Chinese is to avoid using the 被－ sentence whenever possible. Remember that adversity is the key element. Avoid using it unless the semantic reading or the grammatical structure leaves no other choice. Even then, consider the notional passive before adopting the passive proper.

2. The Construction 不但……，而且……

The following pattern may be used to join two sentences together to highlight and reinforce the similarity and association between them. The function of the correlatives is very similar to that of "not only...but also..." in English.

不但　Sentence $_1$，而且　Sentence $_2$。

(1)　　你不但是我的好老师，而且也是我的好朋友。

Nǐ búdàn shì wǒ de hǎo lǎoshī, érqiě yě shì wǒ de hǎo péngyou.

Not only are you my good teacher, you are also my good friend.

(2)　　不但我说你是一个好老师，而且别的老师也都认为你教得很成功。

Búdàn wǒ shuō nǐ shì yíge hǎo lǎoshī, érqiě biéde lǎoshī yě dōu rèn-wéi nǐ jiāo de hěn chénggōng.

Not only do I say you are a good teacher, but the other instructors also claim that you teach effectively.

When the two clauses share the same subject, 你 in the case of sentence (1), the subject sits at the very beginning of the entire sequence. If their subjects are different as in (2), the correlatives generally start off the clauses. Also, the second clause may often contain an adverb 也 or 还 to further underscore the association. The following are more illustrations.

(3)　　这本书不但丰富了我的历史知识，而且也加深了我对新中国的了解。

Zhè běn shū búdàn fēngfùle wǒ de lìshǐ zhīshì, érqiě yě jiāshēnle wǒ duì xīn Zhōngguó de liǎojiě.

This book has not only enriched my knowledge of history, but also deepened my understanding of the new China.

(4)　　这个话剧写的不但是中国旧社会的情况，而且也谈到了现代社会里的黑暗。

Zhè ge huàjù xiě de búdàn shì Zhōngguó jiù shèhuì de qíngkuàng, érqiě yě tándàole xiàndài shèhuìli de hēi'àn.

What this play depicts is not only the conditions in old China but (it) also (deals with) the dark side of contemporary society.

(5)　　前天我弟弟把我的日记拿走了。他不但自己拿去看，而且还把日记带到学校去给同学看。

Qiántiān wǒ dìdi bǎ wǒ de rìjì názǒule. Tā búdàn zìjǐ náqù kàn, ér-qiě hái bǎ rìjì dài dào xuéxiào qù gěi tóngxué kàn.

The day before yesterday, my little brother took away my diary. Not only did he himself take it off to read, he also took the diary to school and showed it to his classmates.

(6)　　中国人过年，不但要吃年夜饭，而且还要去朋友家拜年。

Zhōngguó rén guò nián, búdàn yào chī niányè fàn, érqiě hái yào qù péngyou jiā bài nián.

When the Chinese celebrate the New Year, not only do the families get together on the New Year's eve for reunion dinners, they also have to pay New Year calls to their friends.

(7) 她家里打扫得真干净。不但东西收拾得非常整齐，而且红纸黑字的春
     联也贴在门上了。

Tā jiāli dǎsǎo de zhēn gānjìng. Búdàn dōngxi shōushi de fēicháng
zhěngqí, érqiě hóng zhǐ hēi zì de chūnlián yě tiē zài ménshang le.

Her house was indeed immaculately cleaned. Not only were things
neatly placed in order, the New Year scrolls, black calligraphy on
red paper, had also been posted on the door.

(8) 我们爱看鲁迅的小说，不但是因为他写得好，而且是因为他的故事能
     帮助我们了解中国人关心的问题。

Wǒmen ài kàn Lǔ Xùn de xiǎoshuō, búdàn shì yīnwèi tā xiě de hǎo,
érqiě shì yīnwèi tā de gùshì néng bāngzhù wǒmen liǎojiě Zhōngguó
rén guānxīn de wèntí.

We like to read Lu Xun's fiction, not only because he writes well
but also because his stories can help us understand the kind of problems that concern the Chinese.

3. The Emphatic Marker 连

连 *lián*, a verb literally meaning "to connect" or "to include," may be used as a rhetorical marker for emphasis. Its use is similar to that of "even" in English, as in the
following example.

(1) 连我也不知道。
     Lián wǒ yě bù zhīdao.
     Even I don't know.

As illustrated in the following pattern, the preposition 连 is placed before the element on which the emphasis falls, and the predicate generally includes a reinforcing
adverb 也 or 都.

```
连  +  X  +  也/都  +  Verb
```

The X segment may be anything in the sentence, a subject as in (1) or an Object as
in (2), or any grammatical element as in (3) or (4). The stressed segment invariably
appears before the verb.

(2)　他连衣服都没换。

　　　　Tā lián yīfu dōu méi huàn.

　　　　He didn't even change his clothes.

(3)　她连厨房门上都挂上了春联。

　　　　Tā lián chúfáng ménshang dōu guàshàng le chūnlián.

　　　　She even hung New Year scrolls on the kitchen door.

(4)　我连晚上也要去图书馆工作。

　　　　Wǒ lián wǎnshang yě yào qù túshūguǎn gōngzuò.

　　　　Even in the evenings I have to go to the library to work.

The following are a few more sentences to illustrate the use of the pattern in combination with other constructions.

(5)　她忙得连饭也没吃就走了。

　　　　Tā máng de lián fàn yě méi chī jiù zǒu le.

　　　　She was so busy that she left without even having had her meal.

(6)　他什么都想知道，连我的信他也要看。

　　　　Tā shénme dōu xiǎng zhīdao, lián wǒ de xìn tā yě yào kàn.

　　　　He wants to know everything; he even wants to read my letters.

(7)　这个社会非常黑暗，连爱国的都会被抓，被杀。

　　　　Zhè ge shèhuì fēicháng hēi'àn, lián ài guó de dōu huì bèi zhuā, bèi shā.

　　　　This society is very corrupt. Even patriots are arrested and killed.

(8)　他不但学过中文，而且连鲁迅、老舍的书他都看过。

　　　　Tā búdàn xuéguo Zhōngwén, érqiě lián Lǔ Xùn, Lǎo Shě de shū tā dōu kànguo.

　　　　Not only has he studied the Chinese language, he has even read books by Lu Xun and Lao She.

Please note that in sentence (5) the Object 饭 is in fact part of the compound expression 吃饭 meaning "to eat." The 连 pattern can break up such a Verb—Object compound only when the action is placed under focus. Sentence (9) is another example to illustrate this behavior.

(9)　她忙得连觉也没睡。

　　　　Tā máng de lián jiào yě méi shuì.

　　　　She was so busy that she didn't even get any sleep.

4. The Complement of Extent

As you may recall from Lesson 25, a complement of degree describing the manner or extent of an action is generally formed with an adjective phrase as in the following sentence.

(1)   他写得很难看。
       Tā xiě de hěn nánkàn.
       He writes badly.

Sometimes, to be more descriptive of the degree, the complement may be a more specific characterization of the situation, as in (2).

(2)   他写得谁都看不懂。
       Tā xiě de shéi dōu kàn bu dǒng.
       He writes in such a way that no one can read it.

The complement is unequivocally marked by 得, to be followed by a statement that provides detailed information concerning the outcome or extent of the action. Hence, this kind of complement is referred to as the complement of extent. The complement of extent may consist of a simple verb phrase or a full sentence. It may even be phrased with a complex sentence structure.

(3)   我累得走不动了。
       Wǒ lèi de zǒu bu dòng le.
       I'm so tired that I can't walk any more.

(4)   这个小孩儿哭得连牛奶都不肯吃。
       Zhè ge xiǎoháir kū de lián niúnǎi dōu bù kěn chī.
       The baby cried so much that it wasn't even willing to drink (its) milk.

(5)   她聪明得你说什么她都懂。
       Tā cōngming de nǐ shuō shénme tā dōu dǒng.
       She is so smart that whatever you say, she understands.

(6)   人民没有吃的，没有穿的，被逼得卖儿卖女。
       Rénmín méi yǒu chī de, méi yǒu chuān de, bèi bī de mài ér mài nǚ.
       The people didn't have anything to eat or to wear. They were forced to sell their sons and daughters.

(7)　这个话剧演得好得不但看过的人都很感动，而且还有很多人去看两次
三次的。

Zhè ge huàjù yǎn de hǎo de búdàn kànguo de rén dōu hěn gǎndòng,
érqiě hái yǒu hěn duō rén qù kàn liǎngcì sāncì de.

The play was so well performed that not only was the audience
deeply moved, there were also many who went to see it twice or
three times.

The last sentence actually consists of two complements: the first being 演得……,
describing the outcome of the performance, and the second 好得……, detailing the
degree of the success.

Lesson 50

1. Numeral Approximates

When two successive numerals are put together, the combination stands for an approximate number. For example, 五 六个 *wǔliùge* "five or six items." This pattern of approximation differs from the use of 几 *jǐ* in that the latter may represent anything between one and ten. 十几个人 *shíjǐge rén* is 11 to 19 people but 十一二 个人 *shíyī'èrge rén* is either eleven or twelve people. The pattern is generally used in combination with a measure word and is applicable to a digital figure of any size.

(1)　两 三个画展
　　　liǎngsānge huàzhǎn
　　　two or three art exhibits

(2)　八 九只笔
　　　bājiǔzhī bǐ
　　　eight or nine pens

(3)　二十七 八岁
　　　èrshiqībā suì
　　　twenty-seven or twenty-eight years old

(4)　三四十只兔子
　　　sānsìshizhī tùzi
　　　thirty or forty rabbits

(5)　一百零六 七个演员
　　　yìbǎilíngliùqīge yǎnyuán
　　　a hundred and six or seven actors

(6)　四五百辆汽车
　　　sìwǔbǎiliàng qìchē
　　　four or five hundred cars

(7)   七八千次
       qībāqiāncì
       seven or eight thousand times

(8)   昨天有五六百个人来看画展。
       Zuótiān yǒu wǔliùbǎige rén lái kàn huàzhǎn.
       Five or six hundred people came to see the painting exhibit
       yesterday.

(9)   我虽然已经画了四五笔了，可是我还不知道我要画什么。
       Wǒ suīrán yǐjīng huàle sìwǔbǐ le, kěshì wǒ hái bù zhīdao wǒ yào
       huà shénme.
       Although I've already put down a few strokes, I still don't know
       what I want to draw.

(10)   我把书打开，才看了一两眼，就被吸引住了。用不了两三个小时我就
       把这本三四千页的小说看完了。
       Wǒ bǎ shū dǎkāi, cái kànle yìliǎngyǎn, jiù bèi xīyǐnzhù le. Yòng bu
       liǎo liǎngsānge xiǎoshí, wǒ jiù bǎ zhè běn sānsìqiānyè de xiǎoshuō
       kànwán le.
       I opened the book and had hardly read one or two pages when I
       found myself sucked in by it. Within less than two to three hours, I
       finished reading the novel of three to four thousand pages.

The measure word may of course be a nominal measure, or an action measure as in
sentences (7) and (9).

2. Reduplication of the Measure Word

2.1   A measure word may be reduplicated to convey the meaning "each and every." The use of this pattern is essentially the same as that of " 每 + Measure,"
with a slight difference in emphasis. While " 每 + Measure" is a matter-of-fact
counting of all items, the measure reduplication creates a vivacious tone.

(1)   听见要去动物园了，个个小孩儿都高兴得跳起来了。
       Tīngjiàn yào qù dòngwùyuán le, gègè xiǎoháir dōu gāoxìng de tiào-
       qǐlái le.
       Hearing that they were going to the zoo, all the children jumped up
       in great joy.

(2) 这本书，我不但天天看，而且一天要看两三遍。

Zhè běn shū, wǒ búdàn tiāntiān kàn, érqiě yìtiān yào kàn liǎngsān-
biàn.

Not only do I read this book every day, I read it two or three times
each day.

(3) 春节的时候，家家都团聚过年。

Chūnjié de shíhòu, jiājiā dōu tuánjù guò nián.

During the Spring Festival, each and every family gets together to
celebrate the New Year.

In sentence (3), the measure word is 家, a classifier for households. Unlike 家 or
other measure words, the reduplicated form in (2), namely 天, is a noun by status.
Yet, 天 belongs to a small class of nouns that also possess the behavior characteristic of measure words. They may appear directly after a numeral without an intervening measure as in 一天. Other members of this class include 年 *nián* "year,"
人 *rén* "person," etc. The following example is an exception.

(4) 树树立风雪。

Shù shù lì fēng xuě.

In wind and snow, every tree stands upright.

Sentence (4) is a line from a poem written in the classical style, which does not
necessarily observe the rules of the modern language. When paraphrased into Mandarin, 树树 *shùshù* will become 棵棵树 *kēkē shù* or 株株树 *zhūzhū shù*, with 棵 or
株 as the measure.

2.2 As illustrated in the above examples, a duplicated measure is used primarily as
a nominal in a sentence to be followed by the adverb 都. A numeral－measure
combination, however, may also be repeated and used as an adverbial modifier.

[Numeral－Measure ＋ Numeral－Measure] 地 Verb

The reduplication pattern is a vivid stylistic device for describing the manner or
implement by means of which an action is carried out.

(5) 学生两个两个地进来，检查身体。

Xuésheng liǎngge liǎngge de jìnlái, jiǎnchá shēntǐ.

Two by two, the students came in for their medical checkups.

(6)   你别急，一句一句地说，要不，别人听不懂你说什么。

Nǐ bié jí, yíjù yíjù de shuō; yàobù, biérén tīng bu dǒng nǐ shuō shénme。

Slow down, and say it sentence by sentence. Or else, no one is going to understand you.

(7)   她十块十块地给我，一共给了我五次，所以是五十块钱。

Tā shíkuài shíkuài de gěi wǒ, yígòng gěile wǒ wǔcì. Suǒyǐ shì wǔshikuài qián.

She gave me ten dollars each time for five times. So, the total was fifty dollars.

(8)   我一遍一遍地看，可是怎么看都看不懂这篇文章的意思。

Wǒ yíbiàn yíbiàn de kàn, kěshi zěnme kàn dōu kàn bu dǒng zhè piān wénzhāng de yìsi.

I read it time after time, but no matter what I couldn't make out what this article was trying to say.

(9)   天气一天一天地暖和了。

Tiānqì yìtiān yìtiān de nuǎnhuo le.

The weather is warming up day by day.

Epilogue

Congratulations. You have completed fifty lessons of grammar, including all the basics you need not only for reading elementary teaching texts but also for tackling more advanced levels of language training.

Admittedly prescriptive, and in may ways simplified for pedagogical purposes, this *Grammar* characterizes linguistics operations in Chinese for a general audience and provides a basic reference on nuts and bolts with simple fundamental instructions for assembly. At times, the discussion digresses into more complex premises to explain issues, both grammatical and pragmatic, far beyond the immediate scope of the first year syllabus. Also presented in some detail and with many illustrations are various morphological and syntactic apparatuses by means of which we construct sentences and interpret information. Such knowledge is crucial to forming the comprehensive view of the language that you must eventually acquire to understand not only why we say things in a certain fashion, but more importantly why we don't say things other ways. Although you may not now remember all the rules you have learned or fully comprehend the significance and ramifications of each, in the future when you encounter problems using Chinese you will want to refer to these pages for some plausible explanation. As your studies progress and your exposure to Chinese expands, you also may and probably will enlarge and revise this grammar to accommodate more and newer data.

Language learning is a lifetime enterprise. Fluency in the four basic skills of listening, speaking, reading and writing is acquired only through years of hard work and concentrated effort. You will need to know the sounds, the graphs, the vocabulary, the grammar and, above all, when and how to put every ingredient together in a palatable way that suits a native tongue. Having come this far, you are now adequately equipped to move on to another more challenging level of exploration. 祝你学习成功.

Reference

Chao, Yuen Ren. *A Grammar of Spoken Chinese*. Berkeley and Los Angeles: University of California Press, 1968.

——. *Mandarin Primer*. Cambridge: Harvard University Press, 1964.

Diyijie guoji Hanyu taolunhui lunwenxuan 第一届国际汉语讨论会论文选 (Proceedings of the First International Conference on Chinese Language Teaching). Beijing: Beijing yuyan xueyuan chubanshe 北京语言学院出版社, 1986.

Diyijie shijie Huawen jiaoxue yantaohui lunwenji 第一届世界华文教学研讨会论文集 (Proceedings of the First International Conference on the Teaching of Chinese as a Second Language). Taipei: Shijie Huawen Jiaoyu Xiejinhui 世界华文教育协进会 (World Chinese Language Association), 1985.

Li, Charles N. and Sandra A. Thompson. *Mandarin Chinese: A Functional Reference Grammar*. Berkeley, Los Angeles and London: University of California Press, 1981.

Li, Y. C., Robert L. Cheng, Larry Foster, Shang H. Ho, John Y. Hou and Moira Yip. *Mandarin Chinese: A Practical Reference Grammar for Students and Teachers* (Vol. 1). Taipei: The Crane Publishing Company, 1984.

Liu, Yuehua 刘月华, Pan Wenyu 潘文娱 and Gu Wei 故铧. *Shiyong xiandai Hanyu yufa* 实用现代汉语语法 (A Practical Chinese Grammar). Beijing: Waiyu jiaoxue yu yanjiu chubanshe 外语教学与研究出版社, 1983.

Lü, Shuxiang 吕叔湘. *Xiandai Hanyu babai ci* 现代汉语八百词 (Eight Hundred Words in Modern Chinese). Beijing: Commercial Press, 1983.

Norman, Jerry. *Chinese*. Cambridge: Cambridge University Press, 1988.

Tai, James H. Y. and Frank F. S. Hsueh. *Functionalism and Chinese Grammar*. Chinese Language Teachers Association, Monograph Series No. 1, 1989.

Tang, Ting-chi, Robert L. Cheng and Ying-che Li. *Studies in Chinese Syntax and Semantics: Universe and Scope, Quantification in Chinese*. Taipei: Student Book Company Limited, 1983.

Teng, Shou-hsin. *A Semantic Study of Transitivity Relations in Chinese*. Berkeley and Los Angeles: University of California Press, 1975.

——. *A Basic Course in Chinese Grammar*. San Francisco: Chinese Materials Center, 1979.

Tsao, Feng-fu. *A Functional Study of Topic in Chinese : A First Step towards Discourse Analysis*. Taipei: Student Book Company Limited, 1979.

Index

M

N

pronoun, 9—10, 213, 444; pronoun Object,
 279, 423, 439. *See also dājiā, nín, zìjǐ*
purpose expression, 42—44, 434

Q

qǐ 起 , 417
qiān 千 , 412
qíanbiān 前边 , 147—169
qǐng 请 , 22; as pivotal verb, 105—108
qīngchu 清楚 , 359, 391, 404
qǐng wèn 请问 , 25—26
Q/Q Object, 213—221, 227—230
qù 去 , 35, 78, 91, 165, 282; as directional
 complement, 381, 417
quán 全 , 482—484
quantified Object, 220, 291
quantity complement, 340—344
question, 3—4, 14, 17—18, 19, 26, 39—44,
 101—105. *See* affirmative—negative question;
 alternative question; interrogative word
 question; *ma* question; *ne* question;
 rhetorical question; tag question
question word, *see* interrogative word

R

ràng 让 , passive, 88; pivotal, 105—108
reduplication of adjectives, 388—391
reduplication of measure words, 502—504
reduplication of verbs, 143—145, 169—170,
 189, 282, 391, 457
reference, 213
relative clause construction, 133—138, 213,
 400
rènshi 认识 , 127—129, 460
repetition of verb, affirmative—negative
 question, 40, complement of degree, 180
reported speech, 209

request, 22—23
resultative complement, 351—360, 365—367,
 406, 411, 443, 455, 460, 487
rhetorical question, with *bú shì...ma?* 425;
 with *ma*, 56—57
rì 日 , 116

S

sentence conjoining, 371. *See búdàn...ér-
 qiě...; chúle... yǐwài, yě/hái...; suīrán...
 dànshì/kěshì...; yàoshì... jiù...; yī...jiù ...;
 yīnwèi... suǒyǐ...; yòu...yòu...; zhǐ yǒu...
 cái ...*
sentence *le* 了 , *see* modal particle *le*
sentential predicate, 248—249
sentential unit, 297
sequential use of *shàng* 上 and *xià* 下 , 347—
 349
shàng 上 , 347—349, 381; as directional complement, 417; as resultative complement,
 462—464
shàngbiān 上边 , 147, 168
shàng kè 上课 , 283
shǎo 少 , 99, 342
shéi 谁 , 17—18, 442, 476
shénme 什么 , 19, 476
shì 是 , 11, 14, 40, 85, 104, 125, 144, 154, 205,
 460, 426
shì...de 是……的 , categorical, 72—76, 433—
 442, 494
shì...de 是……的 , past action, 433—442
shì ma? 是吗 ?, 112
short answer, 15, 40
shuāng 双 , 237
shuō 说 , 209, 375
sǐ 死 , 165, 277
simple directional complement, 381—387
specific Object, 217
stative verb, *see* adjective